BLACK BUTLER ⑪

YANA TOBOSO

Translation: Tomo Kimura • Lettering: Alexis Eckerman

KUROSHITSUJI Vol. 11 © 2011 Yana Toboso / SQUARE ENIX CO., LTD. All rights reserved. First published in Japan in 2011 by SQUARE ENIX CO., LTD. English translation rights arranged with SQUARE ENIX CO., LTD. and Hachette Book Group through Tuttle-Mori Agency, Inc.

Translation © 2012 by SQUARE ENIX CO., LTD.

Yen Press
Hachette Book Group
237 Park Avenue, New York, NY 10017

www.HachetteBookGroup.com
www.YenPress.com

Yen Press is an imprint of Hachette Book Group, Inc. The Yen Press name and logo are trademarks of Hachette Book Group, Inc.

First Yen Press Edition: October 2012

ISBN: 978-0-316-22533-5

10 9 8 7 6 5 4

BVG

Printed in the United States of America

Yana Toboso

AUTHOR'S NOTE

"My drawing is nowhere near my ideal devil of a butler. I want to make him a much cooler and nobler, handsome non-human!" ...I've been drawing Sebas by trial and error this whole time, but even after ten volumes, my drawing is far from my ideal, and I can't stop my journey to the ideal Sebas in my head.

I'd like to reach sanctuary already and settle down. But this journey will never end. That's how I feel. And so here's Volume 11, off to a new journey.

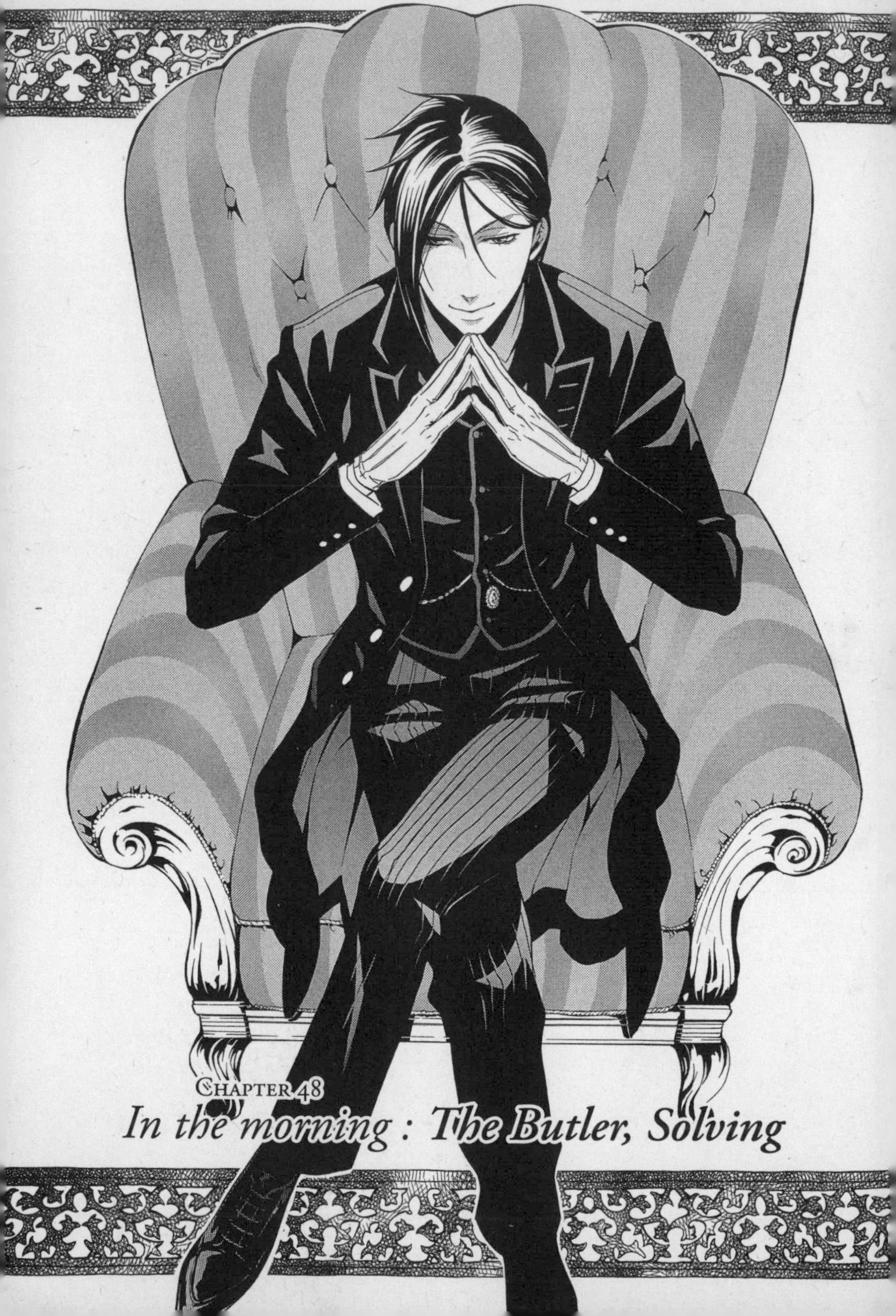
CHAPTER 48
In the morning : The Butler, Solving

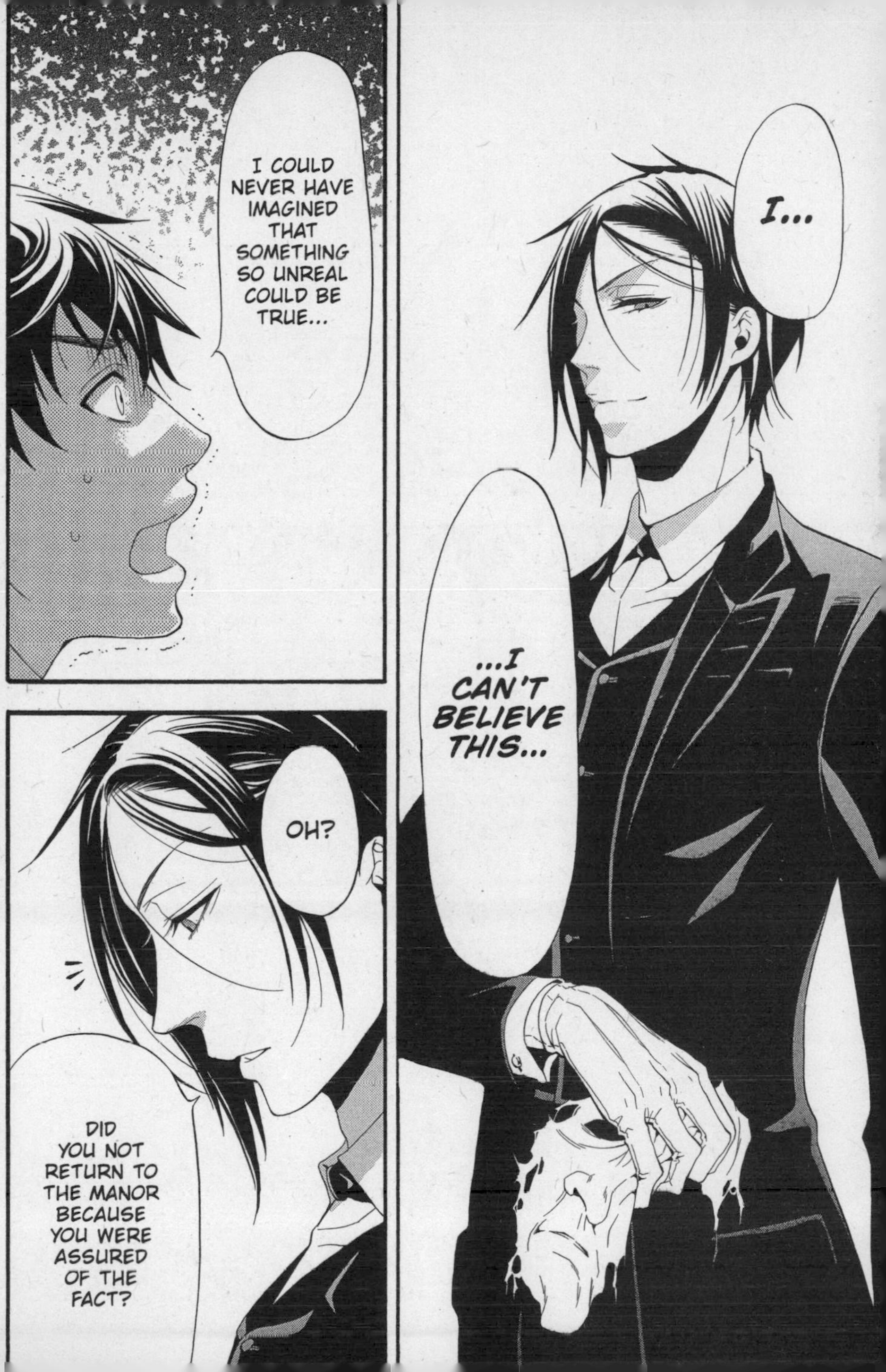
I...
...I CAN'T BELIEVE THIS...
I COULD NEVER HAVE IMAGINED THAT SOMETHING SO UNREAL COULD BE TRUE...
OH?
DID YOU NOT RETURN TO THE MANOR BECAUSE YOU WERE ASSURED OF THE FACT?

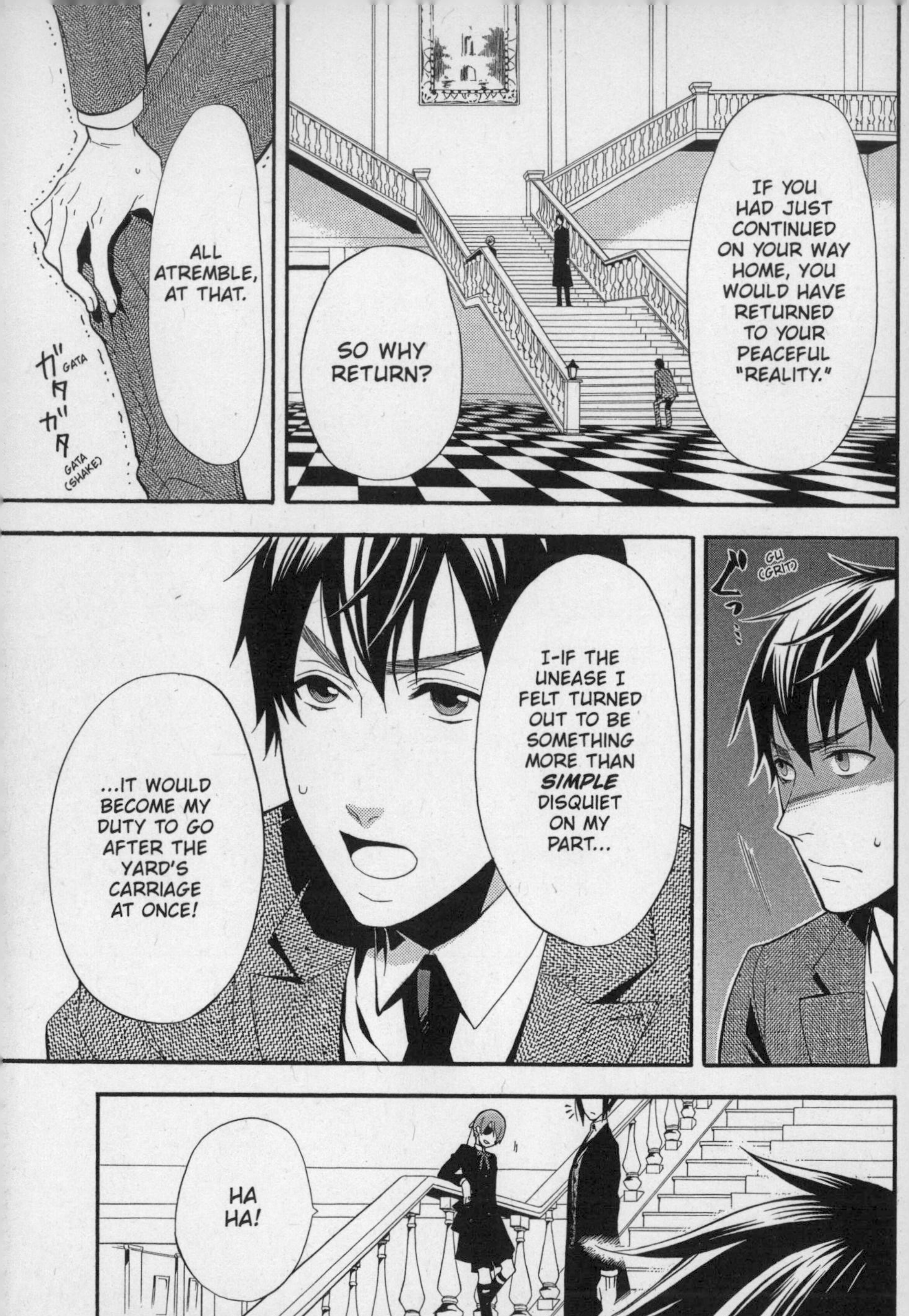

IF YOU HAD JUST CONTINUED ON YOUR WAY HOME, YOU WOULD HAVE RETURNED TO YOUR PEACEFUL "REALITY."
SO WHY RETURN?
ALL ATREMBLE, AT THAT.
ガタガタ GATA GATA (SHAKE)
ぐっ GU (GRIT)
I-IF THE UNEASE I FELT TURNED OUT TO BE SOMETHING MORE THAN *SIMPLE* DISQUIET ON MY PART...
...IT WOULD BECOME MY DUTY TO GO AFTER THE YARD'S CARRIAGE AT ONCE!
HA HA!

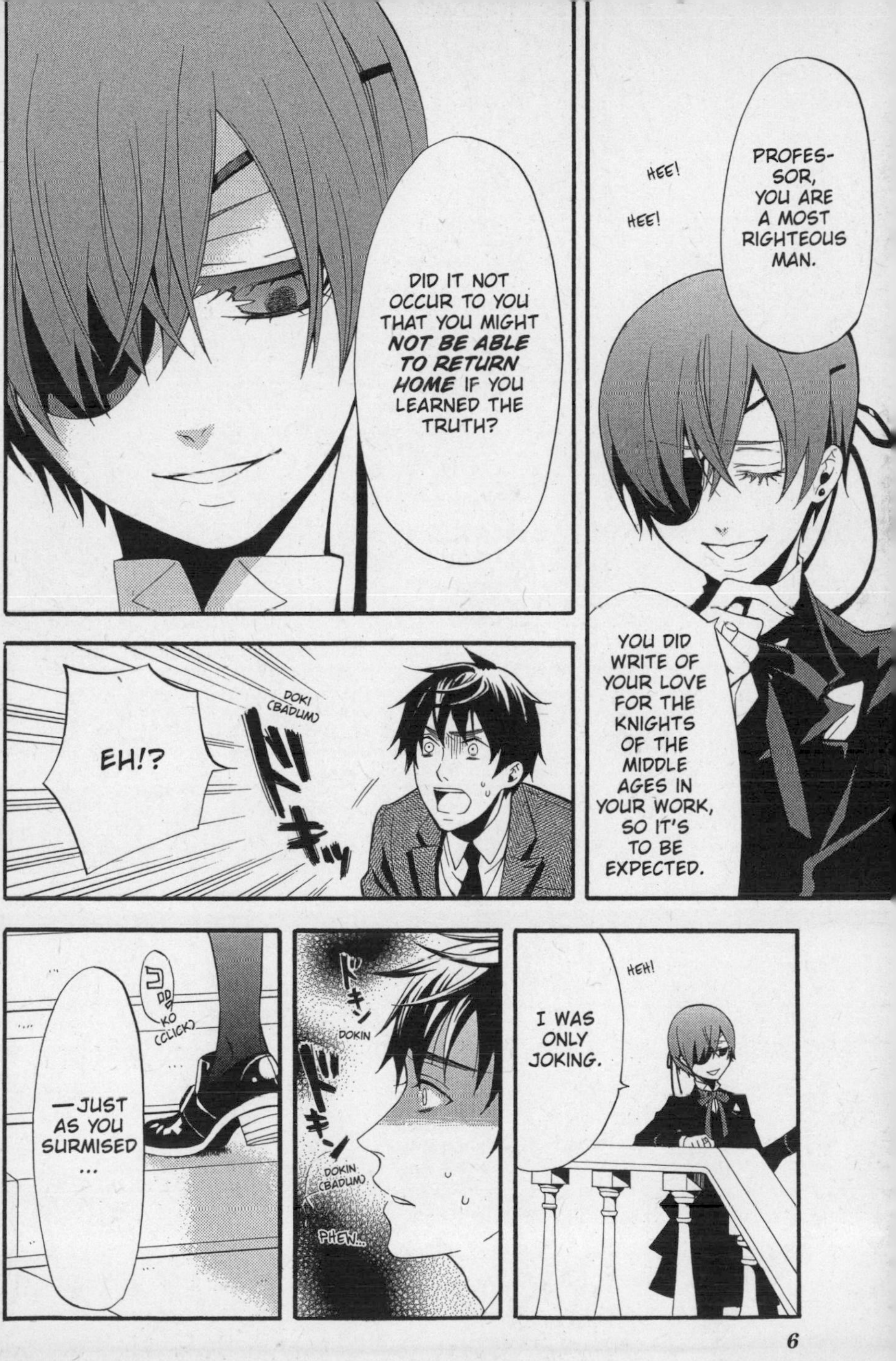
HEE!
HEE!
PROFES-SOR, YOU ARE A MOST RIGHTEOUS MAN.
YOU DID WRITE OF YOUR LOVE FOR THE KNIGHTS OF THE MIDDLE AGES IN YOUR WORK, SO IT'S TO BE EXPECTED.
DID IT NOT OCCUR TO YOU THAT YOU MIGHT ***NOT BE ABLE TO RETURN HOME*** IF YOU LEARNED THE TRUTH?
DOKI (BADUM)
EH!?
HEH!
I WAS ONLY JOKING.
DOKIN
DOKIN (BADUM)
PHEW...
KO (CLICK)
—JUST AS YOU SURMISED ...

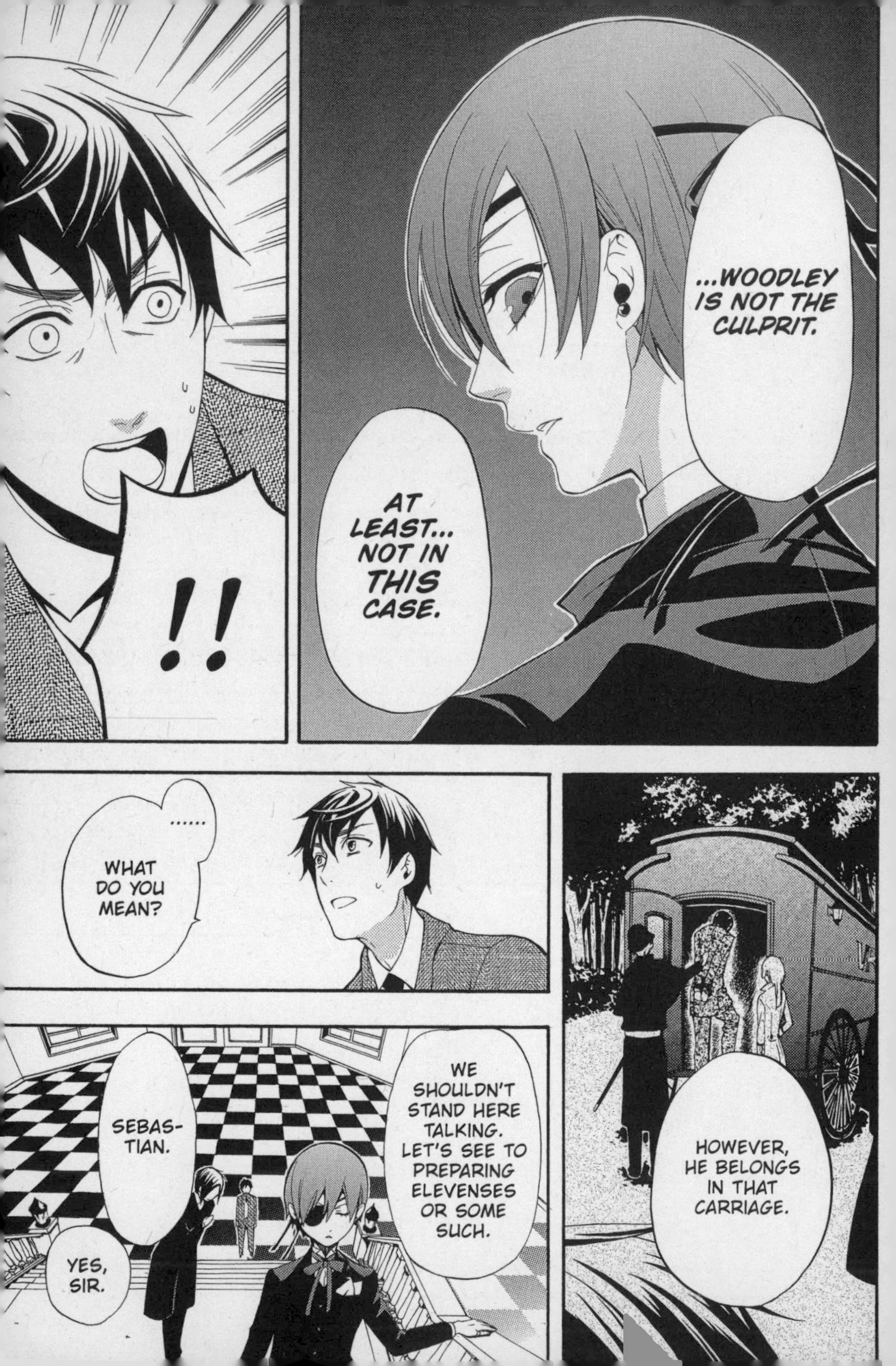
...WOODLEY IS NOT THE CULPRIT.
AT LEAST... NOT IN THIS CASE.
!!
HOWEVER, HE BELONGS IN THAT CARRIAGE.
......
WHAT DO YOU MEAN?
WE SHOULDN'T STAND HERE TALKING. LET'S SEE TO PREPARING ELEVENSES OR SOME SUCH.
SEBAS-TIAN.
YES, SIR.

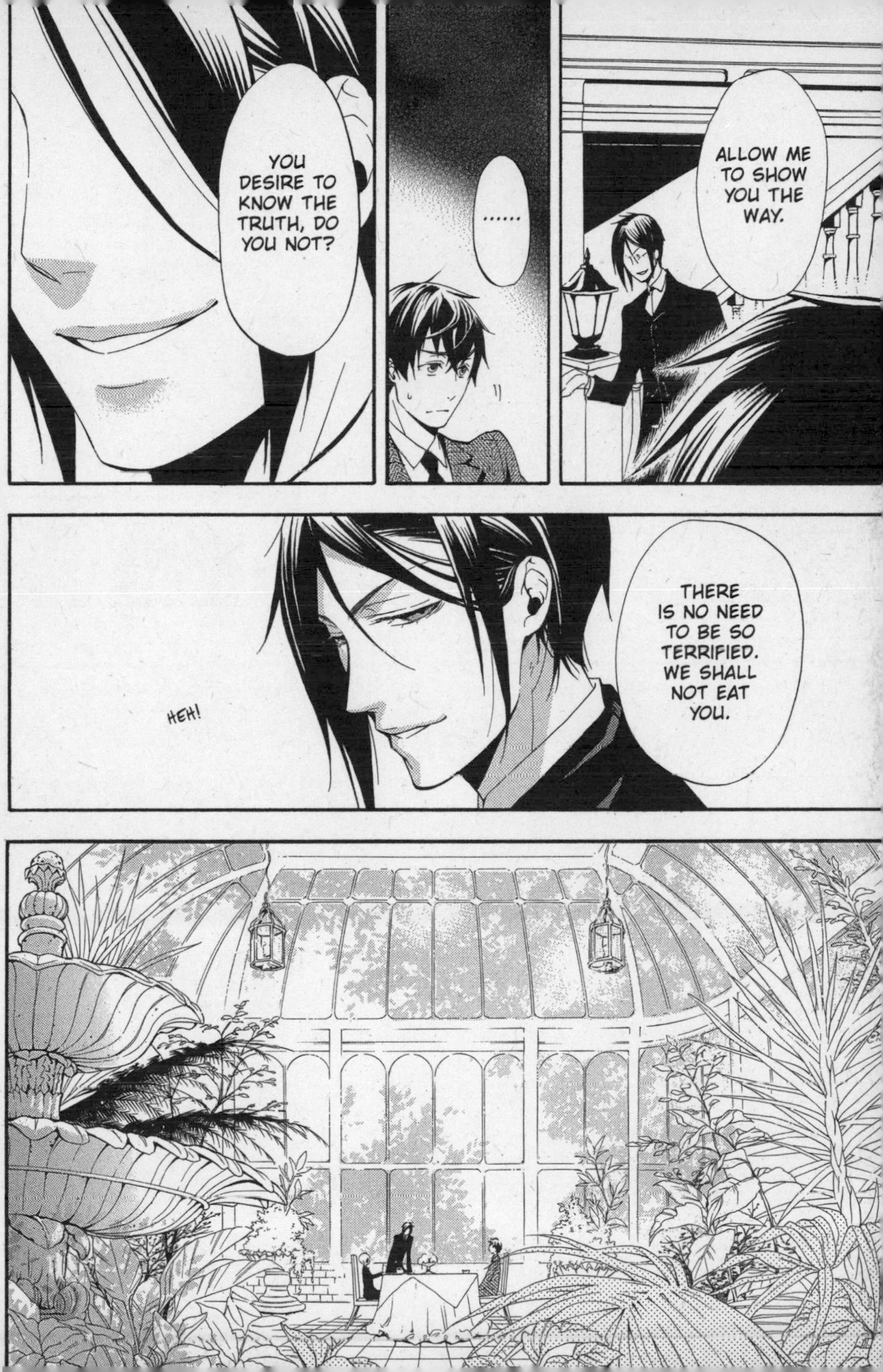
ALLOW ME TO SHOW YOU THE WAY.
......
YOU DESIRE TO KNOW THE TRUTH, DO YOU NOT?
THERE IS NO NEED TO BE SO TERRIFIED. WE SHALL NOT EAT YOU.
HEH!

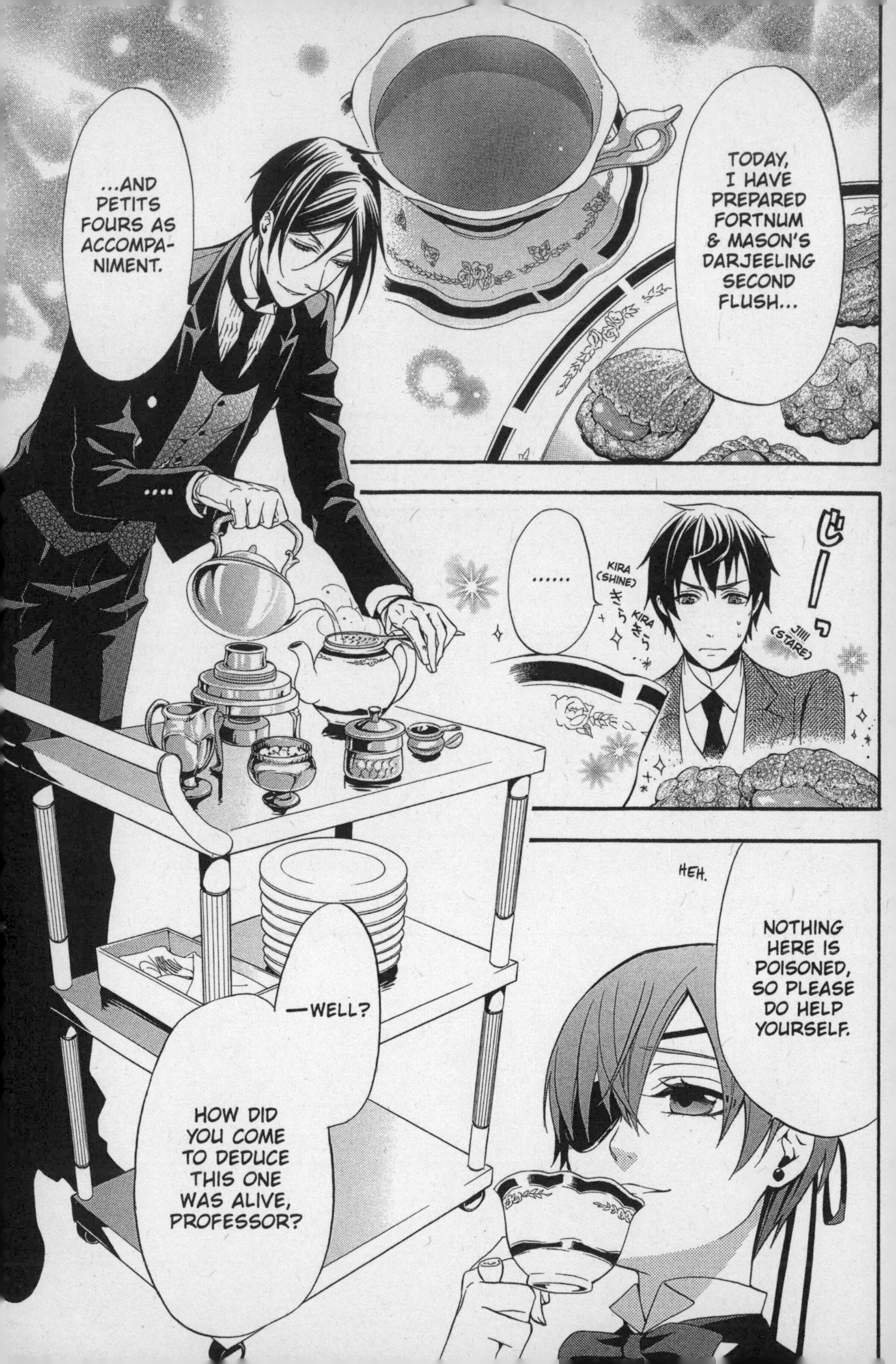
TODAY, I HAVE PREPARED FORTNUM & MASON'S DARJEELING SECOND FLUSH...
...AND PETITS FOURS AS ACCOMPANIMENT.
JIIII (STARE)
KIRA (SHINE)
KIRA
......
HEH.
NOTHING HERE IS POISONED, SO PLEASE DO HELP YOURSELF.
—WELL?
HOW DID YOU COME TO DEDUCE THIS ONE WAS ALIVE, PROFESSOR?

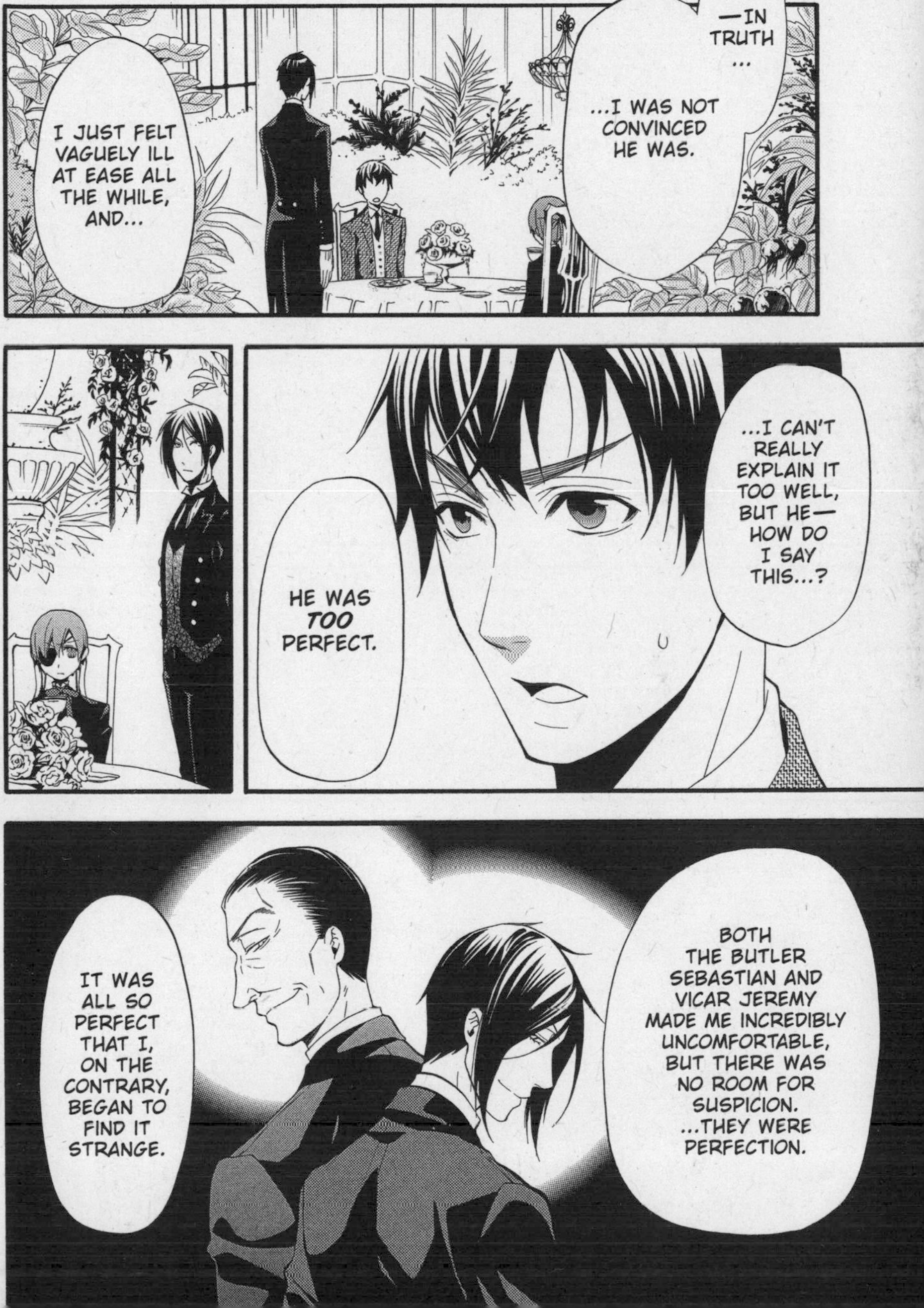
—IN TRUTH...
...I WAS NOT CONVINCED HE WAS.
I JUST FELT VAGUELY ILL AT EASE ALL THE WHILE, AND...
...I CAN'T REALLY EXPLAIN IT TOO WELL, BUT HE—HOW DO I SAY THIS...?
HE WAS *TOO* PERFECT.
BOTH THE BUTLER SEBASTIAN AND VICAR JEREMY MADE ME INCREDIBLY UNCOMFORTABLE, BUT THERE WAS NO ROOM FOR SUSPICION. ...THEY WERE PERFECTION.
IT WAS ALL SO PERFECT THAT I, ON THE CONTRARY, BEGAN TO FIND IT STRANGE.

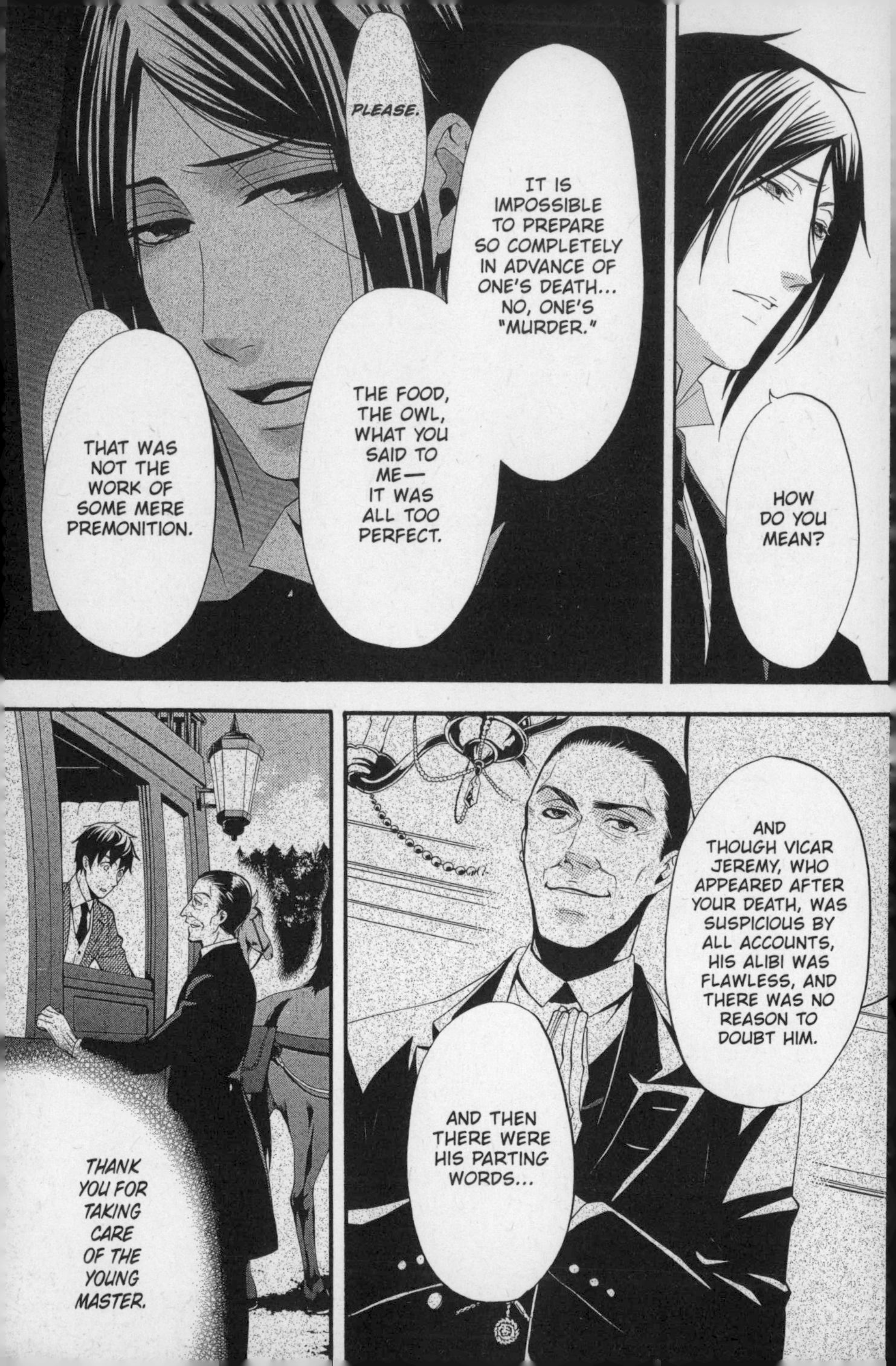
HOW DO YOU MEAN?
PLEASE.
IT IS IMPOSSIBLE TO PREPARE SO COMPLETELY IN ADVANCE OF ONE'S DEATH... NO, ONE'S "MURDER."
THE FOOD, THE OWL, WHAT YOU SAID TO ME— IT WAS ALL TOO PERFECT.
THAT WAS NOT THE WORK OF SOME MERE PREMONITION.
AND THOUGH VICAR JEREMY, WHO APPEARED AFTER YOUR DEATH, WAS SUSPICIOUS BY ALL ACCOUNTS, HIS ALIBI WAS FLAWLESS, AND THERE WAS NO REASON TO DOUBT HIM.
AND THEN THERE WERE HIS PARTING WORDS...
THANK YOU FOR TAKING CARE OF THE YOUNG MASTER.

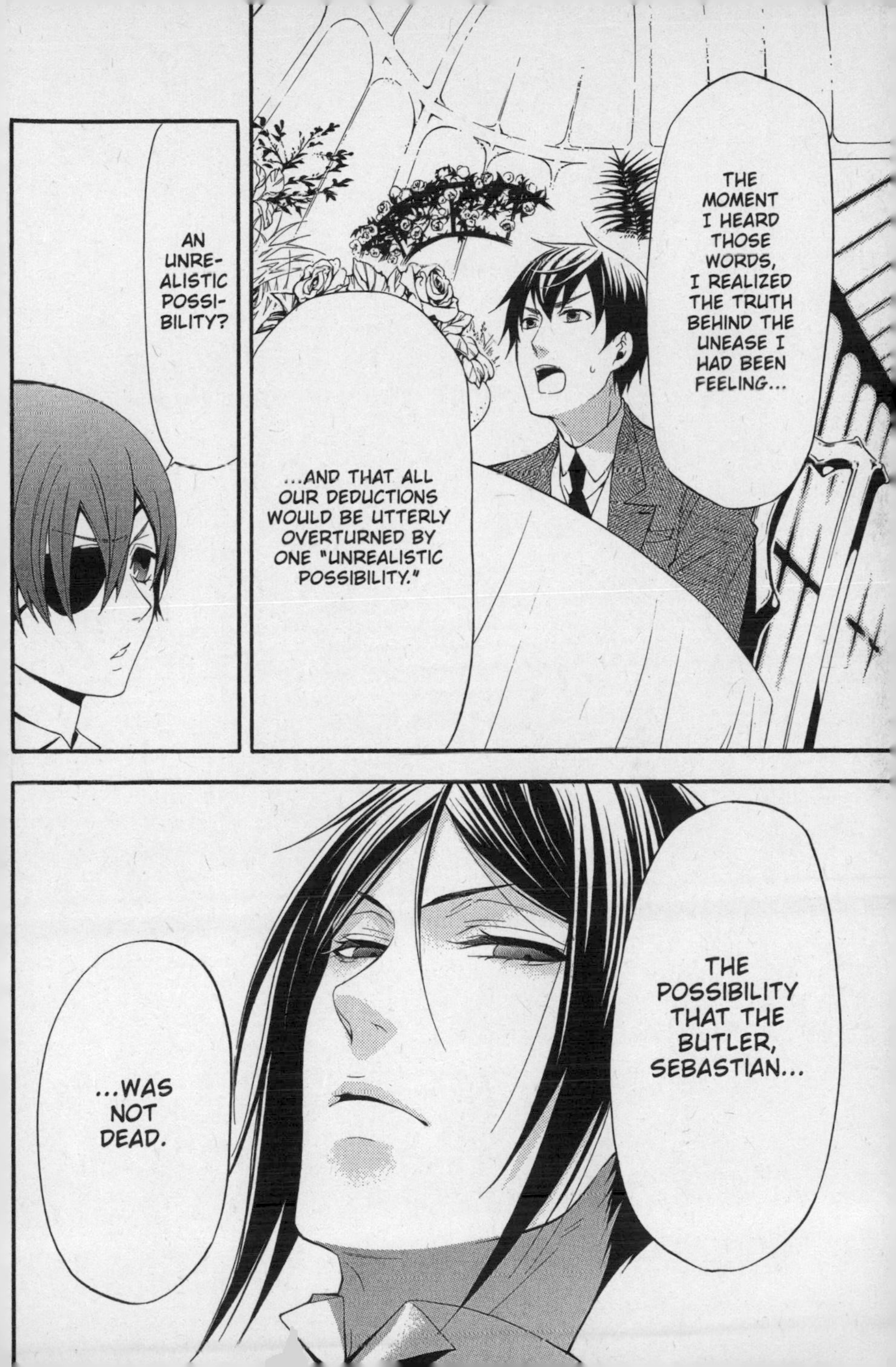
THE MOMENT I HEARD THOSE WORDS, I REALIZED THE TRUTH BEHIND THE UNEASE I HAD BEEN FEELING...
...AND THAT ALL OUR DEDUCTIONS WOULD BE UTTERLY OVERTURNED BY ONE "UNREALISTIC POSSIBILITY."
AN UNRE-ALISTIC POSSI-BILITY?
THE POSSIBILITY THAT THE BUTLER, SEBASTIAN...
...WAS NOT DEAD.

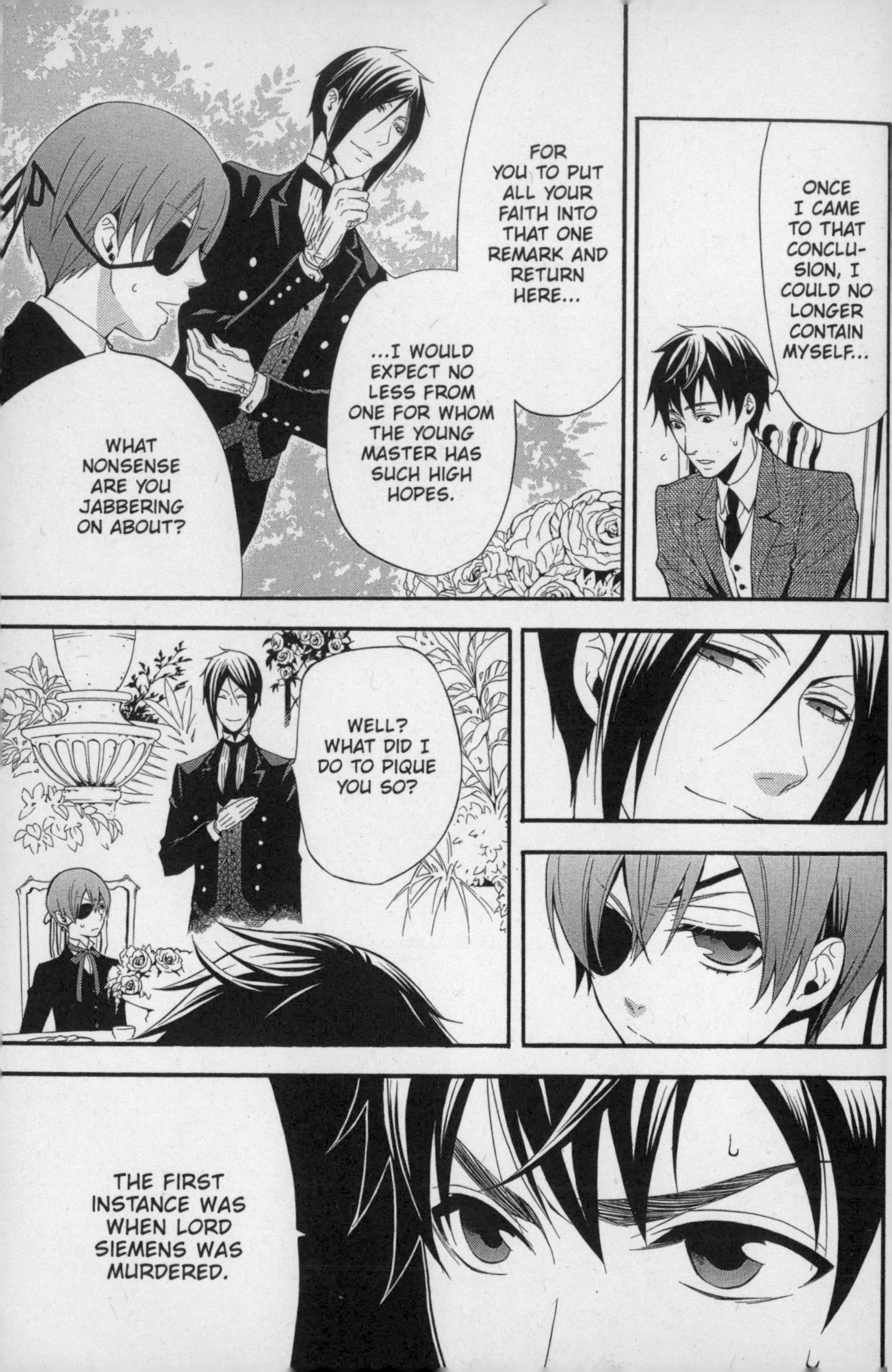
ONCE I CAME TO THAT CONCLUSION, I COULD NO LONGER CONTAIN MYSELF...
FOR YOU TO PUT ALL YOUR FAITH INTO THAT ONE REMARK AND RETURN HERE...
...I WOULD EXPECT NO LESS FROM ONE FOR WHOM THE YOUNG MASTER HAS SUCH HIGH HOPES.
WHAT NONSENSE ARE YOU JABBERING ON ABOUT?
WELL? WHAT DID I DO TO PIQUE YOU SO?
THE FIRST INSTANCE WAS WHEN LORD SIEMENS WAS MURDERED.

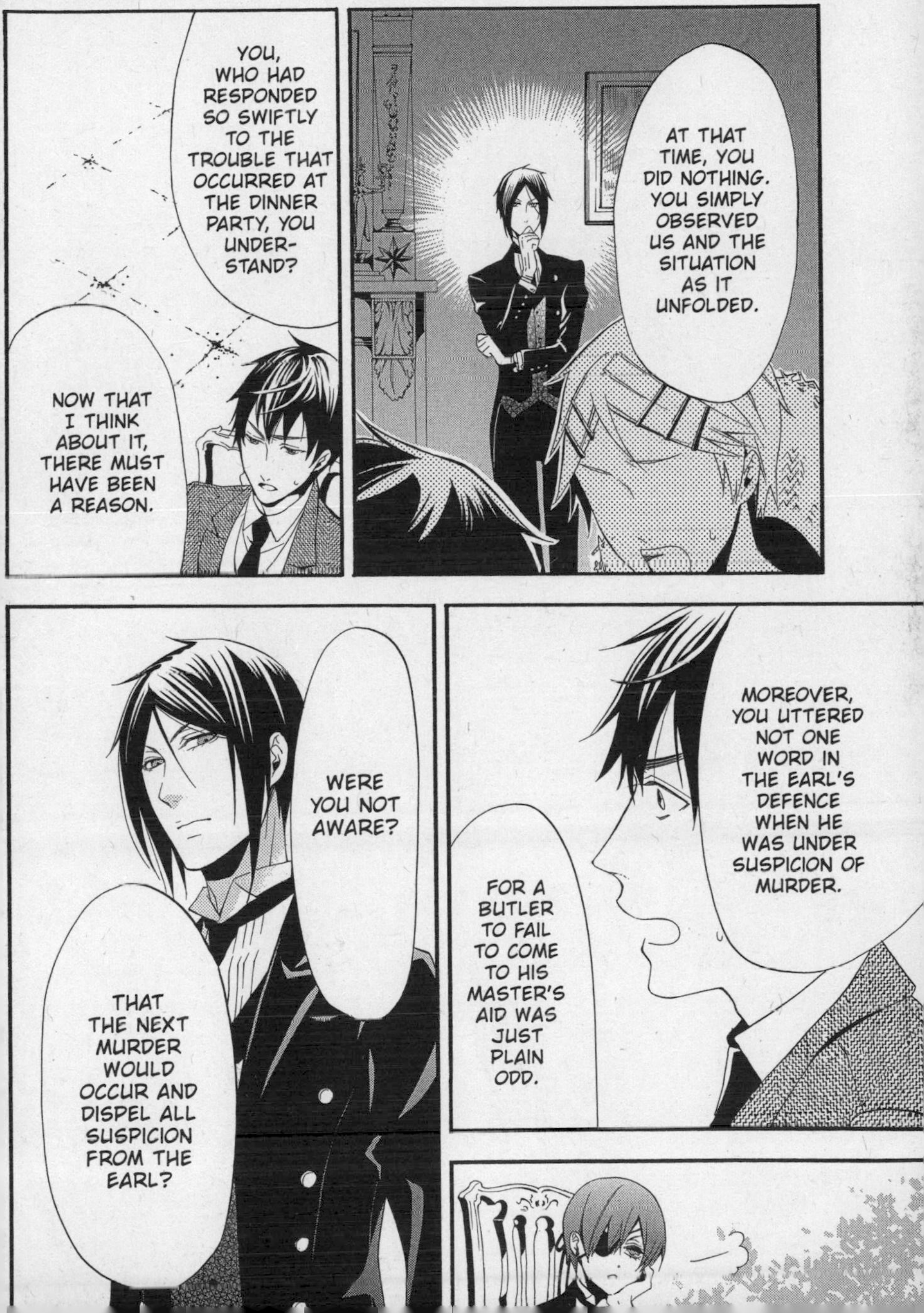
AT THAT TIME, YOU DID NOTHING. YOU SIMPLY OBSERVED US AND THE SITUATION AS IT UNFOLDED.
YOU, WHO HAD RESPONDED SO SWIFTLY TO THE TROUBLE THAT OCCURRED AT THE DINNER PARTY, YOU UNDER-STAND?
NOW THAT I THINK ABOUT IT, THERE MUST HAVE BEEN A REASON.
MOREOVER, YOU UTTERED NOT ONE WORD IN THE EARL'S DEFENCE WHEN HE WAS UNDER SUSPICION OF MURDER.
FOR A BUTLER TO FAIL TO COME TO HIS MASTER'S AID WAS JUST PLAIN ODD.
WERE YOU NOT AWARE?
THAT THE NEXT MURDER WOULD OCCUR AND DISPEL ALL SUSPICION FROM THE EARL?

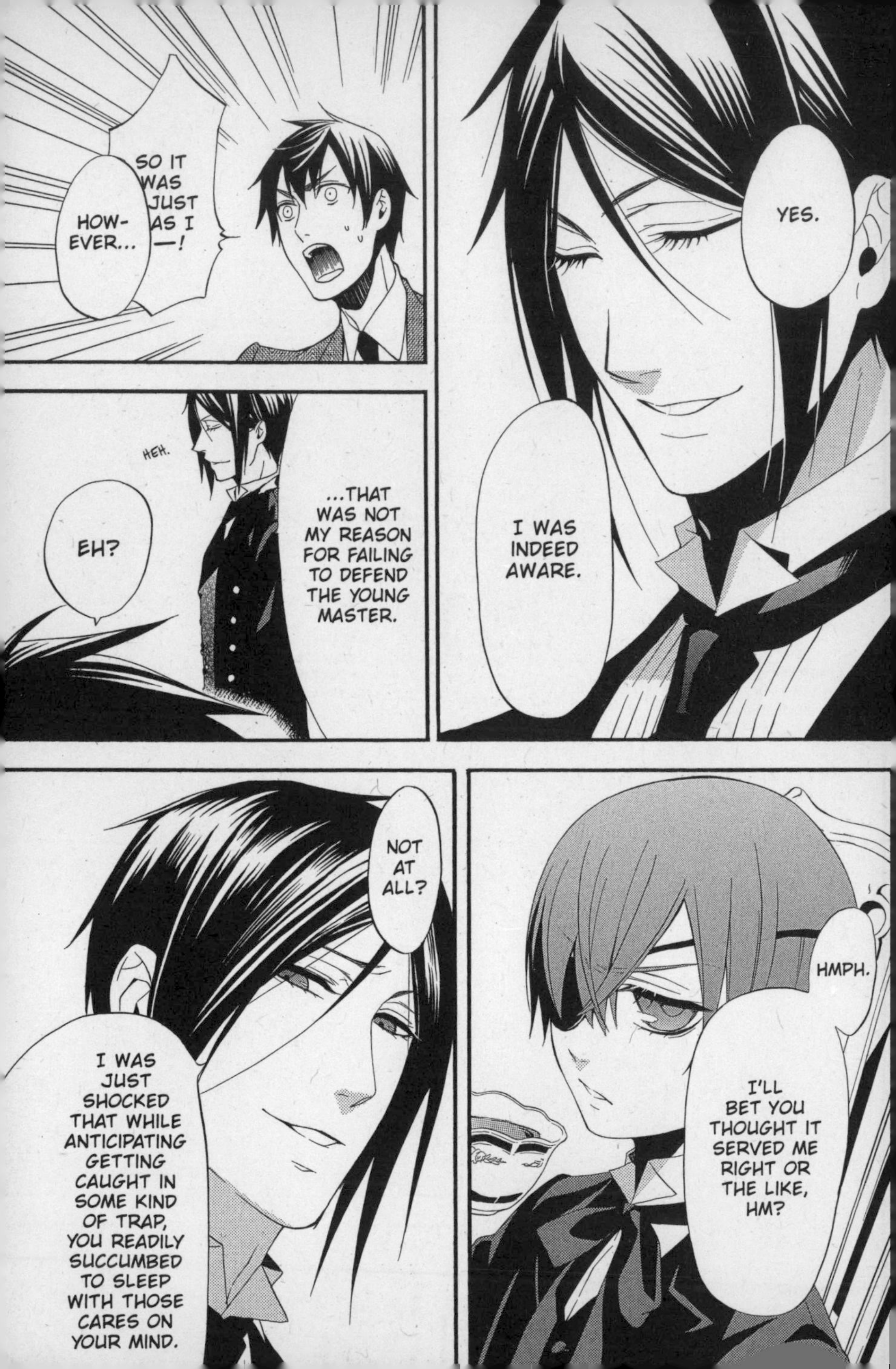
YES.
I WAS INDEED AWARE.
SO IT WAS JUST AS I—!
HOW-EVER...
...THAT WAS NOT MY REASON FOR FAILING TO DEFEND THE YOUNG MASTER.
HEH.
EH?
HMPH.
I'LL BET YOU THOUGHT IT SERVED ME RIGHT OR THE LIKE, HM?
NOT AT ALL?
I WAS JUST SHOCKED THAT WHILE ANTICIPATING GETTING CAUGHT IN SOME KIND OF TRAP, YOU READILY SUCCUMBED TO SLEEP WITH THOSE CARES ON YOUR MIND.

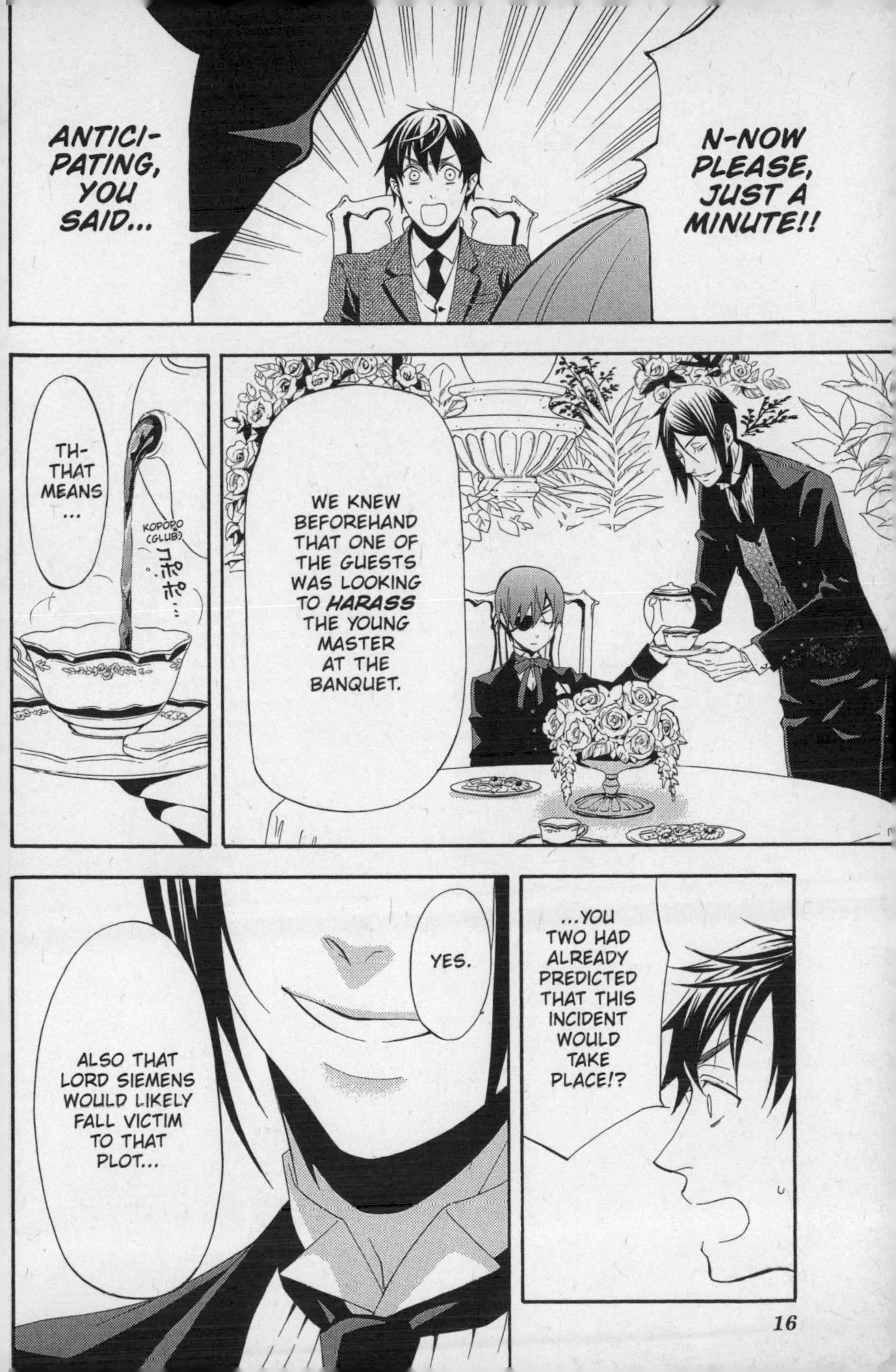
N-NOW PLEASE, JUST A MINUTE!!
ANTICI-PATING, YOU SAID...
WE KNEW BEFOREHAND THAT ONE OF THE GUESTS WAS LOOKING TO *HARASS* THE YOUNG MASTER AT THE BANQUET.
TH- THAT MEANS ...
KOPOPO (GLUB)
コポポ...
...YOU TWO HAD ALREADY PREDICTED THAT THIS INCIDENT WOULD TAKE PLACE!?
YES.
ALSO THAT LORD SIEMENS WOULD LIKELY FALL VICTIM TO THAT PLOT...

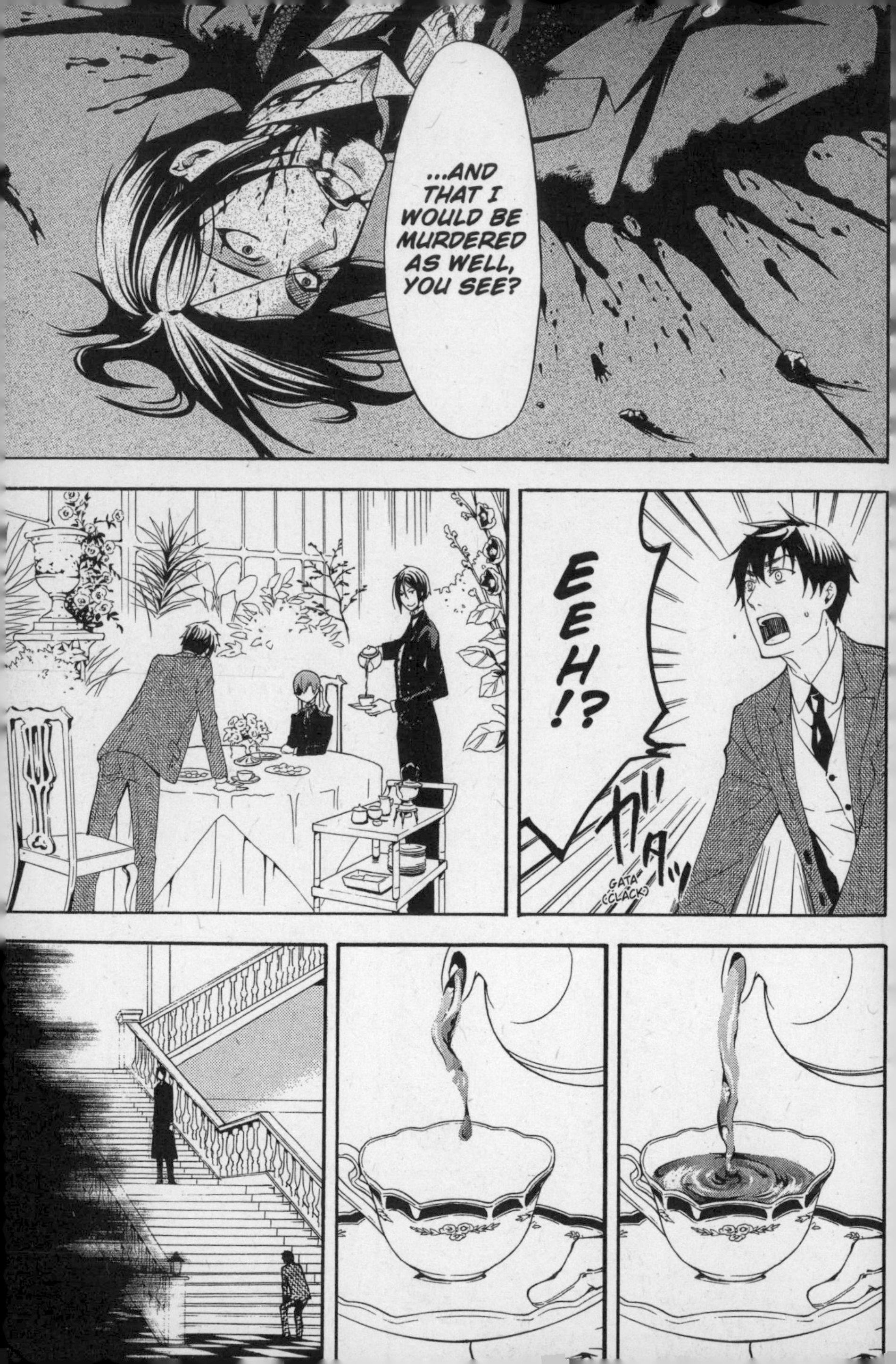
...AND THAT I WOULD BE MURDERED AS WELL, YOU SEE?
EEEH!?
GATA (CLACK)

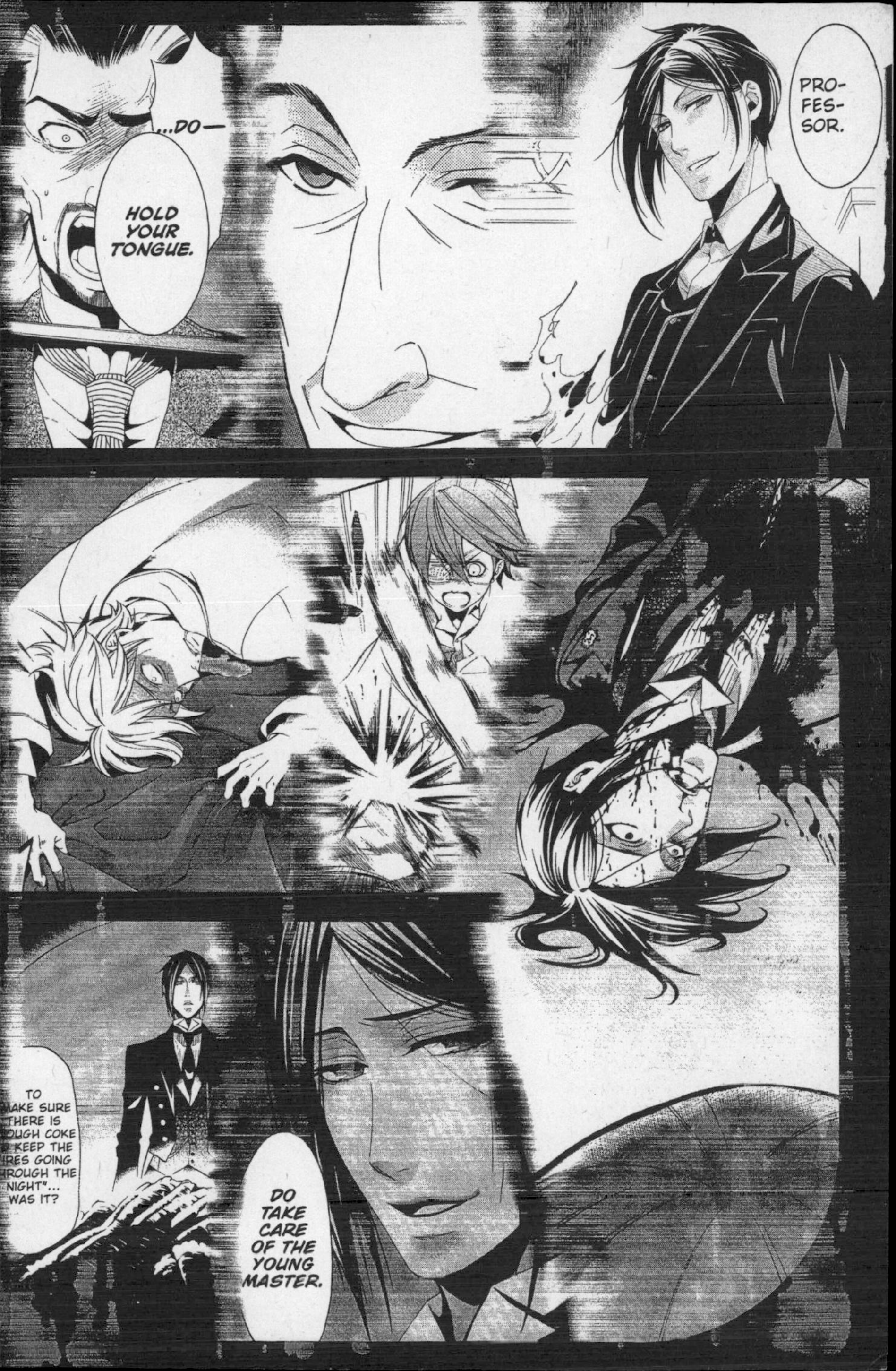
PRO-FES-SOR.
...DO—
HOLD YOUR TONGUE.
DO TAKE CARE OF THE YOUNG MASTER.
TO MAKE SURE THERE IS OUGH COKE KEEP THE RES GOING ROUGH THE NIGHT"... WAS IT?

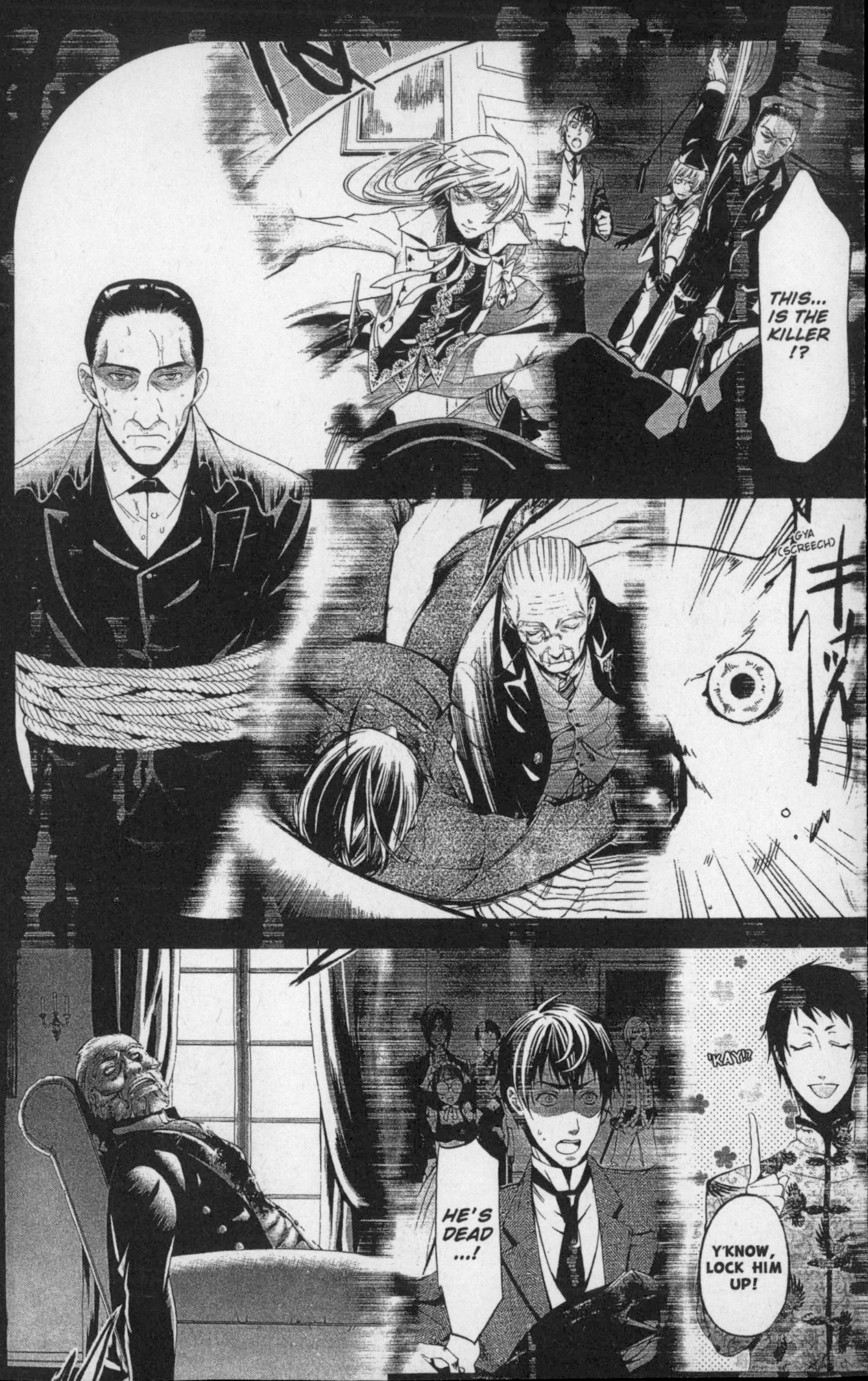
THIS... IS THE KILLER !?
GYA (SCREECH)
'KAY!?
Y'KNOW, LOCK HIM UP!
HE'S DEAD ...!

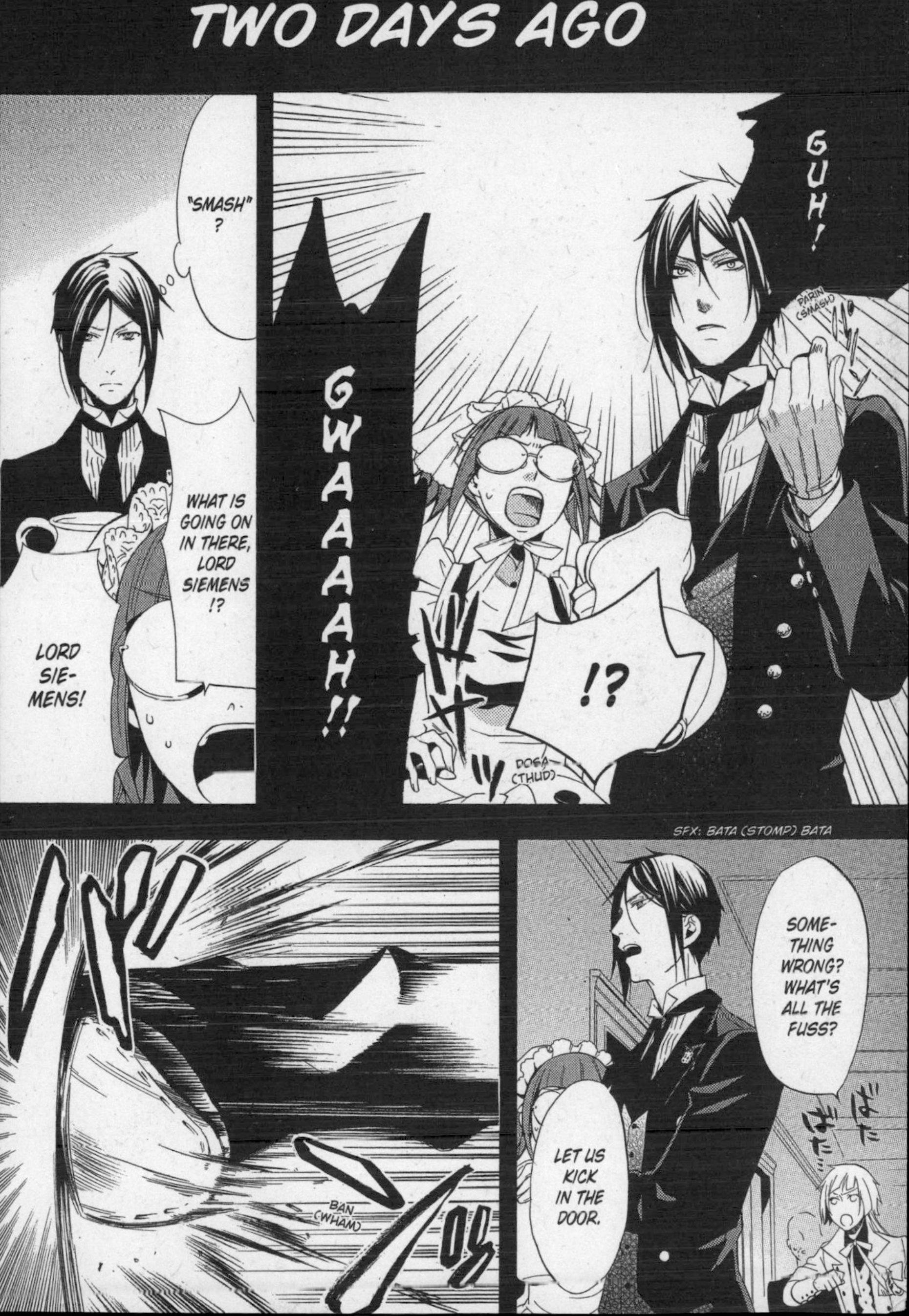
TWO DAYS AGO
GUH!
PARIN (SMASH)
GWAAAAAH!!
!?
DOGA (THUD)
"SMASH"?
WHAT IS GOING ON IN THERE, LORD SIEMENS!?
LORD SIE-MENS!
SFX: BATA (STOMP) BATA
SOME-THING WRONG? WHAT'S ALL THE FUSS?
ばた ばた…
LET US KICK IN THE DOOR.
BAN (WHAM)

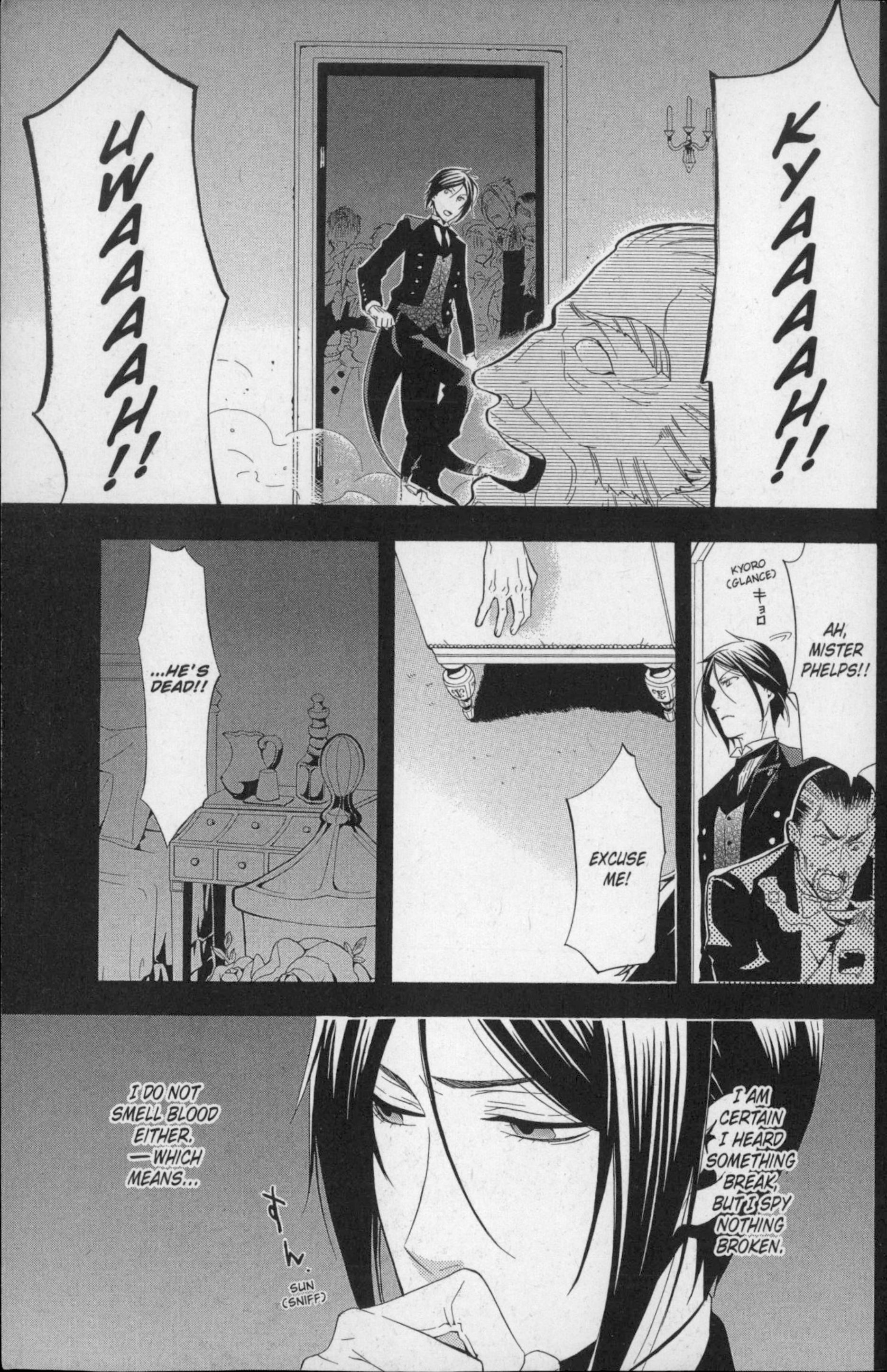
KYAAAAAH!!
UWAAAAAH!!
KYORO (GLANCE)
キョロ
AH, MISTER PHELPS!!
EXCUSE ME!
...HE'S DEAD!!
I AM CERTAIN I HEARD SOMETHING BREAK, BUT I SPY NOTHING BROKEN.
すん
SUN (SNIFF)
I DO NOT SMELL BLOOD EITHER. —WHICH MEANS...

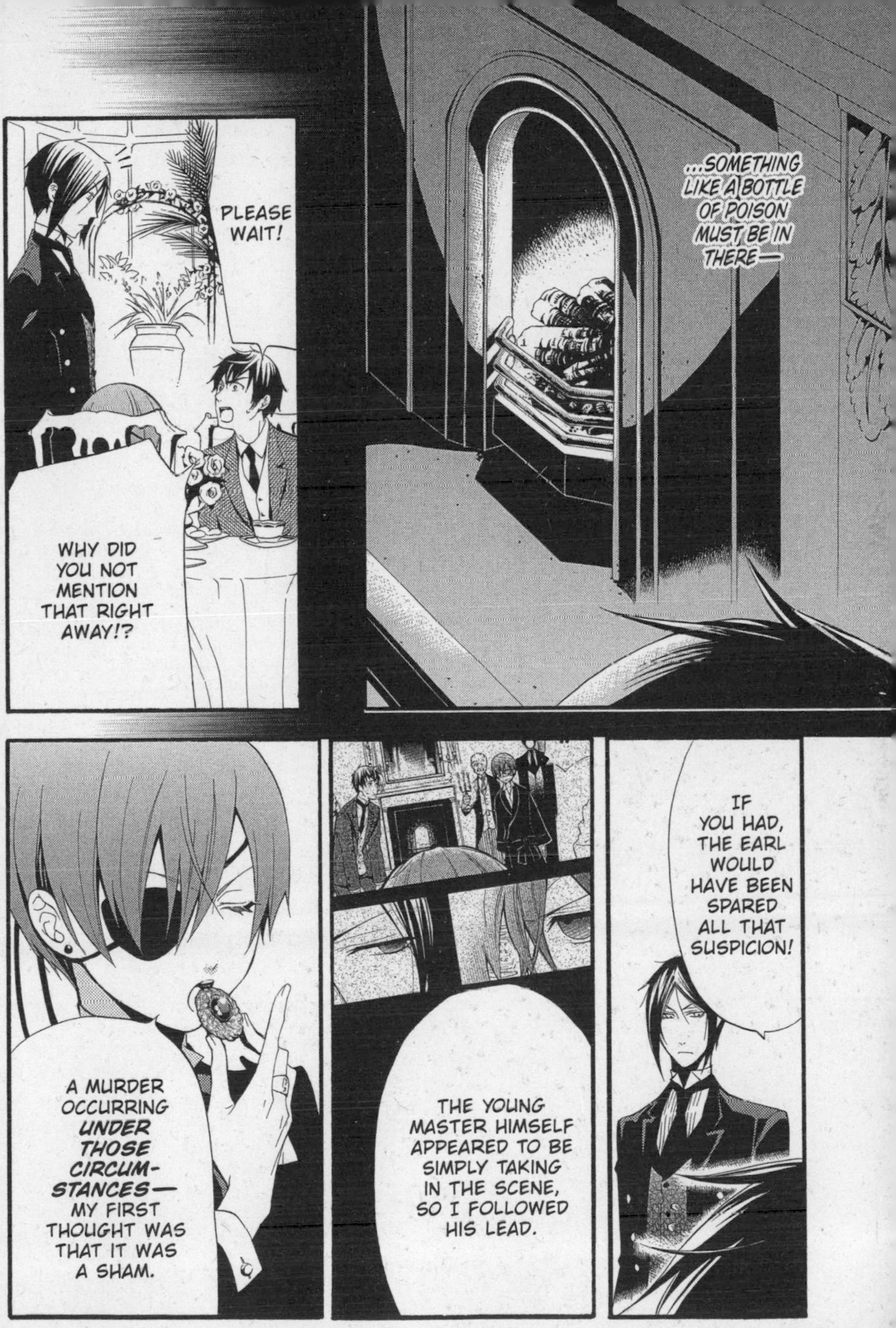
...SOMETHING LIKE A BOTTLE OF POISON MUST BE IN THERE—
PLEASE WAIT!
WHY DID YOU NOT MENTION THAT RIGHT AWAY!?
IF YOU HAD, THE EARL WOULD HAVE BEEN SPARED ALL THAT SUSPICION!
THE YOUNG MASTER HIMSELF APPEARED TO BE SIMPLY TAKING IN THE SCENE, SO I FOLLOWED HIS LEAD.
A MURDER OCCURRING UNDER THOSE CIRCUMSTANCES— MY FIRST THOUGHT WAS THAT IT WAS A SHAM.

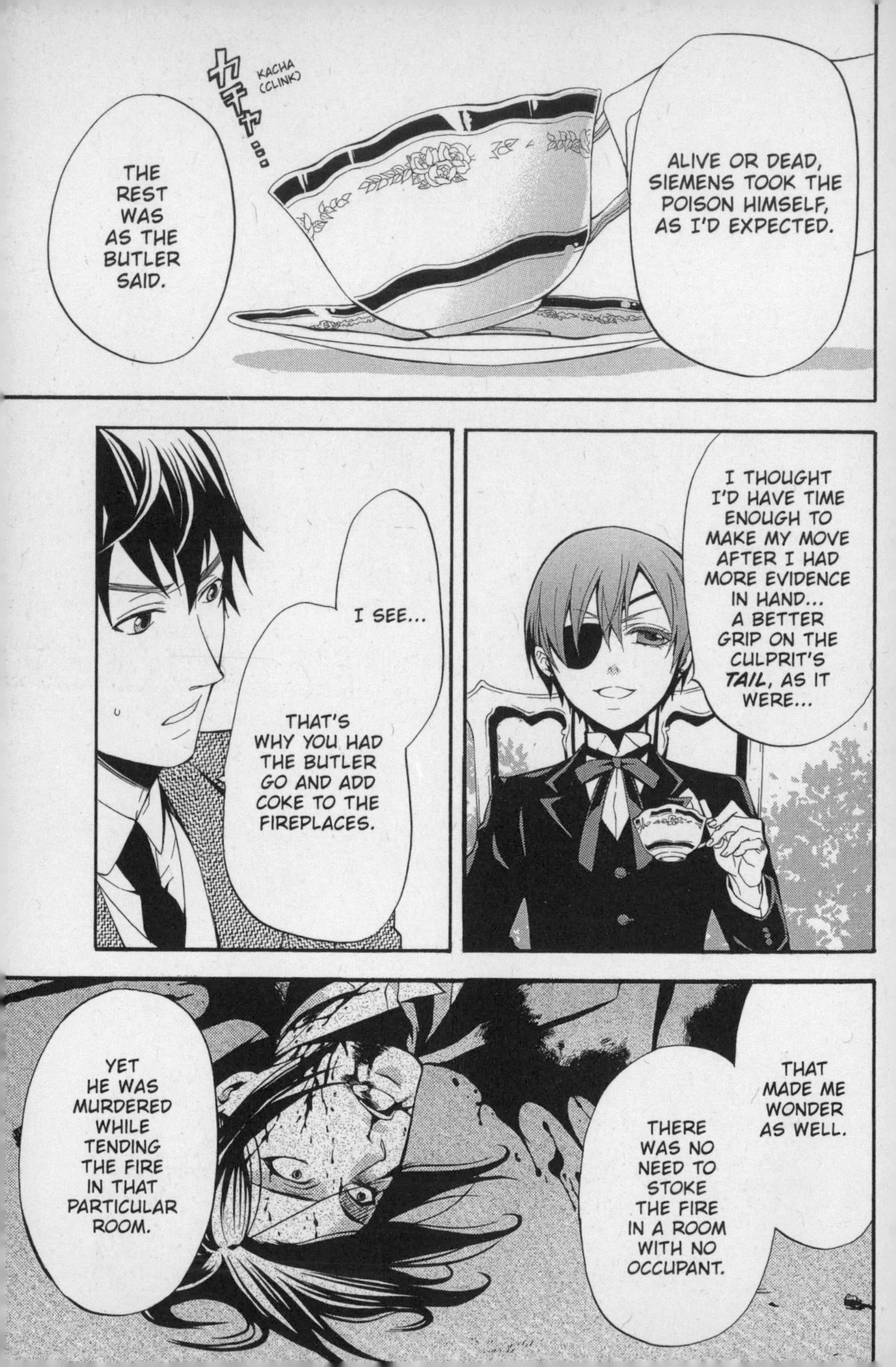
ALIVE OR DEAD, SIEMENS TOOK THE POISON HIMSELF, AS I'D EXPECTED.
カチャ…
KACHA (CLINK)
THE REST WAS AS THE BUTLER SAID.
I THOUGHT I'D HAVE TIME ENOUGH TO MAKE MY MOVE AFTER I HAD MORE EVIDENCE IN HAND... A BETTER GRIP ON THE CULPRIT'S *TAIL*, AS IT WERE...
I SEE...
THAT'S WHY YOU HAD THE BUTLER GO AND ADD COKE TO THE FIREPLACES.
THAT MADE ME WONDER AS WELL.
THERE WAS NO NEED TO STOKE THE FIRE IN A ROOM WITH NO OCCUPANT.
YET HE WAS MURDERED WHILE TENDING THE FIRE IN THAT PARTICULAR ROOM.

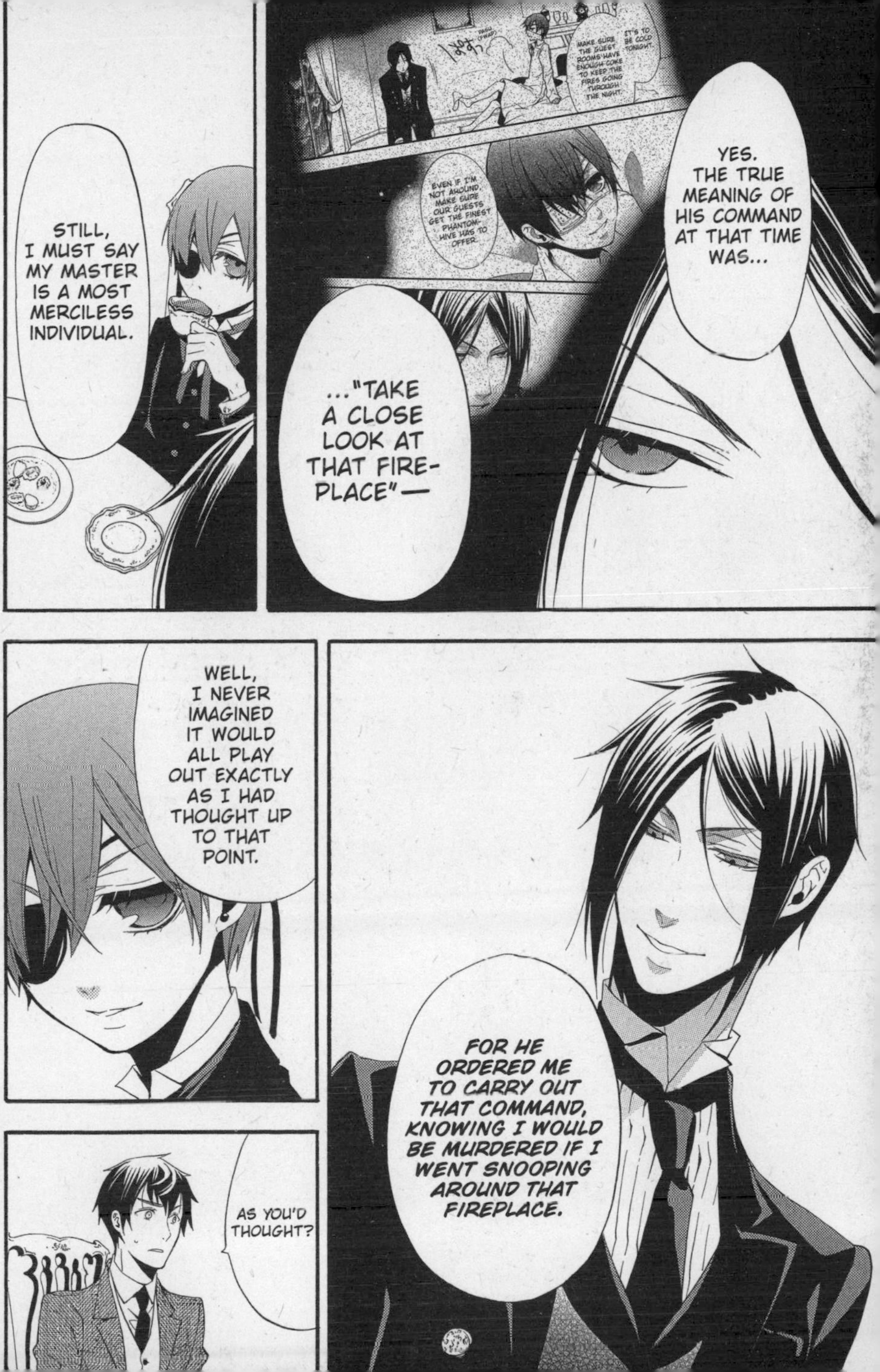
YES.
THE TRUE MEANING OF HIS COMMAND AT THAT TIME WAS...
IT'S TO BE COLD TONIGHT.
MAKE SURE THE GUEST ROOMS HAVE ENOUGH COKE TO KEEP THE FIRES GOING THROUGH THE NIGHT.
PASU (FWAP)
EVEN IF I'M NOT AROUND, MAKE SURE OUR GUESTS GET THE FINEST PHANTOM-HIVE HAS TO OFFER.
..."TAKE A CLOSE LOOK AT THAT FIRE-PLACE"—
STILL, I MUST SAY MY MASTER IS A MOST MERCILESS INDIVIDUAL.
FOR HE ORDERED ME TO CARRY OUT THAT COMMAND, KNOWING I WOULD BE MURDERED IF I WENT SNOOPING AROUND THAT FIREPLACE.
WELL, I NEVER IMAGINED IT WOULD ALL PLAY OUT EXACTLY AS I HAD THOUGHT UP TO THAT POINT.
AS YOU'D THOUGHT?

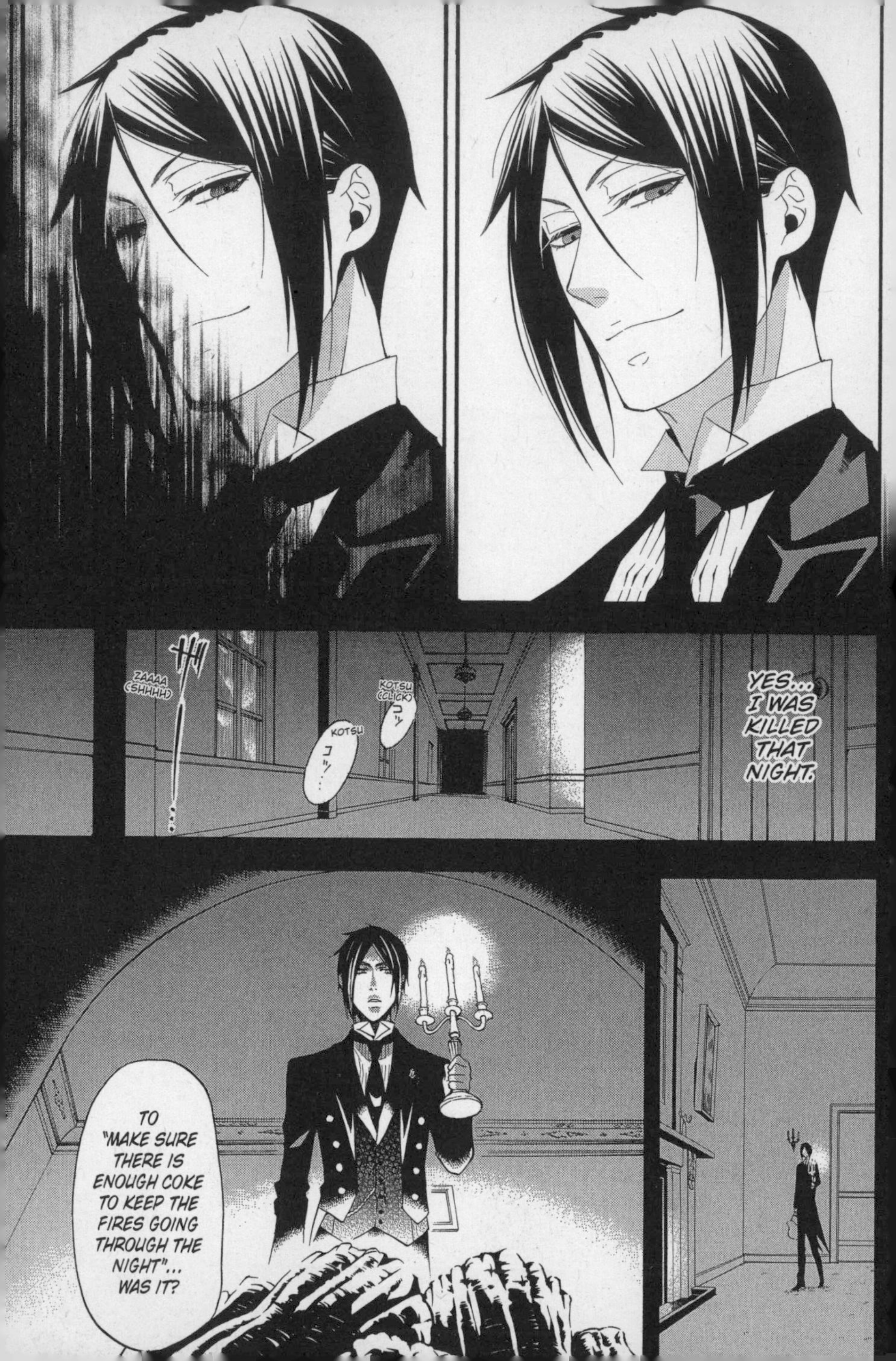
YES... I WAS KILLED THAT NIGHT.
KOTSU (CLICK)
KOTSU
ZAAAA (SHHHH)
TO "MAKE SURE THERE IS ENOUGH COKE TO KEEP THE FIRES GOING THROUGH THE NIGHT"... WAS IT?

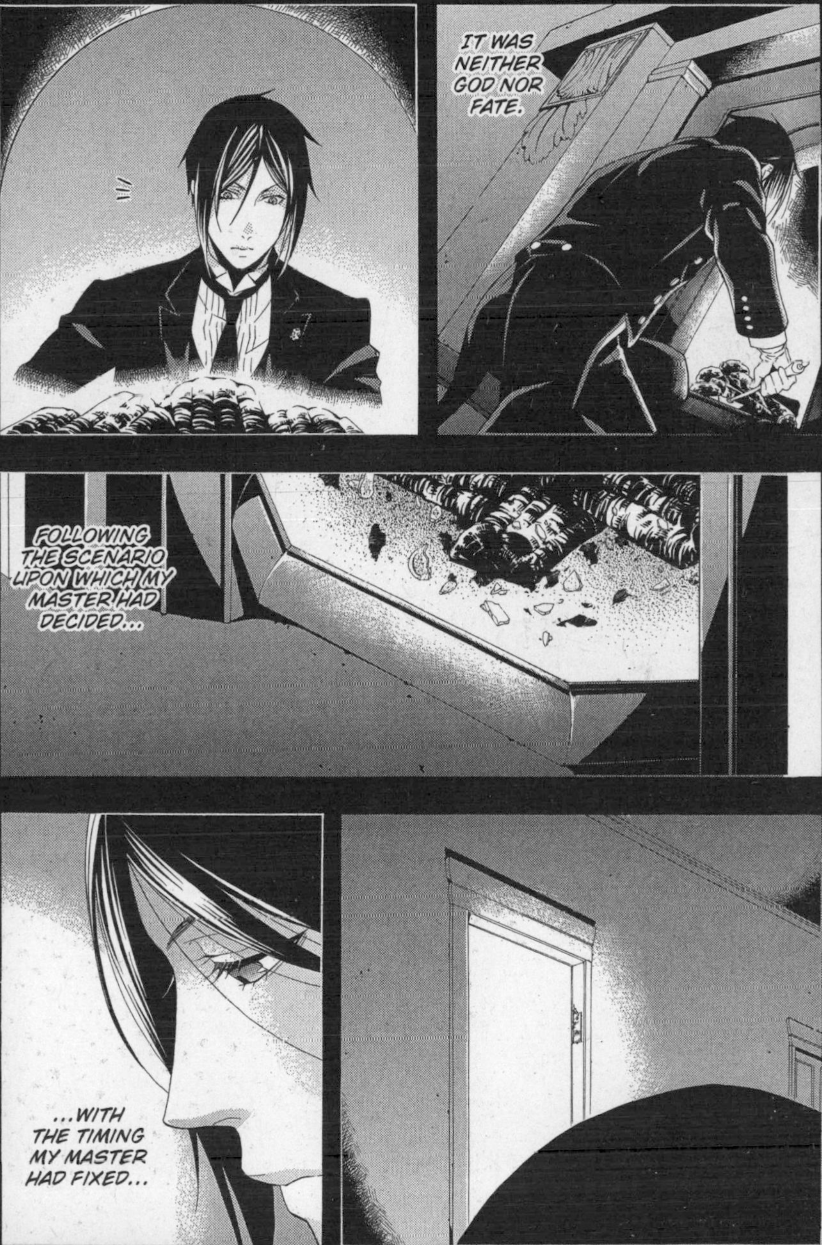
IT WAS NEITHER GOD NOR FATE.
FOLLOWING THE SCENARIO UPON WHICH MY MASTER HAD DECIDED...
...WITH THE TIMING MY MASTER HAD FIXED...

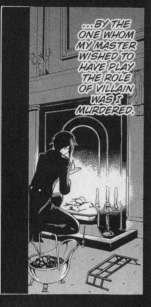

...BY THE ONE WHOM MY MASTER WISHED TO HAVE PLAY THE ROLE OF VILLAIN WAS I MURDERED.
AT THE HANDS OF THE ONE WHO HAD COME ONLY TO TORMENT MY MASTER—
I SHOULD HAVE KNOWN...
YURA (WOBBLE)
ゆら…

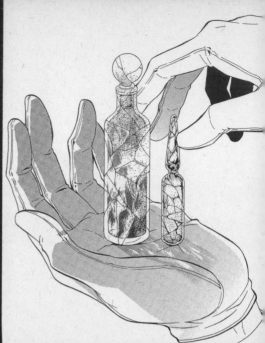

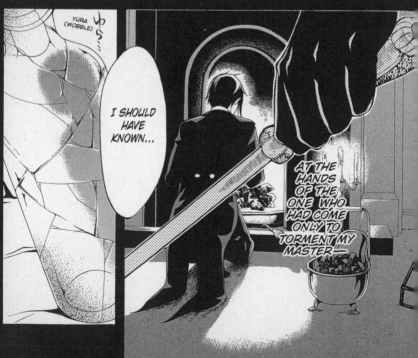

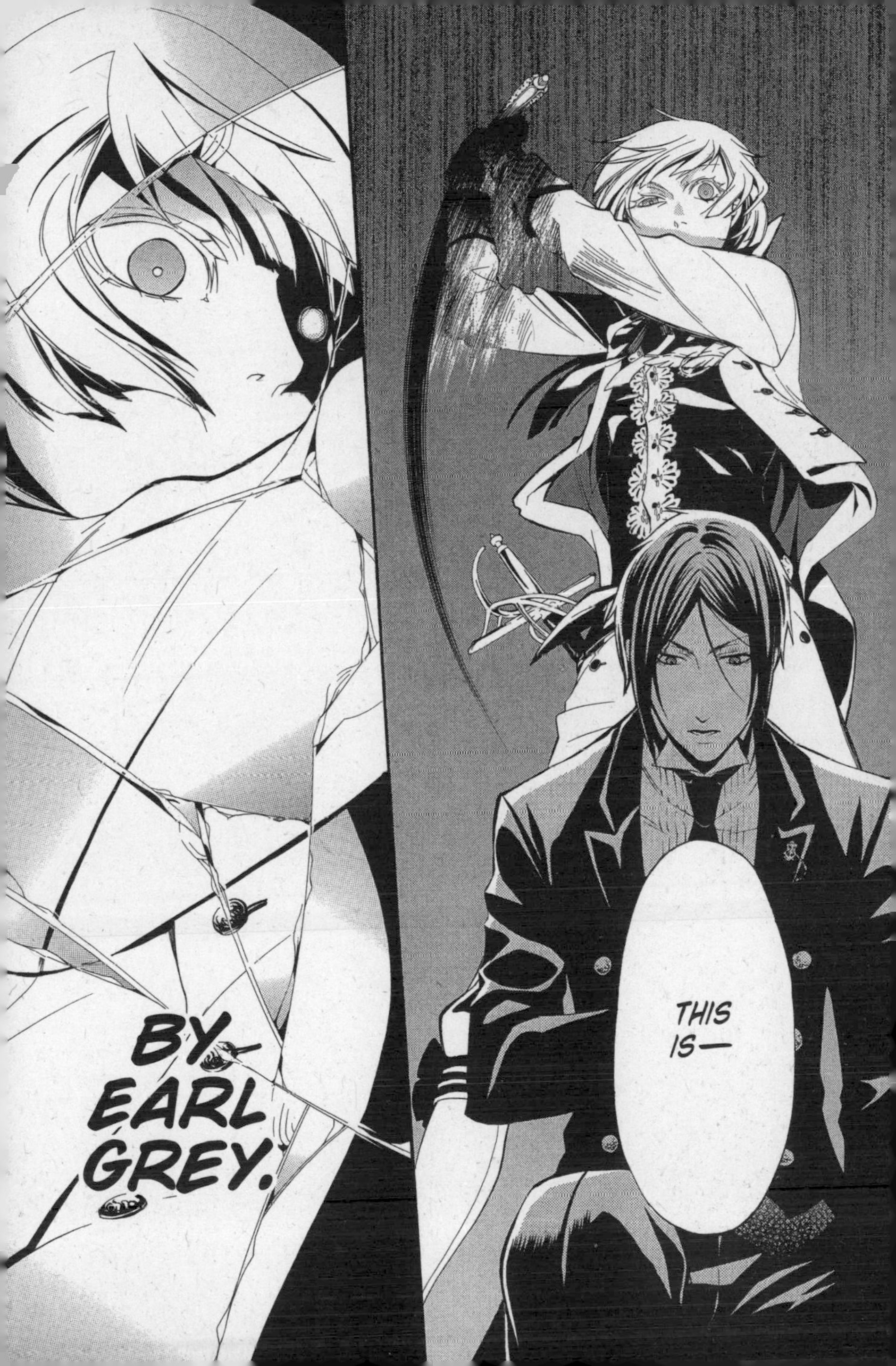
THIS IS—
BY EARL GREY.

Black Butler

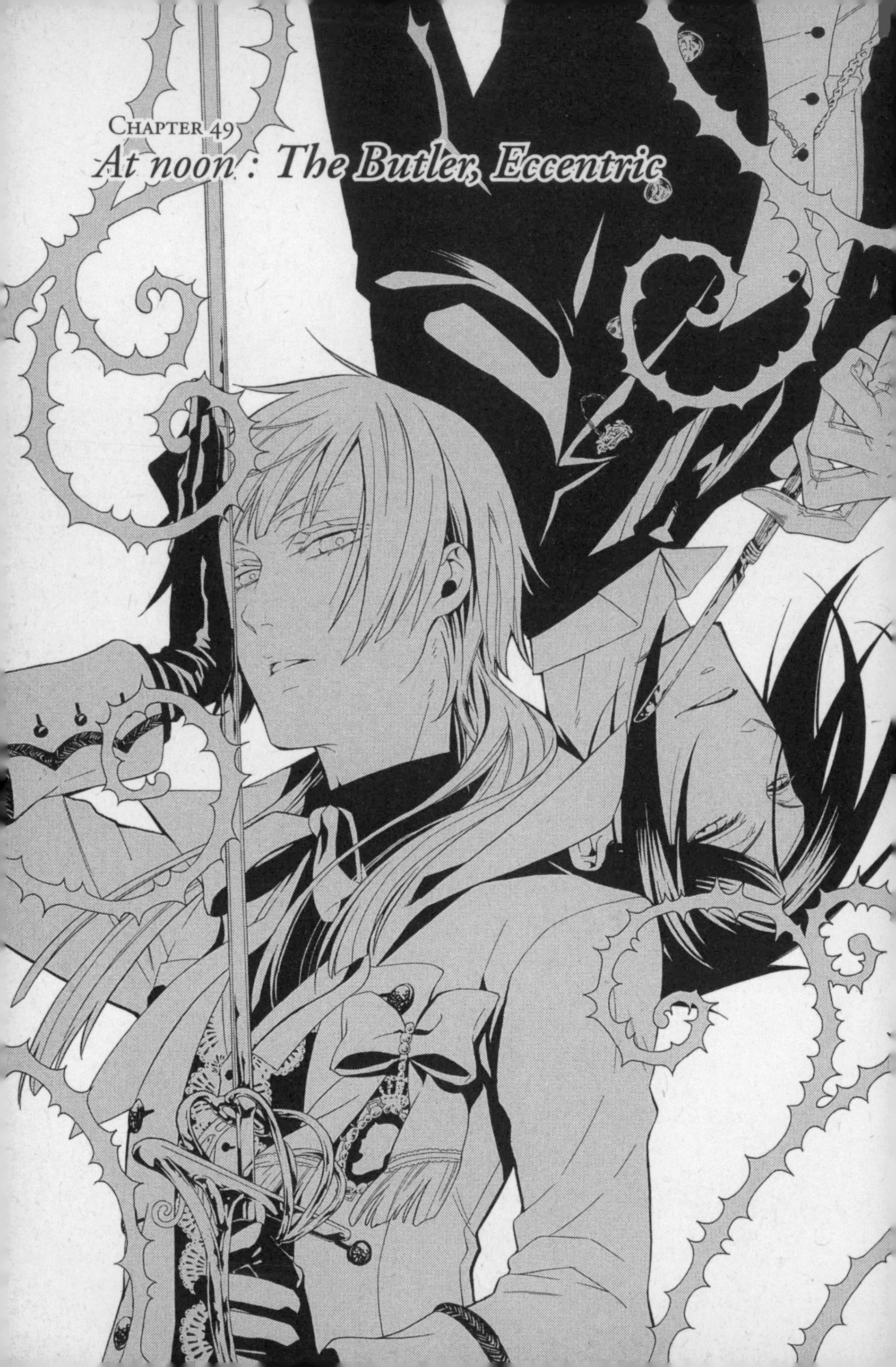
Chapter 49
At noon : The Butler, Eccentric

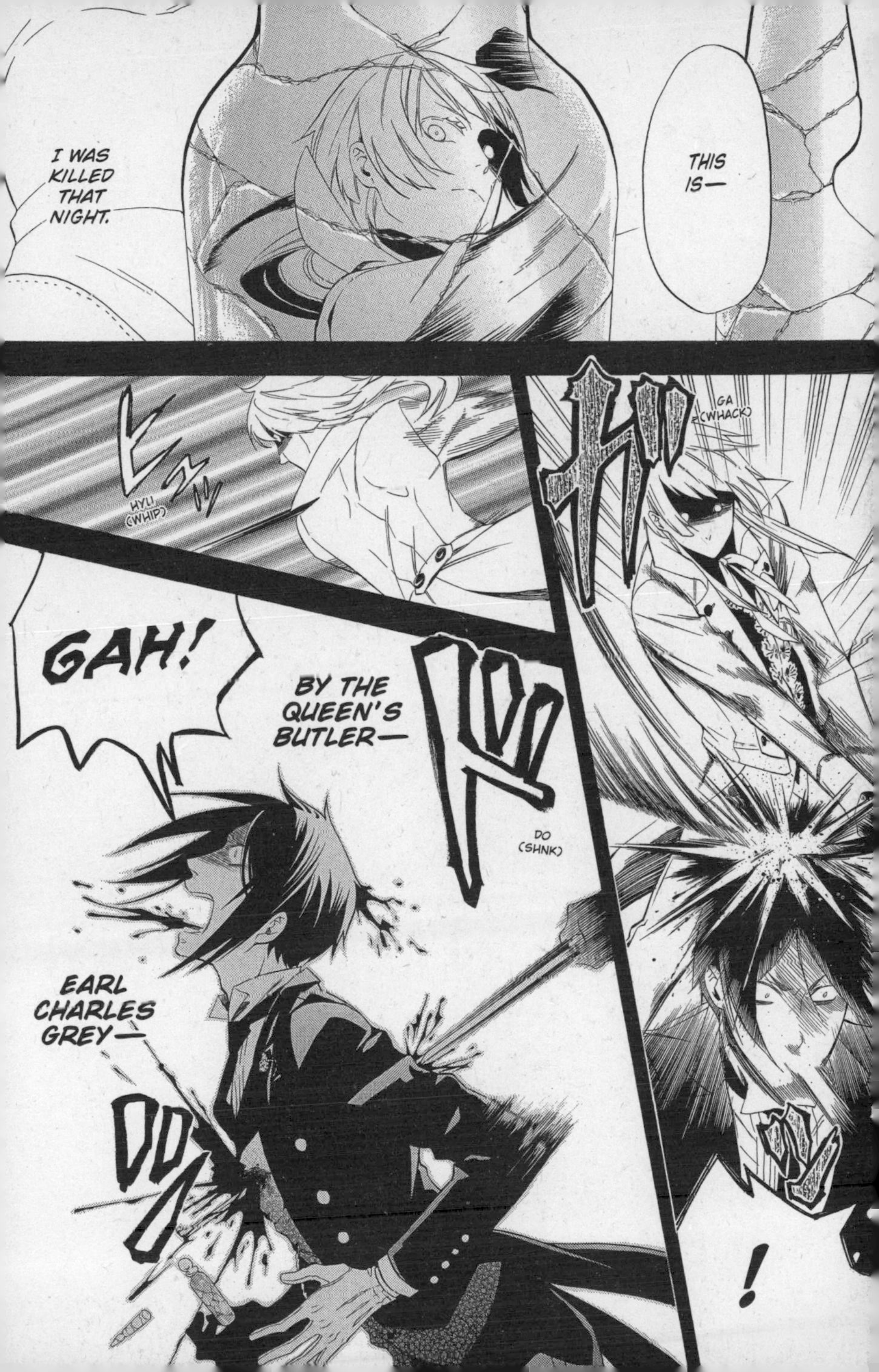
THIS IS—
I WAS KILLED THAT NIGHT.
GA (WHACK)
!
HYU (WHIP)
DO (SHNK)
BY THE QUEEN'S BUTLER—
GAH!
EARL CHARLES GREY—

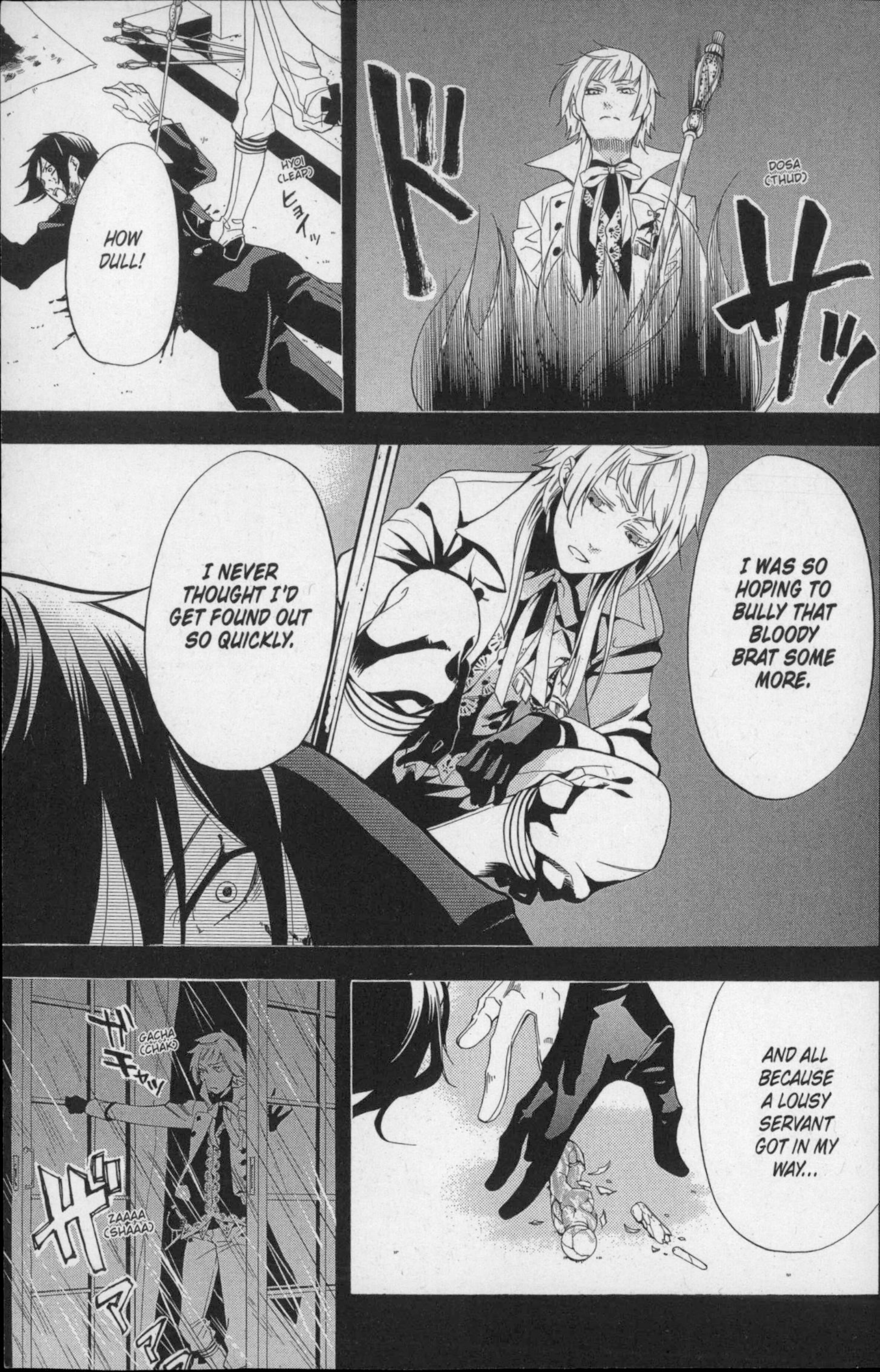
DOSA (THUD)
HYOI (LEAP)
HOW DULL!
I WAS SO HOPING TO BULLY THAT BLOODY BRAT SOME MORE.
I NEVER THOUGHT I'D GET FOUND OUT SO QUICKLY.
AND ALL BECAUSE A LOUSY SERVANT GOT IN MY WAY...
GACHA (CHAK)
ZAAAA (SHAAA)

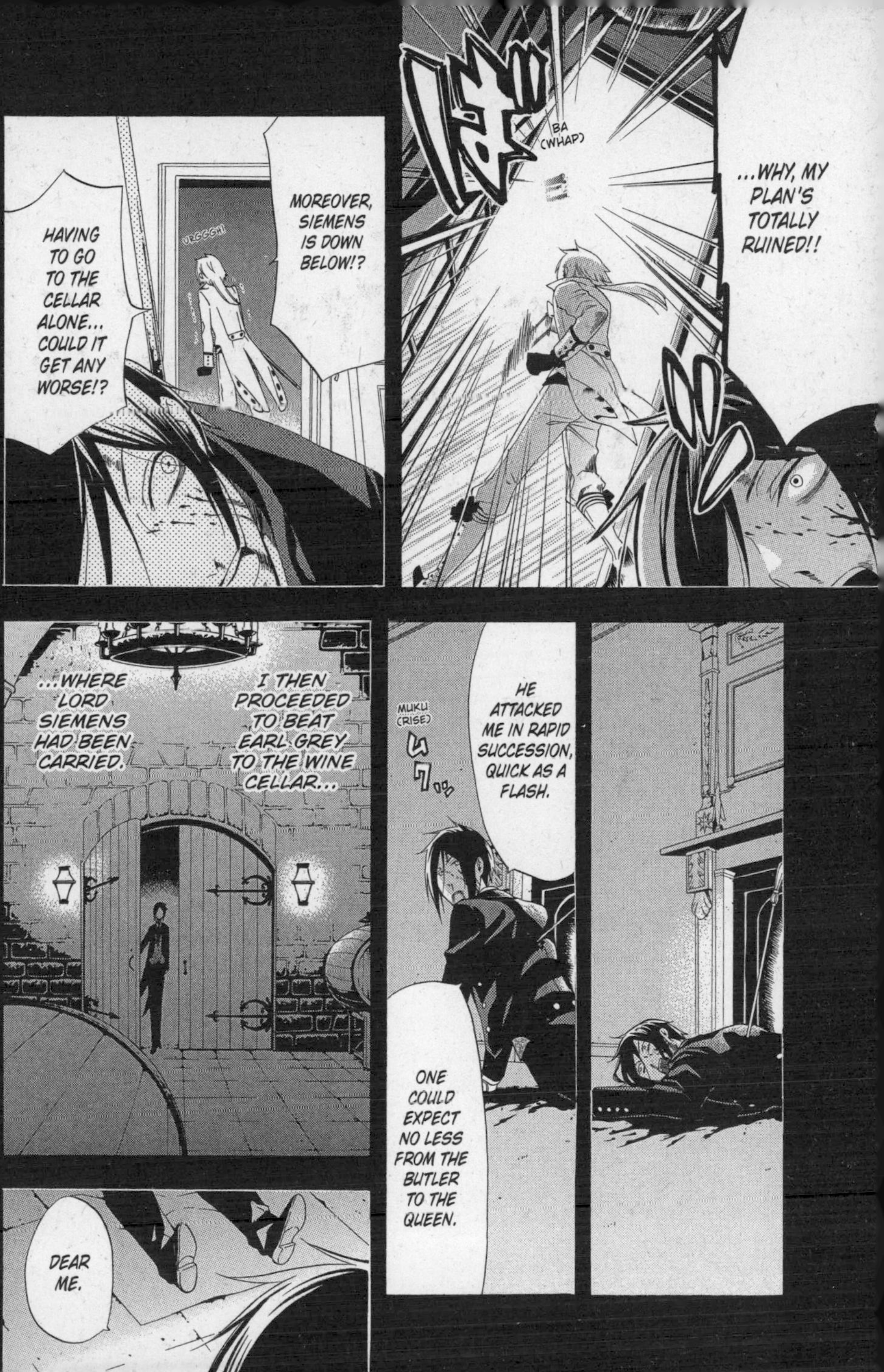
BA (WHAP)
...WHY, MY PLAN'S TOTALLY RUINED!!
MOREOVER, SIEMENS IS DOWN BELOW!?
URGGGH!
HAVING TO GO TO THE CELLAR ALONE... COULD IT GET ANY WORSE!?
HE ATTACKED ME IN RAPID SUCCESSION, QUICK AS A FLASH.
MUKU (RISE)
ONE COULD EXPECT NO LESS FROM THE BUTLER TO THE QUEEN.
I THEN PROCEEDED TO BEAT EARL GREY TO THE WINE CELLAR...
...WHERE LORD SIEMENS HAD BEEN CARRIED.
DEAR ME.

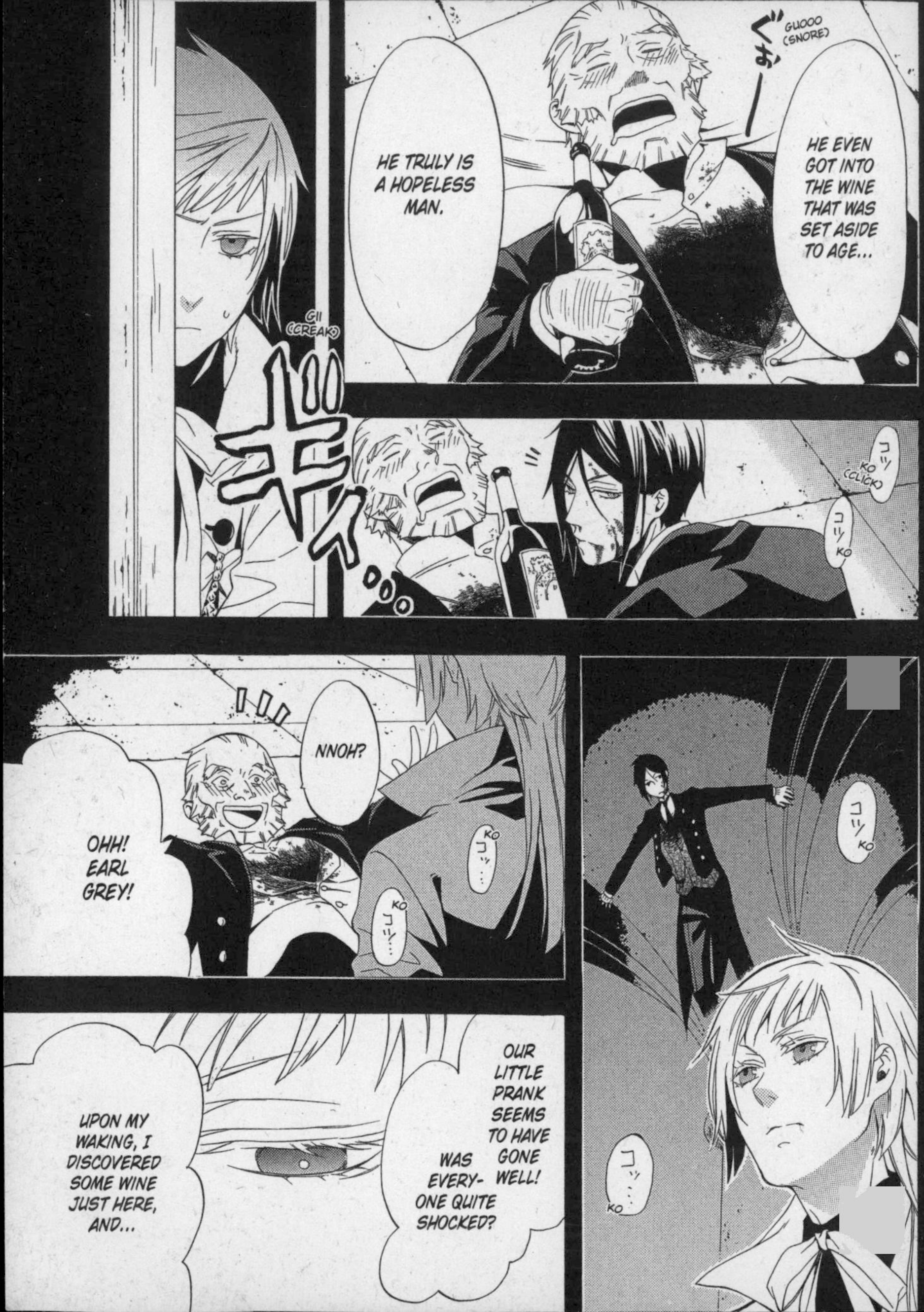
ぐぉー
GUOOO (SNORE)
HE EVEN GOT INTO THE WINE THAT WAS SET ASIDE TO AGE...
HE TRULY IS A HOPELESS MAN.
コツ
KO (CLICK)
コツ
KO
ギィ
GII (CREAK)
コツ
KO
コッ...
KO
NNOH?
KO
コッ...
KO
コッ...
OHH! EARL GREY!
OUR LITTLE PRANK SEEMS TO HAVE GONE WELL!
WAS EVERYONE QUITE SHOCKED?
UPON MY WAKING, I DISCOVERED SOME WINE JUST HERE, AND...

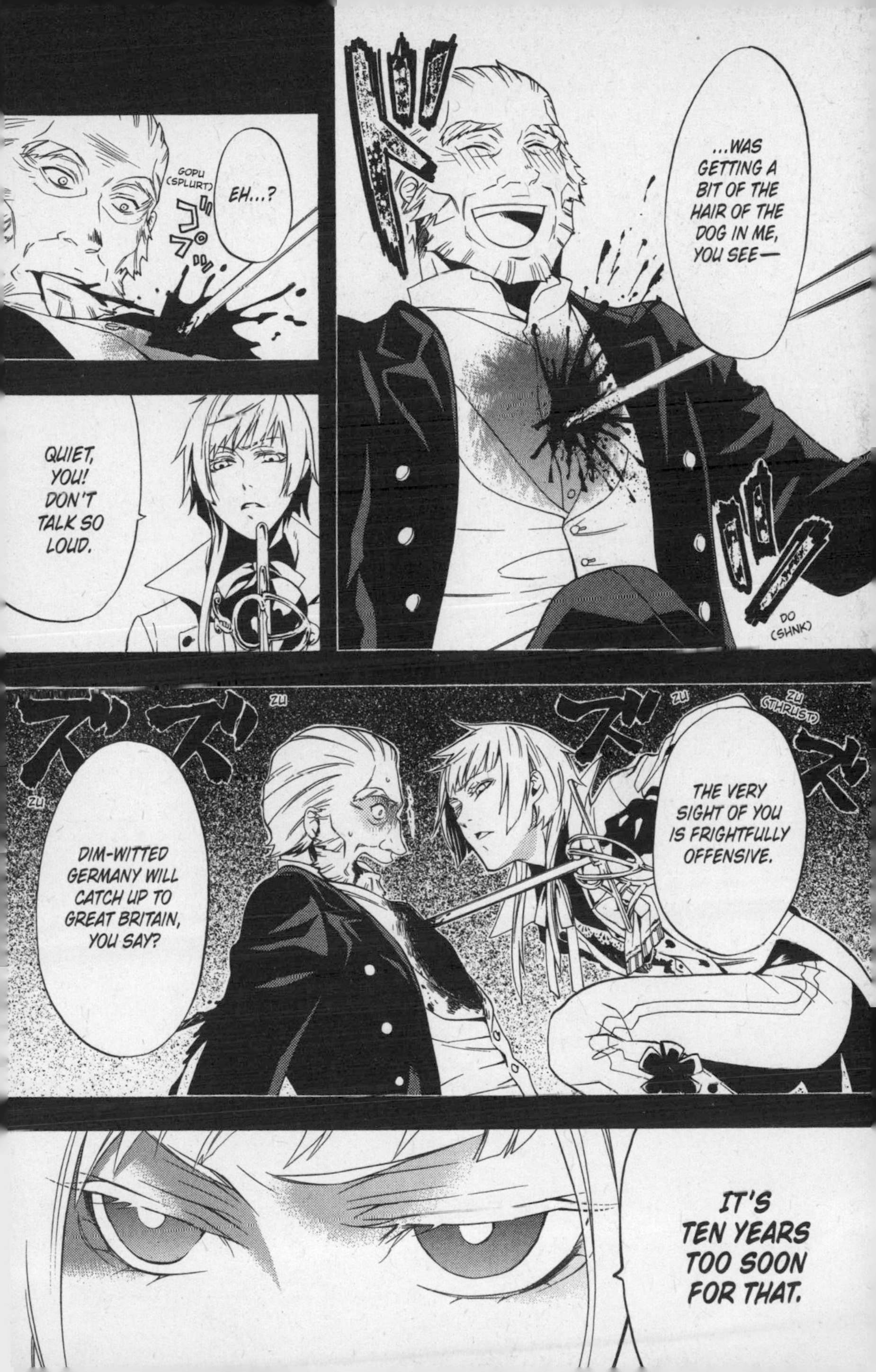
...WAS GETTING A BIT OF THE HAIR OF THE DOG IN ME, YOU SEE—
DO (SHNK)
GOPU (SPLURT)
EH...?
QUIET, YOU! DON'T TALK SO LOUD.
ZU (THRUST)
ZU
THE VERY SIGHT OF YOU IS FRIGHTFULLY OFFENSIVE.
ZU
DIM-WITTED GERMANY WILL CATCH UP TO GREAT BRITAIN, YOU SAY?
ZU
IT'S TEN YEARS TOO SOON FOR THAT.

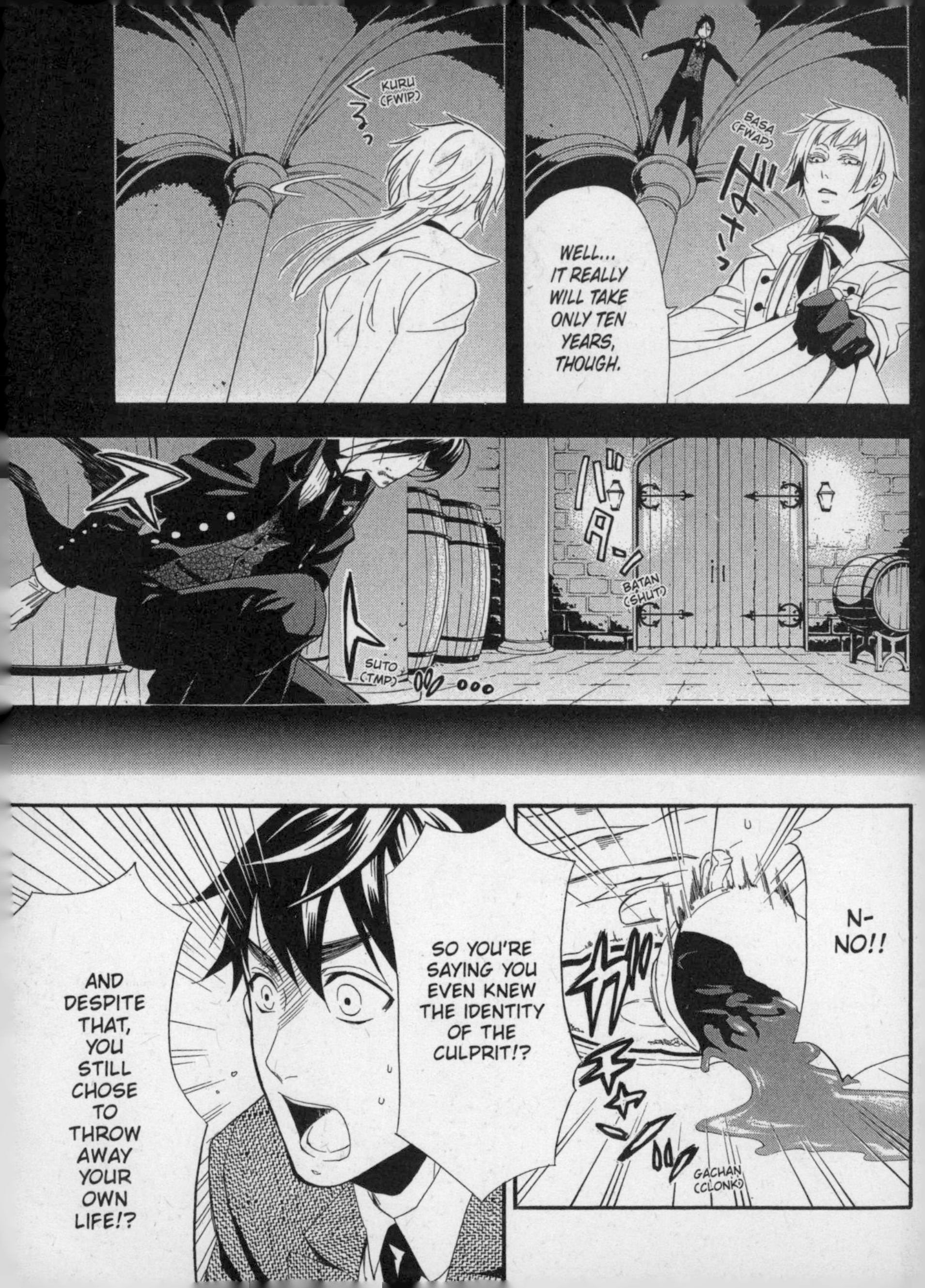
BASA (FWAP)
WELL... IT REALLY WILL TAKE ONLY TEN YEARS, THOUGH.
KURU (FWIP)
BATAN (SHUT)
SUTO (TMP)
N-NO!!
GACHAN (CLONK)
SO YOU'RE SAYING YOU EVEN KNEW THE IDENTITY OF THE CULPRIT!?
AND DESPITE THAT, YOU STILL CHOSE TO THROW AWAY YOUR OWN LIFE!?

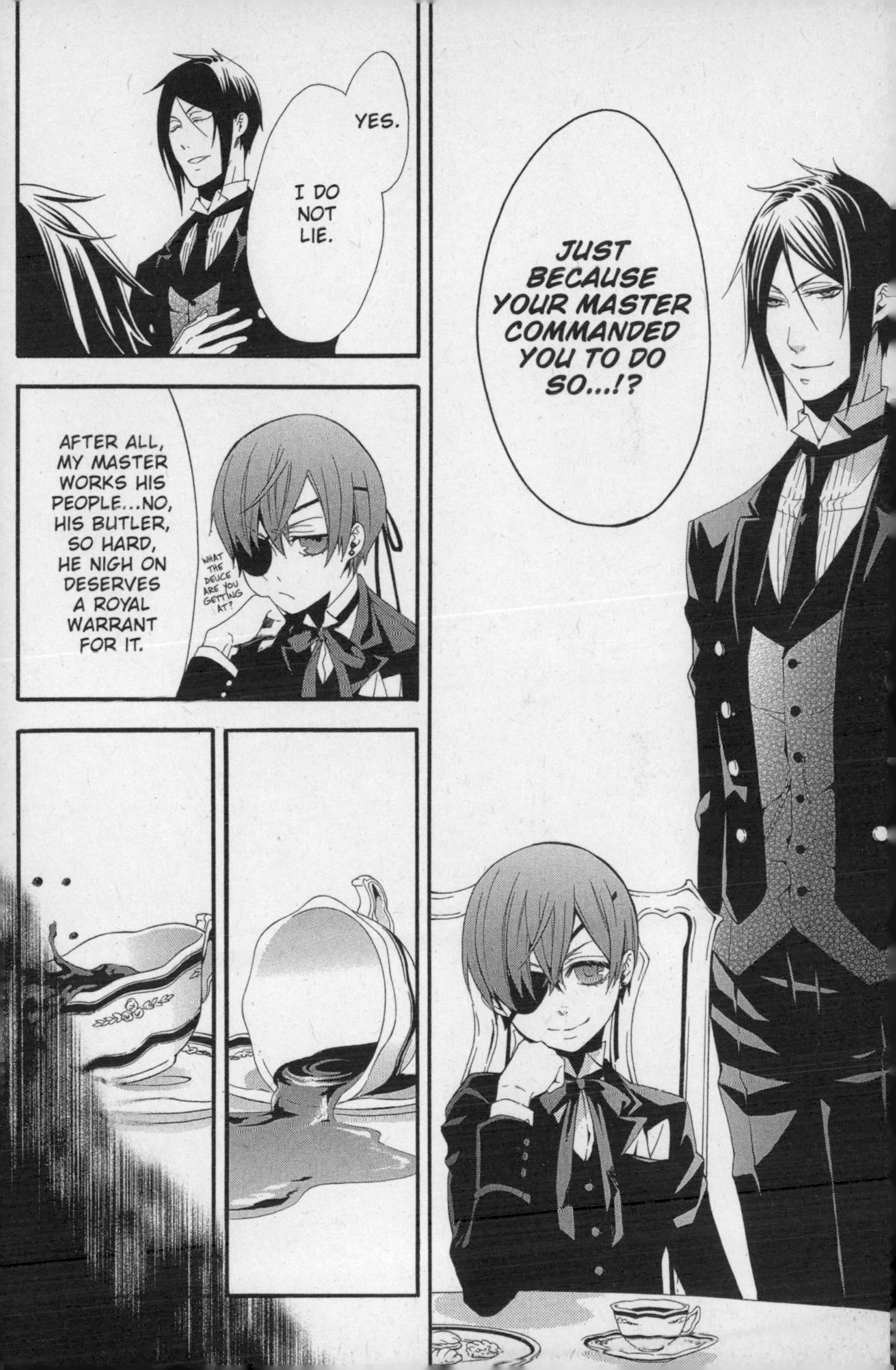
JUST BECAUSE YOUR MASTER COMMANDED YOU TO DO SO...!?
YES.
I DO NOT LIE.
AFTER ALL, MY MASTER WORKS HIS PEOPLE...NO, HIS BUTLER, SO HARD, HE NIGH ON DESERVES A ROYAL WARRANT FOR IT.
WHAT THE DEUCE ARE YOU GETTING AT?

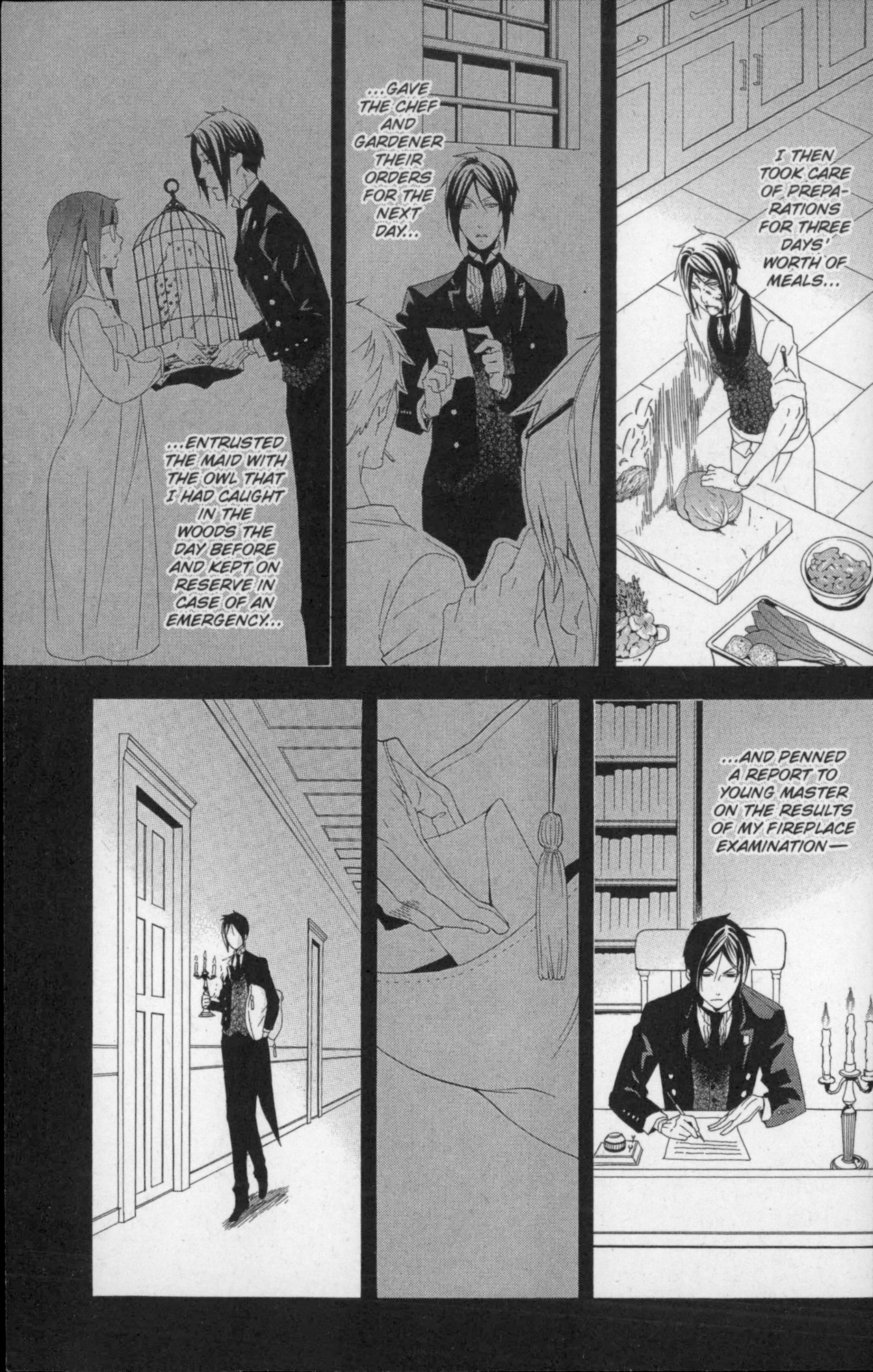
I THEN TOOK CARE OF PREPARATIONS FOR THREE DAYS' WORTH OF MEALS...
...GAVE THE CHEF AND GARDENER THEIR ORDERS FOR THE NEXT DAY...
...ENTRUSTED THE MAID WITH THE OWL THAT I HAD CAUGHT IN THE WOODS THE DAY BEFORE AND KEPT ON RESERVE IN CASE OF AN EMERGENCY...
...AND PENNED A REPORT TO YOUNG MASTER ON THE RESULTS OF MY FIREPLACE EXAMINATION—

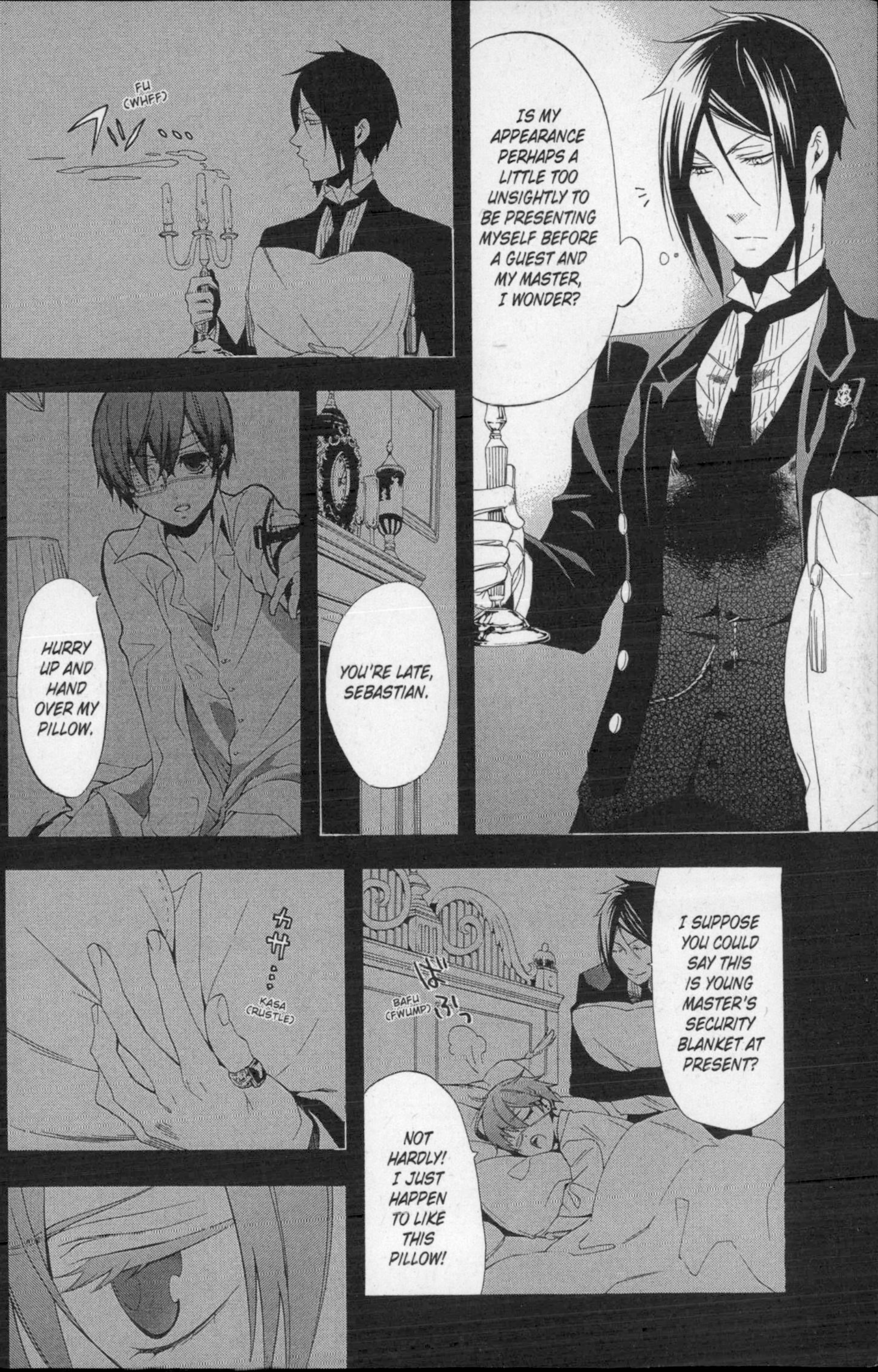
IS MY APPEARANCE PERHAPS A LITTLE TOO UNSIGHTLY TO BE PRESENTING MYSELF BEFORE A GUEST AND MY MASTER, I WONDER?
FU (WHFF)
YOU'RE LATE, SEBASTIAN.
HURRY UP AND HAND OVER MY PILLOW.
BAFU (FWUMP)
I SUPPOSE YOU COULD SAY THIS IS YOUNG MASTER'S SECURITY BLANKET AT PRESENT?
NOT HARDLY! I JUST HAPPEN TO LIKE THIS PILLOW!
KASA (RUSTLE)

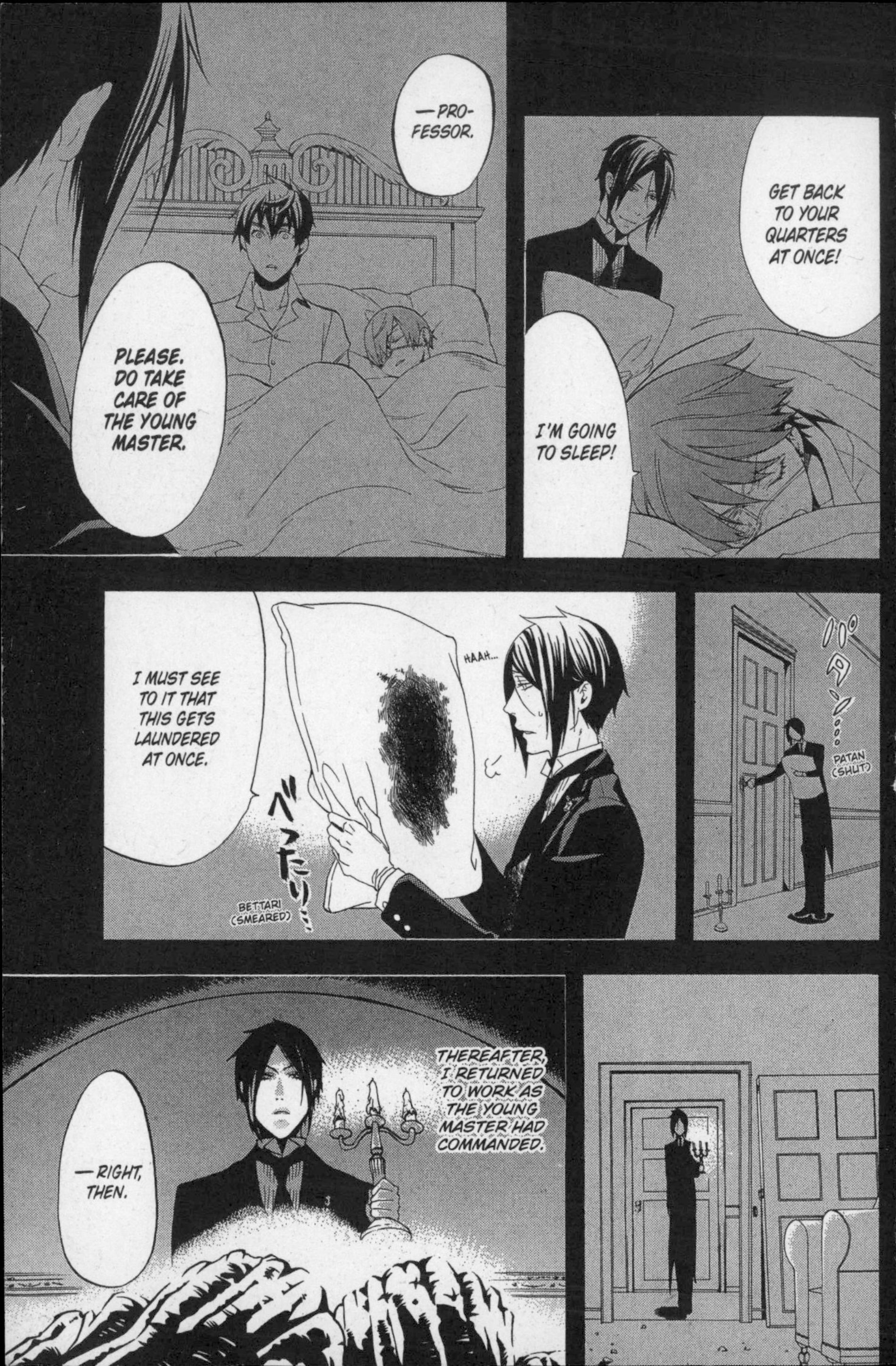

GET BACK TO YOUR QUARTERS AT ONCE!
I'M GOING TO SLEEP!
—PRO-FESSOR.
PLEASE. DO TAKE CARE OF THE YOUNG MASTER.
パタン…
PATAN (SHUT)
HAAH…
I MUST SEE TO IT THAT THIS GETS LAUNDERED AT ONCE.
べったり…
BETTARI (SMEARED)
THEREAFTER, I RETURNED TO WORK AS THE YOUNG MASTER HAD COMMANDED.
—RIGHT, THEN.

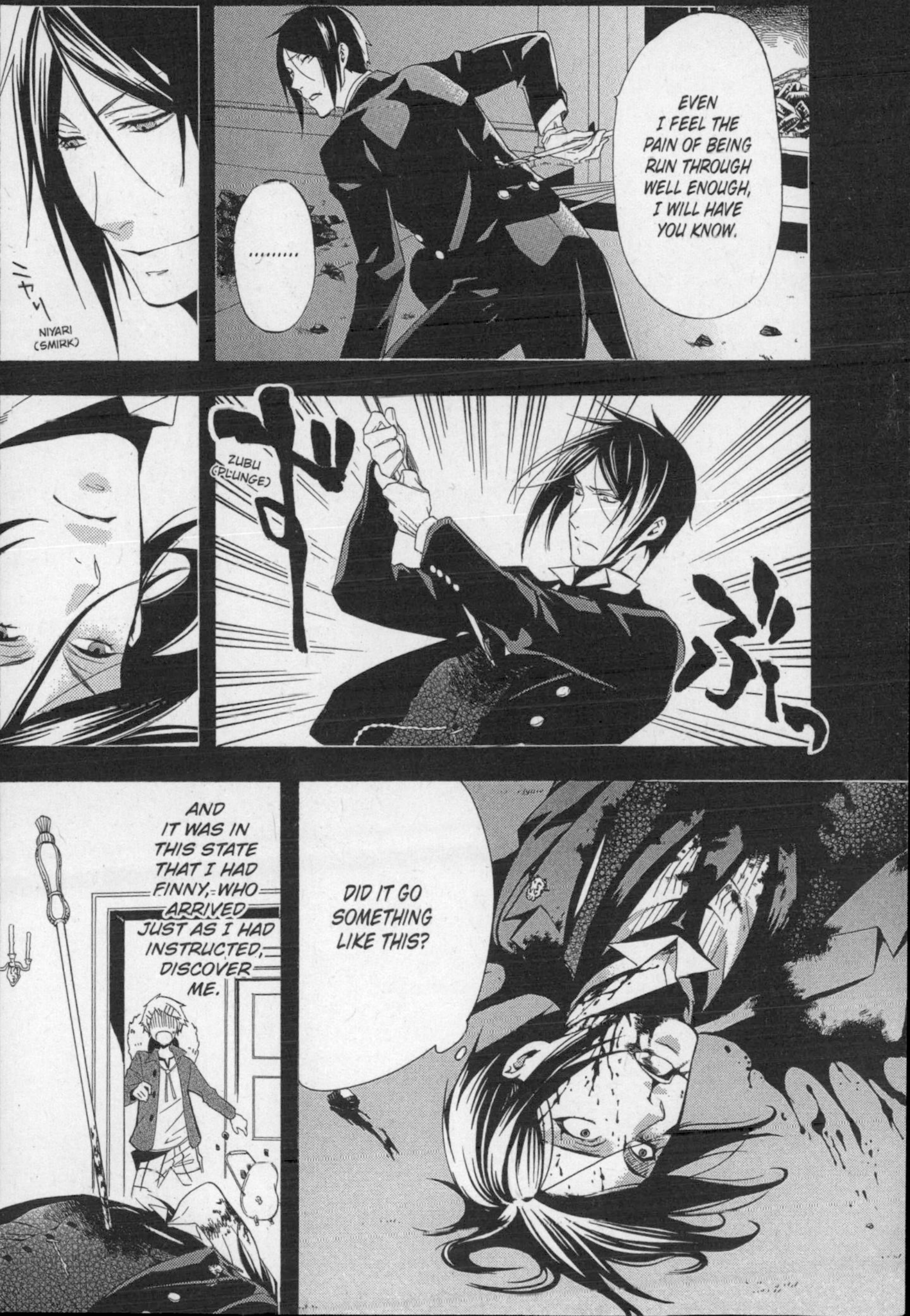
EVEN I FEEL THE PAIN OF BEING RUN THROUGH WELL ENOUGH, I WILL HAVE YOU KNOW.
....
NIYARI (SMIRK)
ZUBU (PLUNGE)
DID IT GO SOMETHING LIKE THIS?
AND IT WAS IN THIS STATE THAT I HAD FINNY, WHO ARRIVED JUST AS I HAD INSTRUCTED, DISCOVER ME.

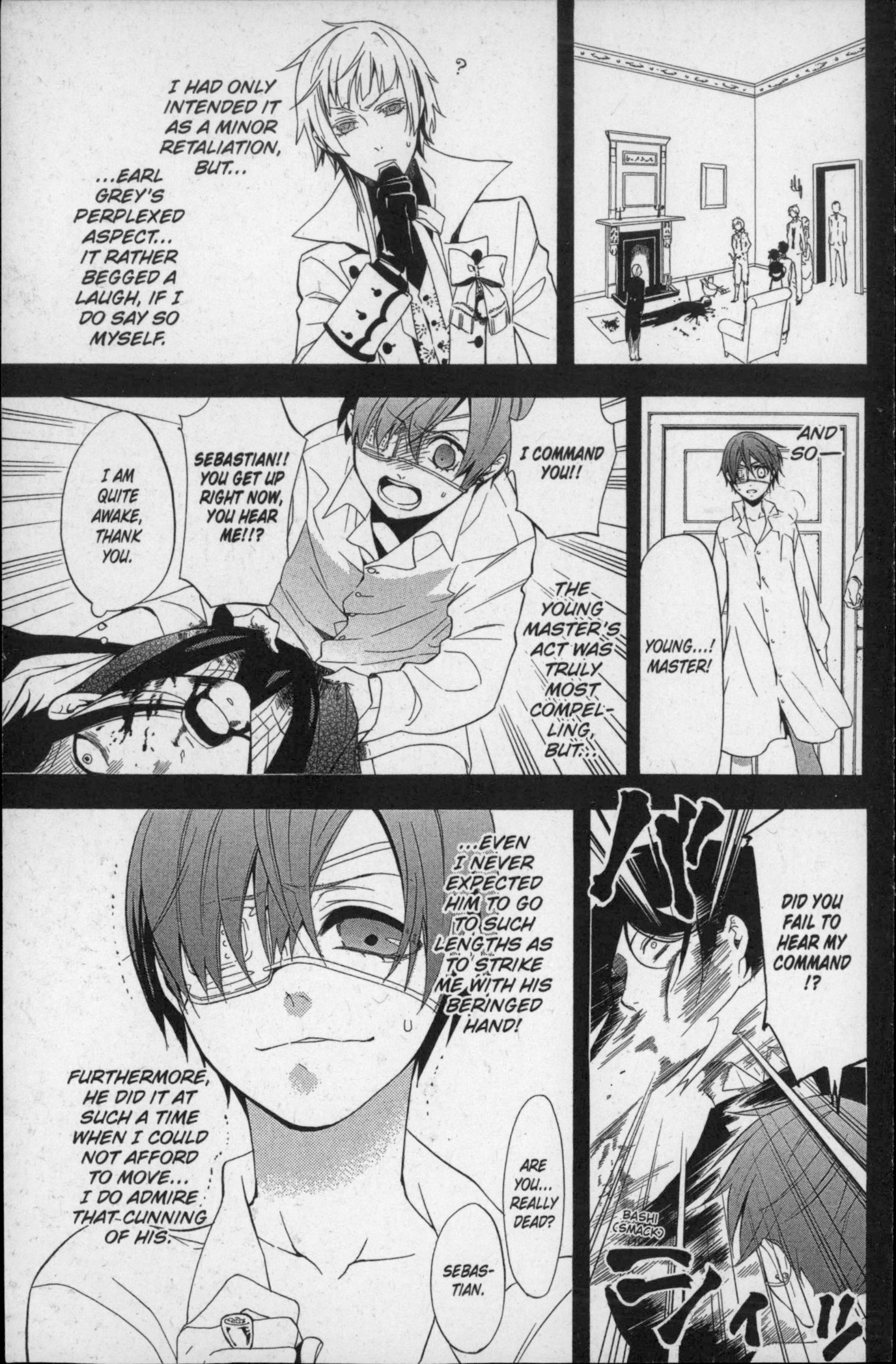

?
I HAD ONLY INTENDED IT AS A MINOR RETALIATION, BUT...
...EARL GREY'S PERPLEXED ASPECT... IT RATHER BEGGED A LAUGH, IF I DO SAY SO MYSELF.
AND SO—
YOUNG...! MASTER!
THE YOUNG MASTER'S ACT WAS TRULY MOST COMPELLING, BUT...
I COMMAND YOU!!
SEBASTIAN!! YOU GET UP RIGHT NOW, YOU HEAR ME!!?
I AM QUITE AWAKE, THANK YOU.
DID YOU FAIL TO HEAR MY COMMAND!?
BASHI (SMACK)
...EVEN I NEVER EXPECTED HIM TO GO TO SUCH LENGTHS AS TO STRIKE ME WITH HIS BERINGED HAND!
ARE YOU... REALLY DEAD?
SEBASTIAN.
FURTHERMORE, HE DID IT AT SUCH A TIME WHEN I COULD NOT AFFORD TO MOVE... I DO ADMIRE THAT CUNNING OF HIS.

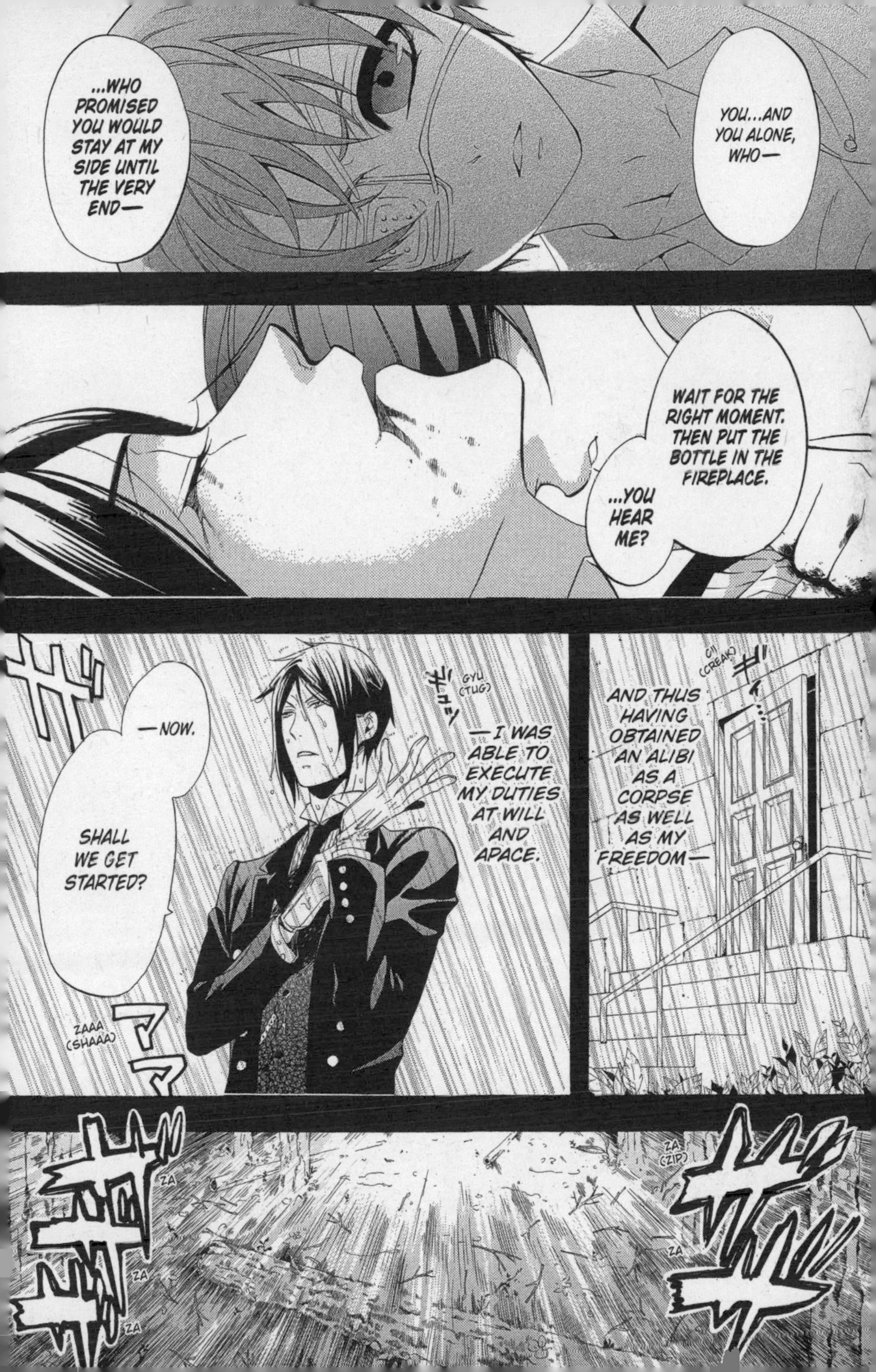
YOU...AND YOU ALONE, WHO—
...WHO PROMISED YOU WOULD STAY AT MY SIDE UNTIL THE VERY END—
WAIT FOR THE RIGHT MOMENT. THEN PUT THE BOTTLE IN THE FIREPLACE.
...YOU HEAR ME?
GII (CREAK)
AND THUS HAVING OBTAINED AN ALIBI AS A CORPSE AS WELL AS MY FREEDOM—
GYU (TUG)
—I WAS ABLE TO EXECUTE MY DUTIES AT WILL AND APACE.
—NOW.
SHALL WE GET STARTED?
ZAAA (SHAAA)
ZA (ZIP)
ZA
ZA
ZA
ZA

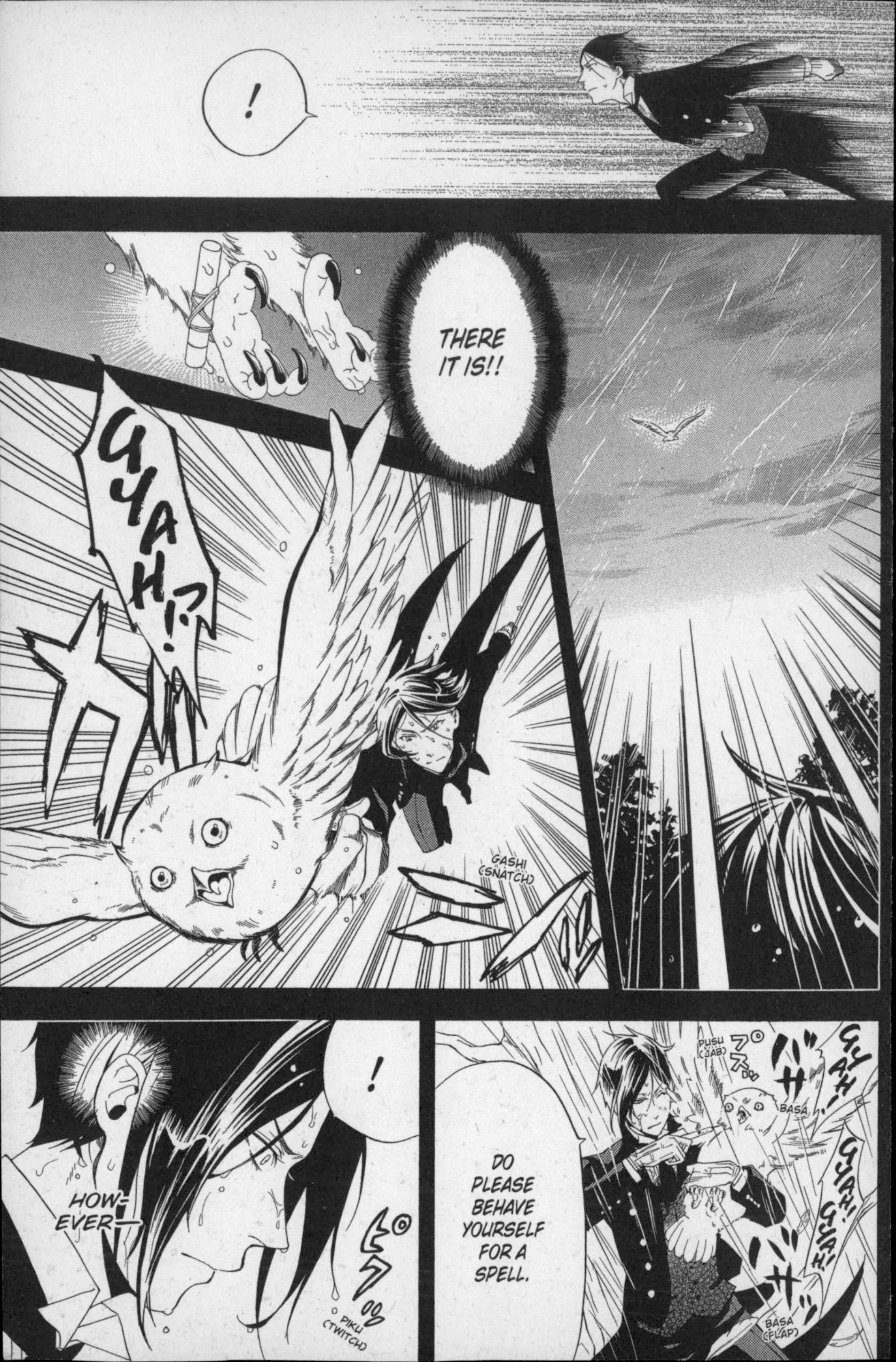
!
THERE IT IS!!
GYAH!?
GASHI (SNATCH)
PUSU (JAB)
GYAH!
BASA
GYAH!
GYAH!
DO PLEASE BEHAVE YOURSELF FOR A SPELL.
BASA (FLAP)
!
HOW-EVER—
PIKU (TWITCH)

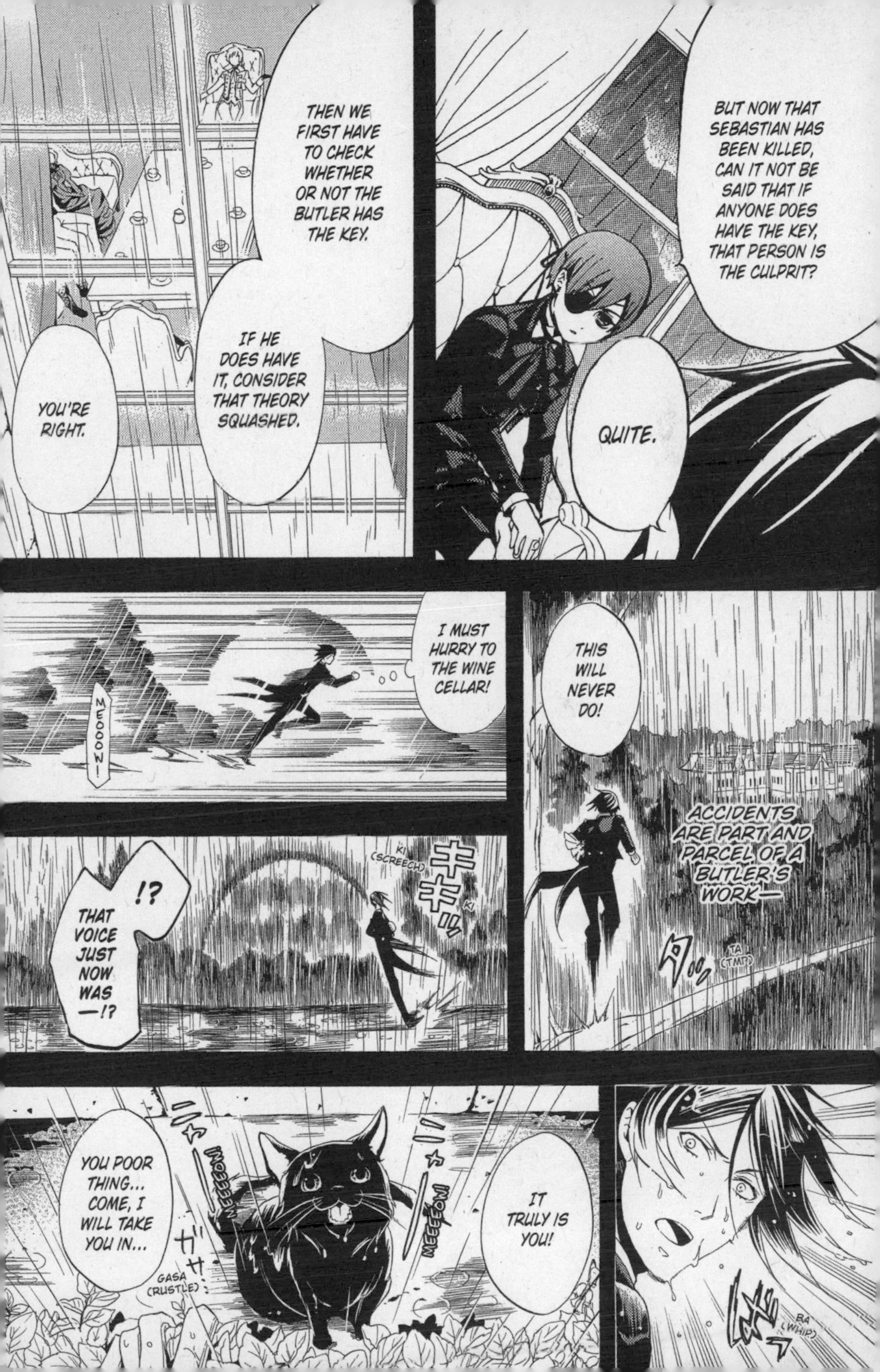

BUT NOW THAT SEBASTIAN HAS BEEN KILLED, CAN IT NOT BE SAID THAT IF ANYONE DOES HAVE THE KEY, THAT PERSON IS THE CULPRIT?
QUITE.
THEN WE FIRST HAVE TO CHECK WHETHER OR NOT THE BUTLER HAS THE KEY.
IF HE DOES HAVE IT, CONSIDER THAT THEORY SQUASHED.
YOU'RE RIGHT.
THIS WILL NEVER DO!
ACCIDENTS ARE PART AND PARCEL OF A BUTLER'S WORK—
TA (TMP)
I MUST HURRY TO THE WINE CELLAR!
MEOOOW!
KI (SCREECH)
KI
!?
THAT VOICE JUST NOW WAS—!?
BA (WHIP)
MEEEEOW!
IT TRULY IS YOU!
MEEEEOW!
YOU POOR THING... COME, I WILL TAKE YOU IN...
GASA (RUSTLE)

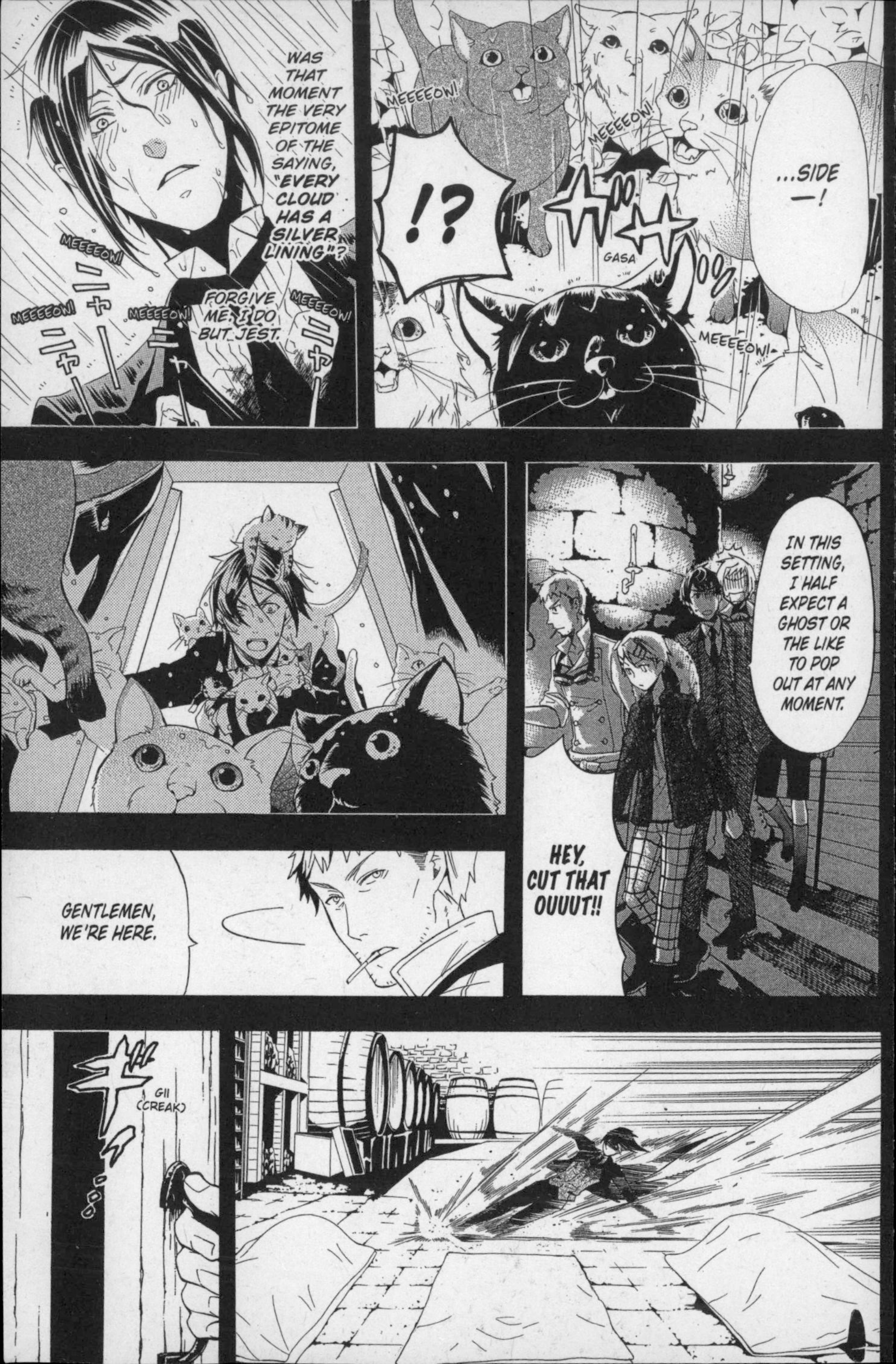
...SIDE —!
MEEEEOW!
MEEEEOW!
!?
GASA
MEEEEOW!
WAS THAT MOMENT THE VERY EPITOME OF THE SAYING, "EVERY CLOUD HAS A SILVER LINING"?
MEEEEOW!
FORGIVE ME. I DO BUT JEST.
MEEEEOW!
MEEEEOW!
MEEEEOW!
IN THIS SETTING, I HALF EXPECT A GHOST OR THE LIKE TO POP OUT AT ANY MOMENT.
HEY, CUT THAT OUUUT!!
GENTLEMEN, WE'RE HERE.
GII (CREAK)

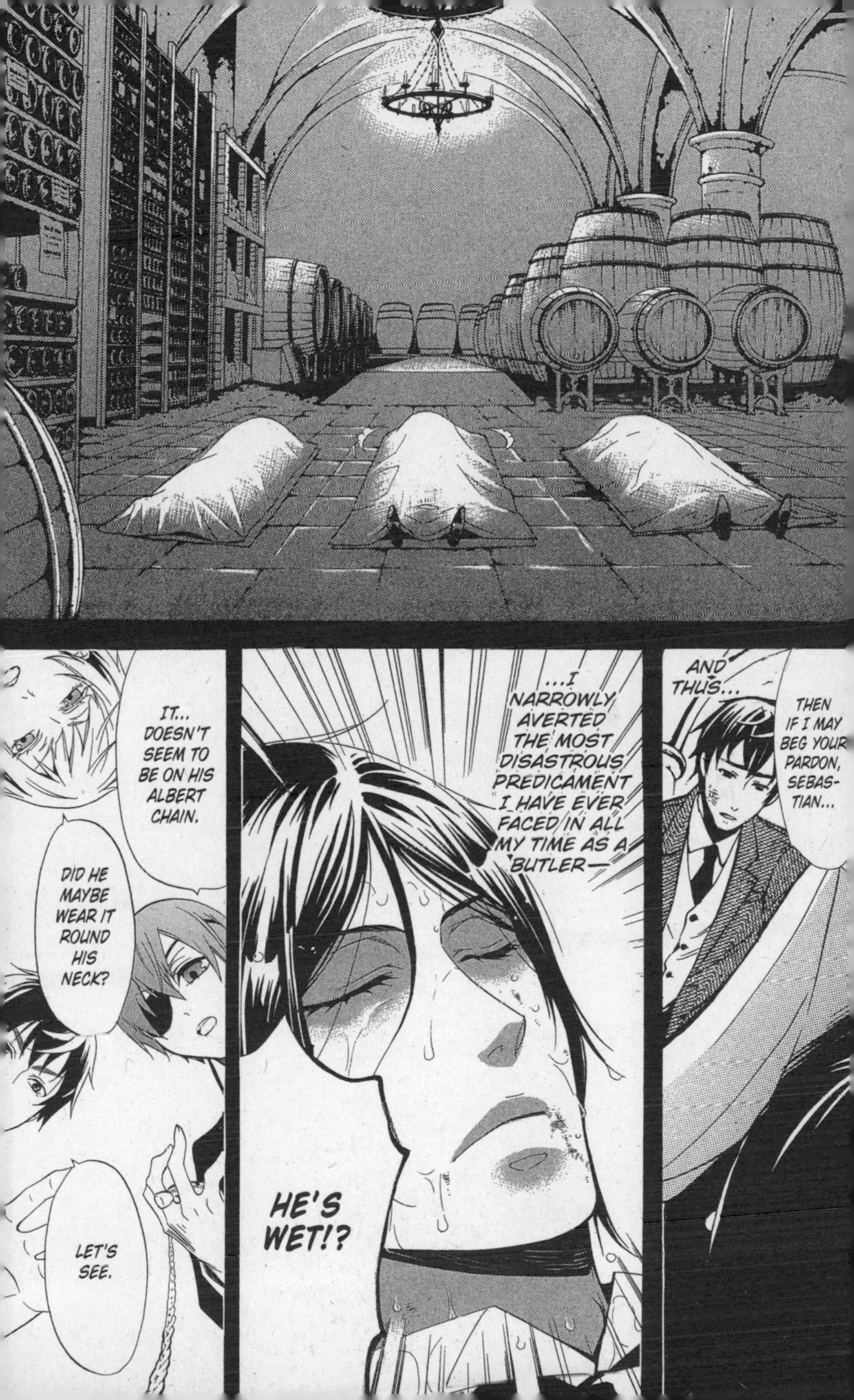
THEN IF I MAY BEG YOUR PARDON, SEBASTIAN...
AND THUS...
...I NARROWLY AVERTED THE MOST DISASTROUS PREDICAMENT I HAVE EVER FACED IN ALL MY TIME AS A BUTLER—
HE'S WET!?
IT... DOESN'T SEEM TO BE ON HIS ALBERT CHAIN.
DID HE MAYBE WEAR IT ROUND HIS NECK?
LET'S SEE.

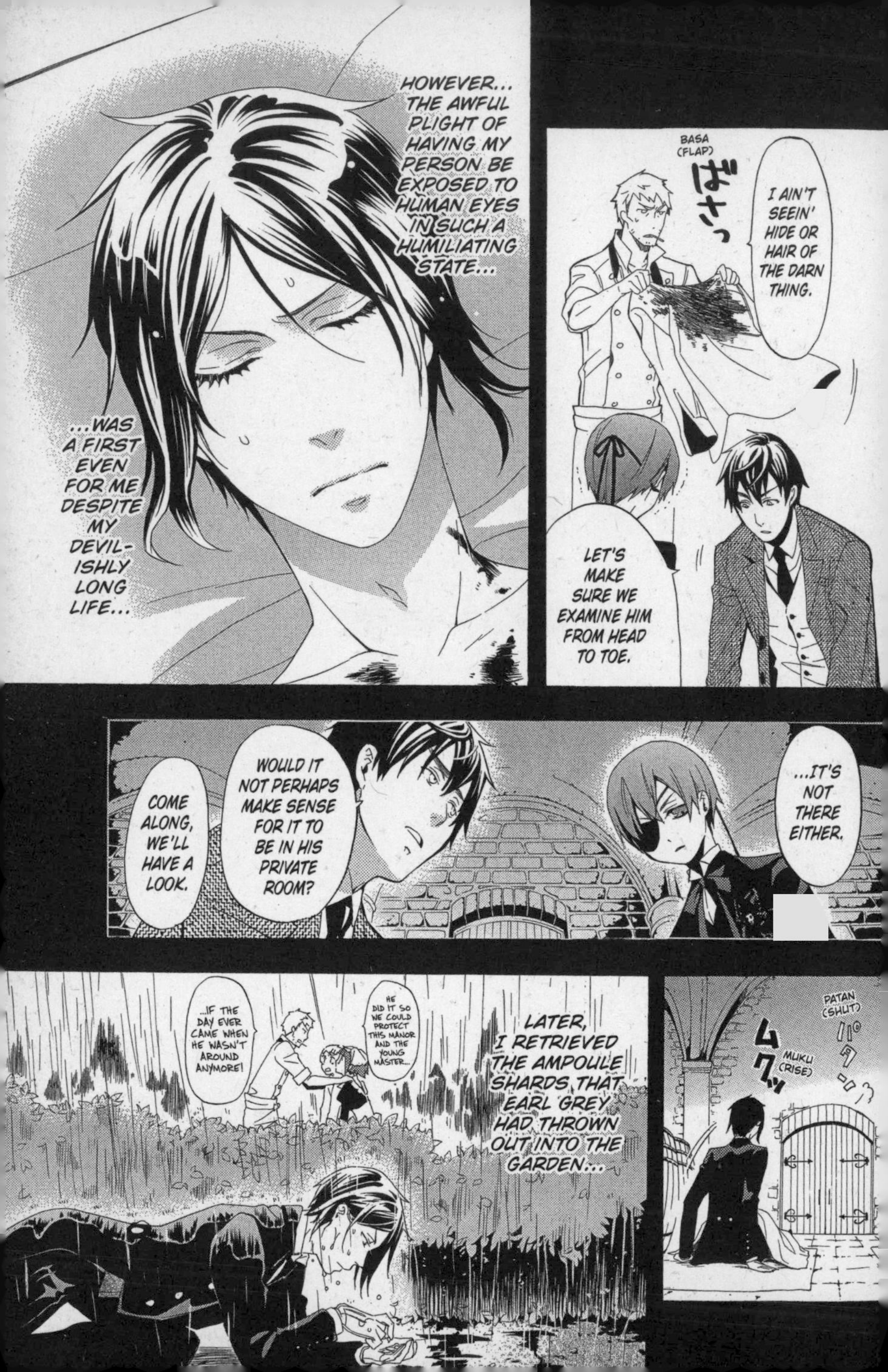
BASA (FLAP)
ばさっ
I AIN'T SEEIN' HIDE OR HAIR OF THE DARN THING.
LET'S MAKE SURE WE EXAMINE HIM FROM HEAD TO TOE.
HOWEVER... THE AWFUL PLIGHT OF HAVING MY PERSON BE EXPOSED TO HUMAN EYES IN SUCH A HUMILIATING STATE...
...WAS A FIRST EVEN FOR ME DESPITE MY DEVIL-ISHLY LONG LIFE...
...IT'S NOT THERE EITHER.
WOULD IT NOT PERHAPS MAKE SENSE FOR IT TO BE IN HIS PRIVATE ROOM?
COME ALONG, WE'LL HAVE A LOOK.
PATAN (SHUT)
パタン
MUKU (RISE)
ムクッ
LATER, I RETRIEVED THE AMPOULE SHARDS THAT EARL GREY HAD THROWN OUT INTO THE GARDEN...
HE DID IT SO WE COULD PROTECT THIS MANOR AND THE YOUNG MASTER...
...IF THE DAY EVER CAME WHEN HE WASN'T AROUND ANYMORE!

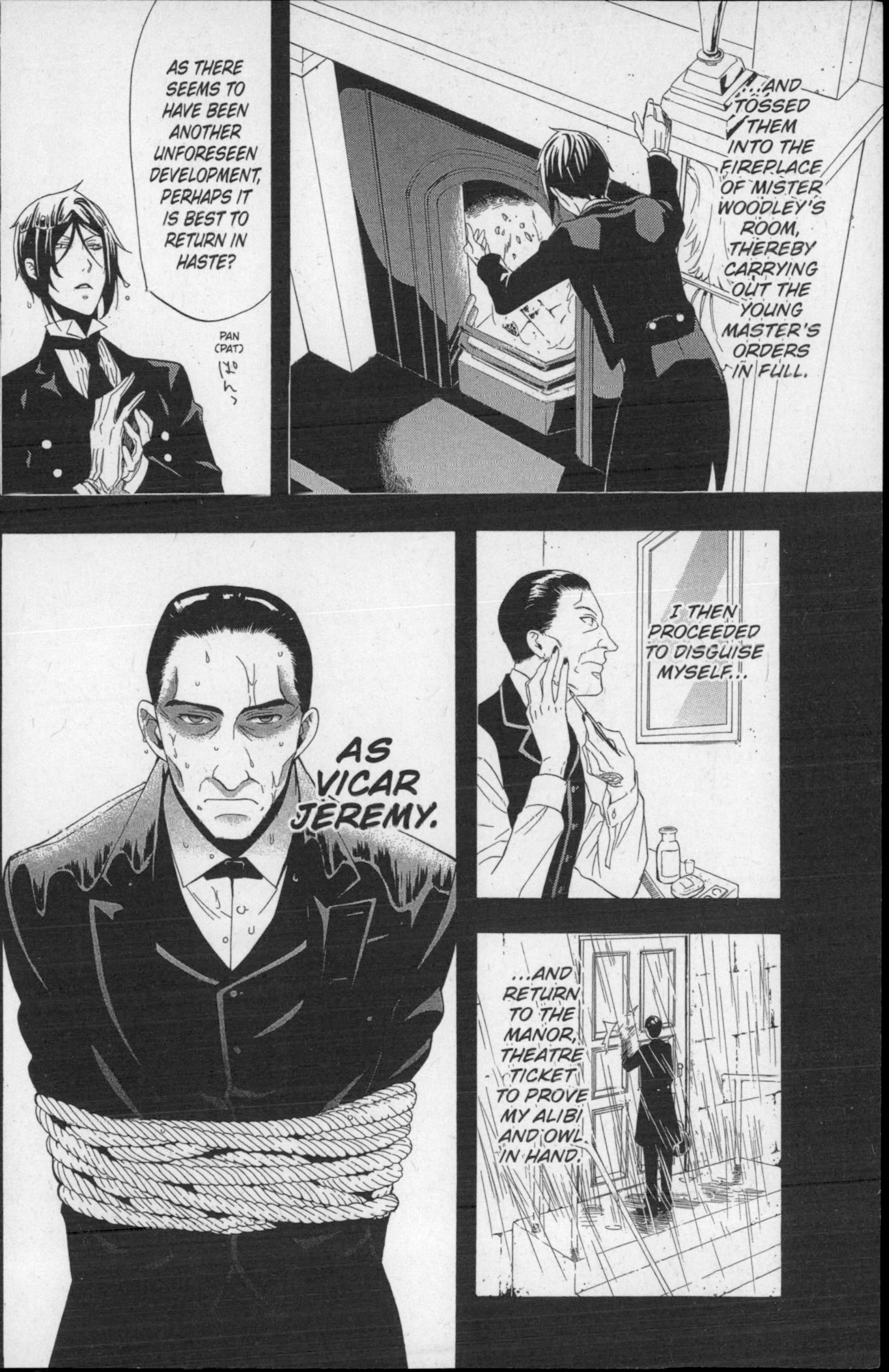
...AND TOSSED THEM INTO THE FIREPLACE OF MISTER WOODLEY'S ROOM, THEREBY CARRYING OUT THE YOUNG MASTER'S ORDERS IN FULL.
AS THERE SEEMS TO HAVE BEEN ANOTHER UNFORESEEN DEVELOPMENT, PERHAPS IT IS BEST TO RETURN IN HASTE?
PAN (PAT)
ぱん
I THEN PROCEEDED TO DISGUISE MYSELF...
...AND RETURN TO THE MANOR, THEATRE TICKET TO PROVE MY ALIBI AND OWL IN HAND.
AS VICAR JEREMY.

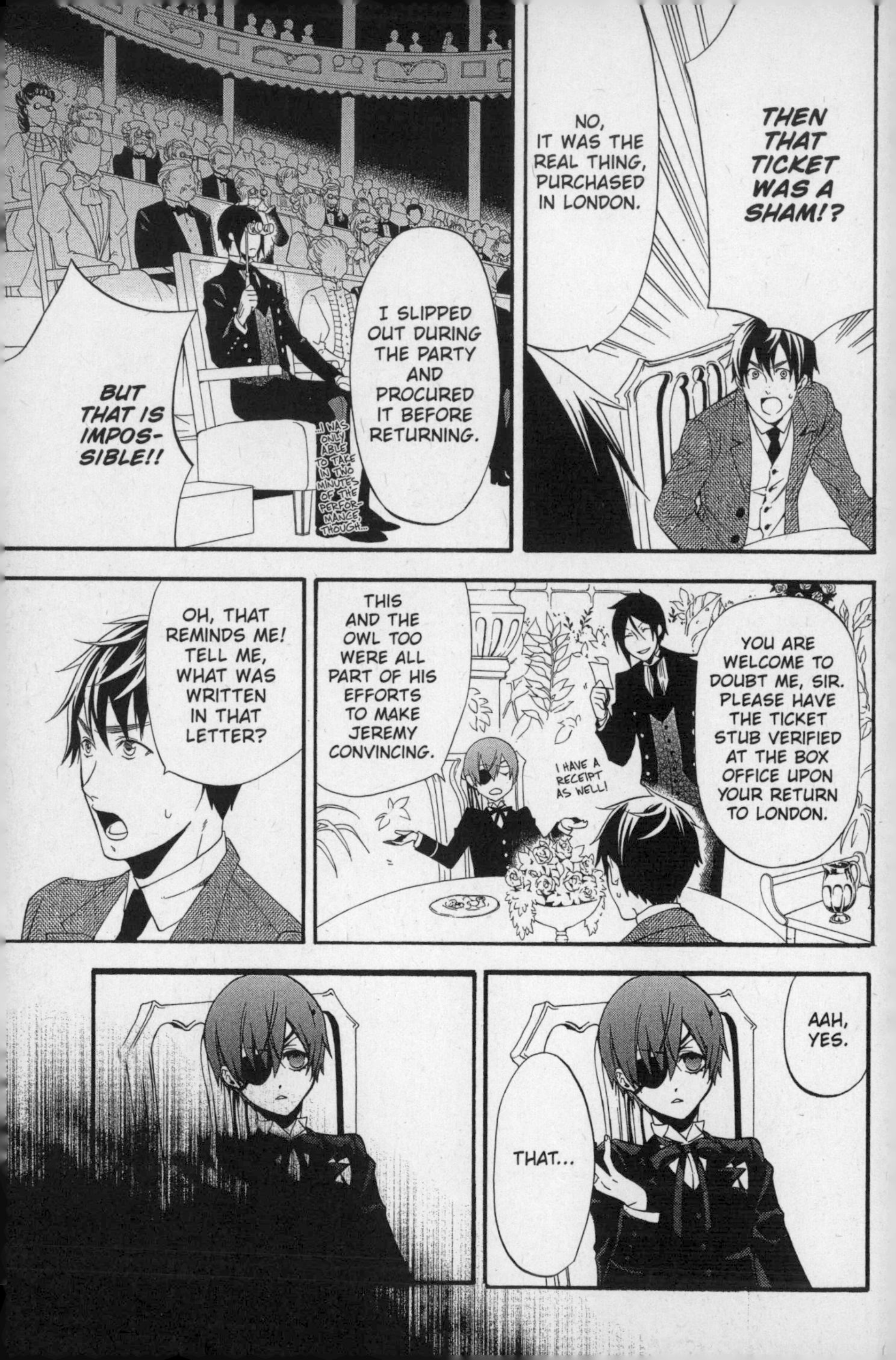
THEN THAT TICKET WAS A SHAM!?
NO, IT WAS THE REAL THING, PURCHASED IN LONDON.
I SLIPPED OUT DURING THE PARTY AND PROCURED IT BEFORE RETURNING.
...I WAS ONLY ABLE TO TAKE IN TWO MINUTES OF THE PERFORMANCE, THOUGH...
BUT THAT IS IMPOSSIBLE!!
YOU ARE WELCOME TO DOUBT ME, SIR. PLEASE HAVE THE TICKET STUB VERIFIED AT THE BOX OFFICE UPON YOUR RETURN TO LONDON.
I HAVE A RECEIPT AS WELL!
THIS AND THE OWL TOO WERE ALL PART OF HIS EFFORTS TO MAKE JEREMY CONVINCING.
OH, THAT REMINDS ME! TELL ME, WHAT WAS WRITTEN IN THAT LETTER?
AAH, YES.
THAT...

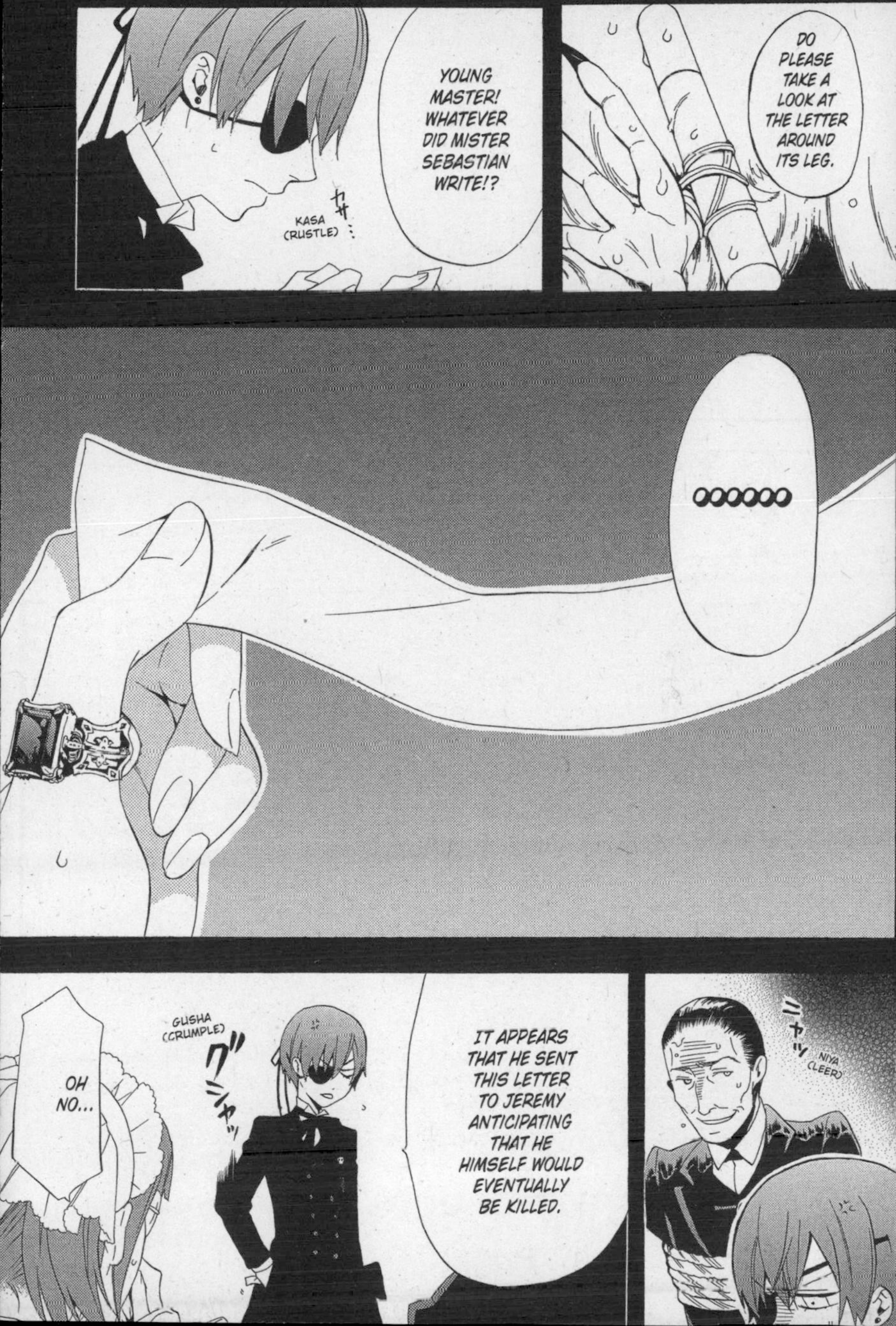
DO PLEASE TAKE A LOOK AT THE LETTER AROUND ITS LEG.
YOUNG MASTER! WHATEVER DID MISTER SEBASTIAN WRITE!?
カサ…
KASA (RUSTLE)
......
ニヤッ
NIYA (LEER)
IT APPEARS THAT HE SENT THIS LETTER TO JEREMY ANTICIPATING THAT HE HIMSELF WOULD EVENTUALLY BE KILLED.
グシャッ
GUSHA (CRUMPLE)
OH NO...

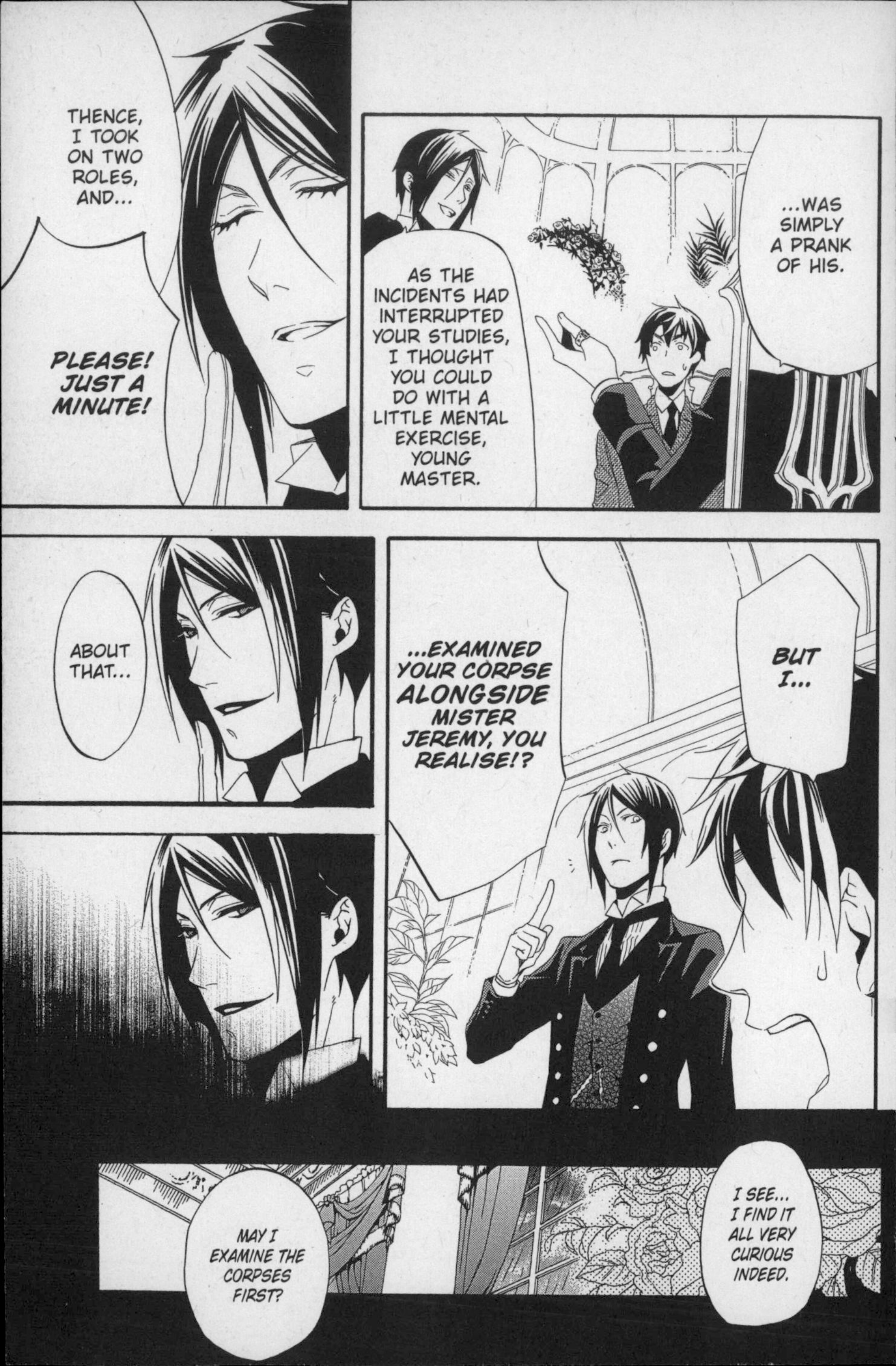
...WAS SIMPLY A PRANK OF HIS.
AS THE INCIDENTS HAD INTERRUPTED YOUR STUDIES, I THOUGHT YOU COULD DO WITH A LITTLE MENTAL EXERCISE, YOUNG MASTER.
THENCE, I TOOK ON TWO ROLES, AND...
PLEASE! JUST A MINUTE!
BUT I...
...EXAMINED YOUR CORPSE ALONGSIDE MISTER JEREMY, YOU REALISE!?
ABOUT THAT...
I SEE... I FIND IT ALL VERY CURIOUS INDEED.
MAY I EXAMINE THE CORPSES FIRST?

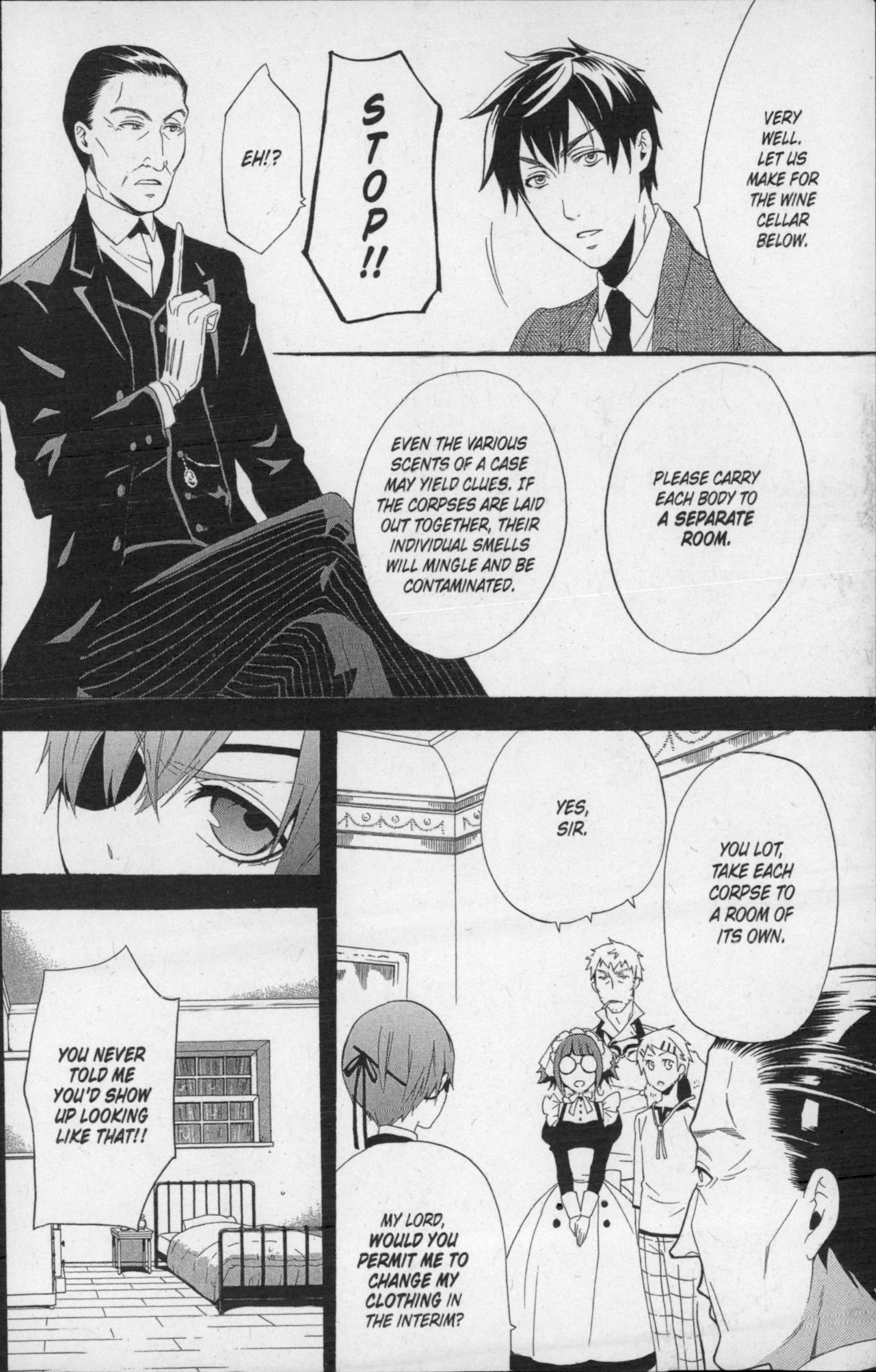
VERY WELL. LET US MAKE FOR THE WINE CELLAR BELOW.
STOP!!
EH!?
PLEASE CARRY EACH BODY TO A SEPARATE ROOM.
EVEN THE VARIOUS SCENTS OF A CASE MAY YIELD CLUES. IF THE CORPSES ARE LAID OUT TOGETHER, THEIR INDIVIDUAL SMELLS WILL MINGLE AND BE CONTAMINATED.
YOU LOT, TAKE EACH CORPSE TO A ROOM OF ITS OWN.
YES, SIR.
MY LORD, WOULD YOU PERMIT ME TO CHANGE MY CLOTHING IN THE INTERIM?
YOU NEVER TOLD ME YOU'D SHOW UP LOOKING LIKE THAT!!

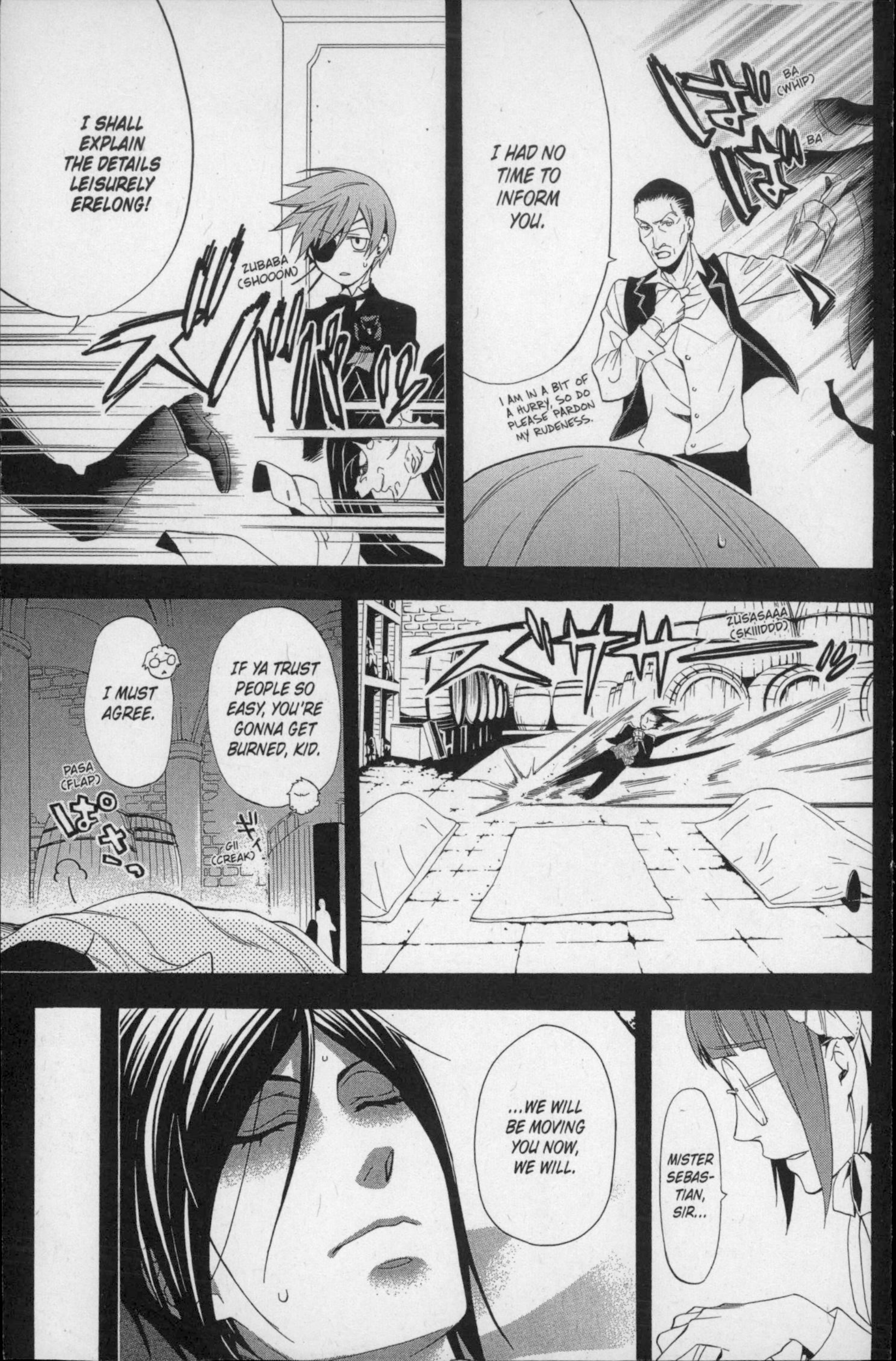
BA (WHIP)
BA
I HAD NO TIME TO INFORM YOU.
I AM IN A BIT OF A HURRY, SO DO PLEASE PARDON MY RUDENESS.
I SHALL EXPLAIN THE DETAILS LEISURELY ERELONG!
ZUBABA (SHOOOM)
ZUSASAAA (SKIIIDDD)
IF YA TRUST PEOPLE SO EASY, YOU'RE GONNA GET BURNED, KID.
I MUST AGREE.
PASA (FLAP)
GII (CREAK)
MISTER SEBAS-TIAN, SIR...
...WE WILL BE MOVING YOU NOW, WE WILL.

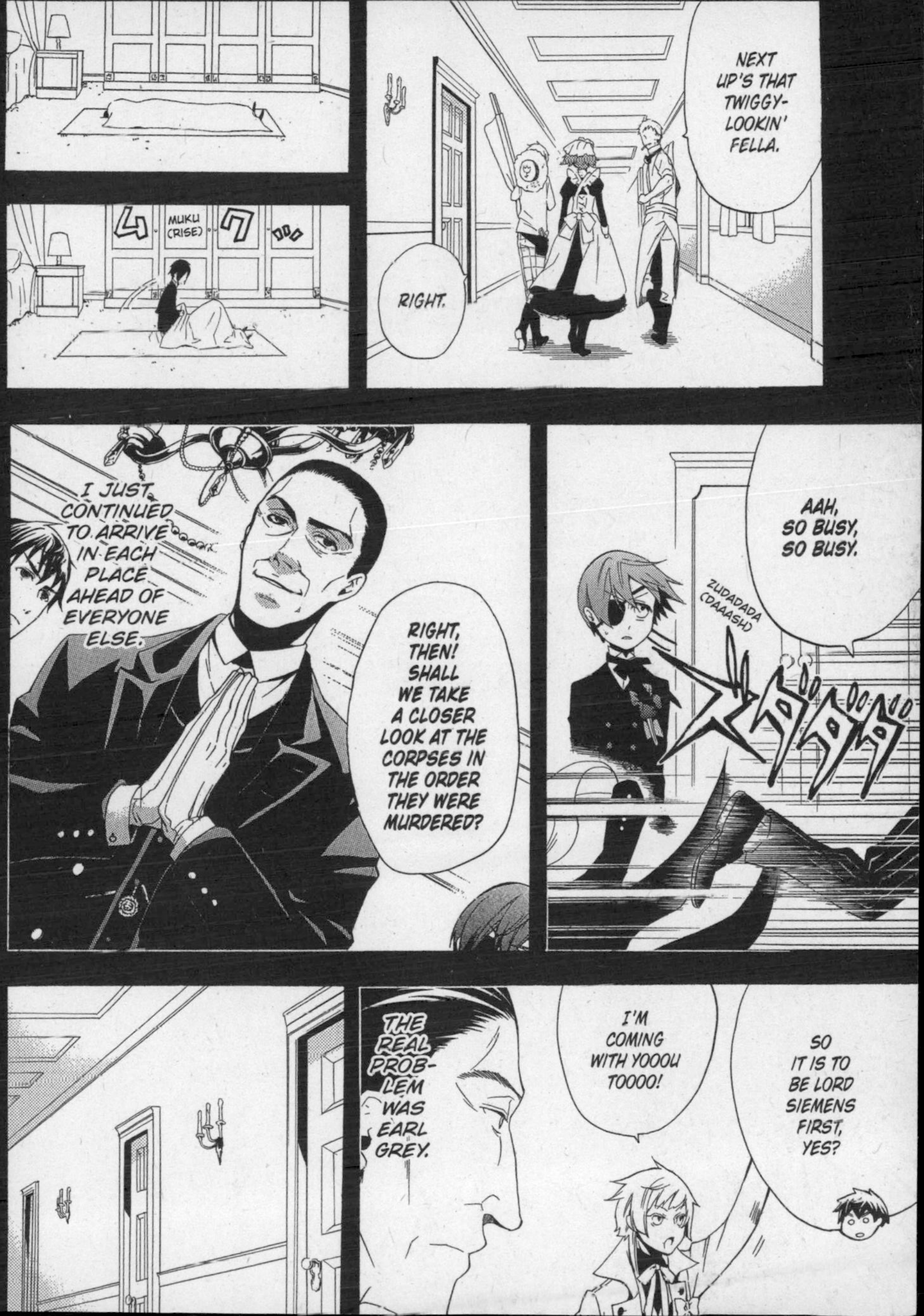
NEXT UP'S THAT TWIGGY-LOOKIN' FELLA.
RIGHT.
MUKU (RISE)
AAH, SO BUSY, SO BUSY.
ZUDADADA (DAAASH)
I JUST CONTINUED TO ARRIVE IN EACH PLACE AHEAD OF EVERYONE ELSE.
RIGHT, THEN! SHALL WE TAKE A CLOSER LOOK AT THE CORPSES IN THE ORDER THEY WERE MURDERED?
SO IT IS TO BE LORD SIEMENS FIRST, YES?
I'M COMING WITH YOOOU TOOOO!
THE REAL PROB-LEM WAS EARL GREY.

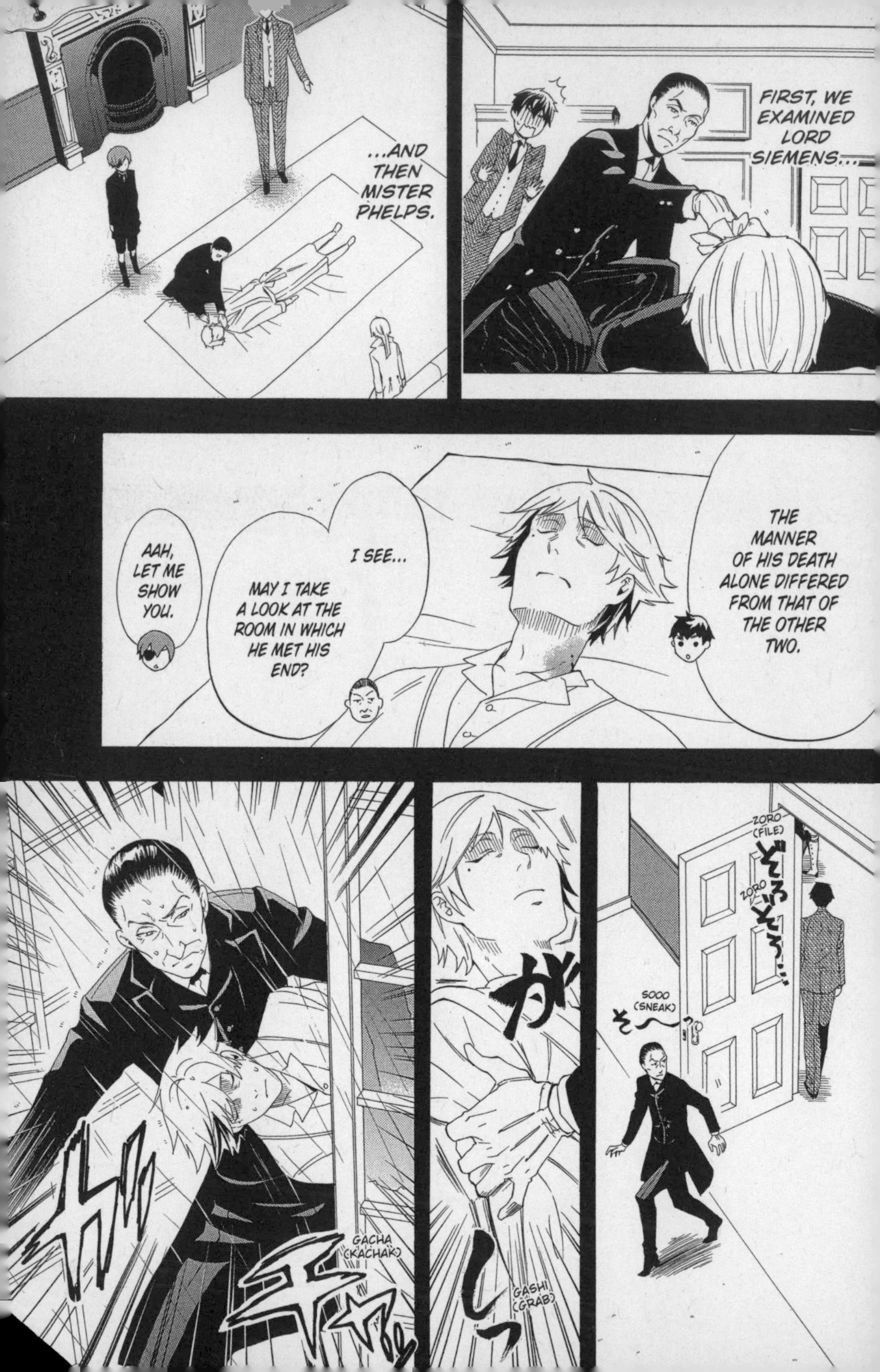
FIRST, WE EXAMINED LORD SIEMENS...
...AND THEN MISTER PHELPS.
THE MANNER OF HIS DEATH ALONE DIFFERED FROM THAT OF THE OTHER TWO.
I SEE...
MAY I TAKE A LOOK AT THE ROOM IN WHICH HE MET HIS END?
AAH, LET ME SHOW YOU.
ZORO (FILE)
ZORO
SOOO (SNEAK)
GASHI (GRAB)
GACHA (KACHAK)

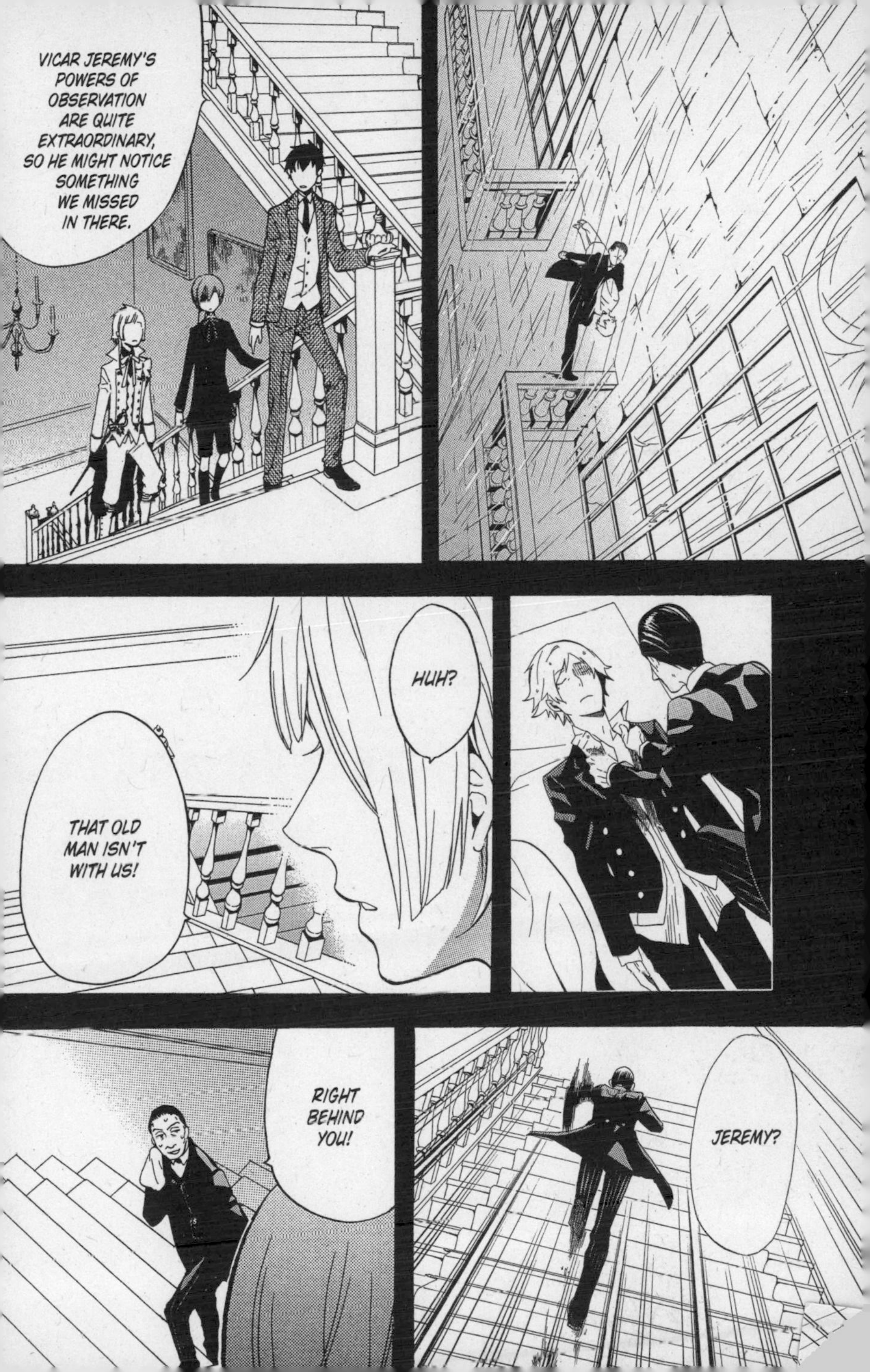
VICAR JEREMY'S POWERS OF OBSERVATION ARE QUITE EXTRAORDINARY, SO HE MIGHT NOTICE SOMETHING WE MISSED IN THERE.
HUH?
THAT OLD MAN ISN'T WITH US!
JEREMY?
RIGHT BEHIND YOU!

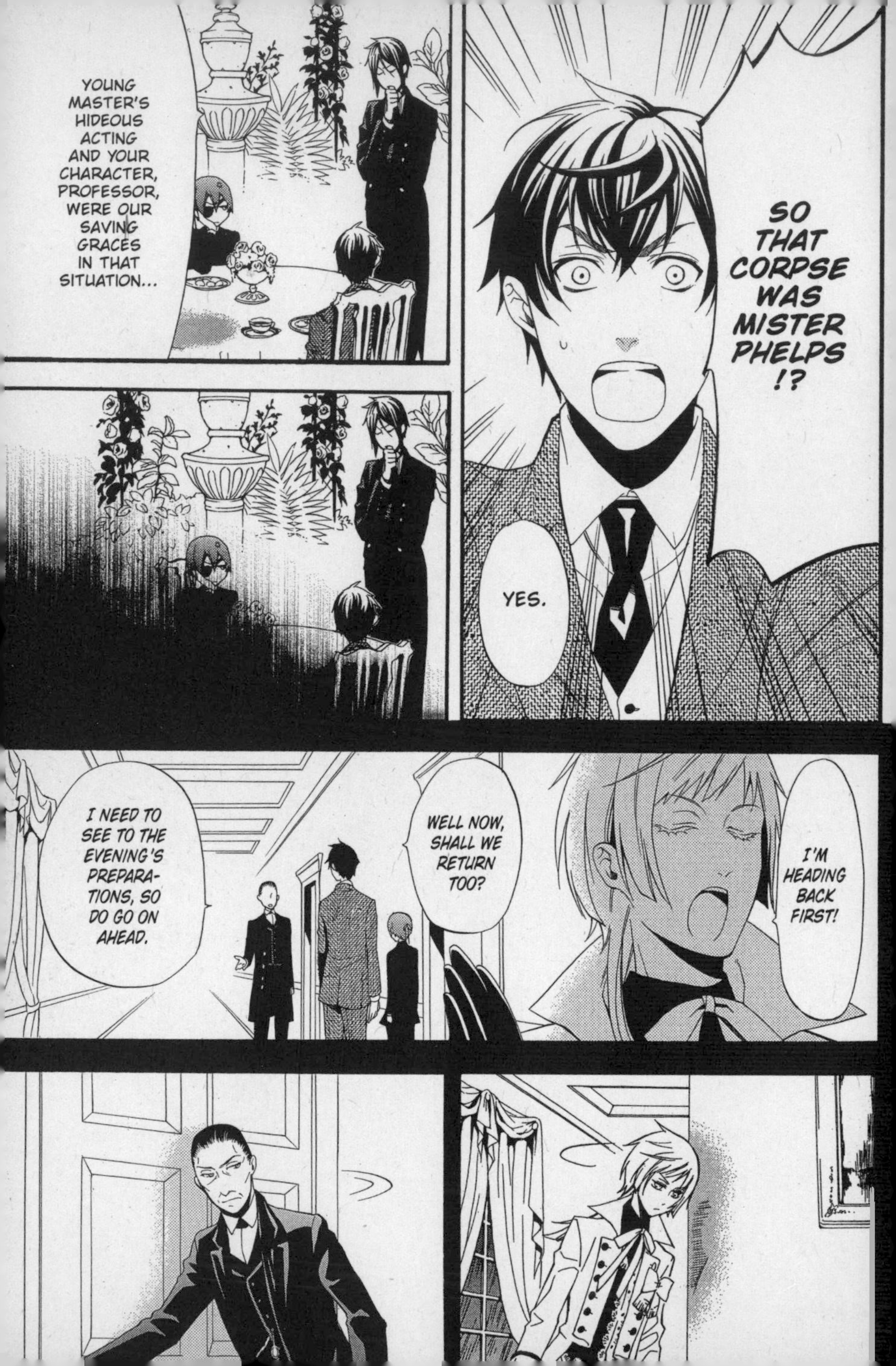
SO THAT CORPSE WAS MISTER PHELPS!?
YES.
YOUNG MASTER'S HIDEOUS ACTING AND YOUR CHARACTER, PROFESSOR, WERE OUR SAVING GRACES IN THAT SITUATION...
I'M HEADING BACK FIRST!
WELL NOW, SHALL WE RETURN TOO?
I NEED TO SEE TO THE EVENING'S PREPARA-TIONS, SO DO GO ON AHEAD.

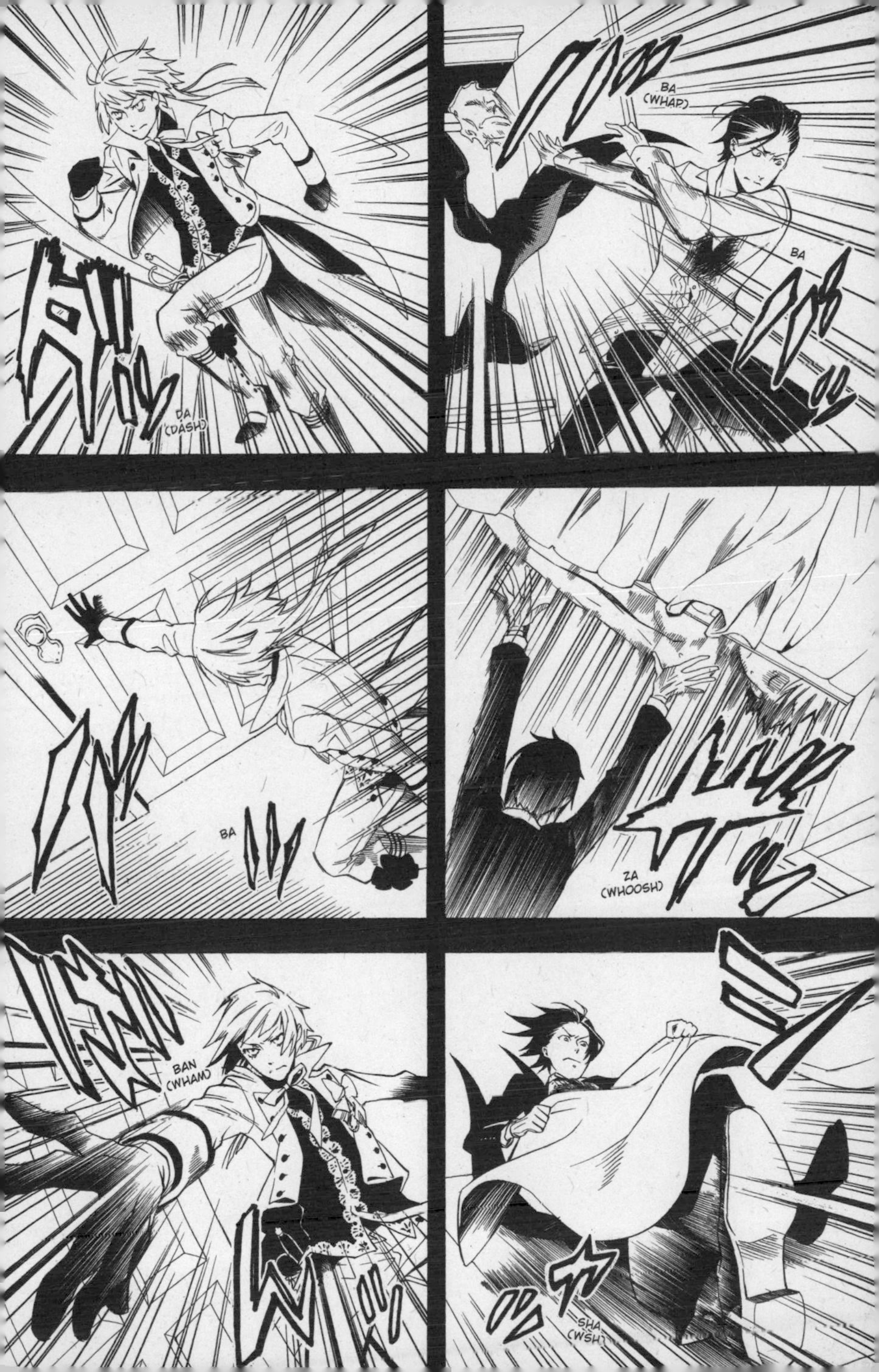
BA (WHAP)
BA
DA (DASH)
ZA (WHOOSH)
BA
SHA (WSH)
BAN (WHAM)

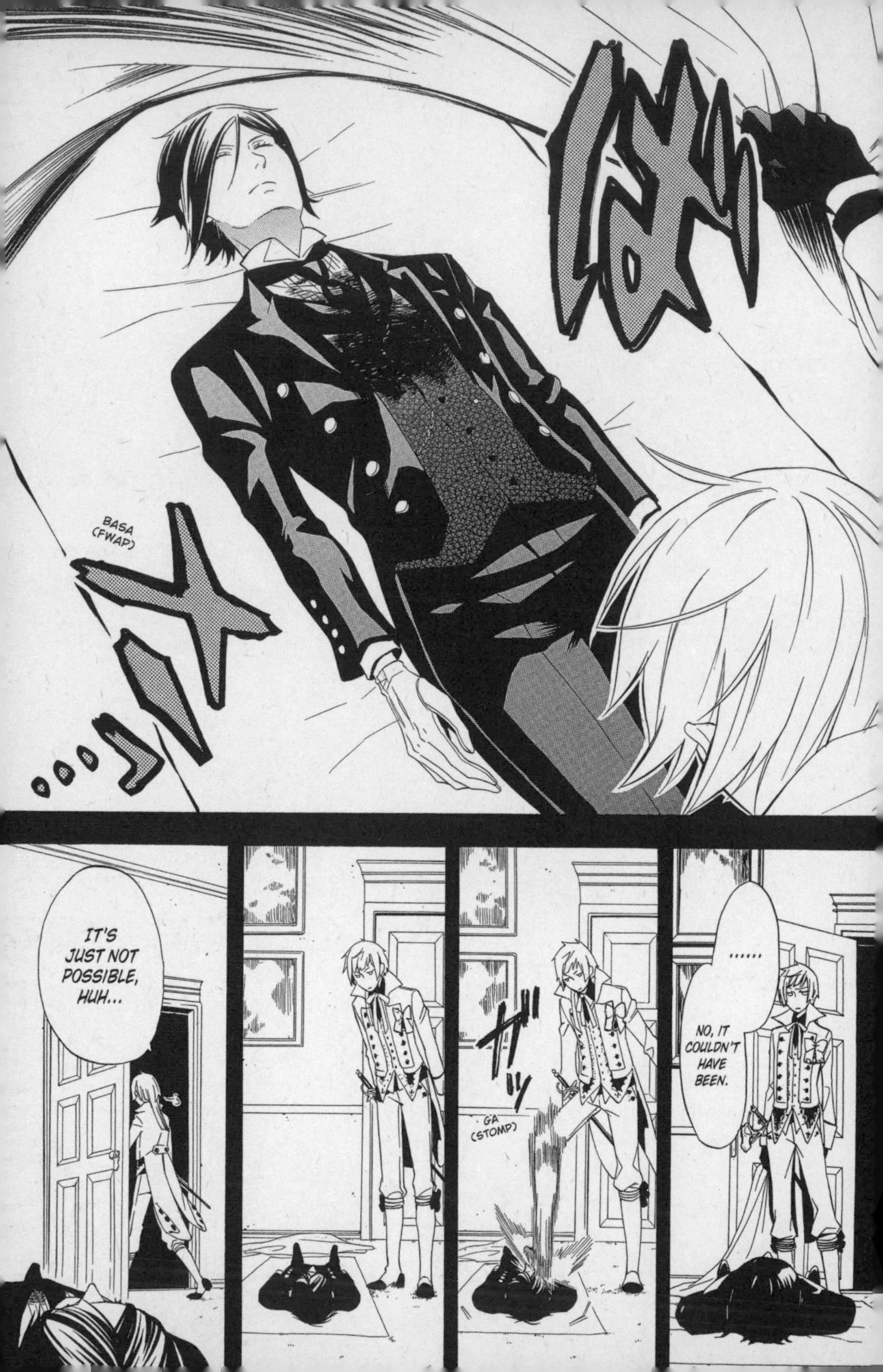
BASA (FWAP)
......
NO, IT COULDN'T HAVE BEEN.
GA (STOMP)
IT'S JUST NOT POSSIBLE, HUH...

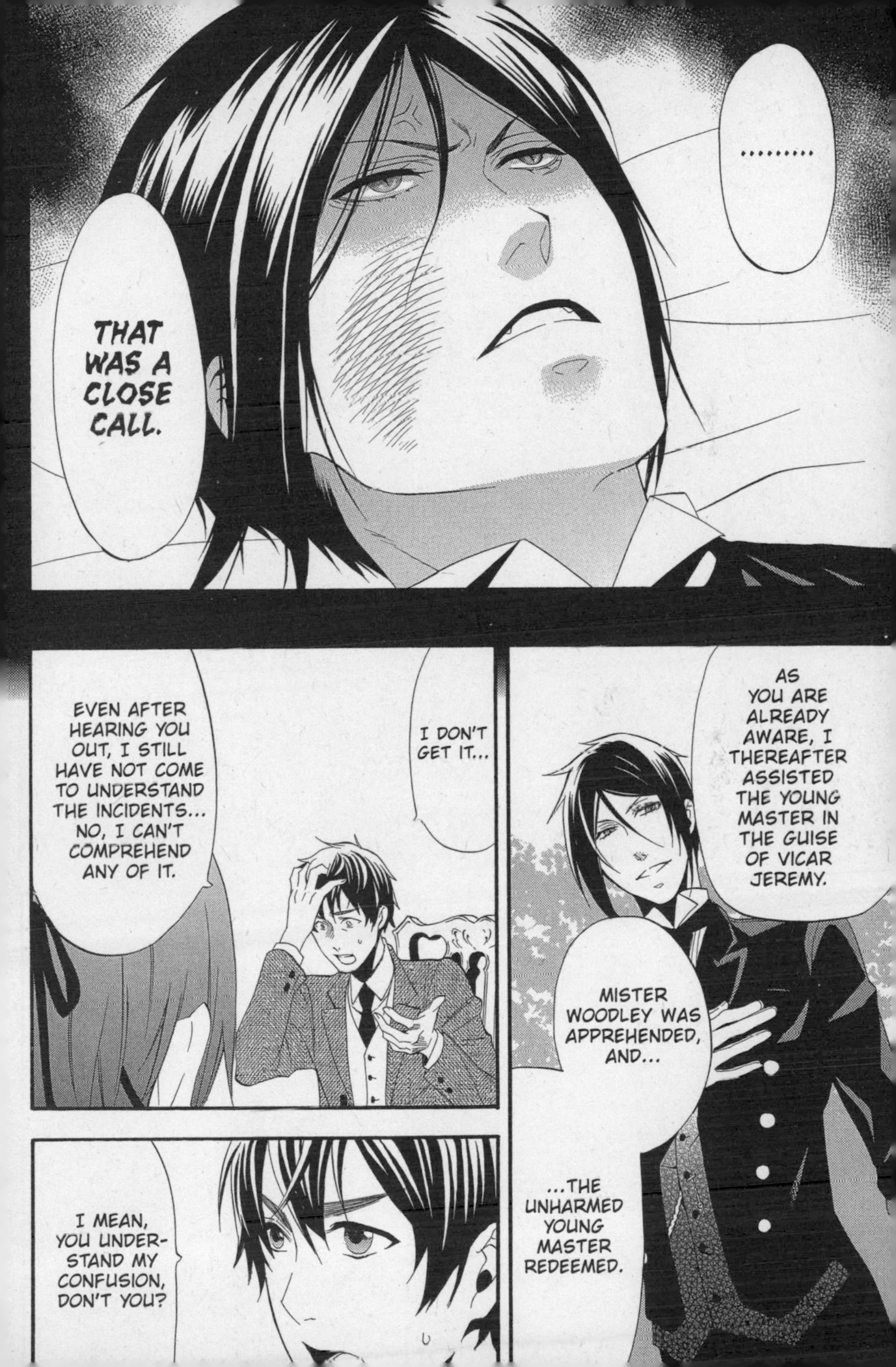
....
THAT WAS A CLOSE CALL.
AS YOU ARE ALREADY AWARE, I THEREAFTER ASSISTED THE YOUNG MASTER IN THE GUISE OF VICAR JEREMY.
MISTER WOODLEY WAS APPREHENDED, AND...
...THE UNHARMED YOUNG MASTER REDEEMED.
I DON'T GET IT...
EVEN AFTER HEARING YOU OUT, I STILL HAVE NOT COME TO UNDERSTAND THE INCIDENTS... NO, I CAN'T COMPREHEND ANY OF IT.
I MEAN, YOU UNDER-STAND MY CONFUSION, DON'T YOU?

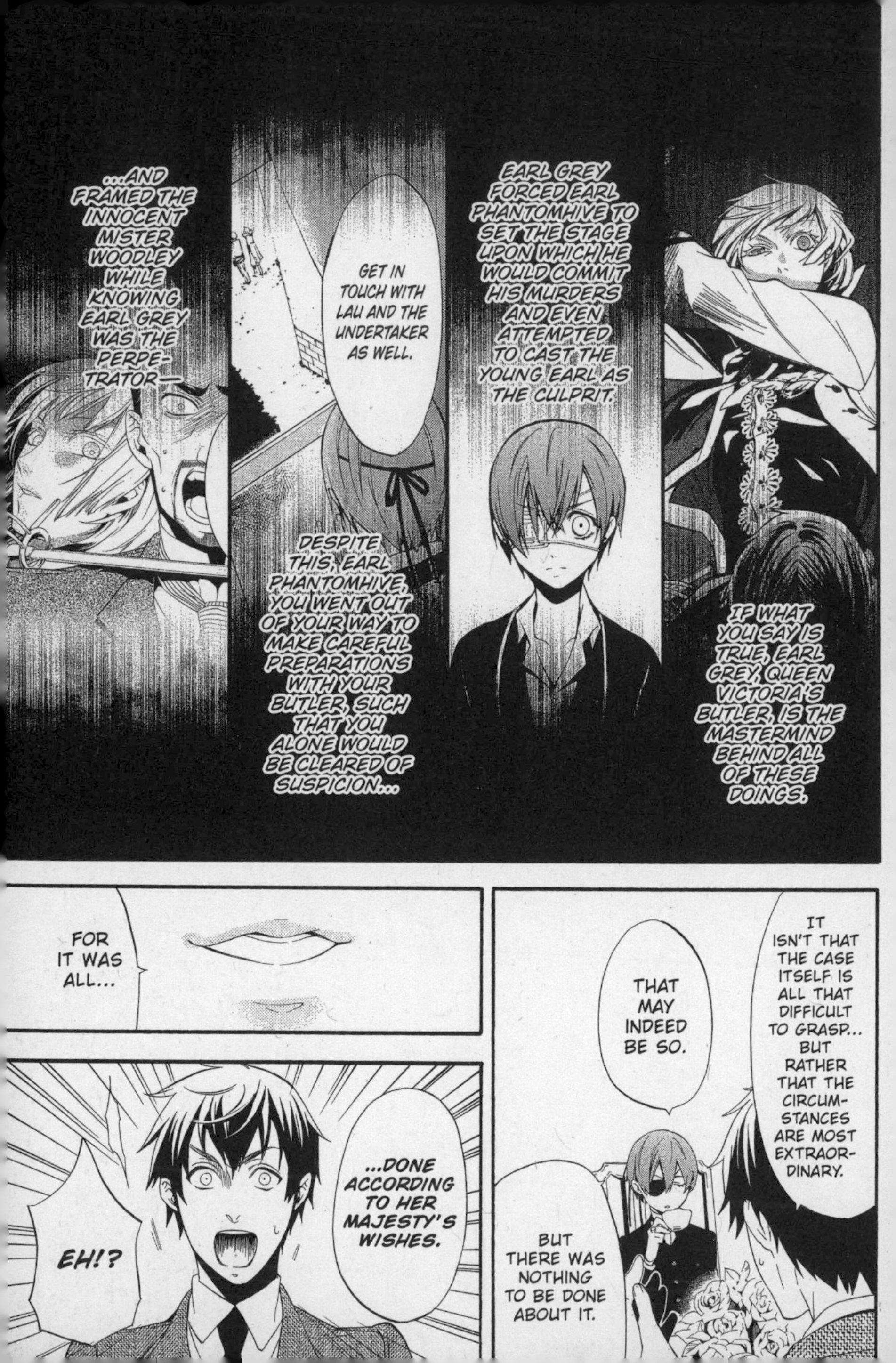
IF WHAT YOU SAY IS TRUE, EARL GREY, QUEEN VICTORIA'S BUTLER, IS THE MASTERMIND BEHIND ALL OF THESE DOINGS.
EARL GREY FORCED EARL PHANTOMHIVE TO SET THE STAGE UPON WHICH HE WOULD COMMIT HIS MURDERS AND EVEN ATTEMPTED TO CAST THE YOUNG EARL AS THE CULPRIT.
GET IN TOUCH WITH LAU AND THE UNDERTAKER AS WELL.
DESPITE THIS, EARL PHANTOMHIVE, YOU WENT OUT OF YOUR WAY TO MAKE CAREFUL PREPARATIONS WITH YOUR BUTLER, SUCH THAT YOU ALONE WOULD BE CLEARED OF SUSPICION...
...AND FRAMED THE INNOCENT MISTER WOODLEY WHILE KNOWING EARL GREY WAS THE PERPE-TRATOR—
IT ISN'T THAT THE CASE ITSELF IS ALL THAT DIFFICULT TO GRASP... BUT RATHER THAT THE CIRCUM-STANCES ARE MOST EXTRAOR-DINARY.
THAT MAY INDEED BE SO.
BUT THERE WAS NOTHING TO BE DONE ABOUT IT.
FOR IT WAS ALL...
...DONE ACCORDING TO HER MAJESTY'S WISHES.
EH!?

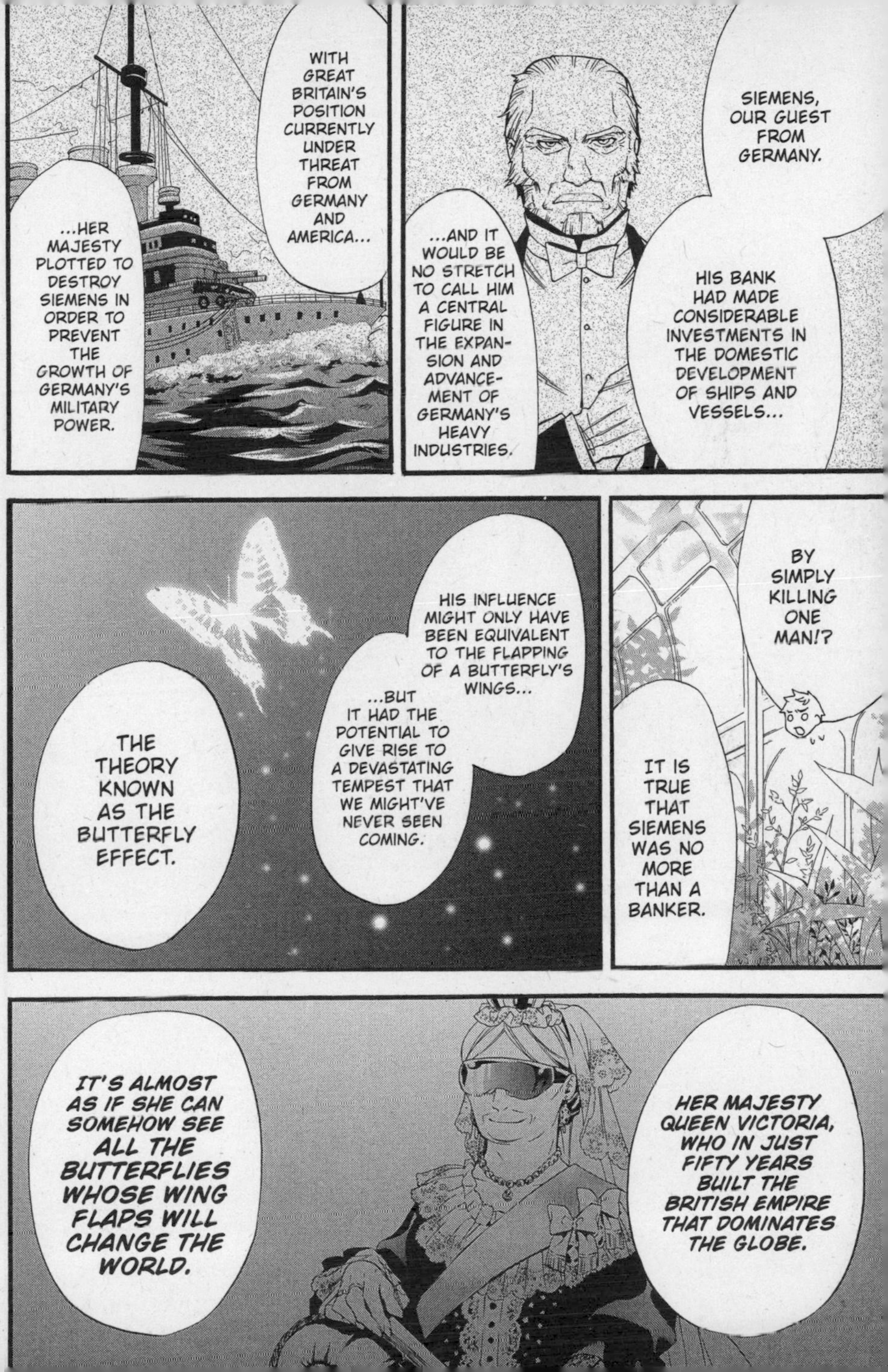
SIEMENS, OUR GUEST FROM GERMANY.
HIS BANK HAD MADE CONSIDERABLE INVESTMENTS IN THE DOMESTIC DEVELOPMENT OF SHIPS AND VESSELS...
...AND IT WOULD BE NO STRETCH TO CALL HIM A CENTRAL FIGURE IN THE EXPANSION AND ADVANCEMENT OF GERMANY'S HEAVY INDUSTRIES.
WITH GREAT BRITAIN'S POSITION CURRENTLY UNDER THREAT FROM GERMANY AND AMERICA...
...HER MAJESTY PLOTTED TO DESTROY SIEMENS IN ORDER TO PREVENT THE GROWTH OF GERMANY'S MILITARY POWER.
BY SIMPLY KILLING ONE MAN!?
IT IS TRUE THAT SIEMENS WAS NO MORE THAN A BANKER.
HIS INFLUENCE MIGHT ONLY HAVE BEEN EQUIVALENT TO THE FLAPPING OF A BUTTERFLY'S WINGS...
...BUT IT HAD THE POTENTIAL TO GIVE RISE TO A DEVASTATING TEMPEST THAT WE MIGHT'VE NEVER SEEN COMING.
THE THEORY KNOWN AS THE BUTTERFLY EFFECT.
HER MAJESTY QUEEN VICTORIA, WHO IN JUST FIFTY YEARS BUILT THE BRITISH EMPIRE THAT DOMINATES THE GLOBE.
IT'S ALMOST AS IF SHE CAN SOMEHOW SEE ALL THE BUTTERFLIES WHOSE WING FLAPS WILL CHANGE THE WORLD.

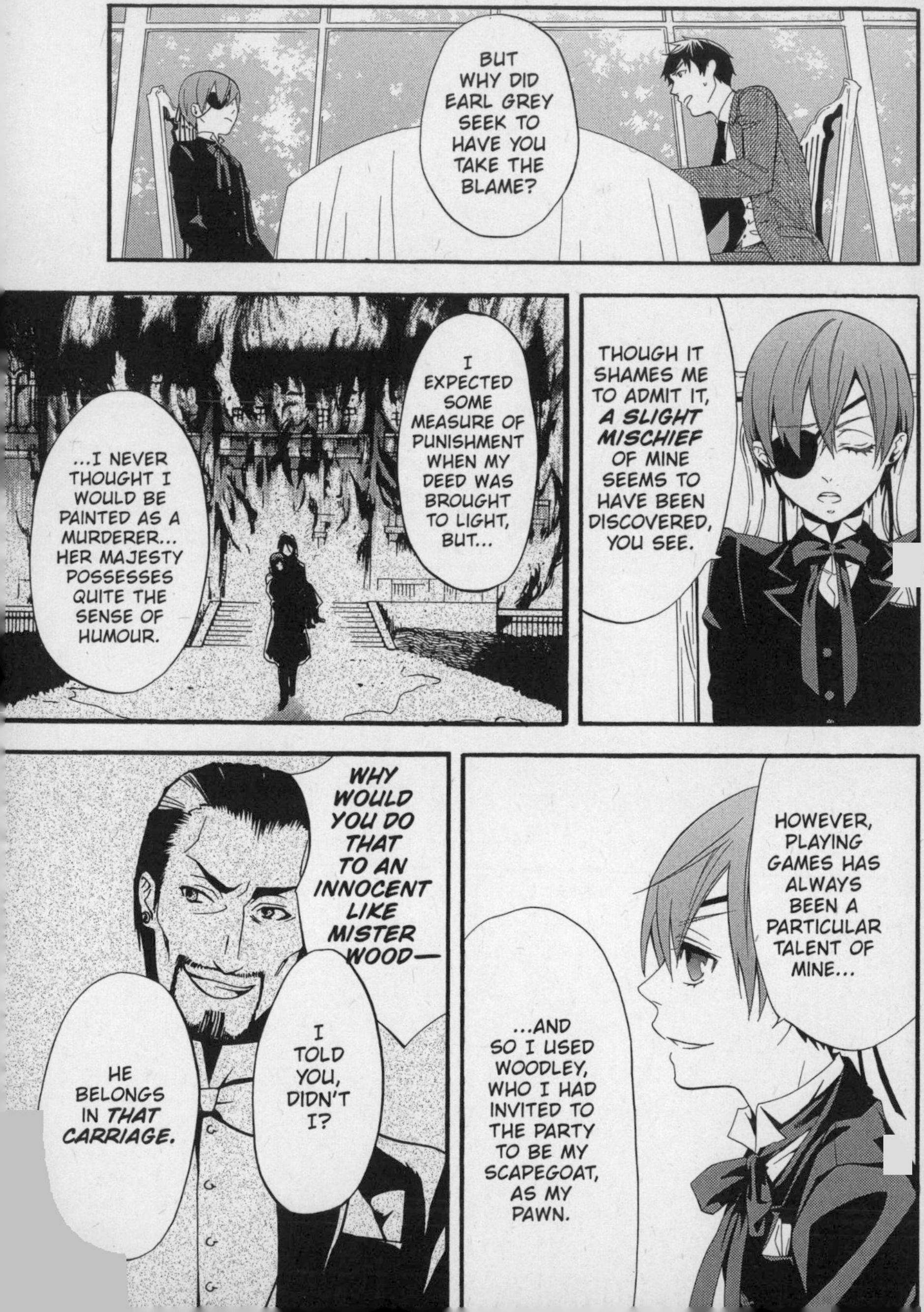
BUT WHY DID EARL GREY SEEK TO HAVE YOU TAKE THE BLAME?
THOUGH IT SHAMES ME TO ADMIT IT, ***A SLIGHT MISCHIEF*** OF MINE SEEMS TO HAVE BEEN DISCOVERED, YOU SEE.
I EXPECTED SOME MEASURE OF PUNISHMENT WHEN MY DEED WAS BROUGHT TO LIGHT, BUT...
...I NEVER THOUGHT I WOULD BE PAINTED AS A MURDERER... HER MAJESTY POSSESSES QUITE THE SENSE OF HUMOUR.
HOWEVER, PLAYING GAMES HAS ALWAYS BEEN A PARTICULAR TALENT OF MINE...
...AND SO I USED WOODLEY, WHO I HAD INVITED TO THE PARTY TO BE MY SCAPEGOAT, AS MY PAWN.
WHY WOULD YOU DO THAT TO AN INNOCENT LIKE MISTER WOOD—
I TOLD YOU, DIDN'T I?
HE BELONGS IN ***THAT CARRIAGE.***

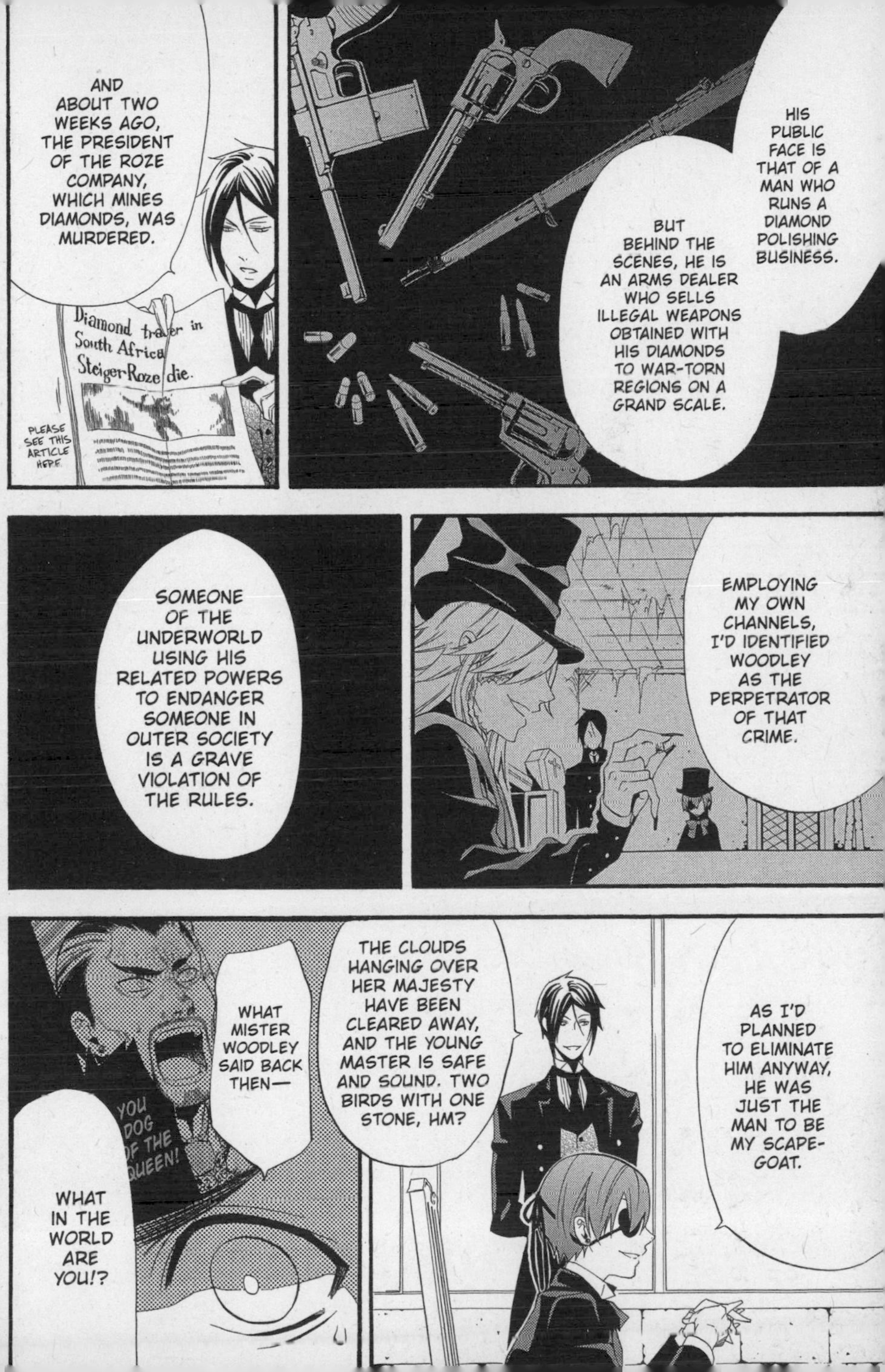
HIS PUBLIC FACE IS THAT OF A MAN WHO RUNS A DIAMOND POLISHING BUSINESS.
BUT BEHIND THE SCENES, HE IS AN ARMS DEALER WHO SELLS ILLEGAL WEAPONS OBTAINED WITH HIS DIAMONDS TO WAR-TORN REGIONS ON A GRAND SCALE.
AND ABOUT TWO WEEKS AGO, THE PRESIDENT OF THE ROZE COMPANY, WHICH MINES DIAMONDS, WAS MURDERED.
Diamond tra er in South Africa Steiger Roze die.
PLEASE SEE THIS ARTICLE HERE.
EMPLOYING MY OWN CHANNELS, I'D IDENTIFIED WOODLEY AS THE PERPETRATOR OF THAT CRIME.
SOMEONE OF THE UNDERWORLD USING HIS RELATED POWERS TO ENDANGER SOMEONE IN OUTER SOCIETY IS A GRAVE VIOLATION OF THE RULES.
AS I'D PLANNED TO ELIMINATE HIM ANYWAY, HE WAS JUST THE MAN TO BE MY SCAPE-GOAT.
THE CLOUDS HANGING OVER HER MAJESTY HAVE BEEN CLEARED AWAY, AND THE YOUNG MASTER IS SAFE AND SOUND. TWO BIRDS WITH ONE STONE, HM?
WHAT MISTER WOODLEY SAID BACK THEN—
YOU DOG OF THE QUEEN!
WHAT IN THE WORLD ARE YOU!?

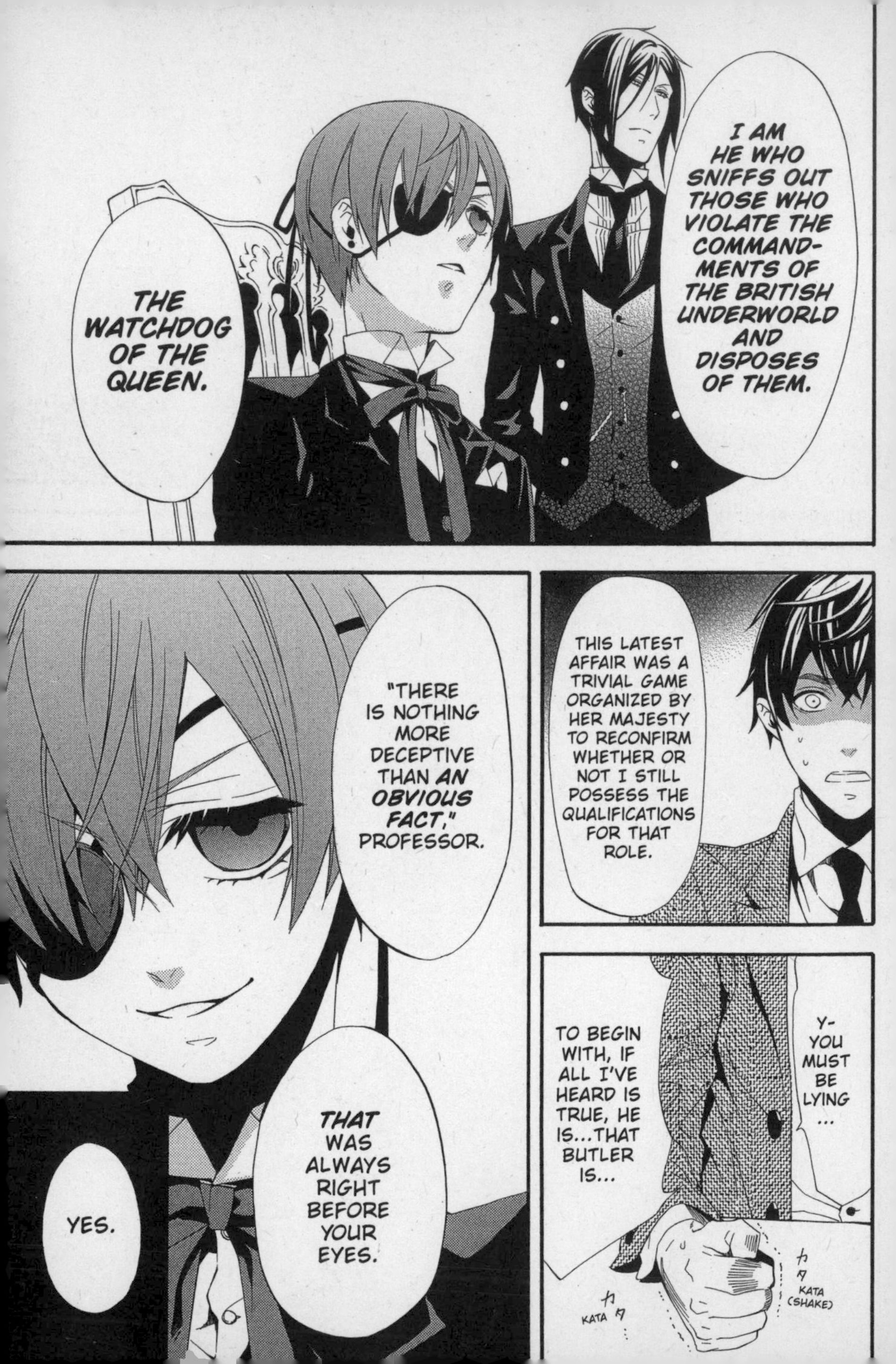
I AM HE WHO SNIFFS OUT THOSE WHO VIOLATE THE COMMAND-MENTS OF THE BRITISH UNDERWORLD AND DISPOSES OF THEM.
THE WATCHDOG OF THE QUEEN.
THIS LATEST AFFAIR WAS A TRIVIAL GAME ORGANIZED BY HER MAJESTY TO RECONFIRM WHETHER OR NOT I STILL POSSESS THE QUALIFICATIONS FOR THAT ROLE.
Y-YOU MUST BE LYING...
TO BEGIN WITH, IF ALL I'VE HEARD IS TRUE, HE IS...THAT BUTLER IS...
カタ KATA (SHAKE)
カタ KATA
"THERE IS NOTHING MORE DECEPTIVE THAN AN OBVIOUS FACT," PROFESSOR.
THAT WAS ALWAYS RIGHT BEFORE YOUR EYES.
YES.

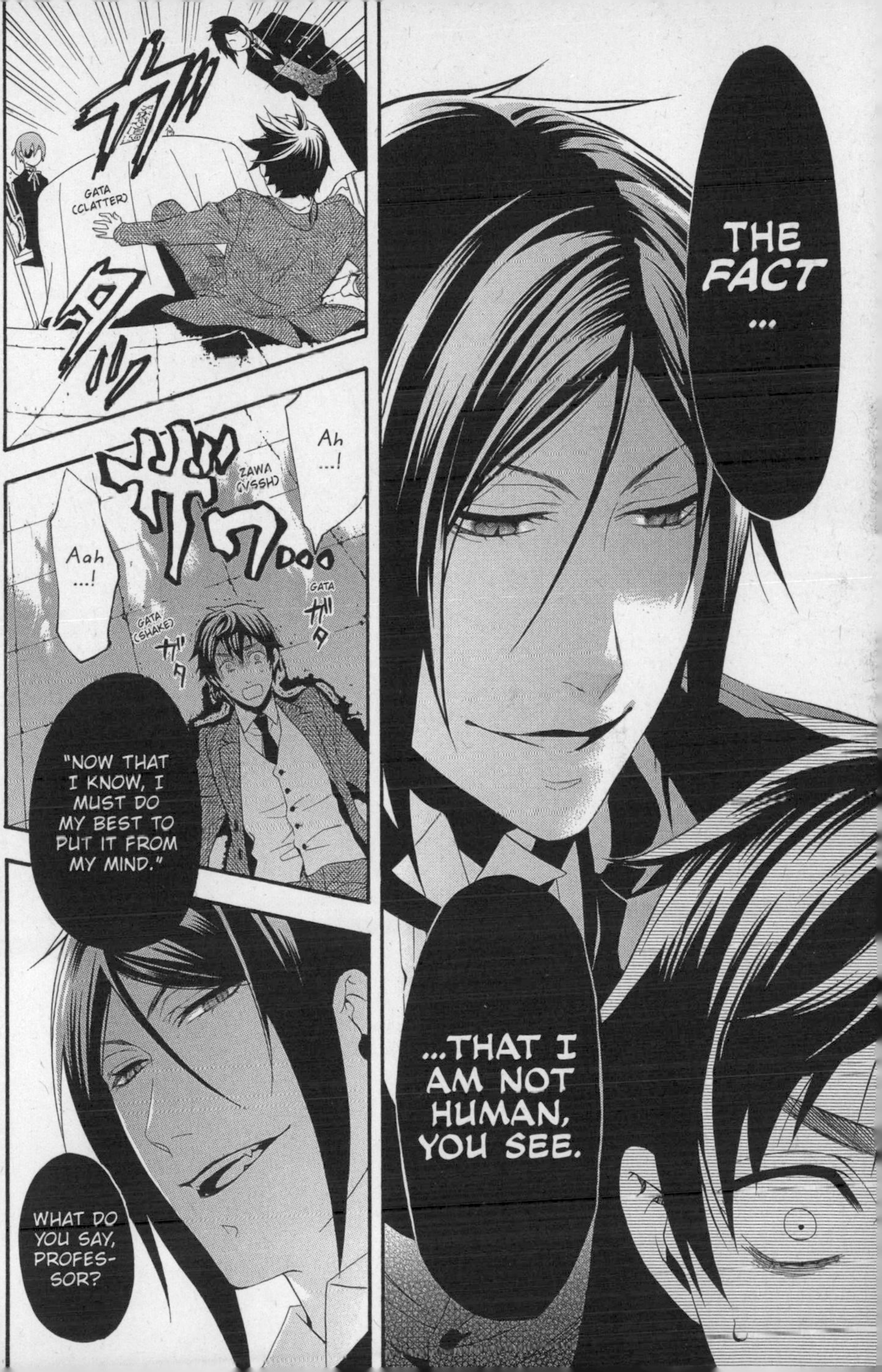
THE FACT ...
...THAT I AM NOT HUMAN, YOU SEE.
GATA (CLATTER)
Ah ...!
ZAWA (VSSH)
Aah ...!
GATA
GATA (SHAKE)
"NOW THAT I KNOW, I MUST DO MY BEST TO PUT IT FROM MY MIND."
WHAT DO YOU SAY, PROFES-SOR?

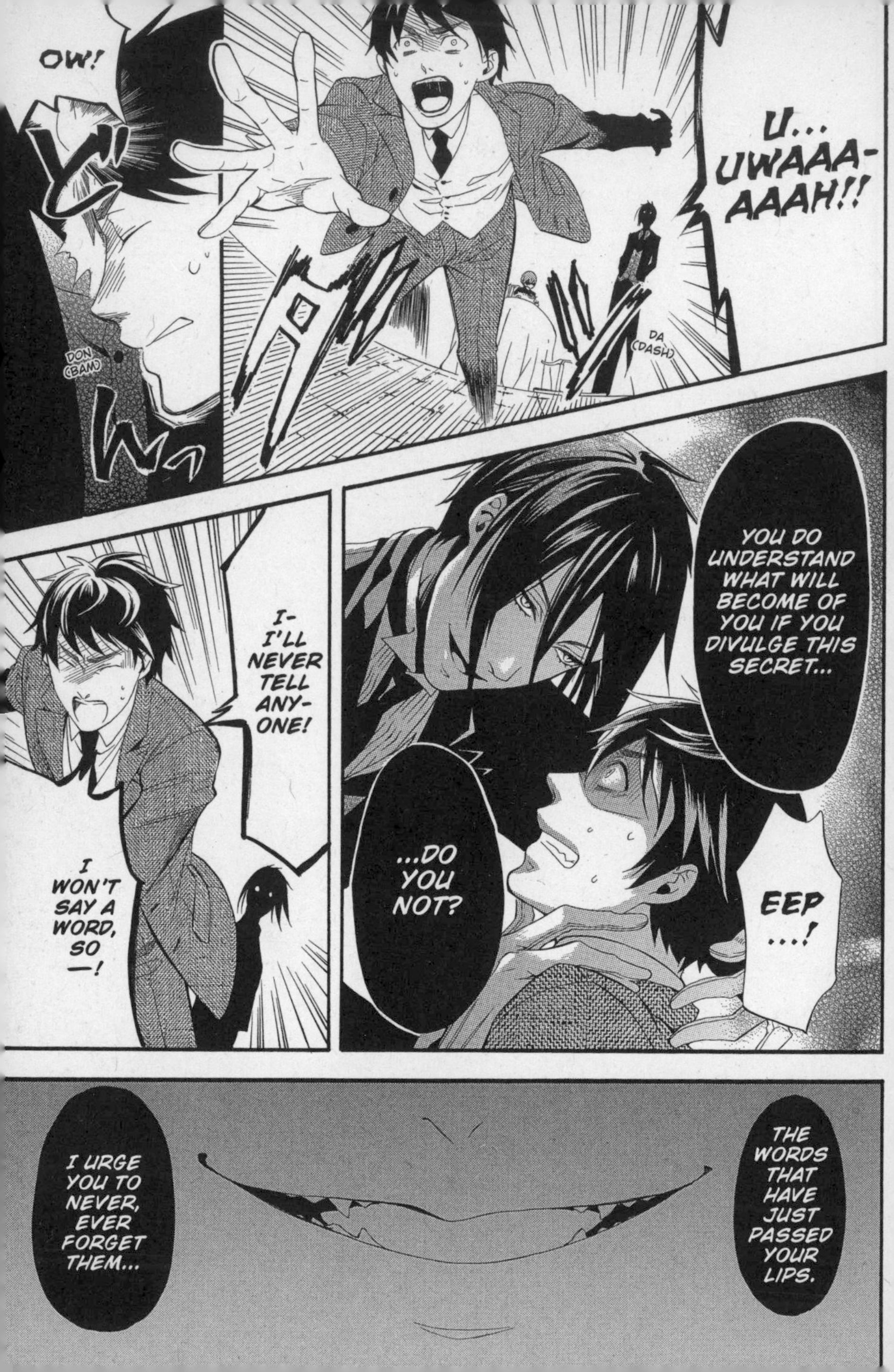
U... UWAAA-AAAH!!
DA (DASH)
OW!
DON (BAM)
YOU DO UNDERSTAND WHAT WILL BECOME OF YOU IF YOU DIVULGE THIS SECRET...
...DO YOU NOT?
EEP ...!
I-I'LL NEVER TELL ANY-ONE!
I WON'T SAY A WORD, SO—!
THE WORDS THAT HAVE JUST PASSED YOUR LIPS.
I URGE YOU TO NEVER, EVER FORGET THEM...

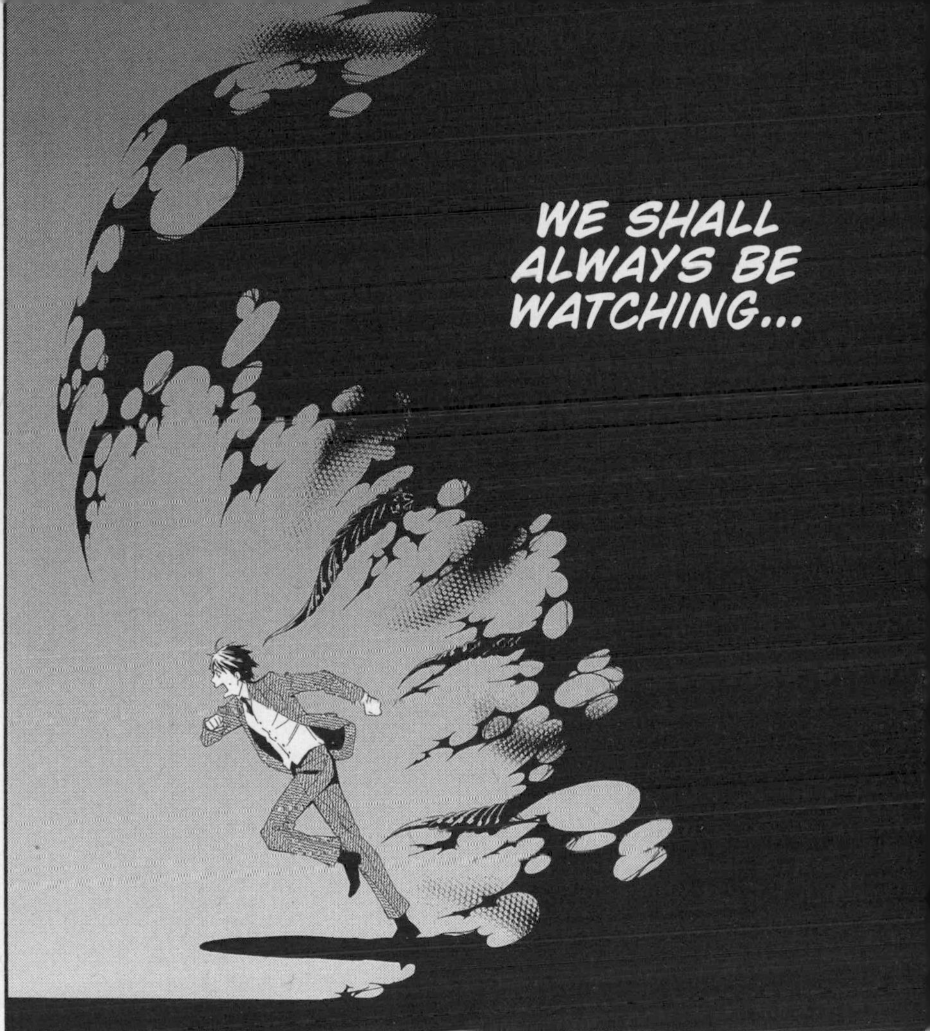
WE SHALL ALWAYS BE WATCHING...
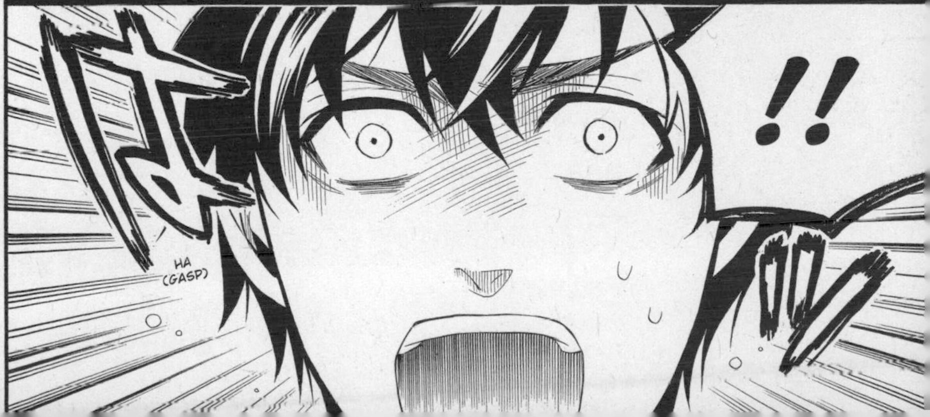
!!
HA (GASP)

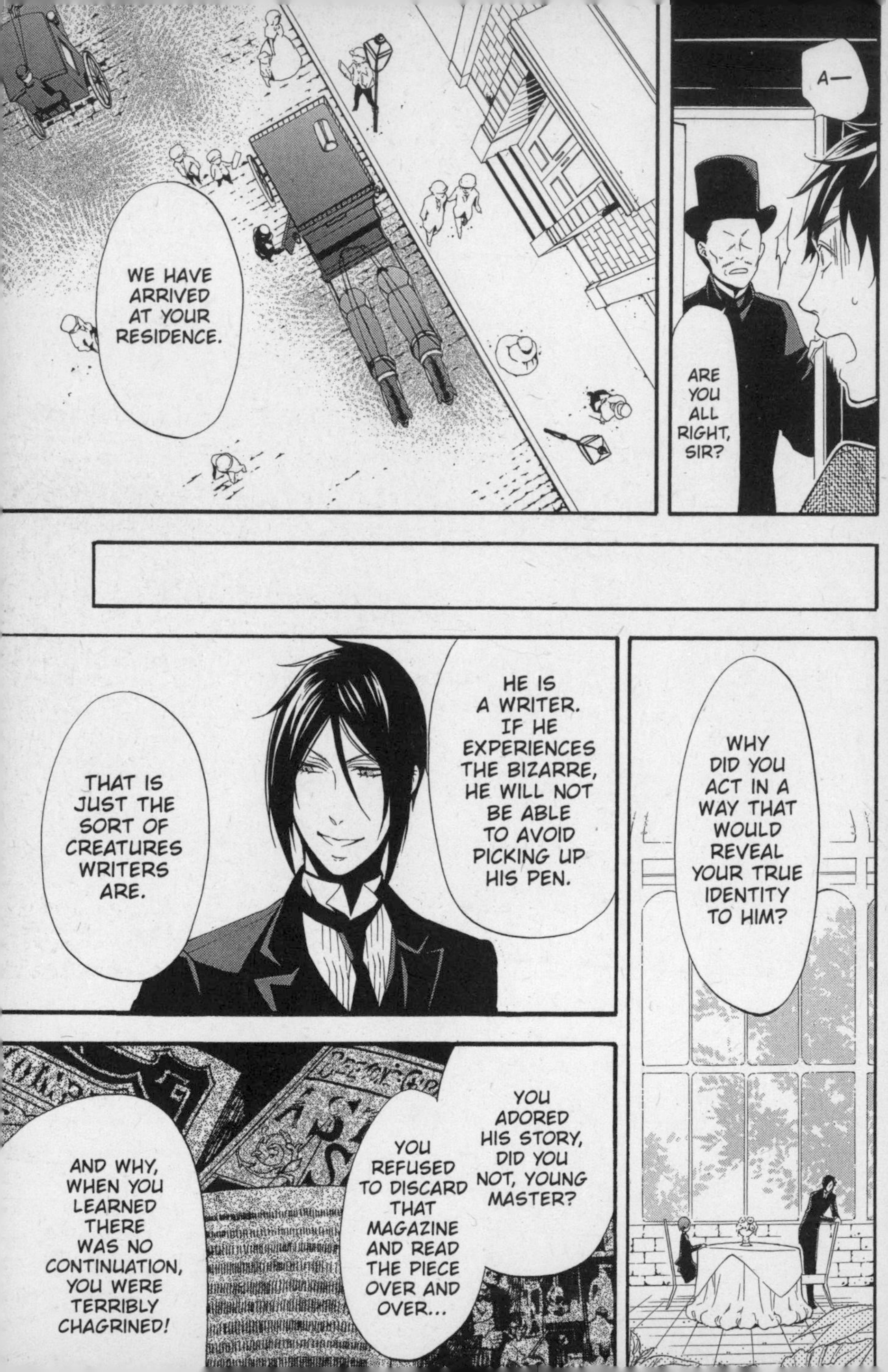
A—
ARE YOU ALL RIGHT, SIR?
WE HAVE ARRIVED AT YOUR RESIDENCE.
WHY DID YOU ACT IN A WAY THAT WOULD REVEAL YOUR TRUE IDENTITY TO HIM?
HE IS A WRITER. IF HE EXPERIENCES THE BIZARRE, HE WILL NOT BE ABLE TO AVOID PICKING UP HIS PEN.
THAT IS JUST THE SORT OF CREATURES WRITERS ARE.
YOU ADORED HIS STORY, DID YOU NOT, YOUNG MASTER?
YOU REFUSED TO DISCARD THAT MAGAZINE AND READ THE PIECE OVER AND OVER...
AND WHY, WHEN YOU LEARNED THERE WAS NO CONTINUATION, YOU WERE TERRIBLY CHAGRINED!

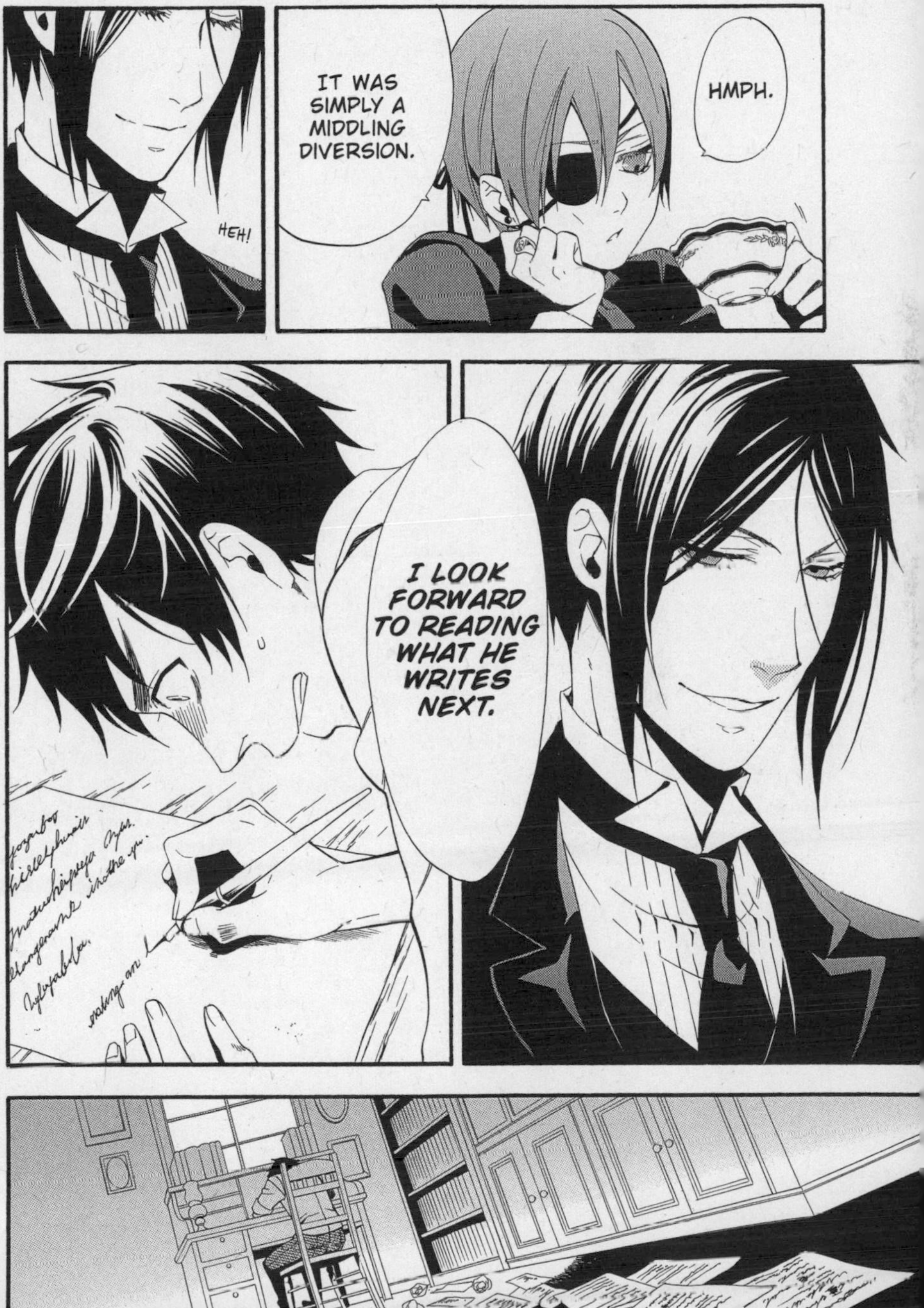
HMPH.
IT WAS SIMPLY A MIDDLING DIVERSION.
HEH!
I LOOK FORWARD TO READING WHAT HE WRITES NEXT.

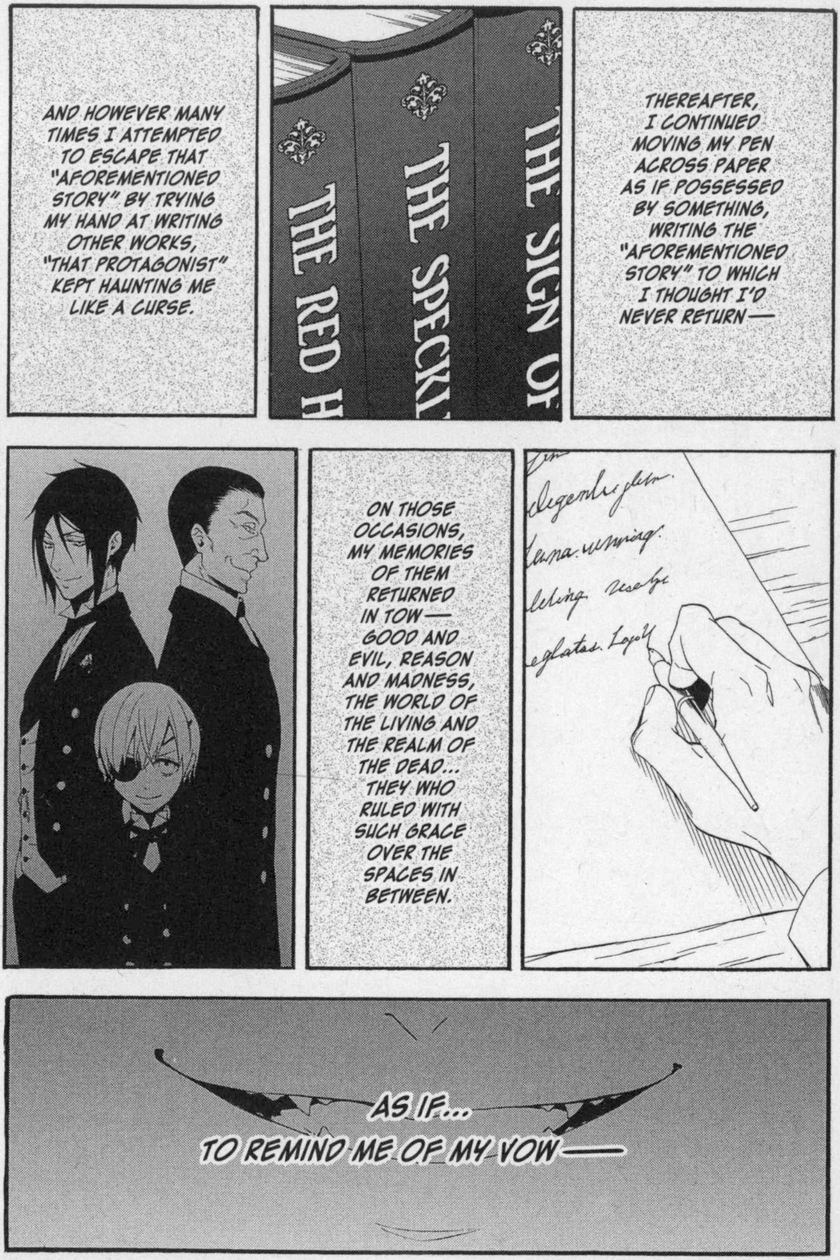

THEREAFTER, I CONTINUED MOVING MY PEN ACROSS PAPER AS IF POSSESSED BY SOMETHING, WRITING THE "AFOREMENTIONED STORY" TO WHICH I THOUGHT I'D NEVER RETURN—
THE SIGN OF
THE SPECKL
THE RED H
AND HOWEVER MANY TIMES I ATTEMPTED TO ESCAPE THAT "AFOREMENTIONED STORY" BY TRYING MY HAND AT WRITING OTHER WORKS, "THAT PROTAGONIST" KEPT HAUNTING ME LIKE A CURSE.
ON THOSE OCCASIONS, MY MEMORIES OF THEM RETURNED IN TOW— GOOD AND EVIL, REASON AND MADNESS, THE WORLD OF THE LIVING AND THE REALM OF THE DEAD... THEY WHO RULED WITH SUCH GRACE OVER THE SPACES IN BETWEEN.
AS IF... TO REMIND ME OF MY VOW—

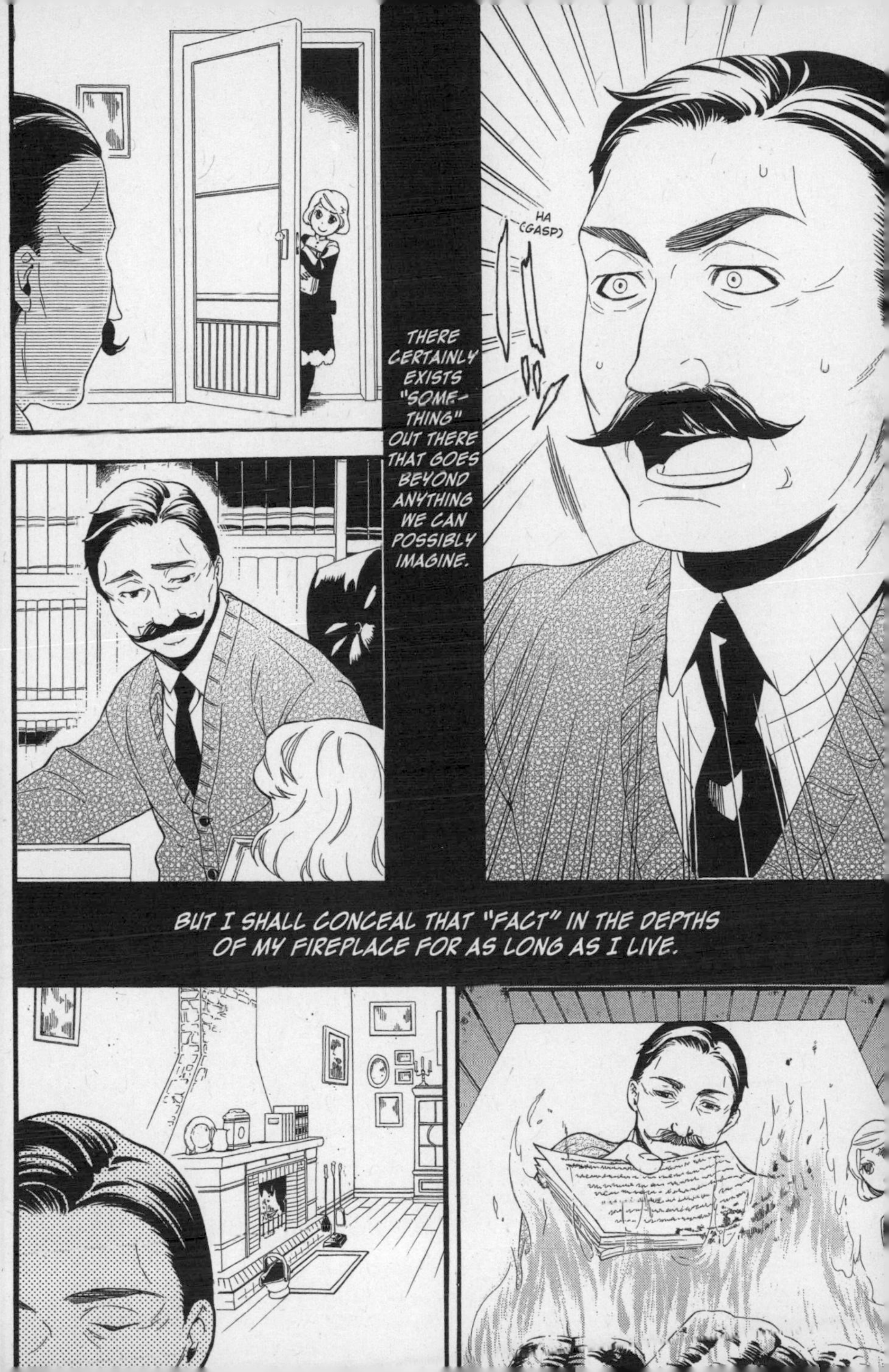
HA (GASP)
THERE CERTAINLY EXISTS "SOME-THING" OUT THERE THAT GOES BEYOND ANYTHING WE CAN POSSIBLY IMAGINE.
BUT I SHALL CONCEAL THAT "FACT" IN THE DEPTHS OF MY FIREPLACE FOR AS LONG AS I LIVE.

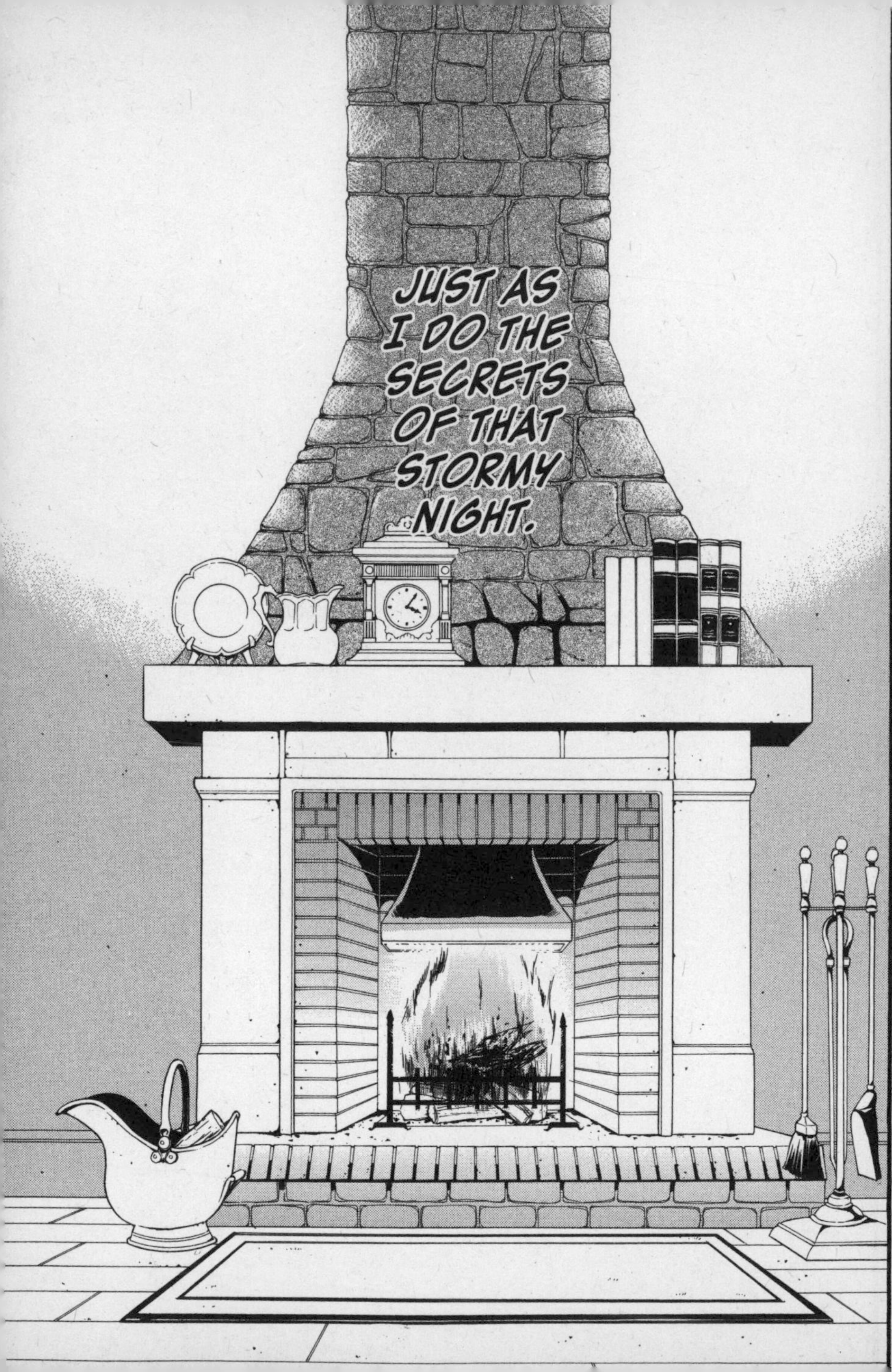
JUST AS I DO THE SECRETS OF THAT STORMY NIGHT.

Black Butler

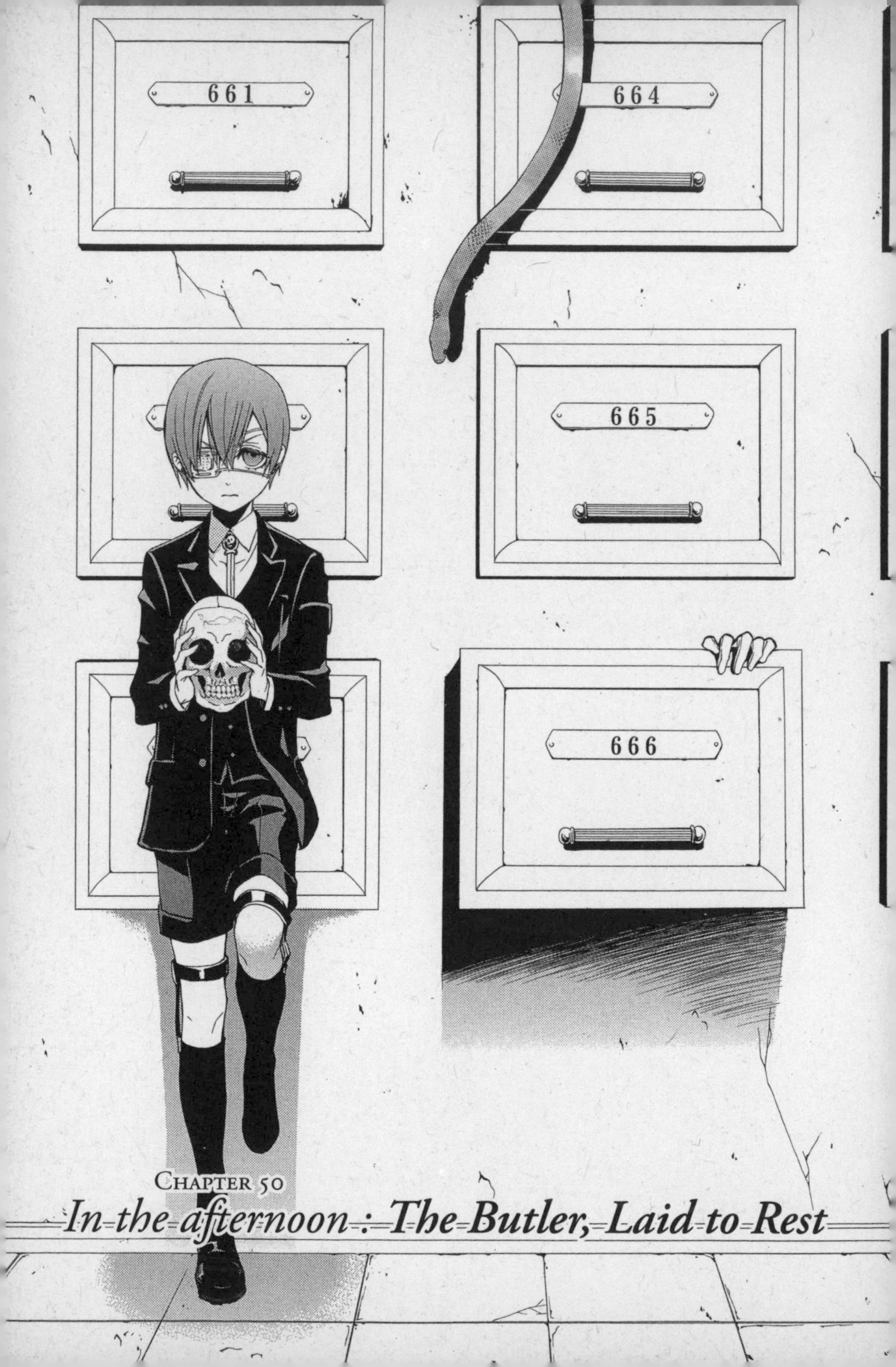
661
664
665
666
CHAPTER 50
In the afternoon : The Butler, Laid to Rest

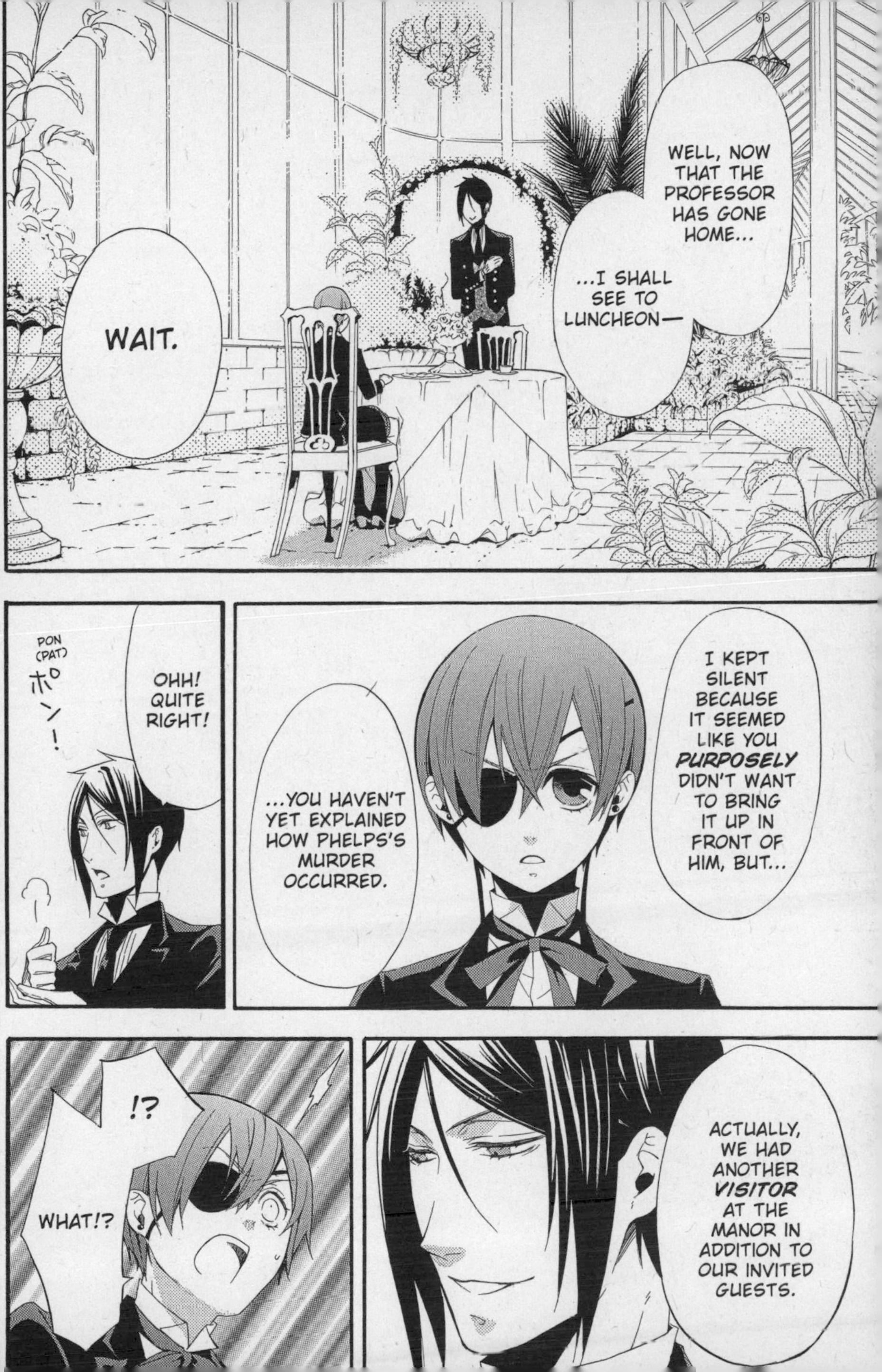
WELL, NOW THAT THE PROFESSOR HAS GONE HOME...
...I SHALL SEE TO LUNCHEON—
WAIT.
I KEPT SILENT BECAUSE IT SEEMED LIKE YOU PURPOSELY DIDN'T WANT TO BRING IT UP IN FRONT OF HIM, BUT...
...YOU HAVEN'T YET EXPLAINED HOW PHELPS'S MURDER OCCURRED.
OHH! QUITE RIGHT!
PON (PAT)
ポン!
ACTUALLY, WE HAD ANOTHER VISITOR AT THE MANOR IN ADDITION TO OUR INVITED GUESTS.
!?
WHAT!?

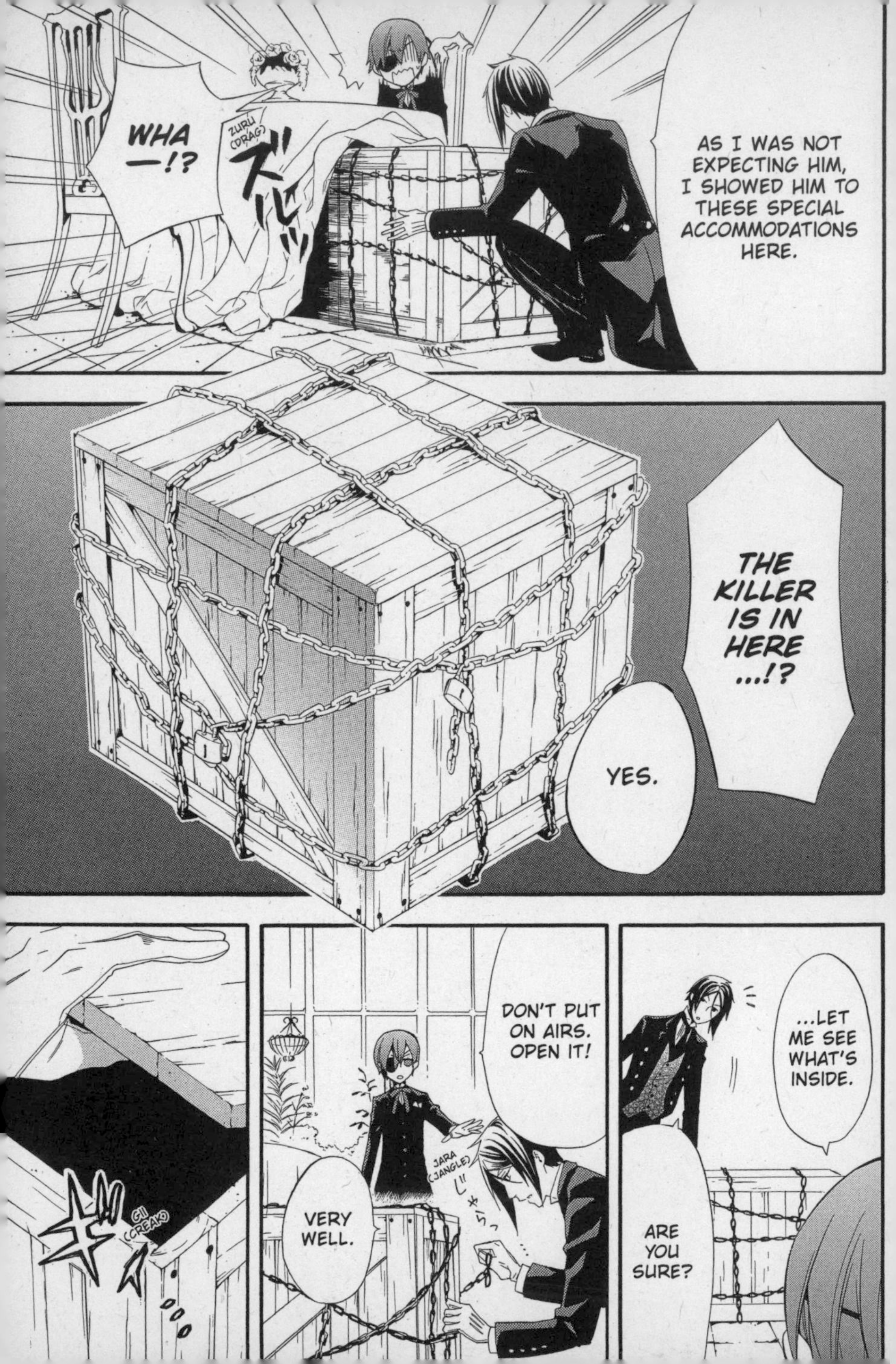
AS I WAS NOT EXPECTING HIM, I SHOWED HIM TO THESE SPECIAL ACCOMMODATIONS HERE.
ZURU (DRAG)
WHA—!?
THE KILLER IS IN HERE...!?
YES.
...LET ME SEE WHAT'S INSIDE.
ARE YOU SURE?
DON'T PUT ON AIRS. OPEN IT!
JARA (JANGLE)
VERY WELL.
GII (CREAK)

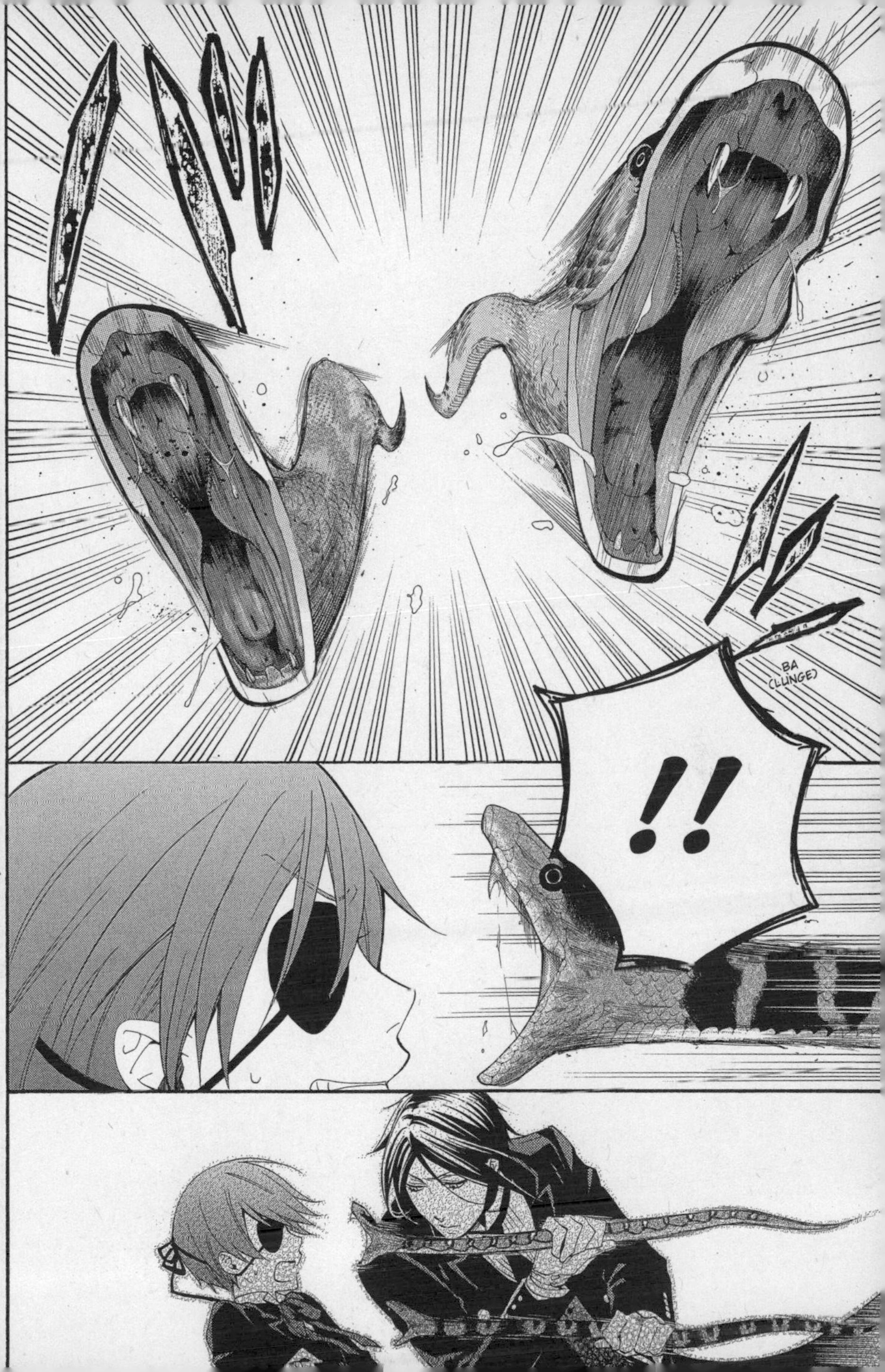
BA
(LUNGE)
!!

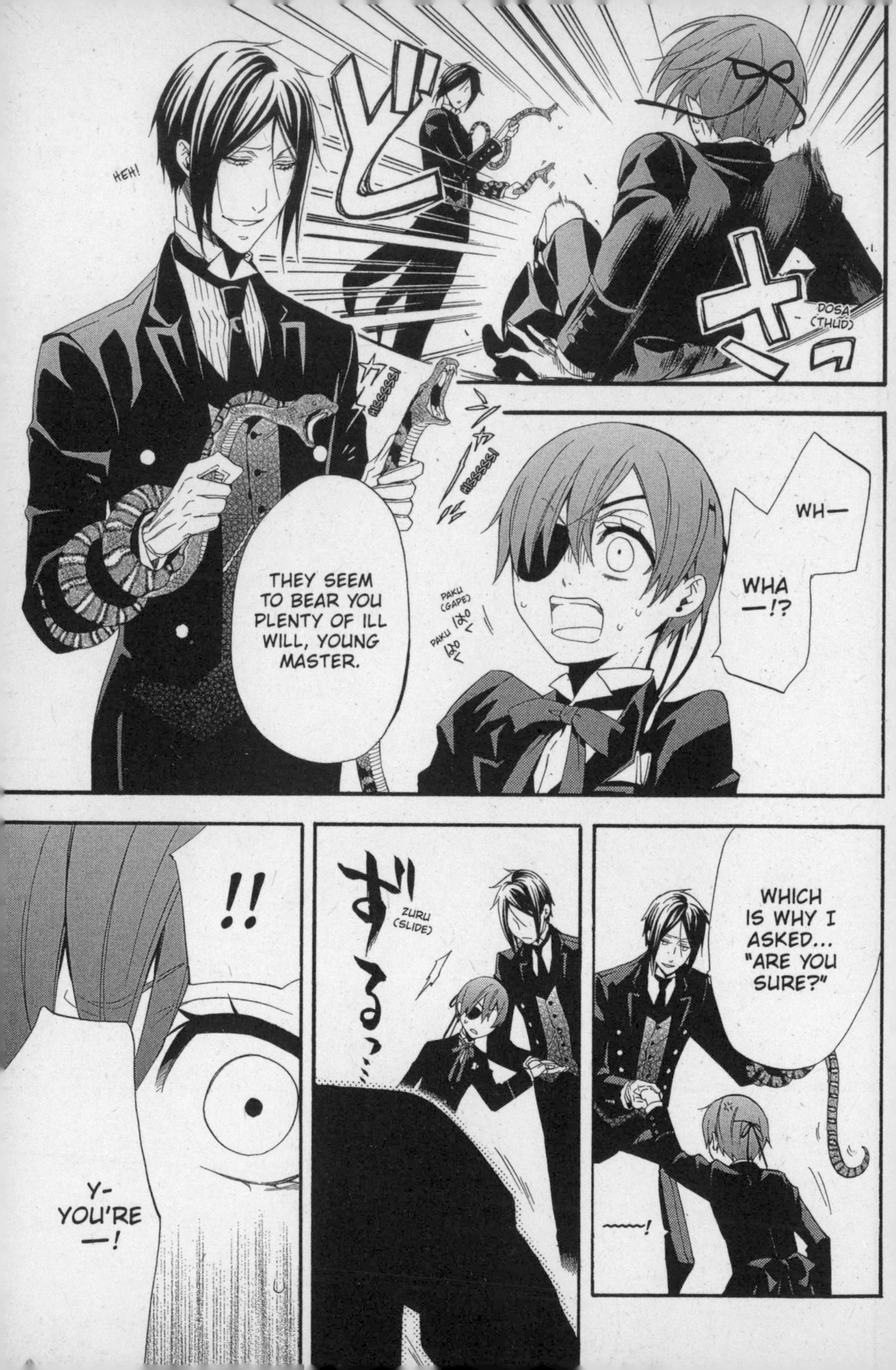

DOSA (THUD)
WH—
WHA—!?
PAKU PAKU (GAPE)
HEH!
HISSSSS!
HISSSSS!
THEY SEEM TO BEAR YOU PLENTY OF ILL WILL, YOUNG MASTER.
WHICH IS WHY I ASKED... "ARE YOU SURE?"
~~~~!
ZURU (SLIDE)
!!
Y-YOU'RE—!
~~~~

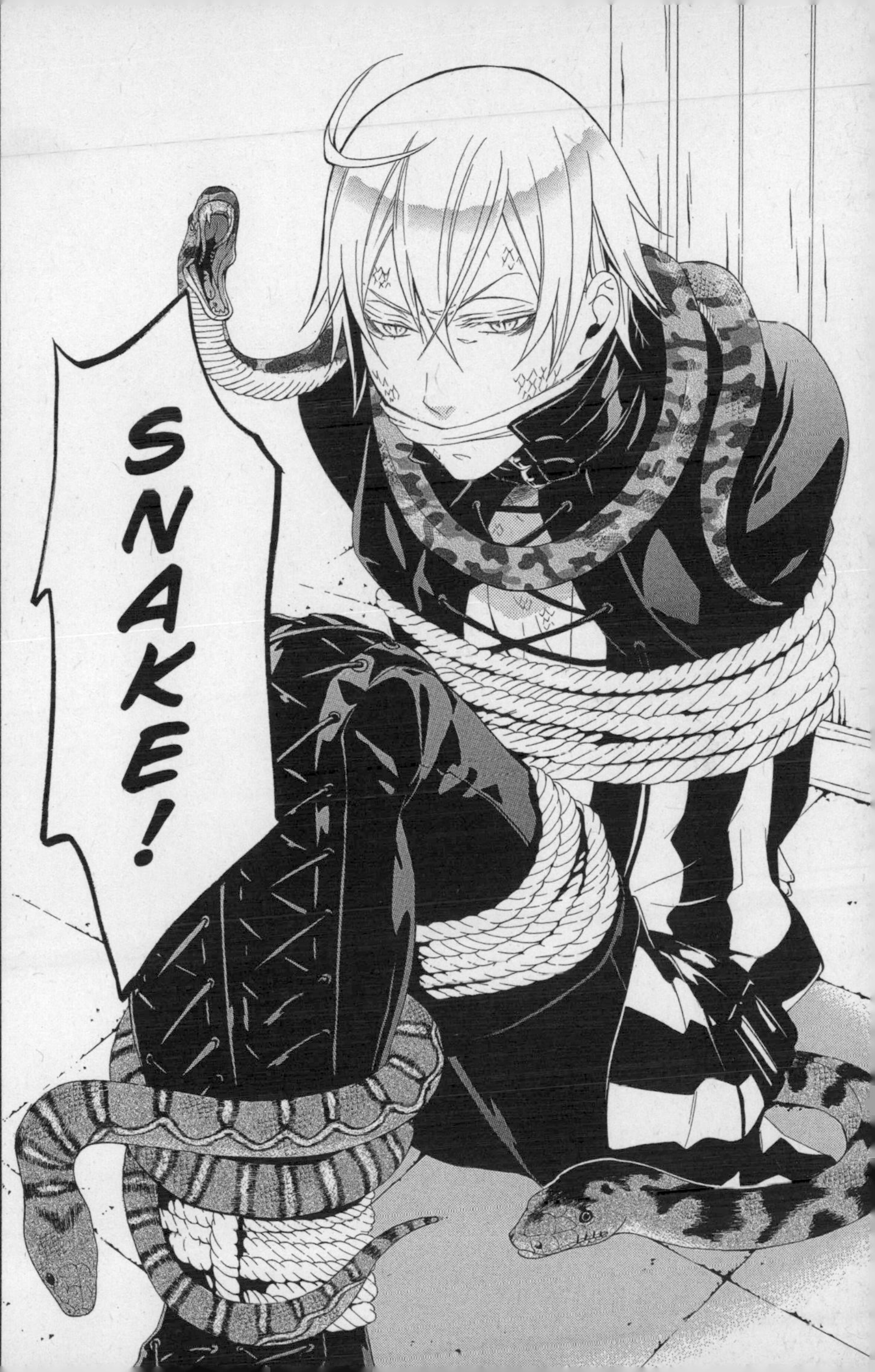
SNAKE!

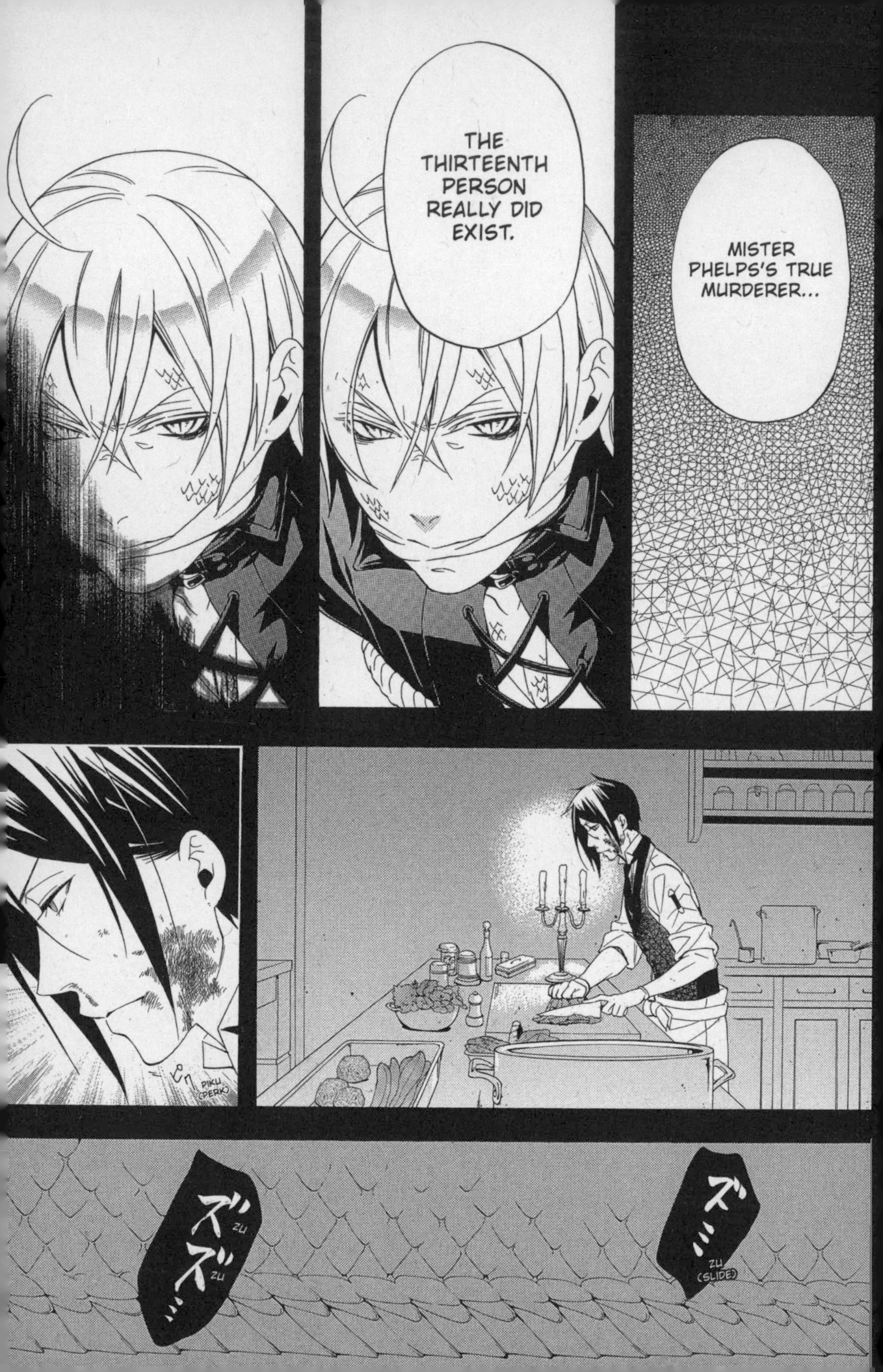
MISTER PHELPS'S TRUE MURDERER...
THE THIRTEENTH PERSON REALLY DID EXIST.
PIKU (PERK)
ズ…
ZU (SLIDE)
ズズ…
ZU
ZU

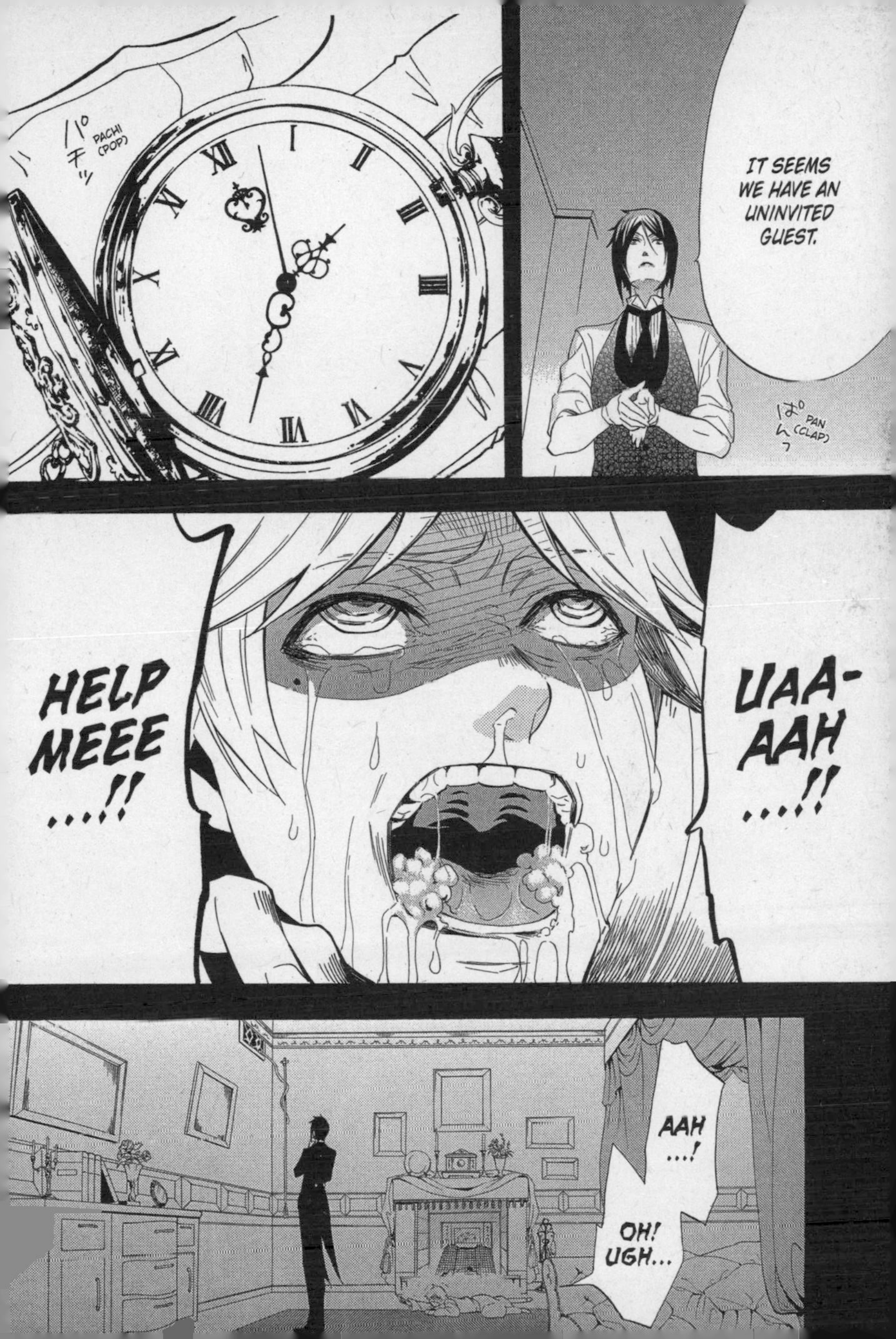
IT SEEMS WE HAVE AN UNINVITED GUEST.
ぱんっ
PAN (CLAP)
パチッ
PACHI (POP)
UAA-AAH ...!!
HELP MEEE ...!!
AAH ...!
OH! UGH...

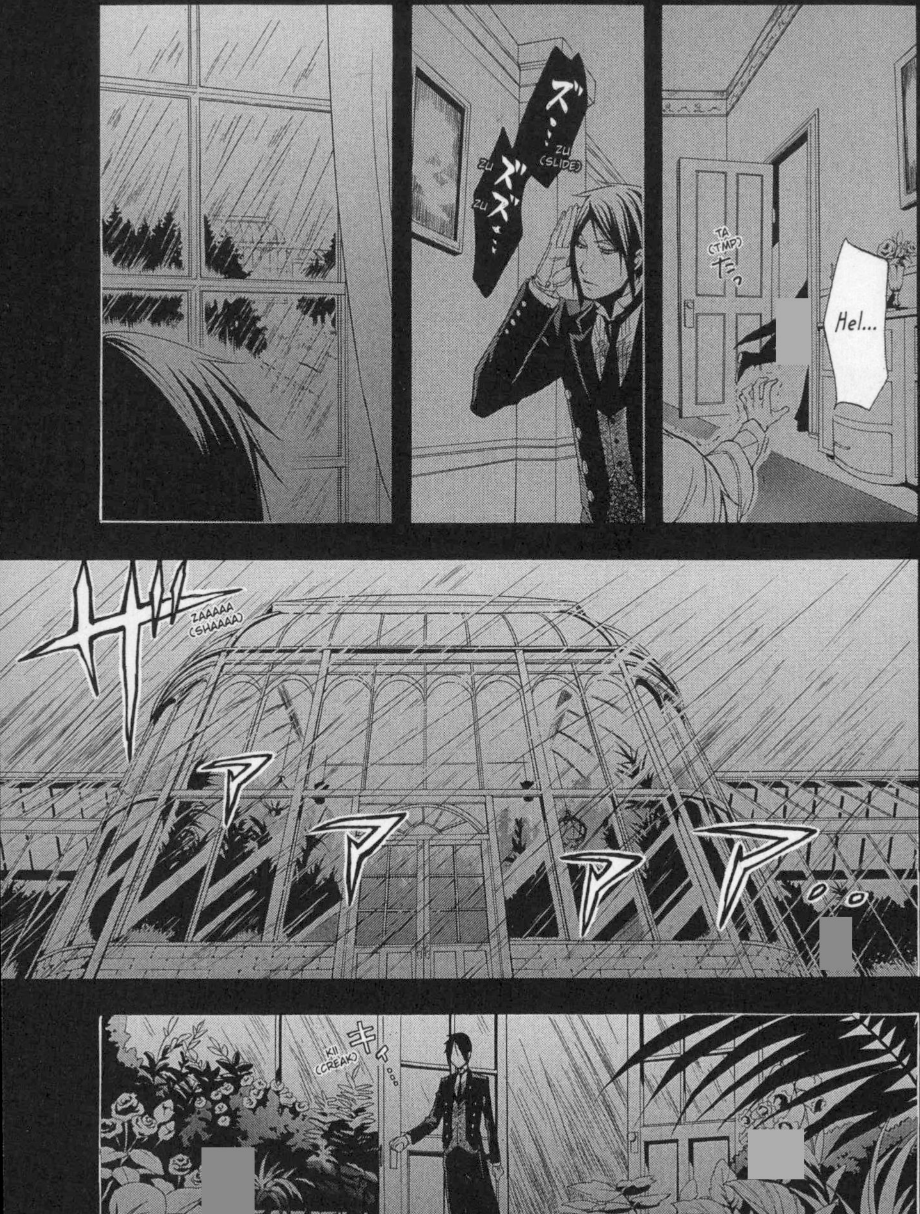
TA (TMP) たっ
Hel...
ズ… ZU (SLIDE)
ズズ… ZU ZU
ZAAAAA (SHAAAA)
キィ… KII (CREAK)

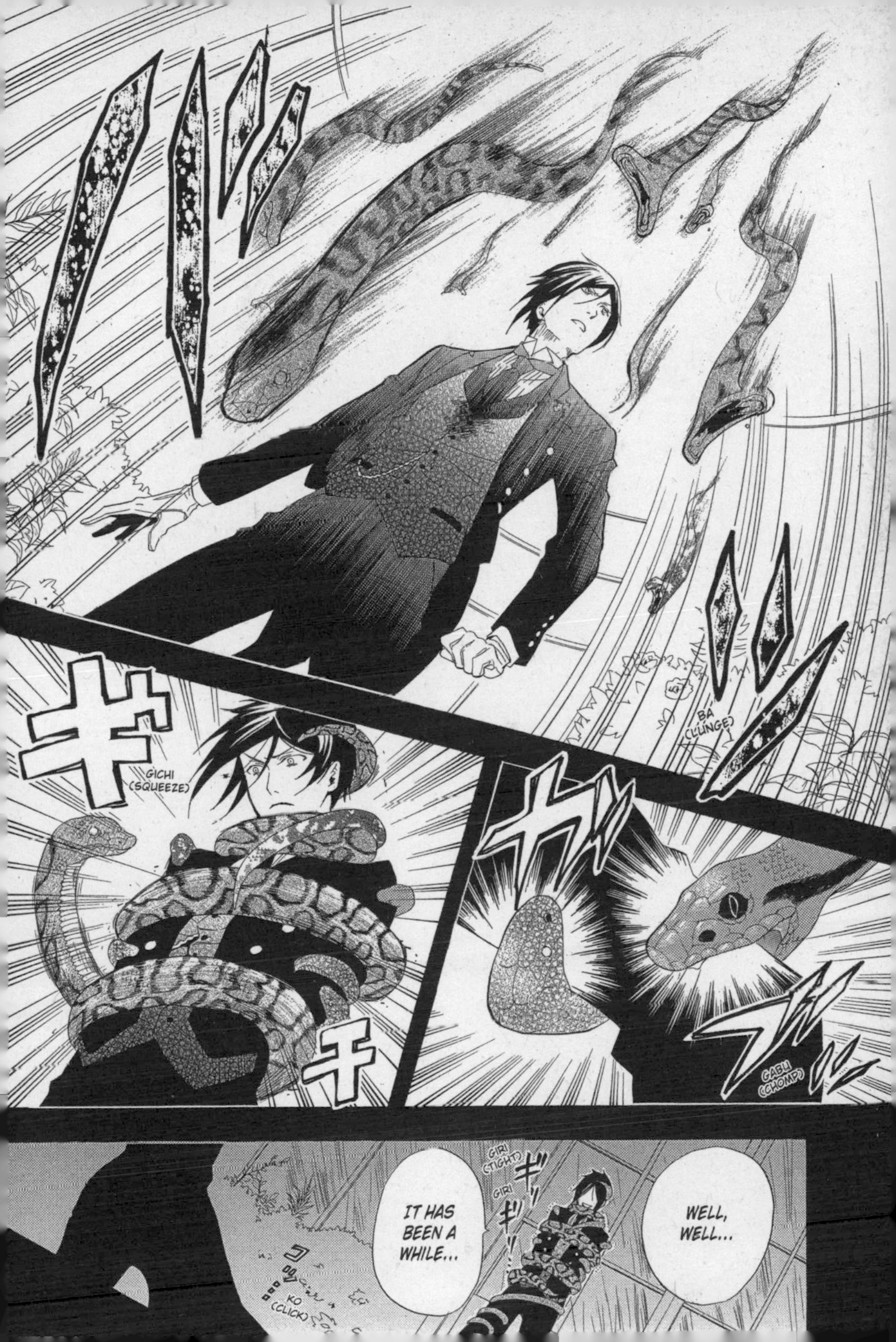
BA (LUNGE)
GABU (CHOMP)
GICHI (SQUEEZE)
WELL, WELL...
GIRI (TIGHT)
GIRI
IT HAS BEEN A WHILE...
KO (CLICK)

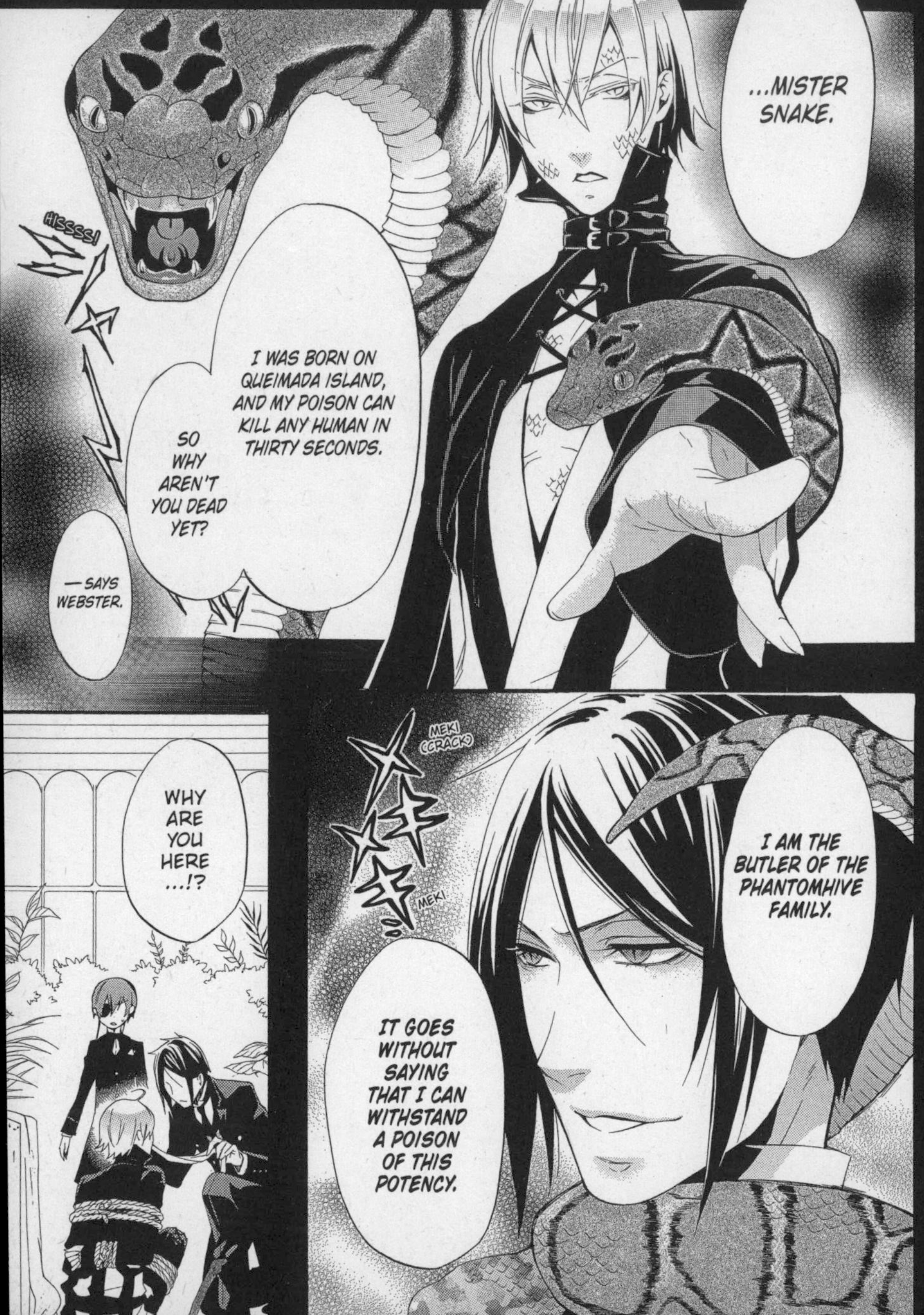
...MISTER SNAKE.
HISSSS!
I WAS BORN ON QUEIMADA ISLAND, AND MY POISON CAN KILL ANY HUMAN IN THIRTY SECONDS.
SO WHY AREN'T YOU DEAD YET?
—SAYS WEBSTER.
MEKI (CRACK)
I AM THE BUTLER OF THE PHANTOMHIVE FAMILY.
MEKI
IT GOES WITHOUT SAYING THAT I CAN WITHSTAND A POISON OF THIS POTENCY.
WHY ARE YOU HERE ...!?

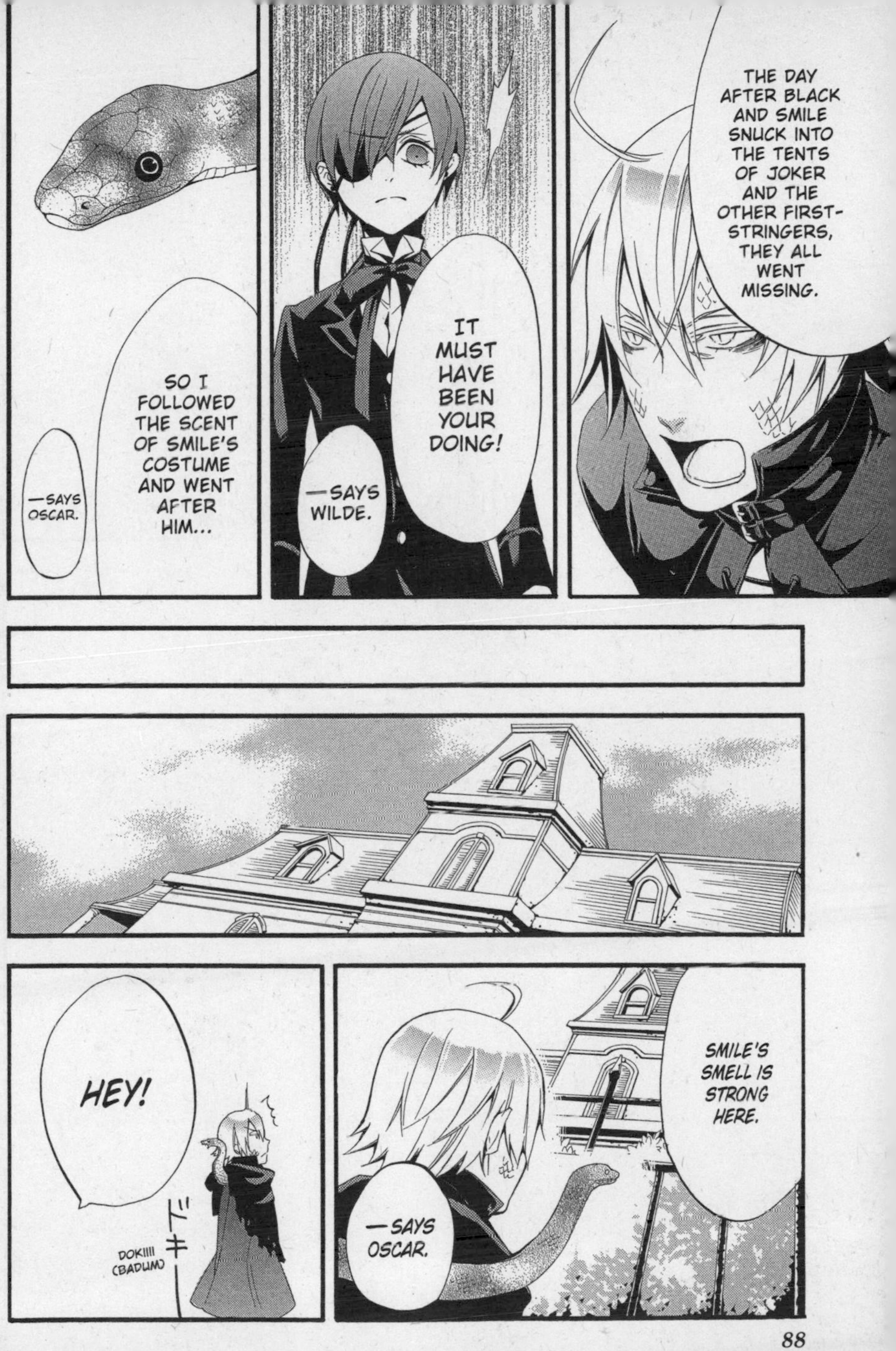
THE DAY AFTER BLACK AND SMILE SNUCK INTO THE TENTS OF JOKER AND THE OTHER FIRST-STRINGERS, THEY ALL WENT MISSING.
IT MUST HAVE BEEN YOUR DOING!
—SAYS WILDE.
SO I FOLLOWED THE SCENT OF SMILE'S COSTUME AND WENT AFTER HIM...
—SAYS OSCAR.
SMILE'S SMELL IS STRONG HERE.
—SAYS OSCAR.
HEY!
ドキ
DOKIIII (BADUM)

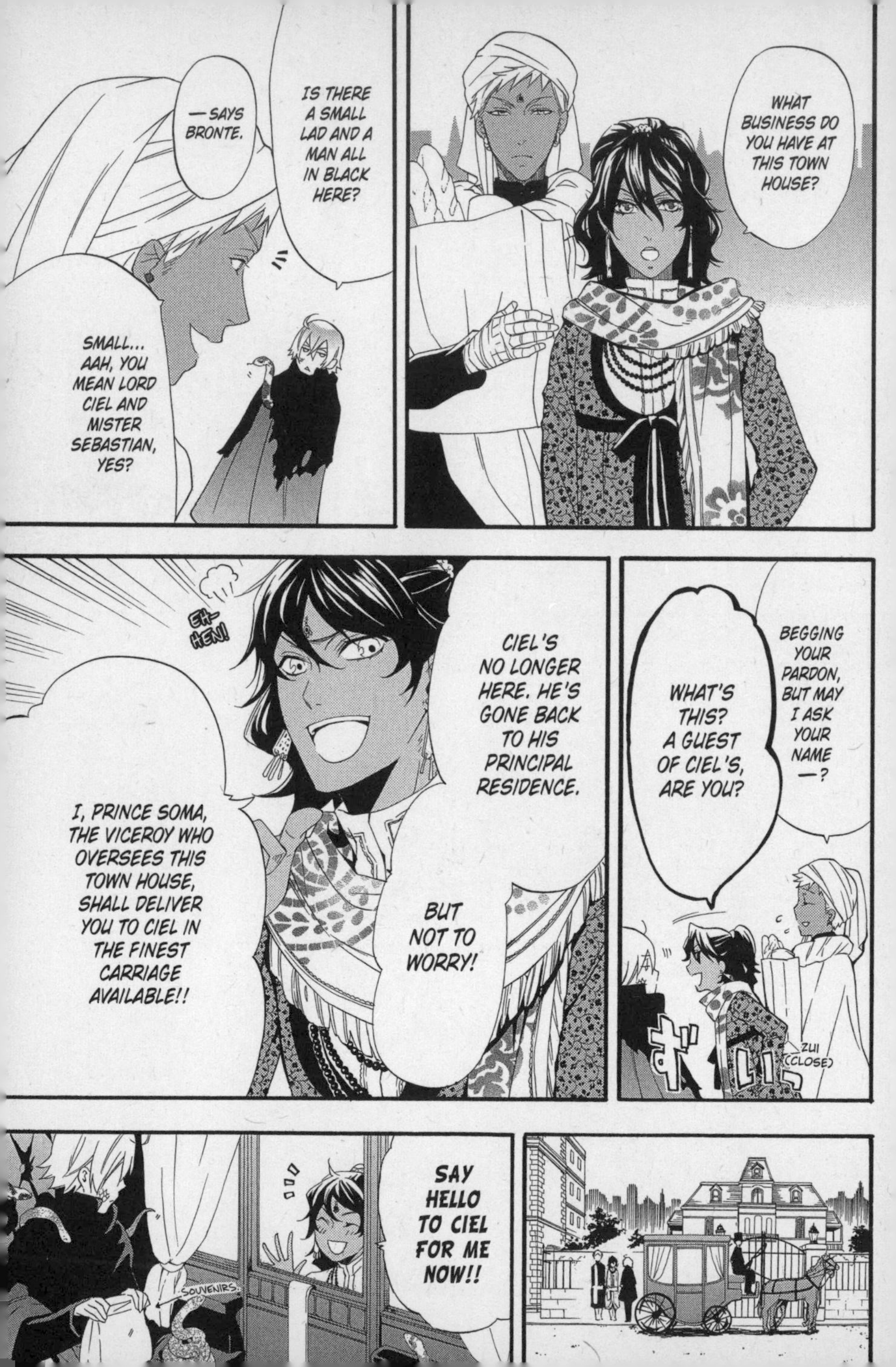
WHAT BUSINESS DO YOU HAVE AT THIS TOWN HOUSE?
IS THERE A SMALL LAD AND A MAN ALL IN BLACK HERE?
—SAYS BRONTE.
SMALL... AAH, YOU MEAN LORD CIEL AND MISTER SEBASTIAN, YES?
BEGGING YOUR PARDON, BUT MAY I ASK YOUR NAME—?
WHAT'S THIS? A GUEST OF CIEL'S, ARE YOU?
ZUI (CLOSE)
CIEL'S NO LONGER HERE. HE'S GONE BACK TO HIS PRINCIPAL RESIDENCE.
EH-HEN!
BUT NOT TO WORRY!
I, PRINCE SOMA, THE VICEROY WHO OVERSEES THIS TOWN HOUSE, SHALL DELIVER YOU TO CIEL IN THE FINEST CARRIAGE AVAILABLE!!
SAY HELLO TO CIEL FOR ME NOW!!
SOUVENIRS

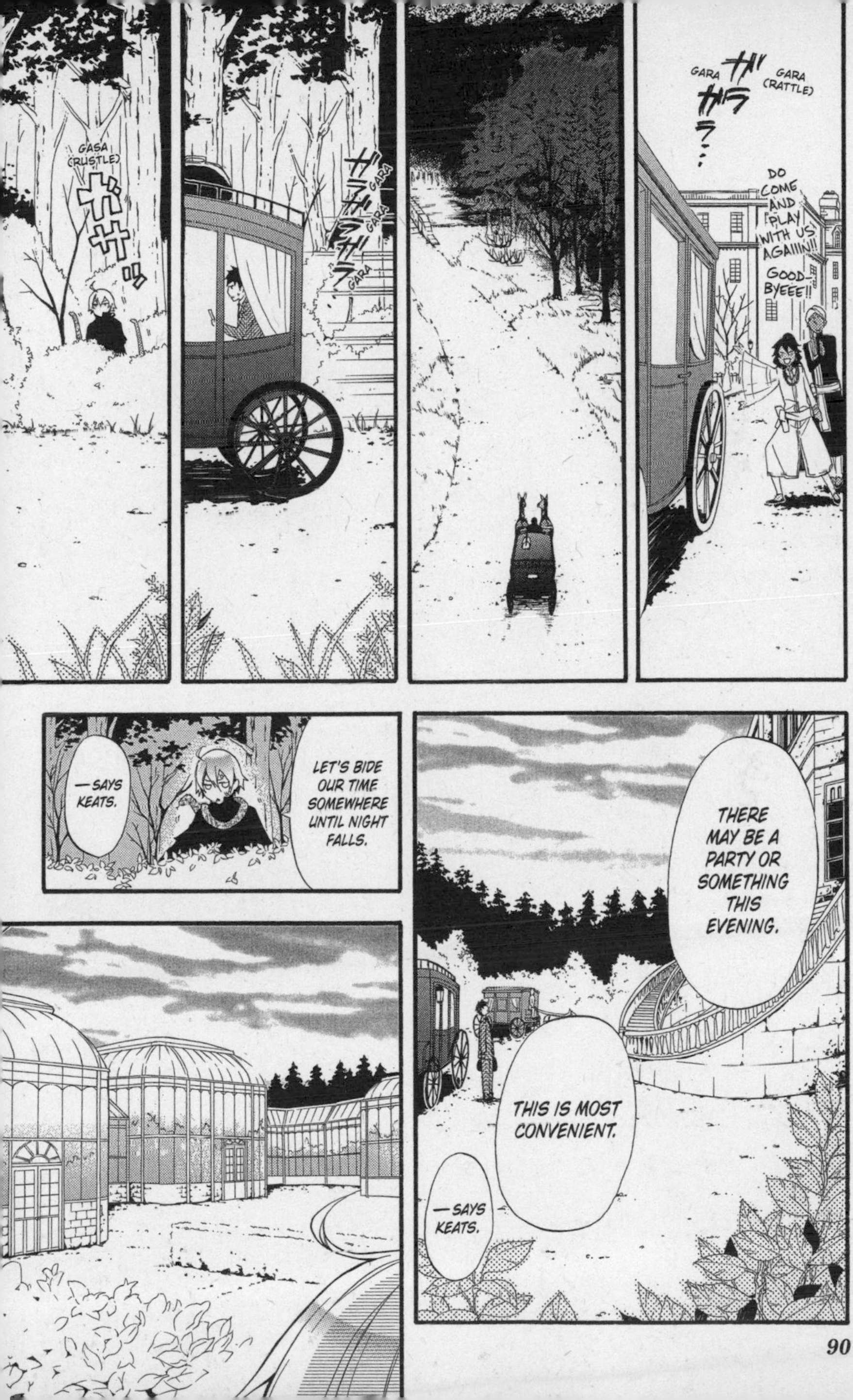
GARA GARA (RATTLE)
DO COME AND PLAY WITH US AGAIIIN!!
GOOD-BYEEE!!
GARA GARA GARA
GASA (RUSTLE)
THERE MAY BE A PARTY OR SOMETHING THIS EVENING.
THIS IS MOST CONVENIENT.
—SAYS KEATS.
LET'S BIDE OUR TIME SOMEWHERE UNTIL NIGHT FALLS.
—SAYS KEATS.

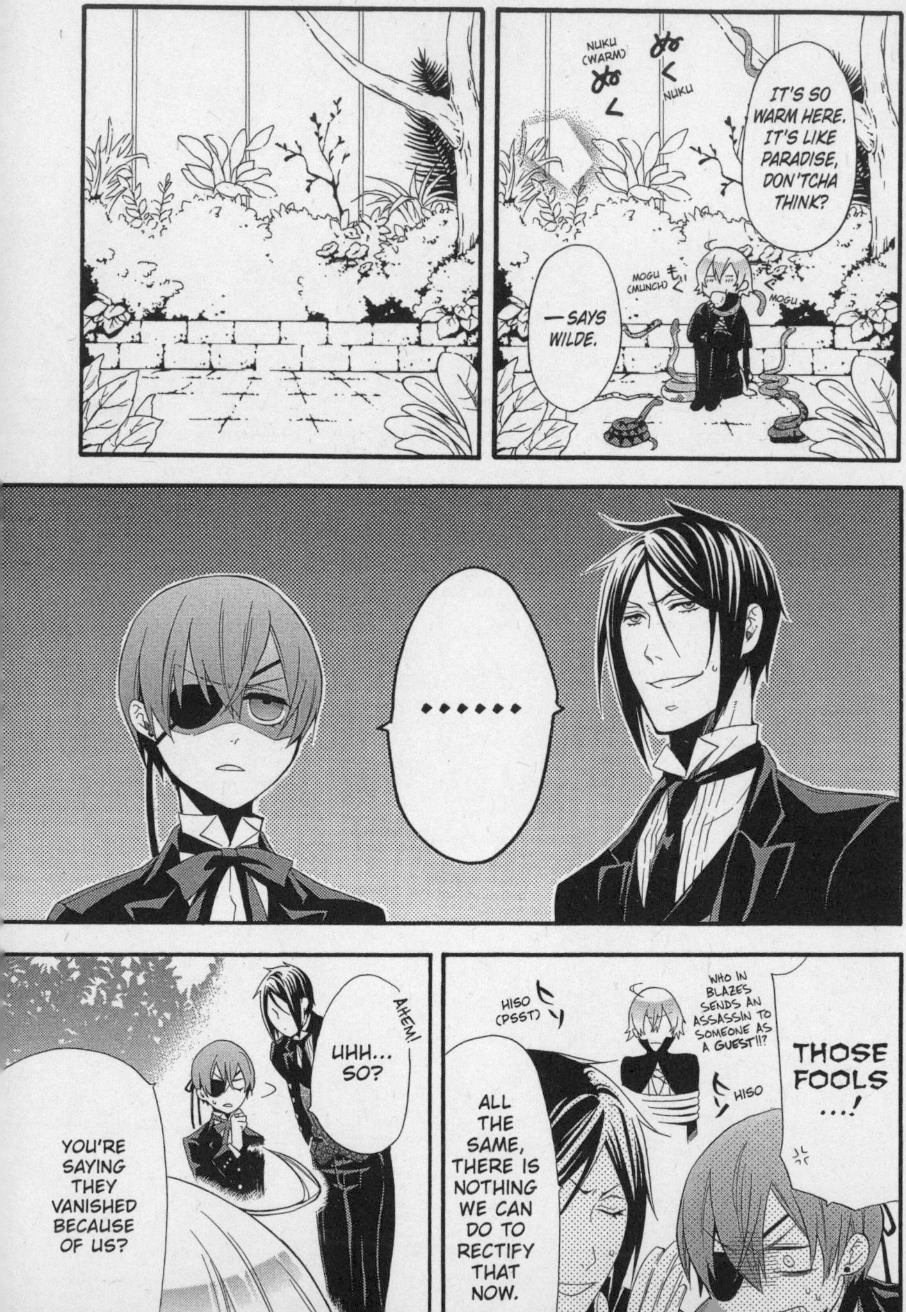

IT'S SO WARM HERE. IT'S LIKE PARADISE, DON'TCHA THINK?
ぬく NUKU
NUKU (WARM) ぬく
もぐ MOGU
MOGU (MUNCH) もぐ
—SAYS WILDE.
......
THOSE FOOLS...!
WHO IN BLAZES SENDS AN ASSASSIN TO SOMEONE AS A GUEST!!?
HISO (PSST)
HISO
ALL THE SAME, THERE IS NOTHING WE CAN DO TO RECTIFY THAT NOW.
AHEM!
UHH... SO?
YOU'RE SAYING THEY VANISHED BECAUSE OF US?

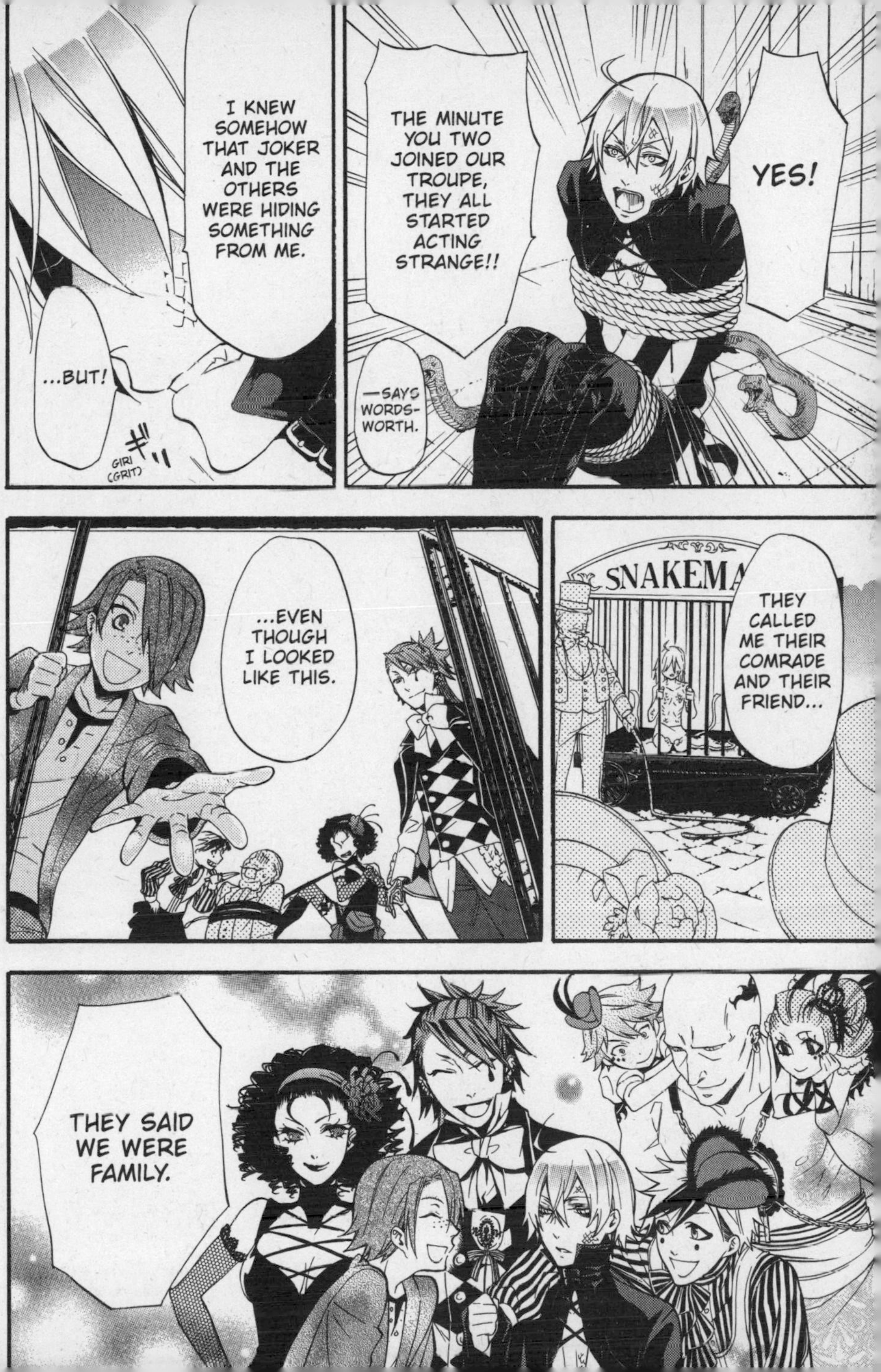
YES!
THE MINUTE YOU TWO JOINED OUR TROUPE, THEY ALL STARTED ACTING STRANGE!!
—SAYS WORDS-WORTH.
I KNEW SOMEHOW THAT JOKER AND THE OTHERS WERE HIDING SOMETHING FROM ME.
...BUT!
GIRI (GRIT)
SNAKEMA
THEY CALLED ME THEIR COMRADE AND THEIR FRIEND...
...EVEN THOUGH I LOOKED LIKE THIS.
THEY SAID WE WERE FAMILY.

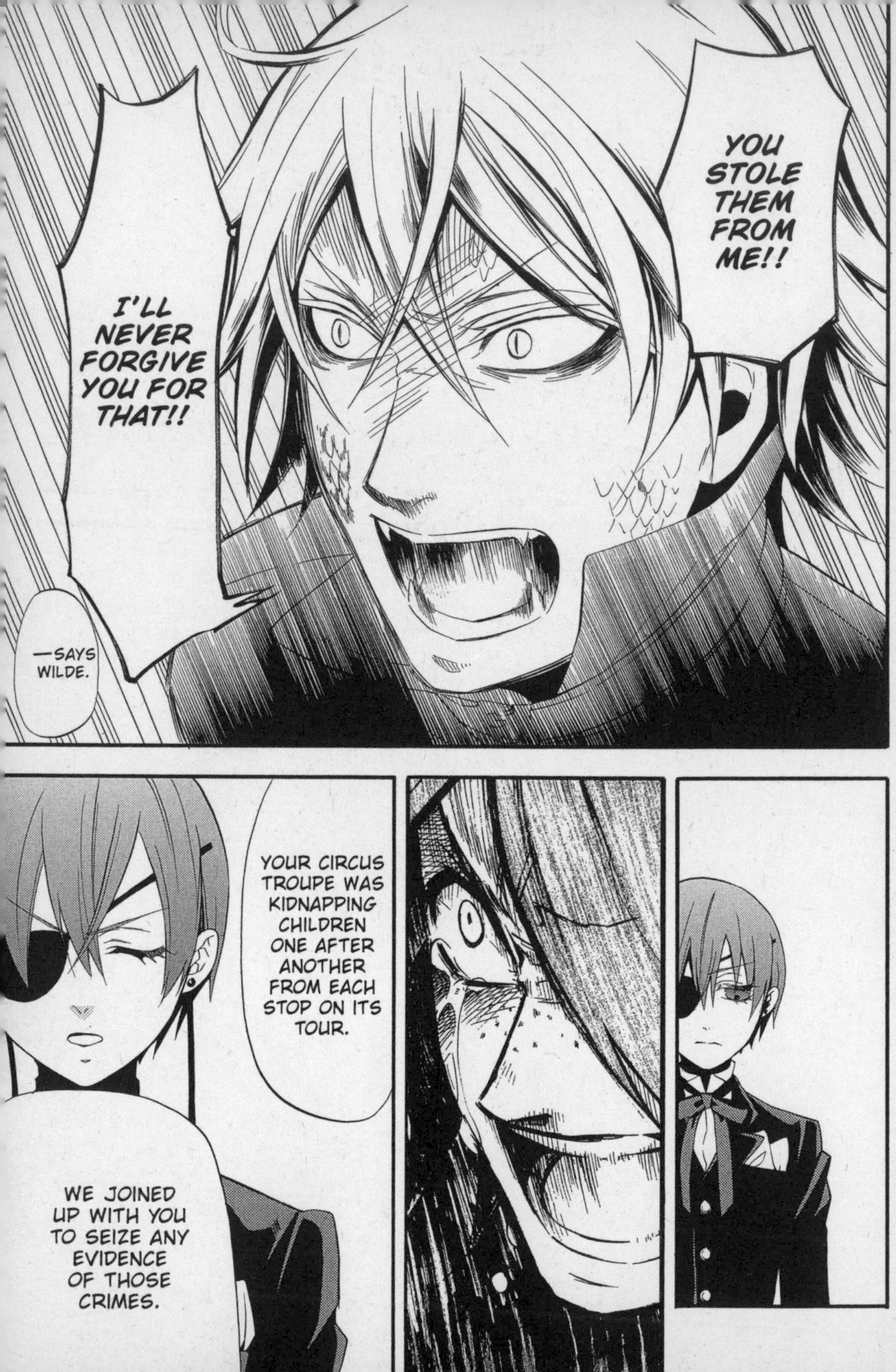
YOU STOLE THEM FROM ME!!
I'LL NEVER FORGIVE YOU FOR THAT!!
—SAYS WILDE.
YOUR CIRCUS TROUPE WAS KIDNAPPING CHILDREN ONE AFTER ANOTHER FROM EACH STOP ON ITS TOUR.
WE JOINED UP WITH YOU TO SEIZE ANY EVIDENCE OF THOSE CRIMES.

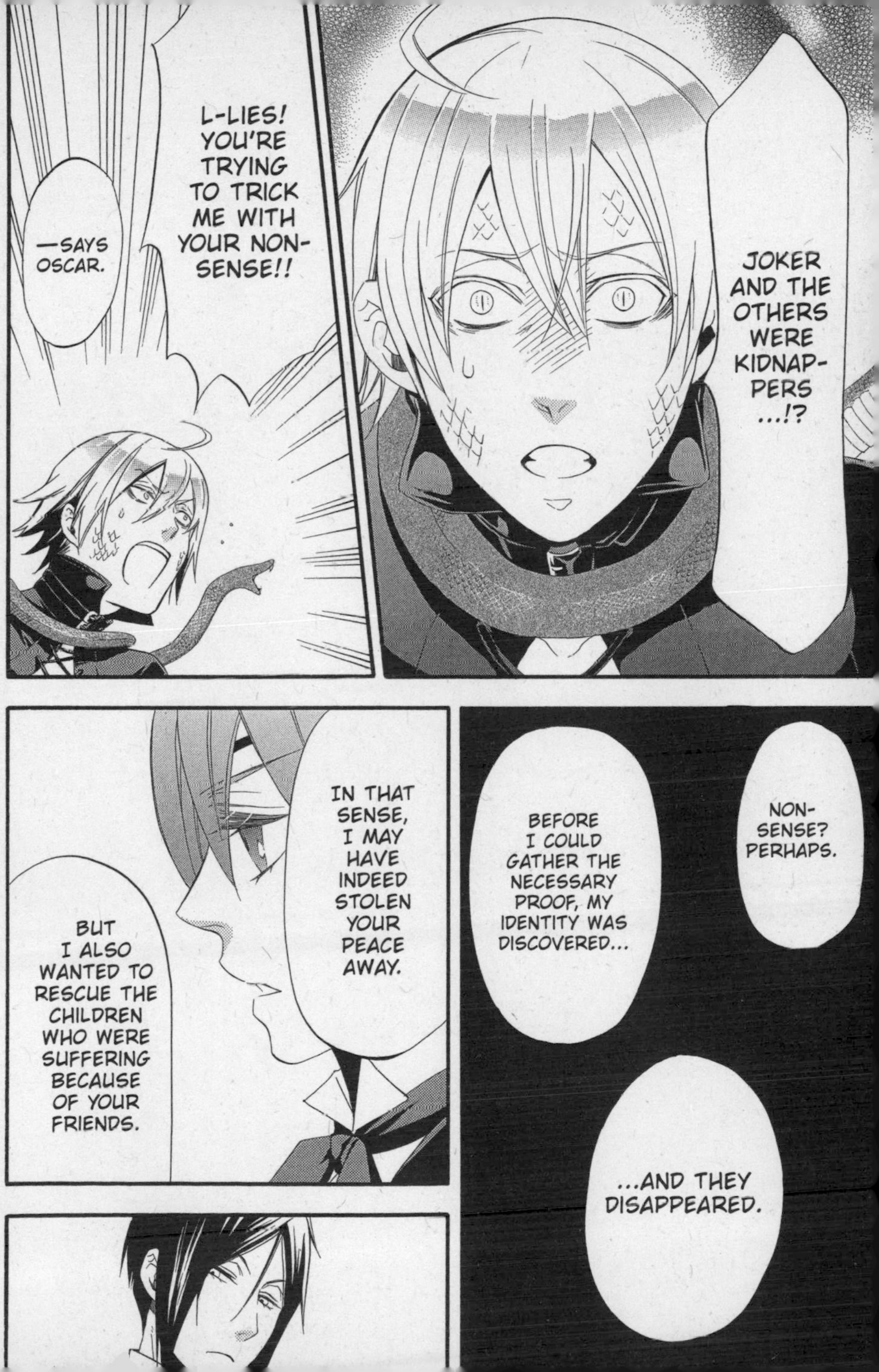
JOKER AND THE OTHERS WERE KIDNAP-PERS ...!?
L-LIES! YOU'RE TRYING TO TRICK ME WITH YOUR NON-SENSE!!
—SAYS OSCAR.
NON-SENSE? PERHAPS.
BEFORE I COULD GATHER THE NECESSARY PROOF, MY IDENTITY WAS DISCOVERED...
...AND THEY DISAPPEARED.
IN THAT SENSE, I MAY HAVE INDEED STOLEN YOUR PEACE AWAY.
BUT I ALSO WANTED TO RESCUE THE CHILDREN WHO WERE SUFFERING BECAUSE OF YOUR FRIENDS.

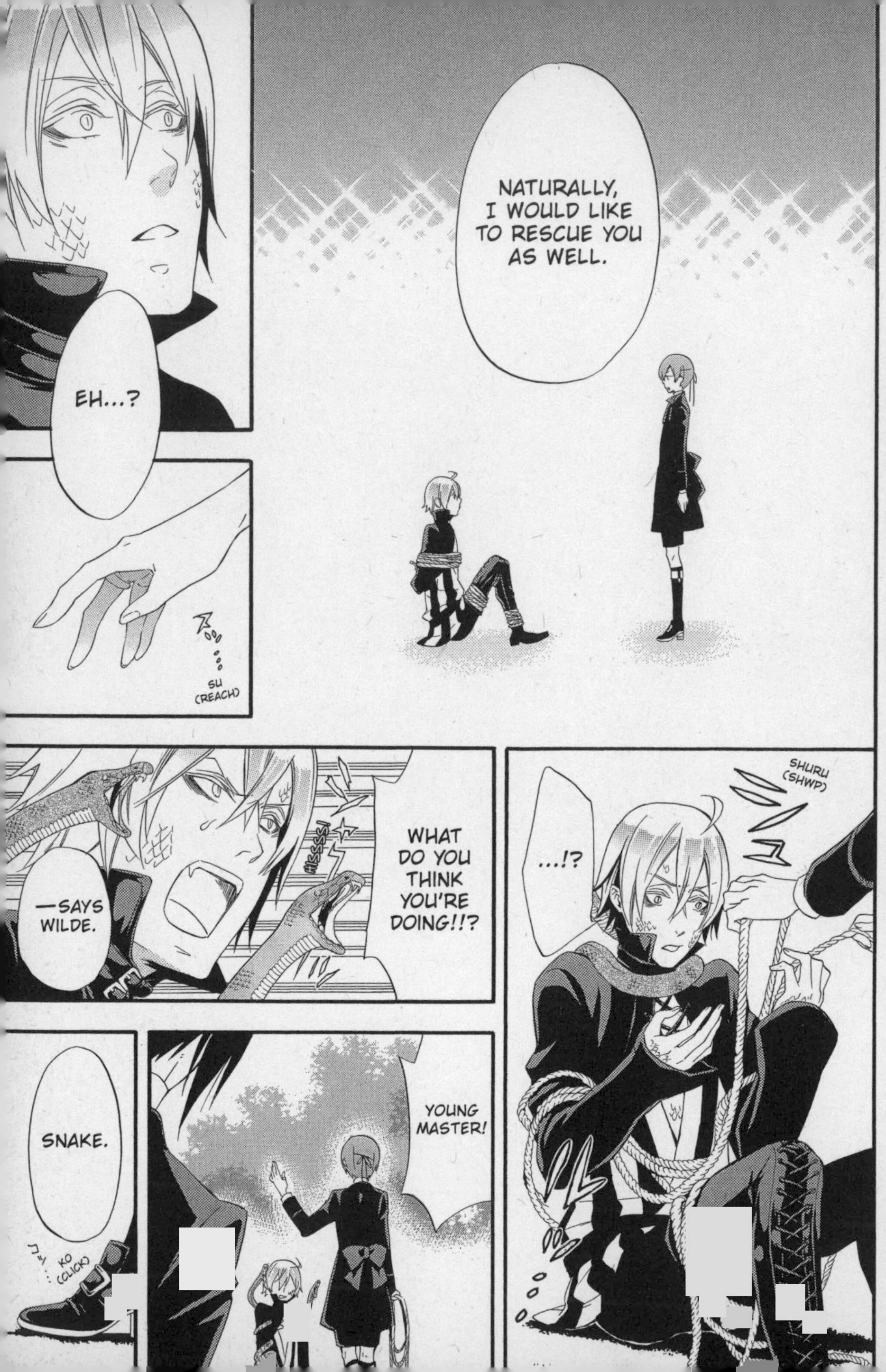
NATURALLY, I WOULD LIKE TO RESCUE YOU AS WELL.
EH...?
SU (REACH)
SHURU (SHWP)
...!?
WHAT DO YOU THINK YOU'RE DOING!!?
HISSS!
—SAYS WILDE.
YOUNG MASTER!
SNAKE.
KO (CLICK)

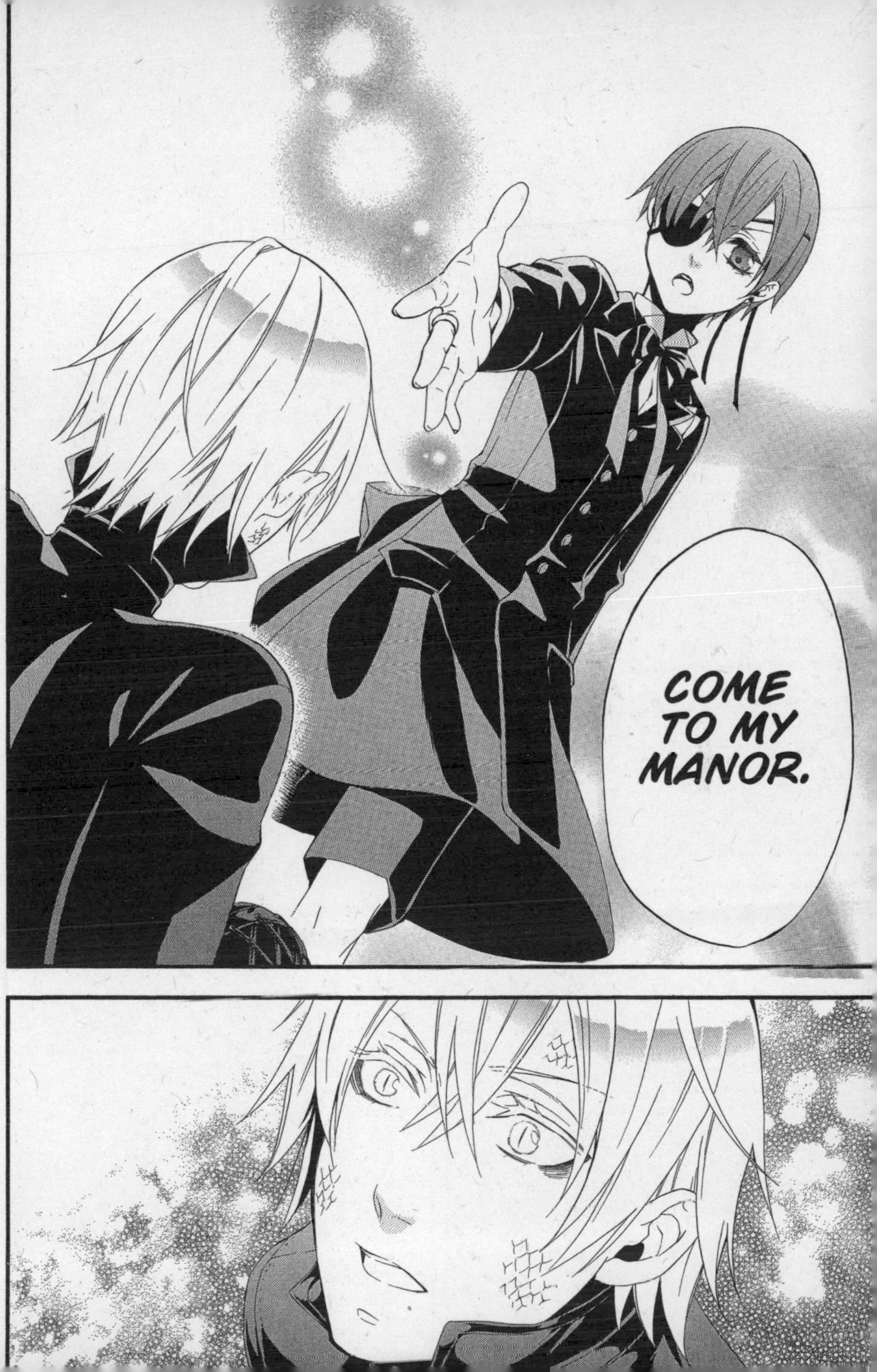
COME TO MY MANOR.

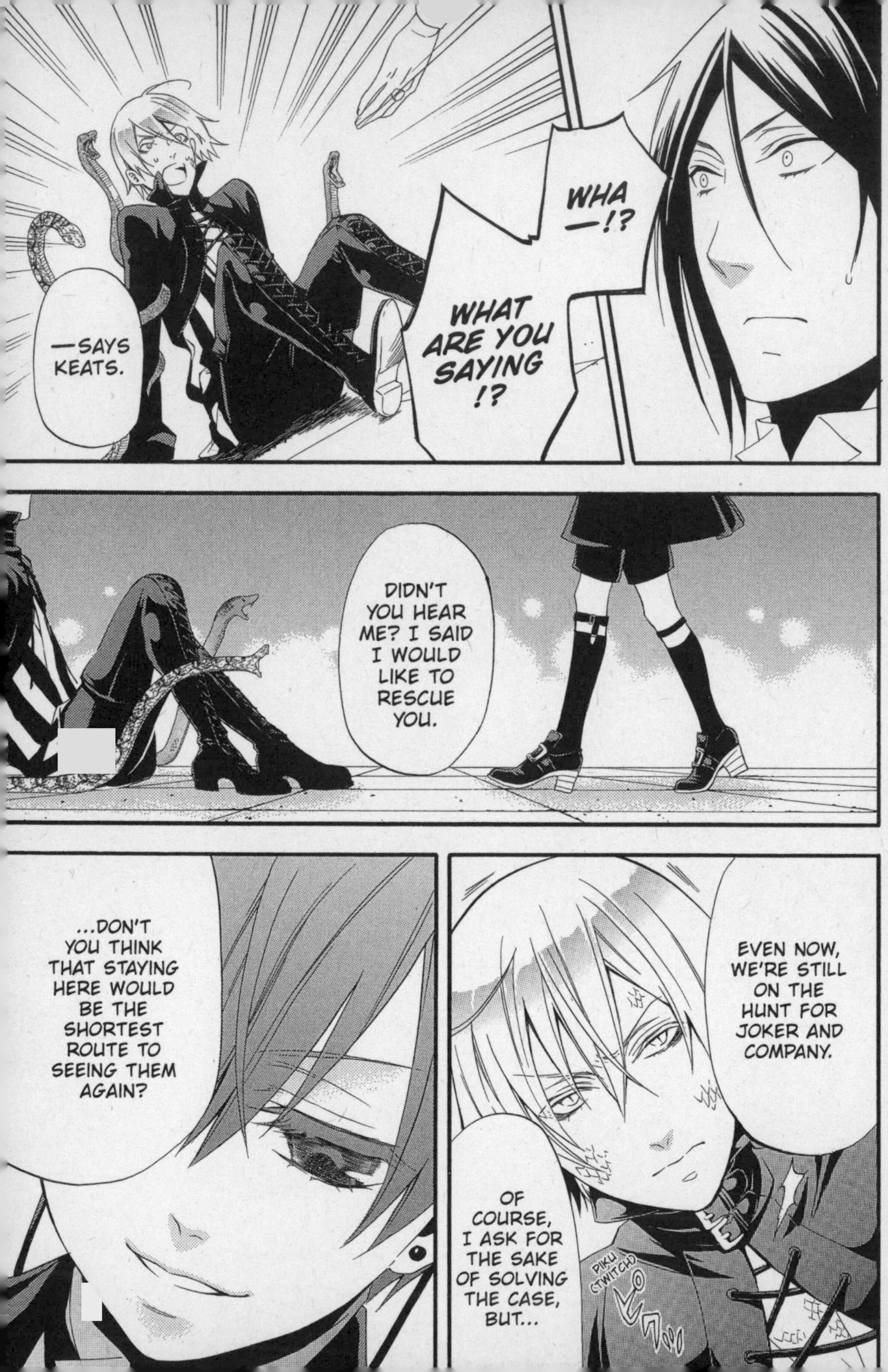
WHA—!?
WHAT ARE YOU SAYING !?
—SAYS KEATS.
DIDN'T YOU HEAR ME? I SAID I WOULD LIKE TO RESCUE YOU.
EVEN NOW, WE'RE STILL ON THE HUNT FOR JOKER AND COMPANY.
OF COURSE, I ASK FOR THE SAKE OF SOLVING THE CASE, BUT...
PIKU (TWITCH)
...DON'T YOU THINK THAT STAYING HERE WOULD BE THE SHORTEST ROUTE TO SEEING THEM AGAIN?

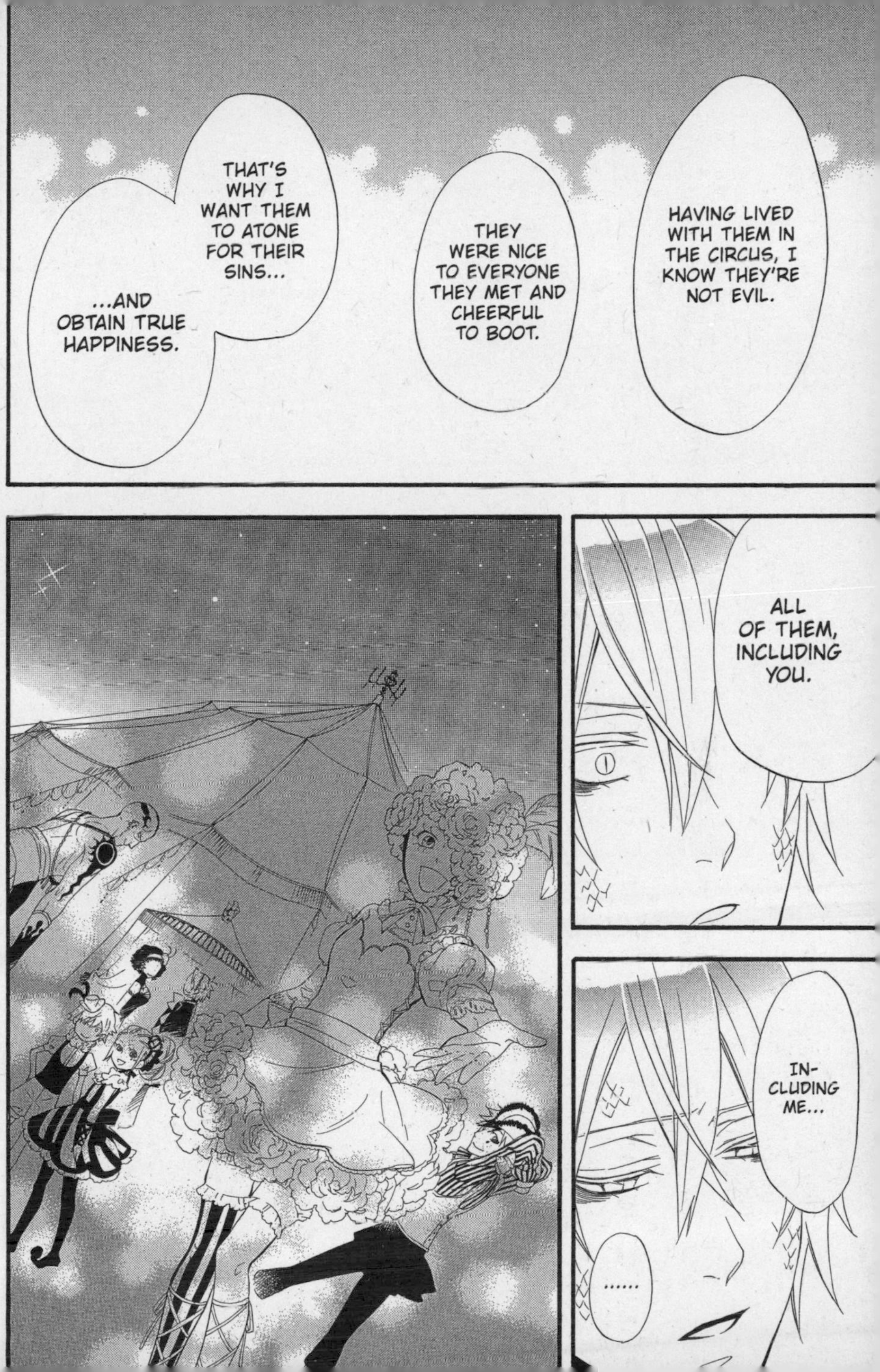
HAVING LIVED WITH THEM IN THE CIRCUS, I KNOW THEY'RE NOT EVIL.
THEY WERE NICE TO EVERYONE THEY MET AND CHEERFUL TO BOOT.
THAT'S WHY I WANT THEM TO ATONE FOR THEIR SINS...
...AND OBTAIN TRUE HAPPINESS.
ALL OF THEM, INCLUDING YOU.
IN-CLUDING ME...
......

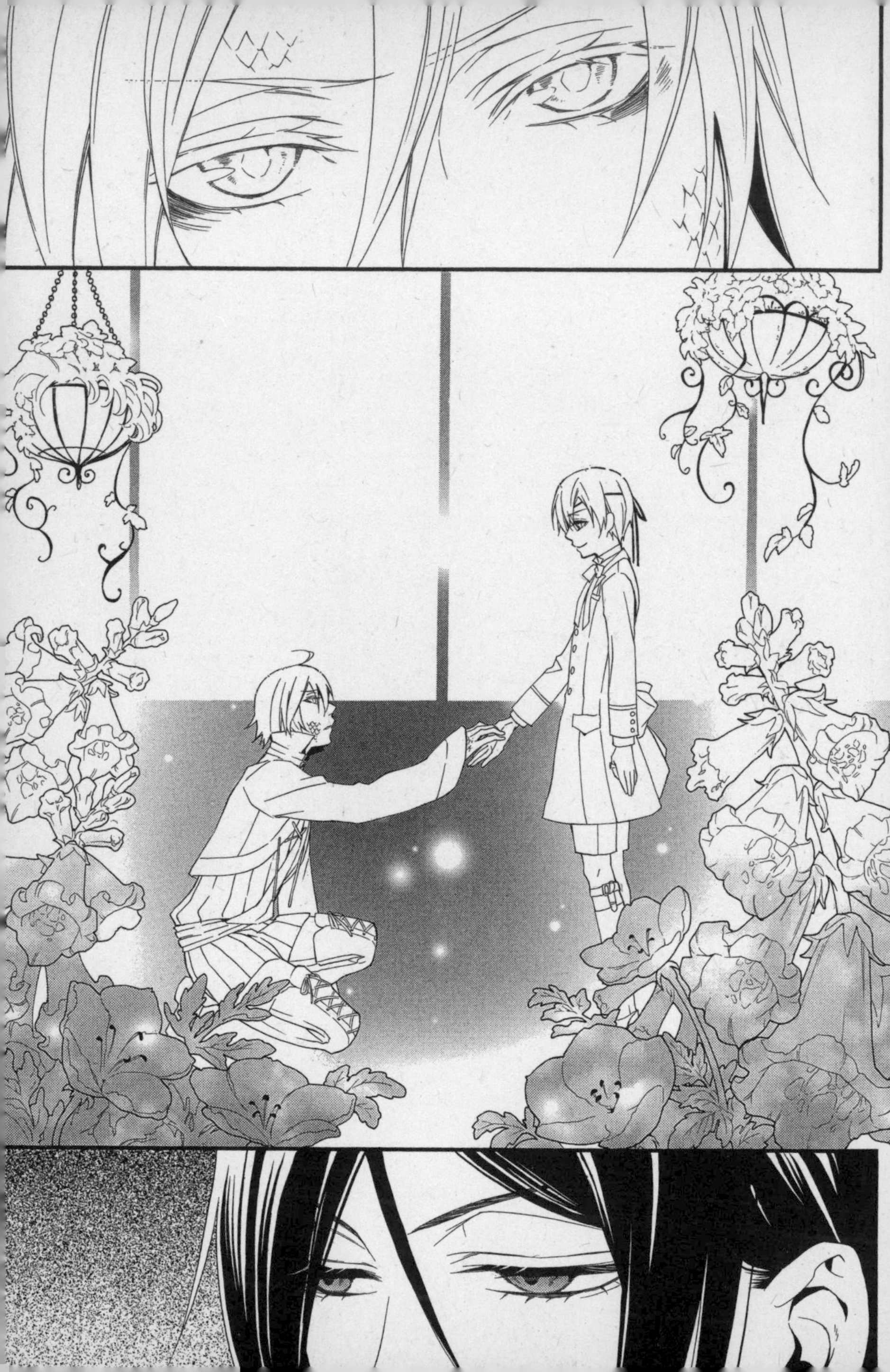

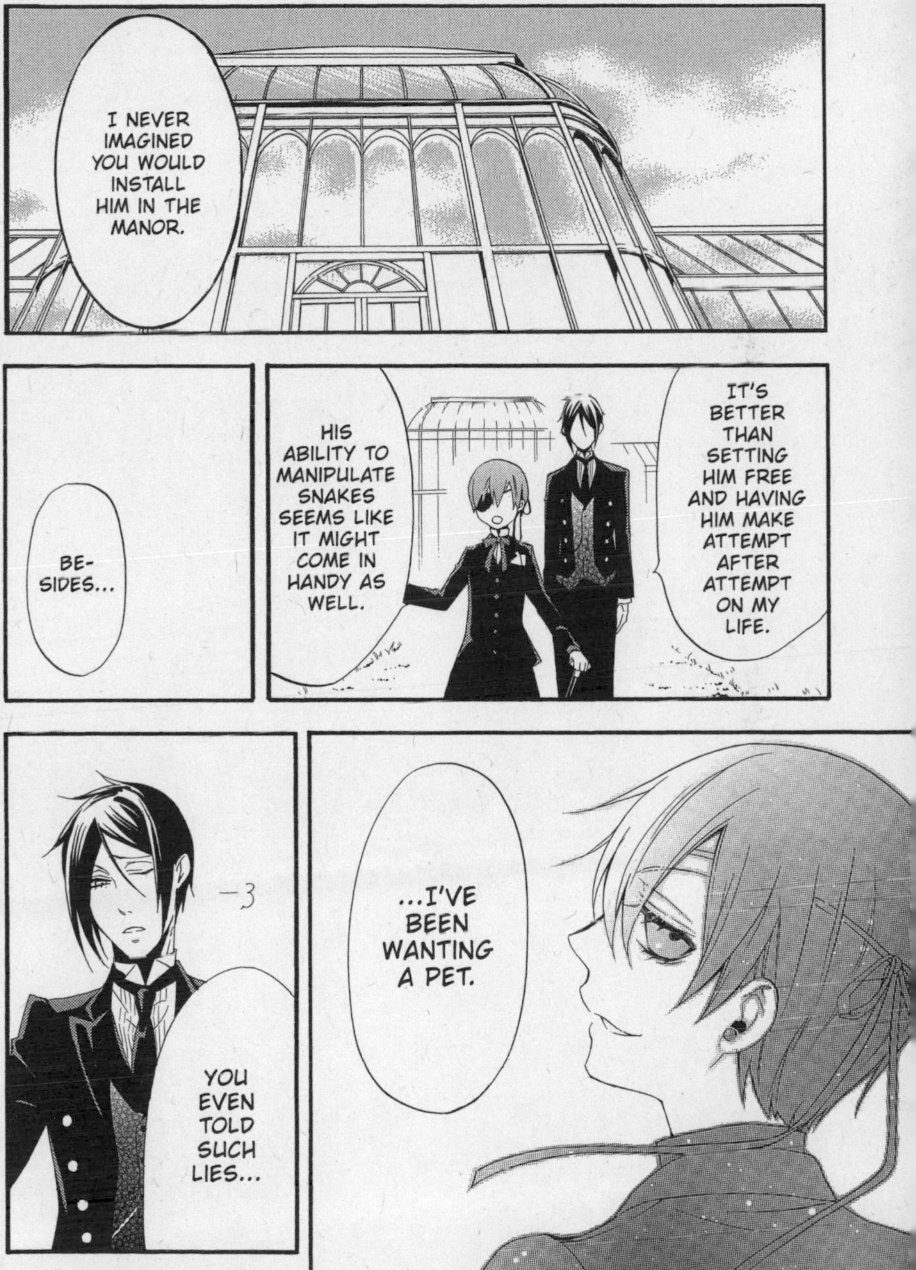
I NEVER IMAGINED YOU WOULD INSTALL HIM IN THE MANOR.
IT'S BETTER THAN SETTING HIM FREE AND HAVING HIM MAKE ATTEMPT AFTER ATTEMPT ON MY LIFE.
HIS ABILITY TO MANIPULATE SNAKES SEEMS LIKE IT MIGHT COME IN HANDY AS WELL.
BE-SIDES...
...I'VE BEEN WANTING A PET.
YOU EVEN TOLD SUCH LIES...

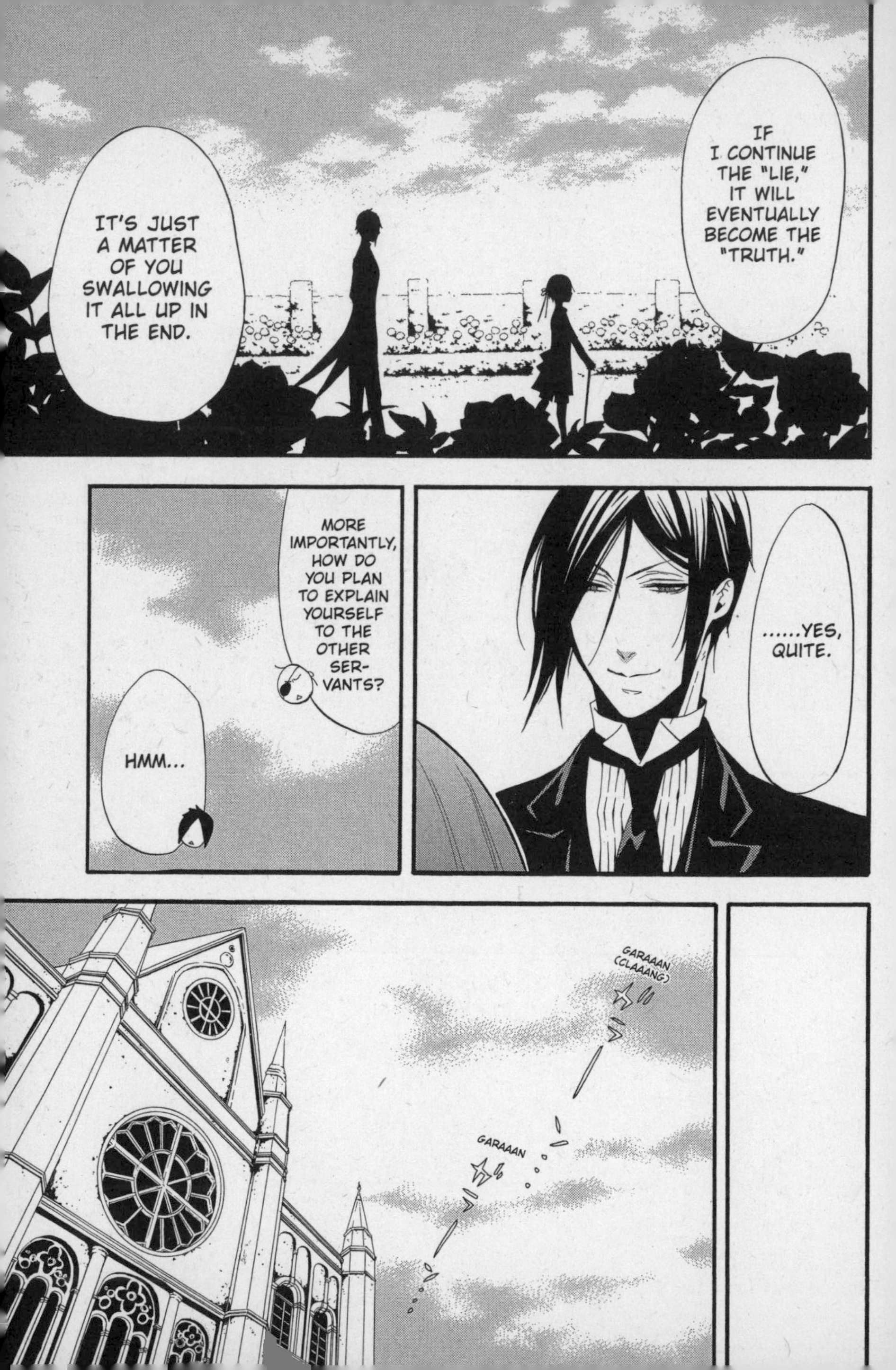
IF I CONTINUE THE "LIE," IT WILL EVENTUALLY BECOME THE "TRUTH."
IT'S JUST A MATTER OF YOU SWALLOWING IT ALL UP IN THE END.
......YES, QUITE.
MORE IMPORTANTLY, HOW DO YOU PLAN TO EXPLAIN YOURSELF TO THE OTHER SER-VANTS?
HMM...
GARAAAN (CLAAANG)
GARAAAN

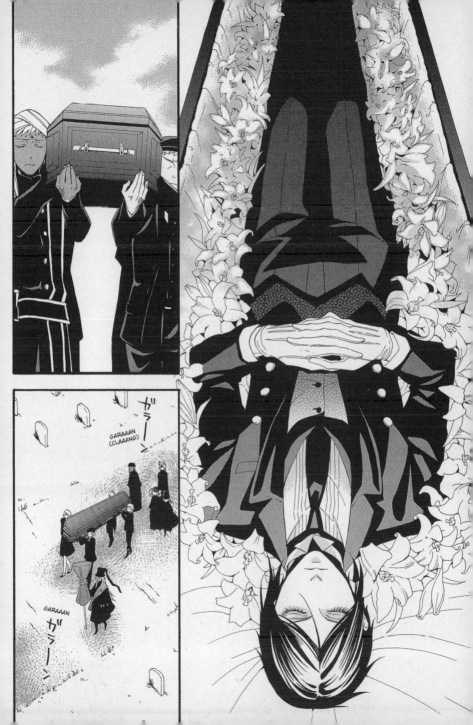

GARAAAN
(CLAAANG)

GARAAAN

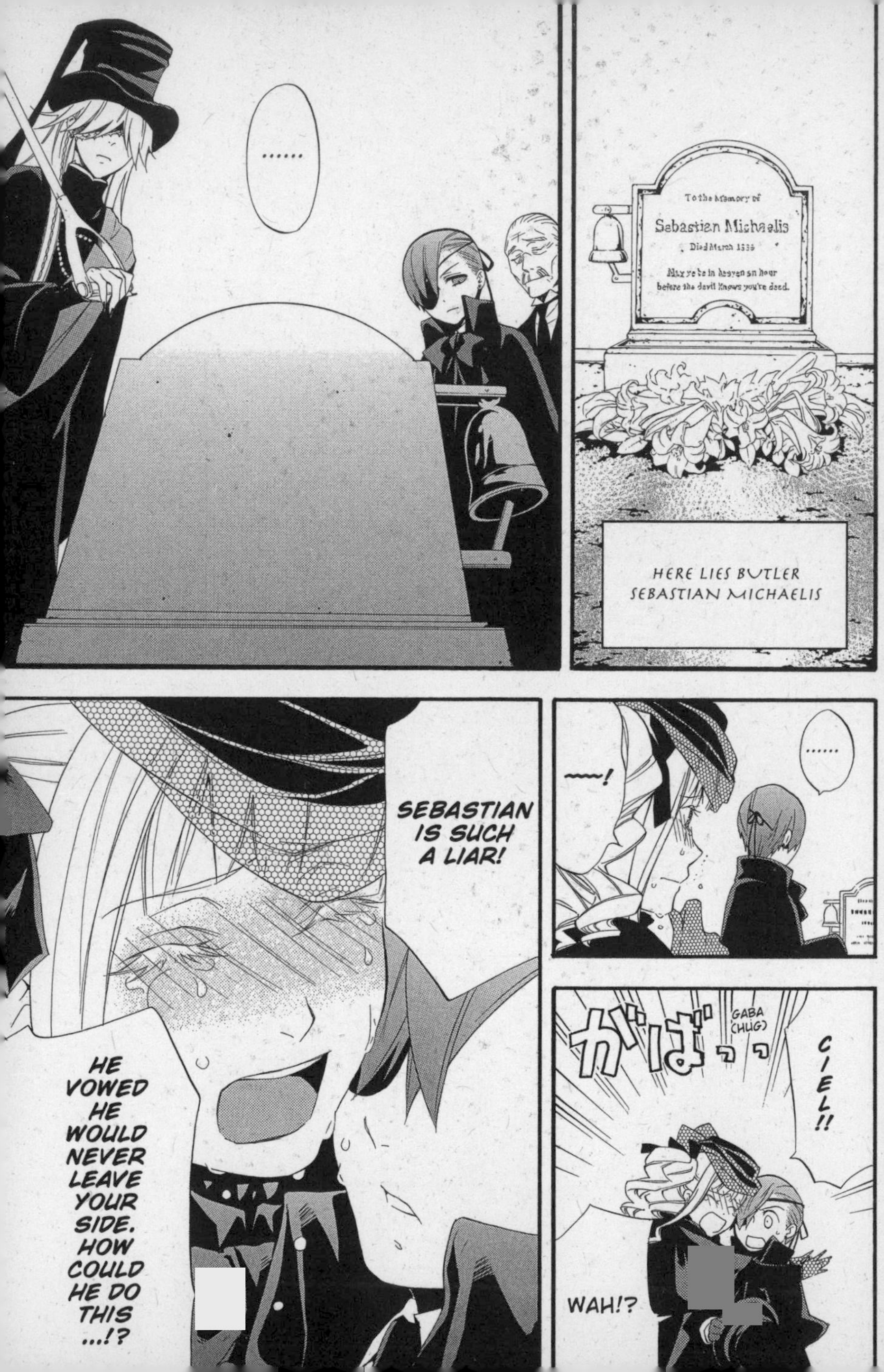
To the Memory of
Sebastian Michaelis
Died March
May ye be in heaven an hour before the devil knows you're dead.
HERE LIES BUTLER SEBASTIAN MICHAELIS
......
......
~~~!
GABA (HUG)
CIEL!!
WAH!?
SEBASTIAN IS SUCH A LIAR!
HE VOWED HE WOULD NEVER LEAVE YOUR SIDE. HOW COULD HE DO THIS ...!?
~~~

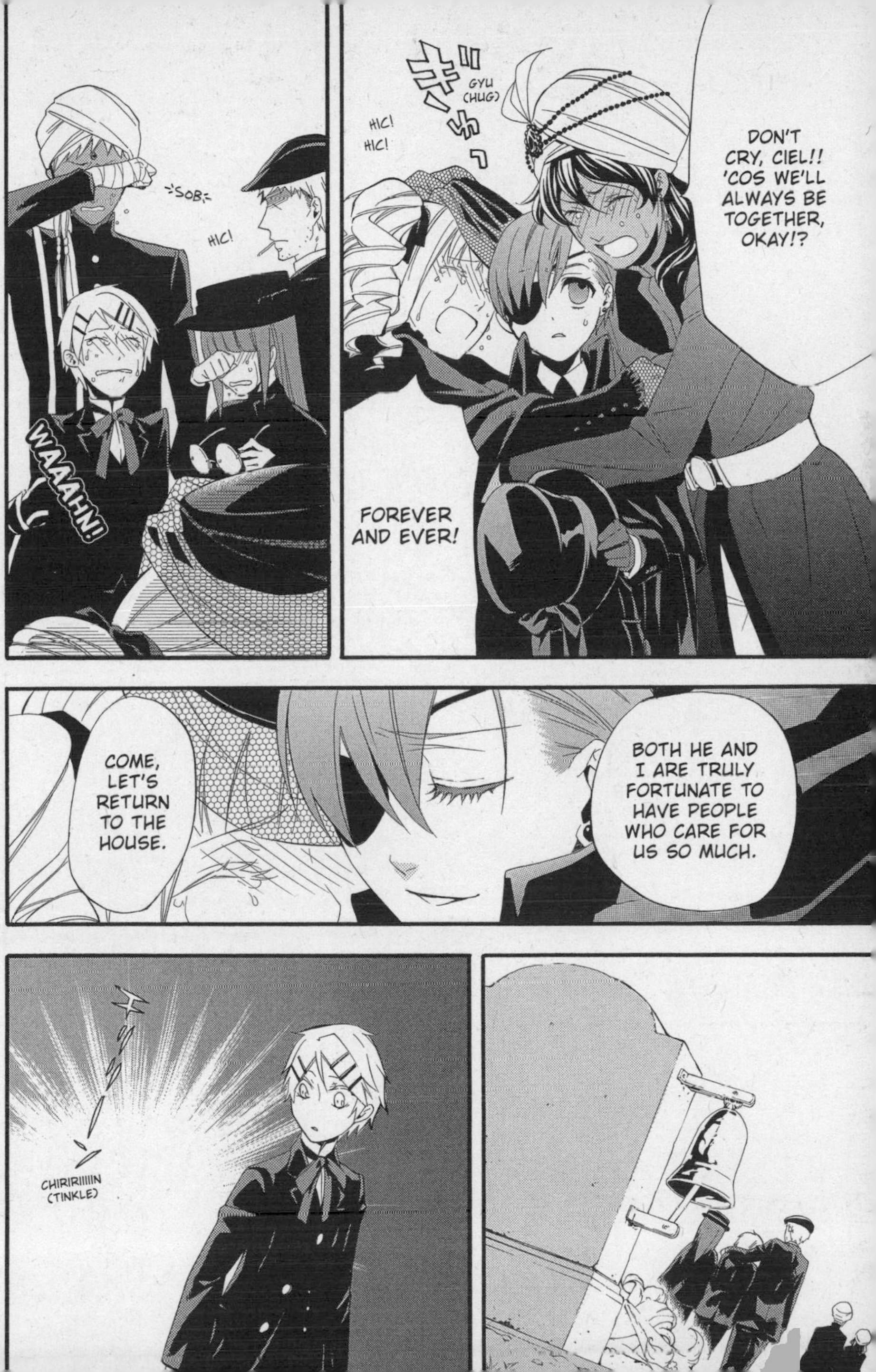
GYU (HUG)
HIC! HIC!
DON'T CRY, CIEL!! 'COS WE'LL ALWAYS BE TOGETHER, OKAY!?
FOREVER AND EVER!
SOB
HIC!
WAAAAHN!
BOTH HE AND I ARE TRULY FORTUNATE TO HAVE PEOPLE WHO CARE FOR US SO MUCH.
COME, LET'S RETURN TO THE HOUSE.
CHIRIRIIIIN (TINKLE)

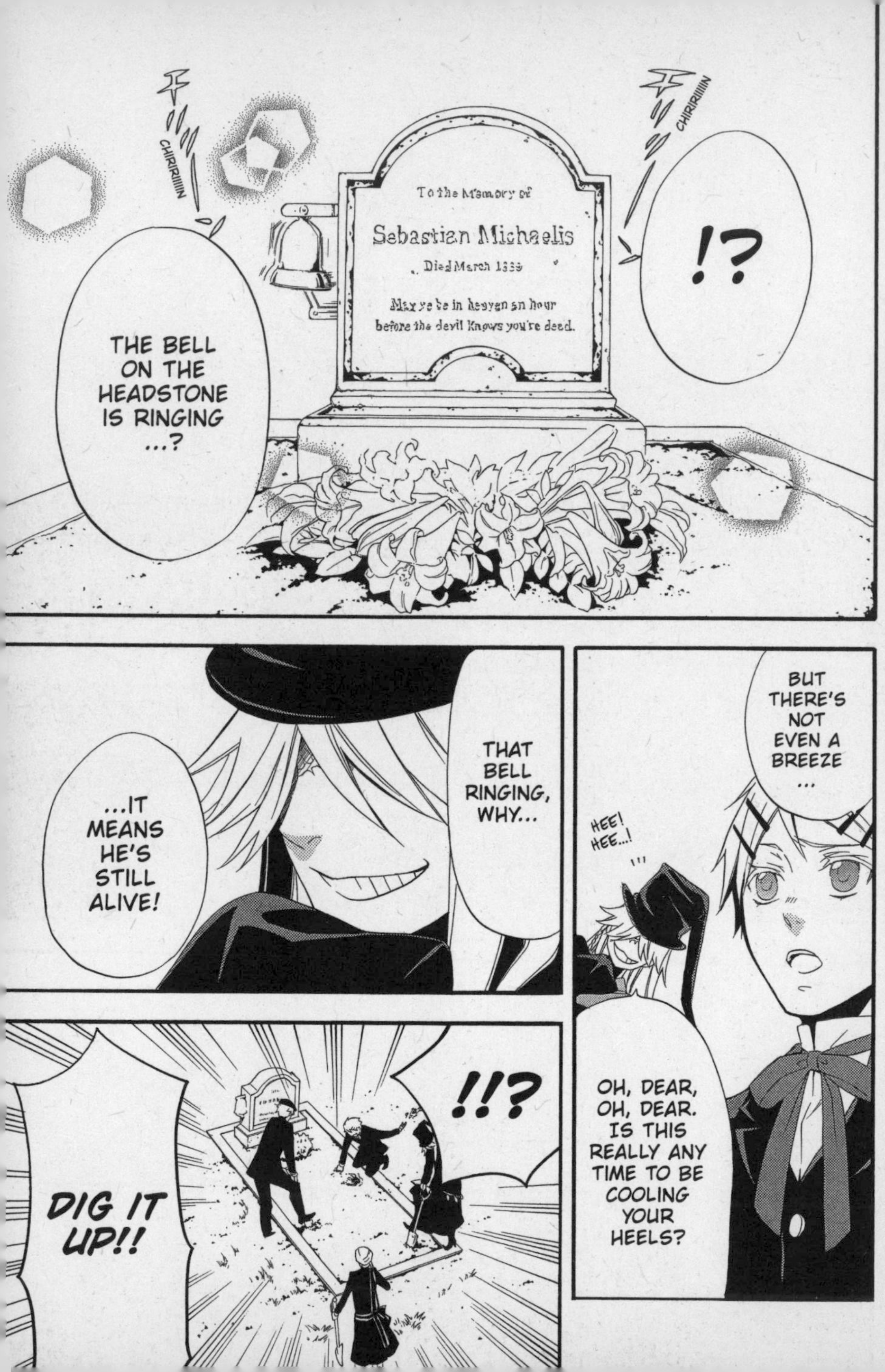
CHIRIIIIN
!?
To the Memory of
Sebastian Michaelis
Died March 1889
May ye be in heaven an hour before the devil knows you're dead.
CHIRIIIIN
THE BELL ON THE HEADSTONE IS RINGING ...?
BUT THERE'S NOT EVEN A BREEZE ...
HEE! HEE...!
OH, DEAR, OH, DEAR. IS THIS REALLY ANY TIME TO BE COOLING YOUR HEELS?
THAT BELL RINGING, WHY...
...IT MEANS HE'S STILL ALIVE!
!!?
DIG IT UP!!

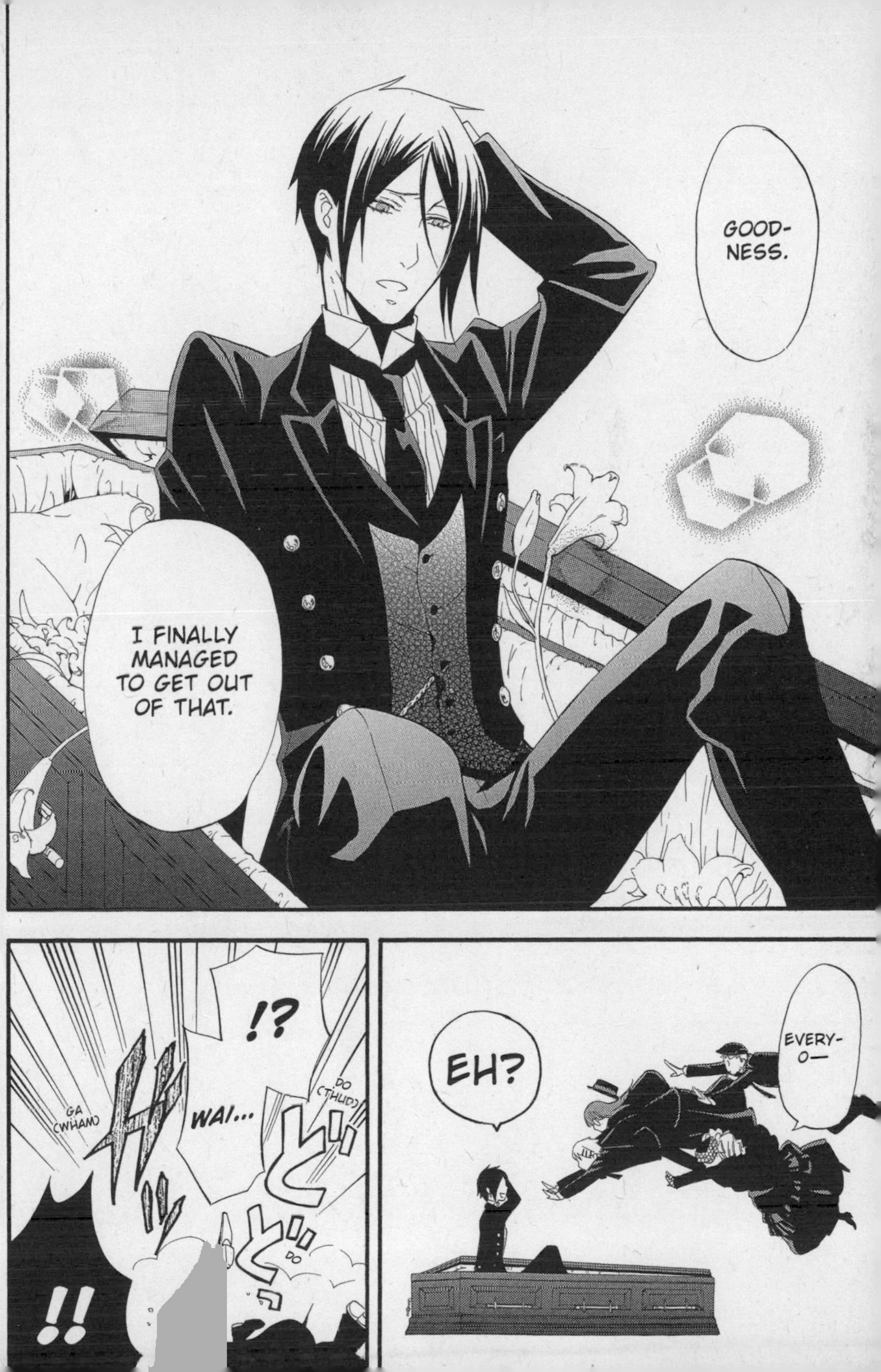
GOOD-
NESS.
I FINALLY MANAGED TO GET OUT OF THAT.
EVERY-
O—
EH?
!?
DO (THUD)
WAI...
GA (WHAM)
DO
!!

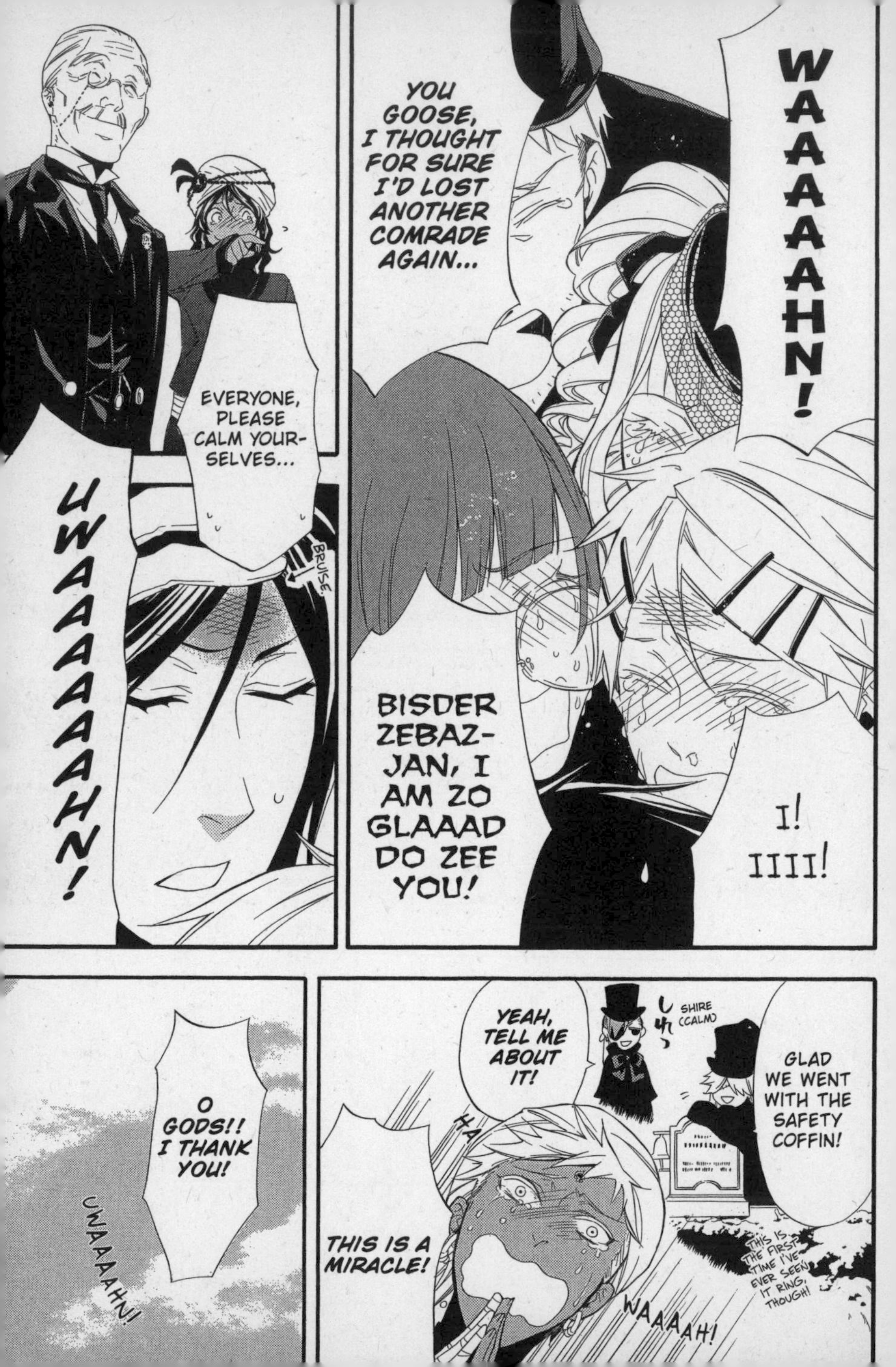
WAAAAAAHN!
YOU GOOSE, I THOUGHT FOR SURE I'D LOST ANOTHER COMRADE AGAIN...
BISDER ZEBAZ-JAN, I AM ZO GLAAAD DO ZEE YOU!
I! IIII!
EVERYONE, PLEASE CALM YOUR-SELVES...
BRUISE.
UWAAAAAAAAHN!
GLAD WE WENT WITH THE SAFETY COFFIN!
YEAH, TELL ME ABOUT IT!
しれっ
SHIRE (CALM)
HA
THIS IS THE FIRST TIME I'VE EVER SEEN IT RING, THOUGH!
THIS IS A MIRACLE!
WAAAAH!
O GODS!! I THANK YOU!
UWAAAAAHN!

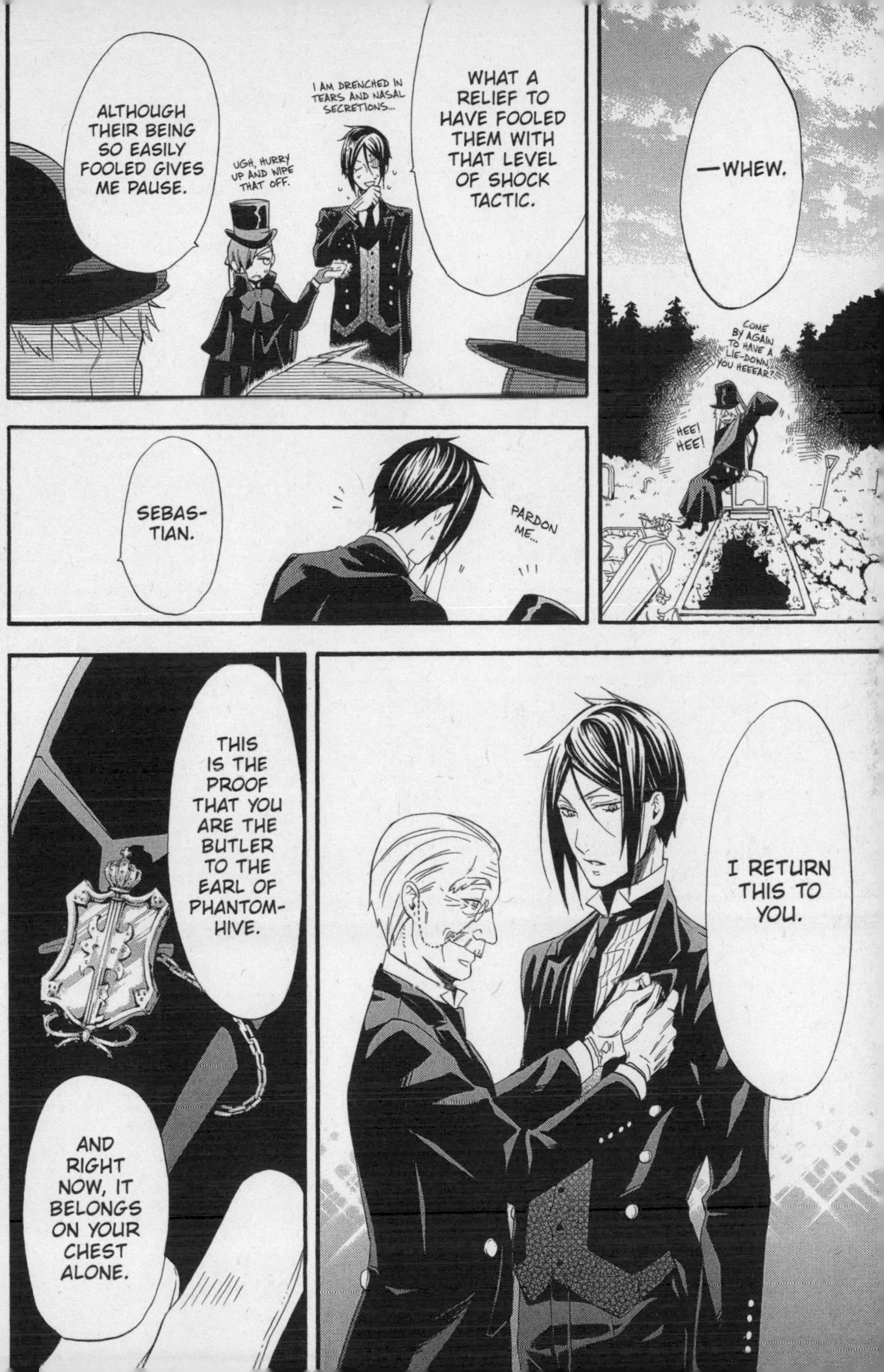
—WHEW.
COME BY AGAIN TO HAVE A LIE-DOWN, YOU HEEEAR?
HEE! HEE!
WHAT A RELIEF TO HAVE FOOLED THEM WITH THAT LEVEL OF SHOCK TACTIC.
I AM DRENCHED IN TEARS AND NASAL SECRETIONS...
UGH, HURRY UP AND WIPE THAT OFF.
ALTHOUGH THEIR BEING SO EASILY FOOLED GIVES ME PAUSE.
PARDON ME...
SEBAS-TIAN.
I RETURN THIS TO YOU.
THIS IS THE PROOF THAT YOU ARE THE BUTLER TO THE EARL OF PHANTOM-HIVE.
AND RIGHT NOW, IT BELONGS ON YOUR CHEST ALONE.

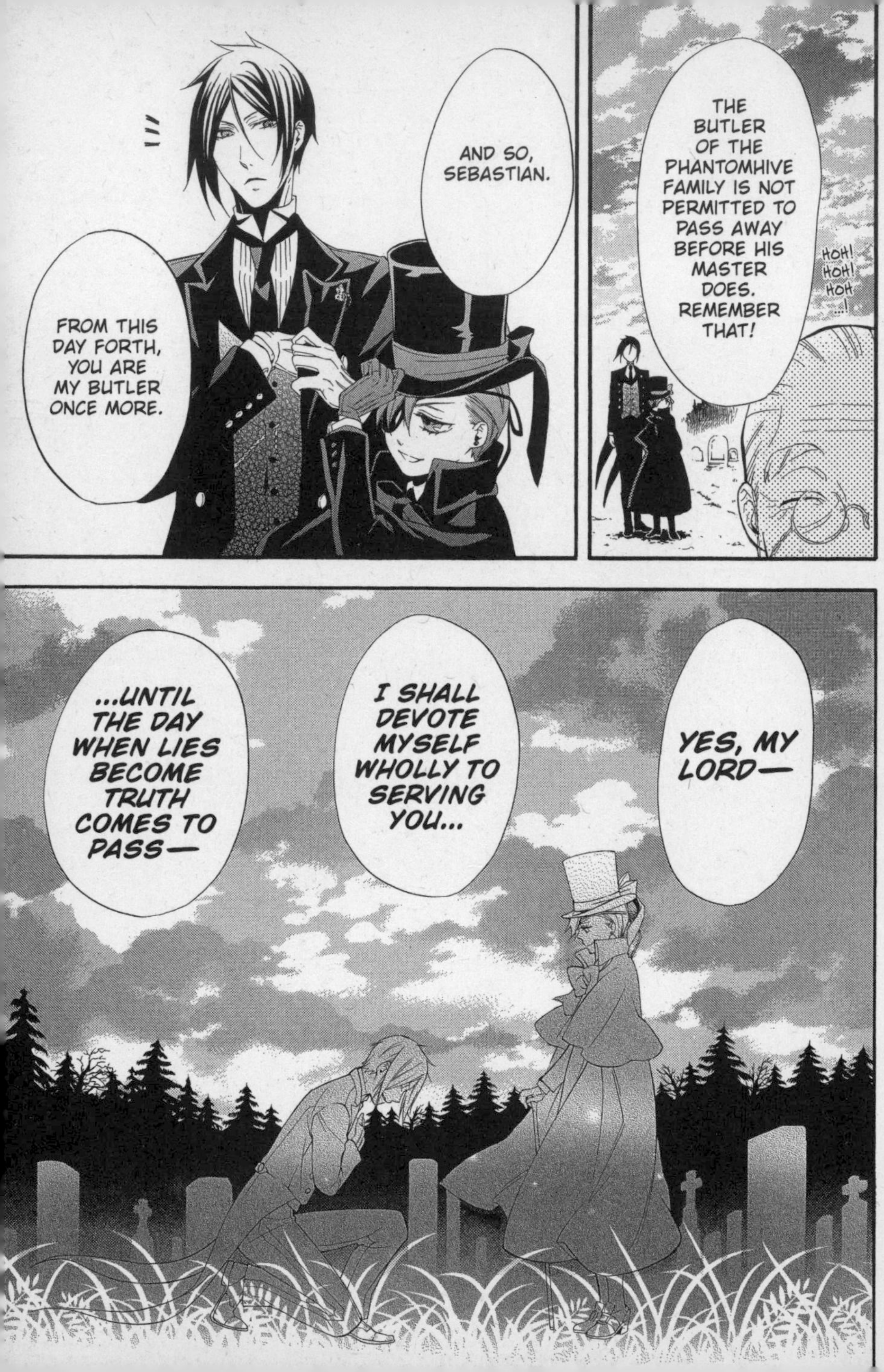
THE BUTLER OF THE PHANTOMHIVE FAMILY IS NOT PERMITTED TO PASS AWAY BEFORE HIS MASTER DOES. REMEMBER THAT!
HOH! HOH! HOH...!
AND SO, SEBASTIAN.
FROM THIS DAY FORTH, YOU ARE MY BUTLER ONCE MORE.
YES, MY LORD—
I SHALL DEVOTE MYSELF WHOLLY TO SERVING YOU...
...UNTIL THE DAY WHEN LIES BECOME TRUTH COMES TO PASS—

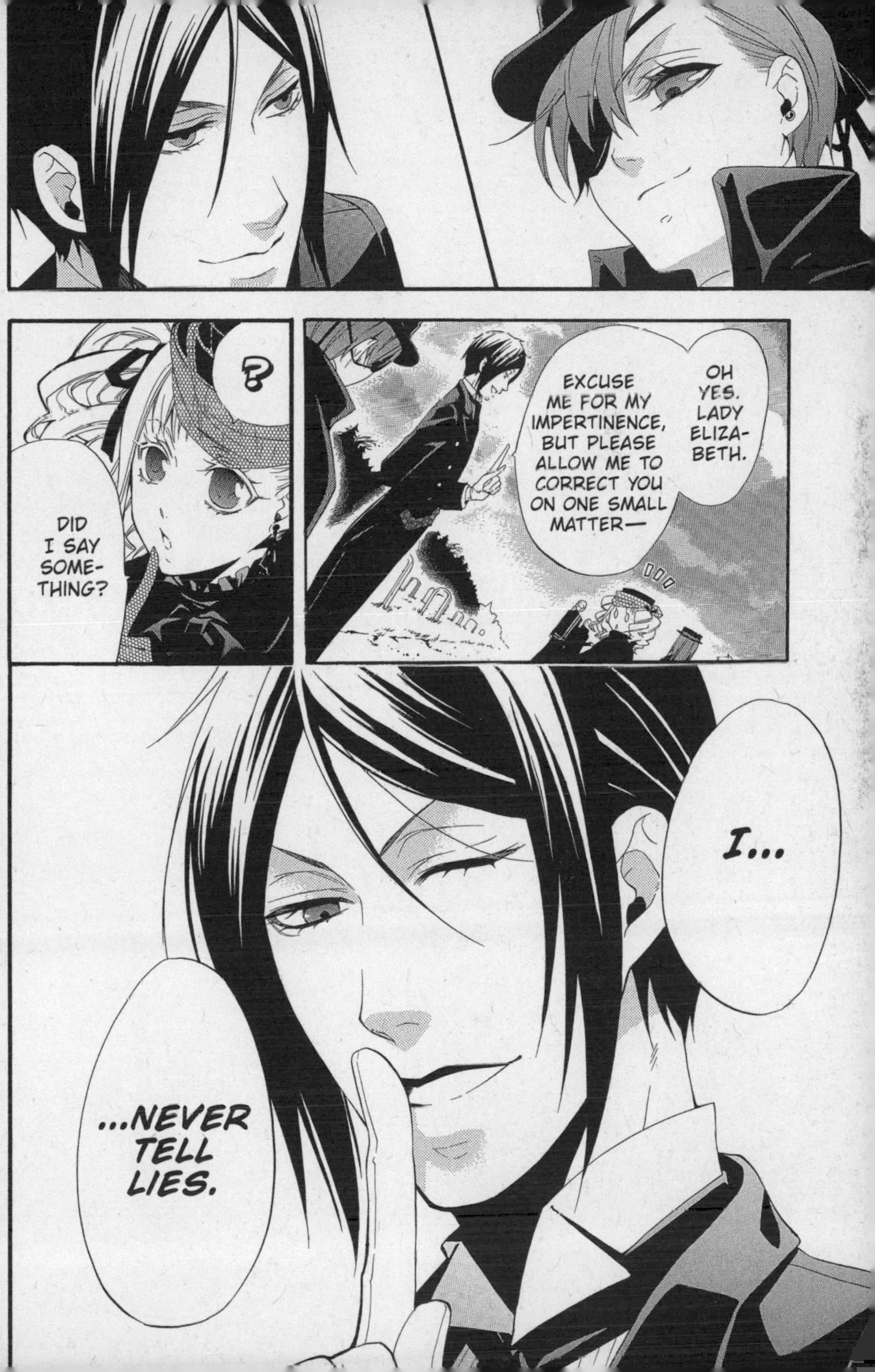
OH YES. LADY ELIZABETH.
EXCUSE ME FOR MY IMPERTINENCE, BUT PLEASE ALLOW ME TO CORRECT YOU ON ONE SMALL MATTER—
?
DID I SAY SOMETHING?
I...
...NEVER TELL LIES.

Black Butler

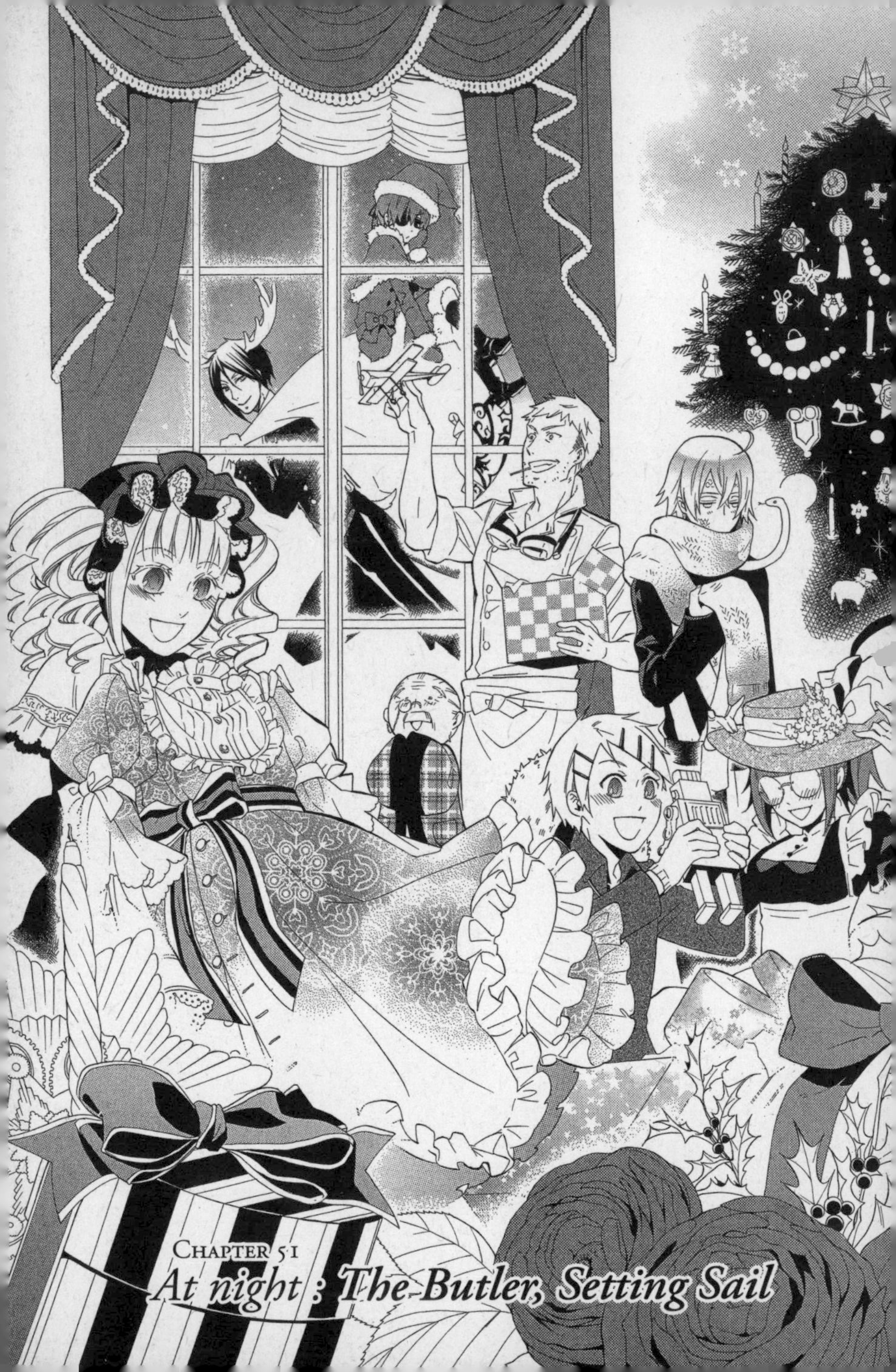

Chapter 51
At night : The Butler, Setting Sail

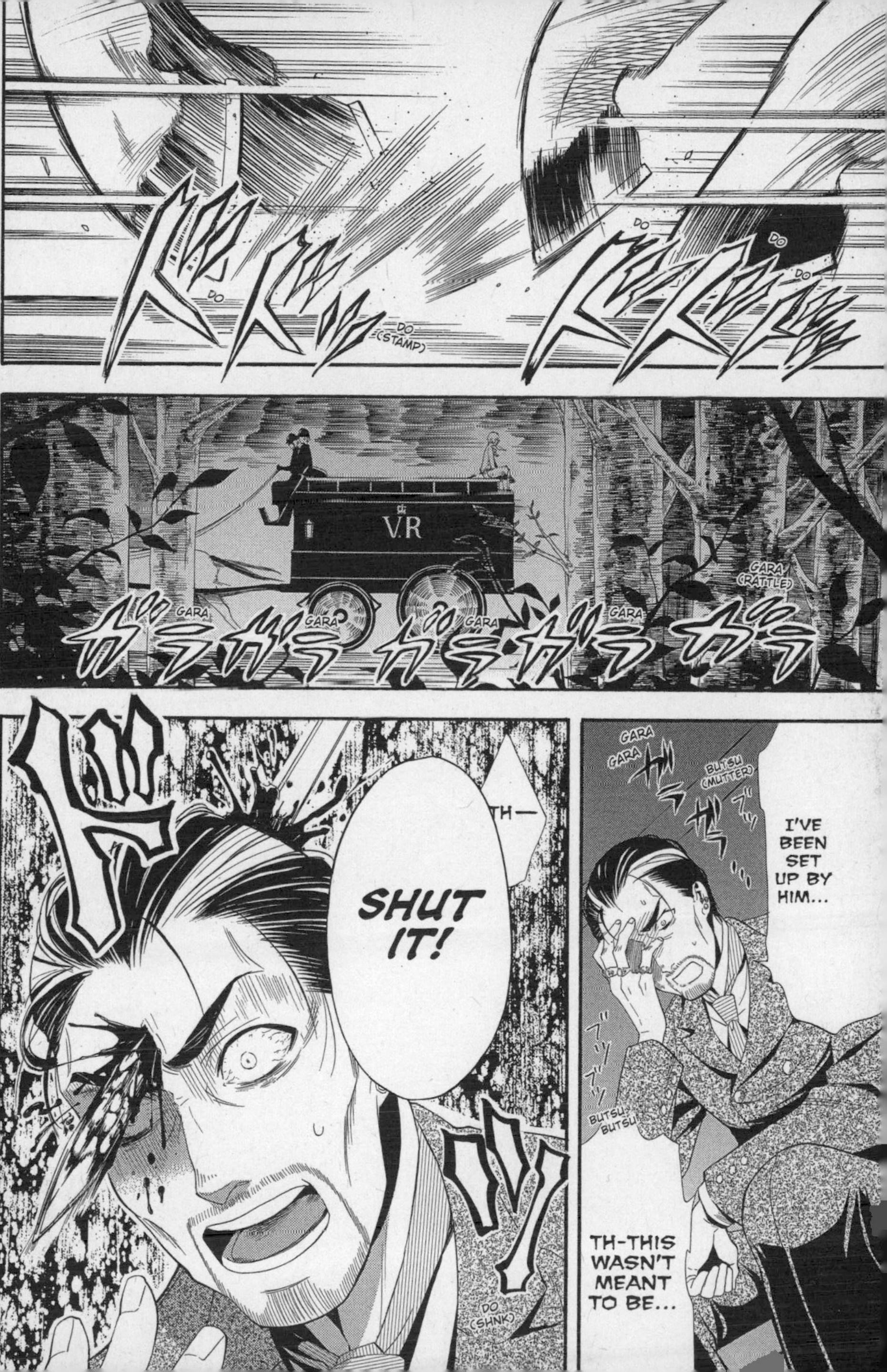
DO
DO
DO
DO
DO (STAMP)
V.R
GARA (RATTLE)
GARA
GARA
GARA
GARA
GARA GARA
BUTSU (MUTTER)
I'VE BEEN SET UP BY HIM...
BUTSU BUTSU
TH-THIS WASN'T MEANT TO BE...
TH—
SHUT IT!
DO (SHNK)

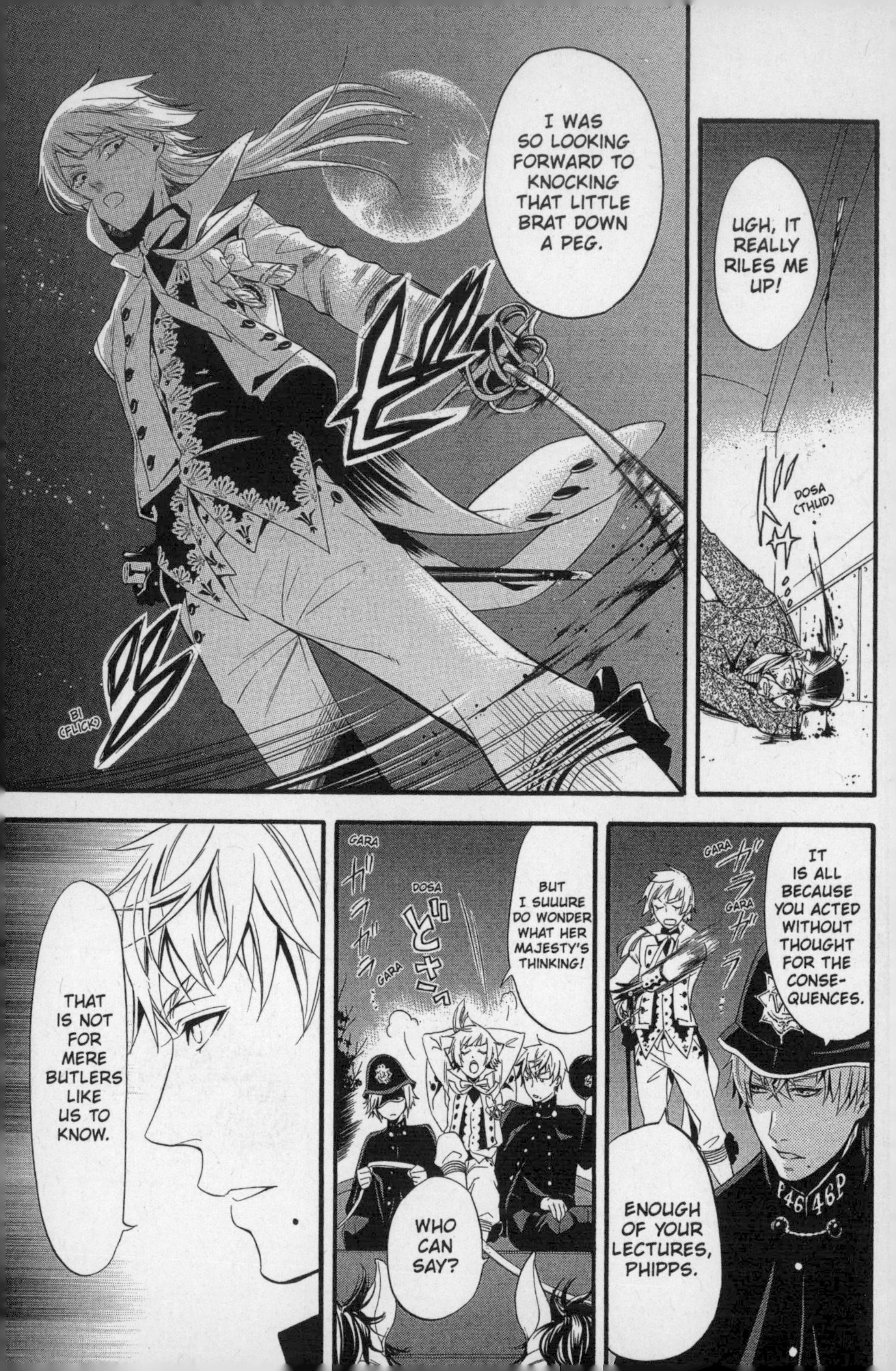
UGH, IT REALLY RILES ME UP!
DOSA (THUD)
I WAS SO LOOKING FORWARD TO KNOCKING THAT LITTLE BRAT DOWN A PEG.
BI (FLICK)
GARA
GARA
IT IS ALL BECAUSE YOU ACTED WITHOUT THOUGHT FOR THE CONSE-QUENCES.
ENOUGH OF YOUR LECTURES, PHIPPS.
GARA
DOSA
GARA
BUT I SUUURE DO WONDER WHAT HER MAJESTY'S THINKING!
WHO CAN SAY?
THAT IS NOT FOR MERE BUTLERS LIKE US TO KNOW.

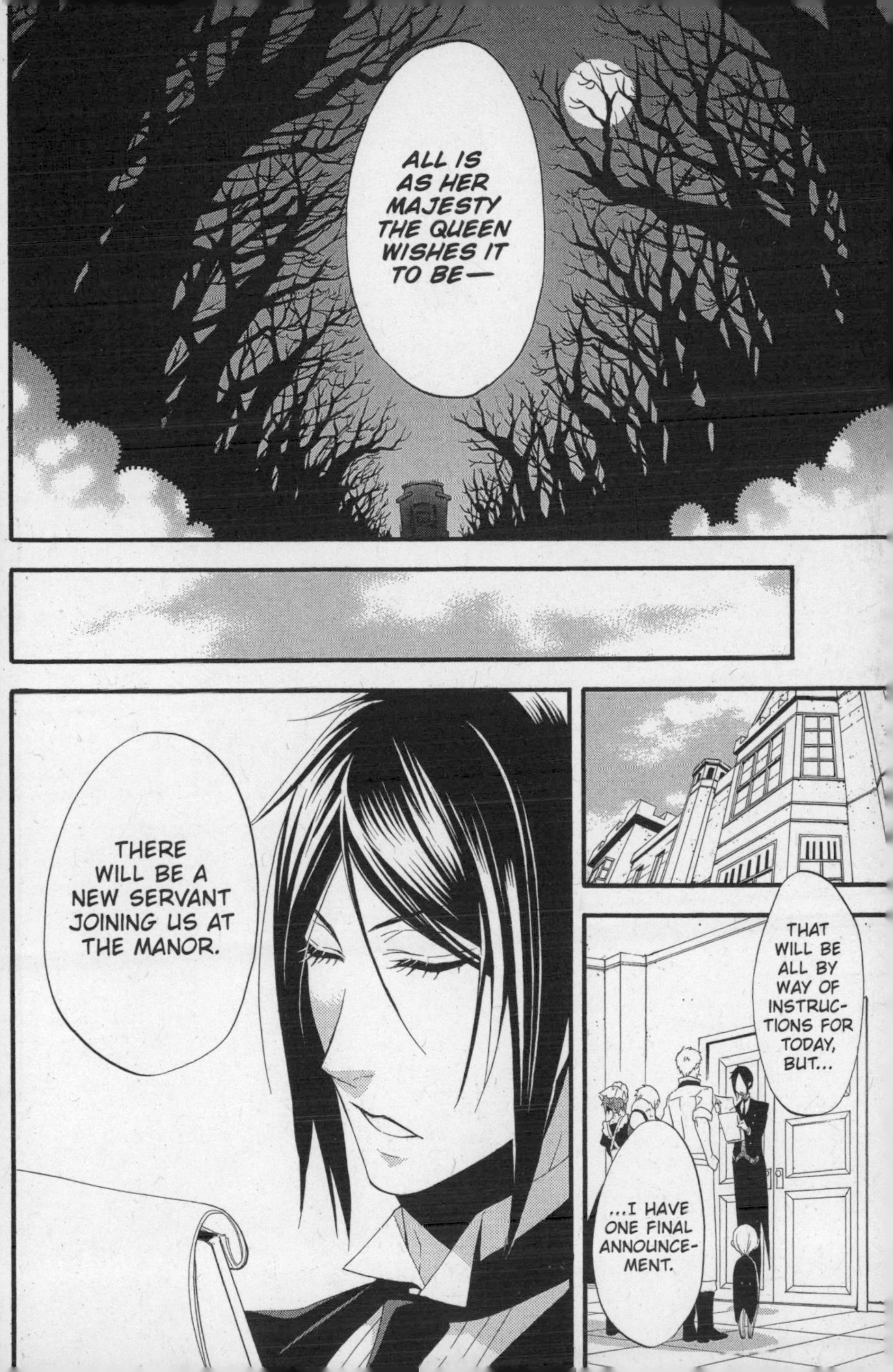
ALL IS AS HER MAJESTY THE QUEEN WISHES IT TO BE—
THAT WILL BE ALL BY WAY OF INSTRUCTIONS FOR TODAY, BUT...
...I HAVE ONE FINAL ANNOUNCEMENT.
THERE WILL BE A NEW SERVANT JOINING US AT THE MANOR.

ガチャ GACHA (CLICK)

COME IN.

EH!?

GYAAAH!

ZORO ズズズ

YIIIKES, SNAAA-AAKES!

ZORO ズズズ

WAH!!

ZORO ズズズ

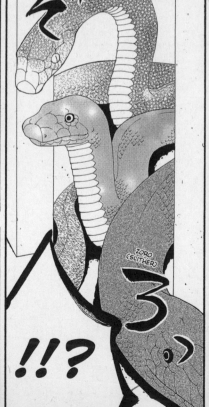

ズズ

ZORO (SLITHER)

ズ

!!!?

HE?

THEY WILL NOT BITE UNTIL HE COMMANDS THEM TO DO SO.

DO PIPE DOWN.

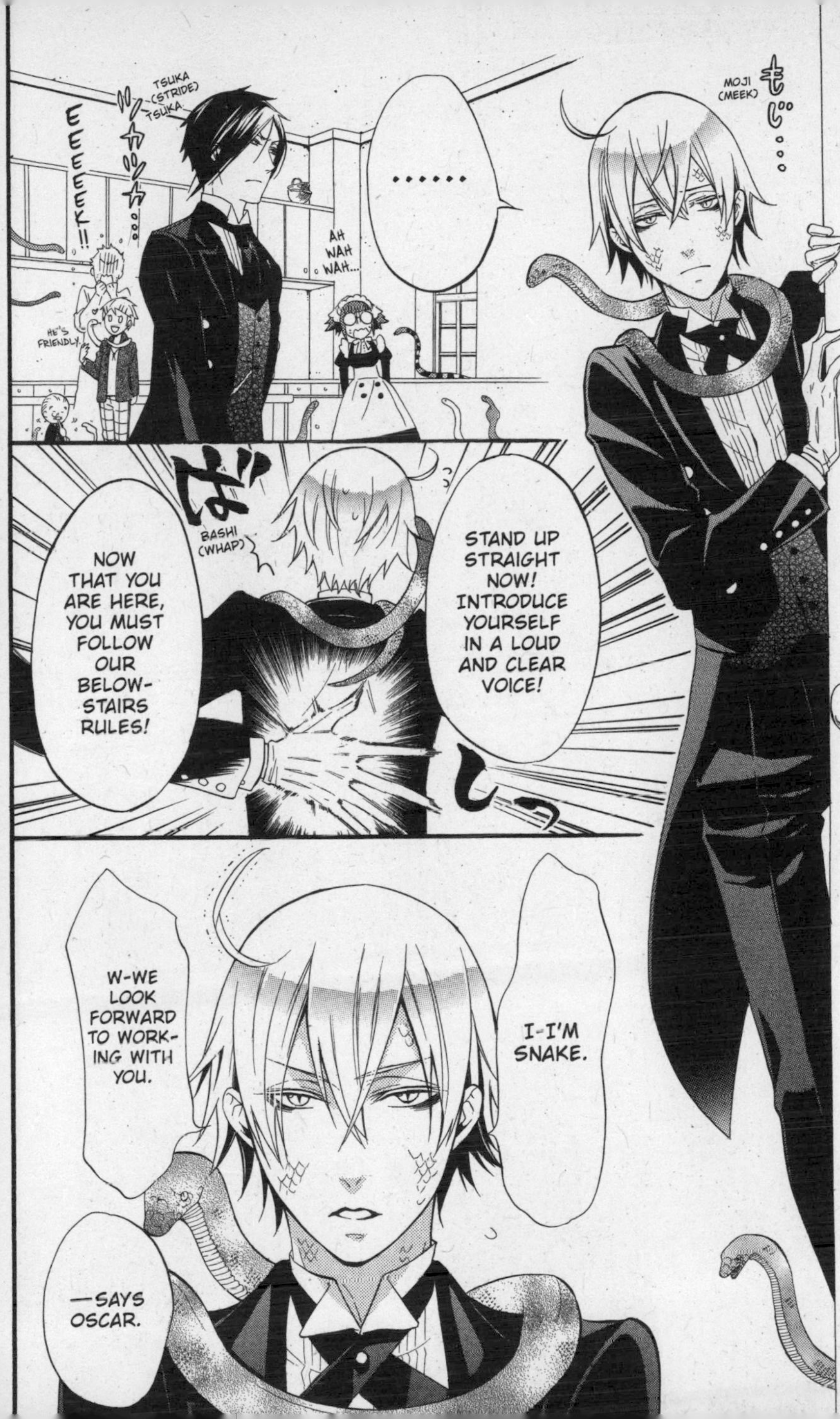
MOJI (MEEK)
......
TSUKA (STRIDE) TSUKA
EEEEEK!!
AH WAH WAH...
HE'S FRIENDLY.
STAND UP STRAIGHT NOW! INTRODUCE YOURSELF IN A LOUD AND CLEAR VOICE!
BASHI (WHAP)
NOW THAT YOU ARE HERE, YOU MUST FOLLOW OUR BELOW-STAIRS RULES!
I-I'M SNAKE.
W-WE LOOK FORWARD TO WORKING WITH YOU.
—SAYS OSCAR.

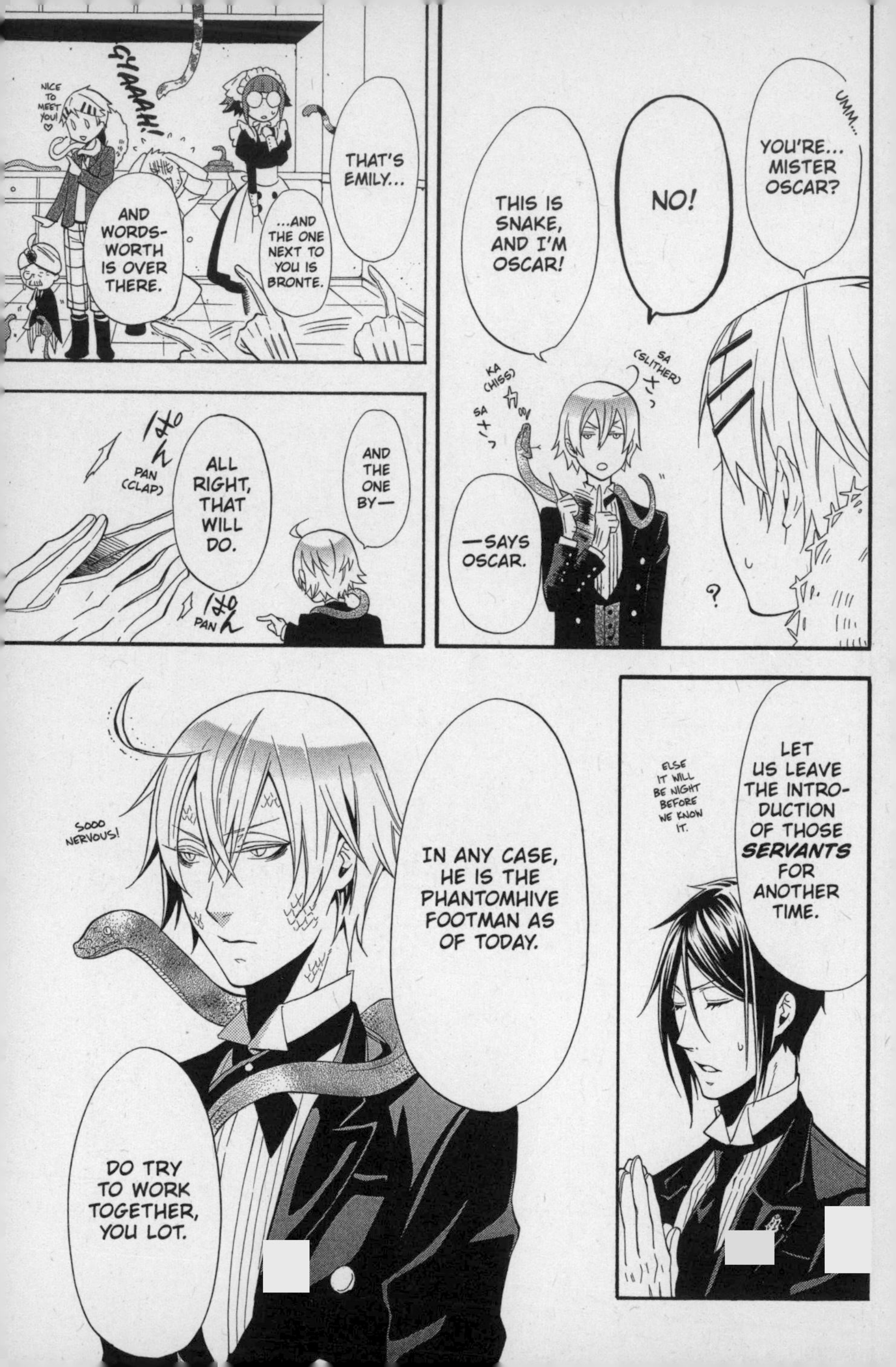
UMM...
YOU'RE... MISTER OSCAR?
NO!
THIS IS SNAKE, AND I'M OSCAR!
SA (SLITHER)
KA (HISS)
SA
—SAYS OSCAR.
?
THAT'S EMILY...
...AND THE ONE NEXT TO YOU IS BRONTE.
AND WORDS-WORTH IS OVER THERE.
GYAAAH!
NICE TO MEET YOU! ♡
AND THE ONE BY—
ALL RIGHT, THAT WILL DO.
PAN (CLAP)
PAN
LET US LEAVE THE INTRO-DUCTION OF THOSE ***SERVANTS*** FOR ANOTHER TIME.
ELSE IT WILL BE NIGHT BEFORE WE KNOW IT.
IN ANY CASE, HE IS THE PHANTOMHIVE FOOTMAN AS OF TODAY.
SOOO NERVOUS!
DO TRY TO WORK TOGETHER, YOU LOT.

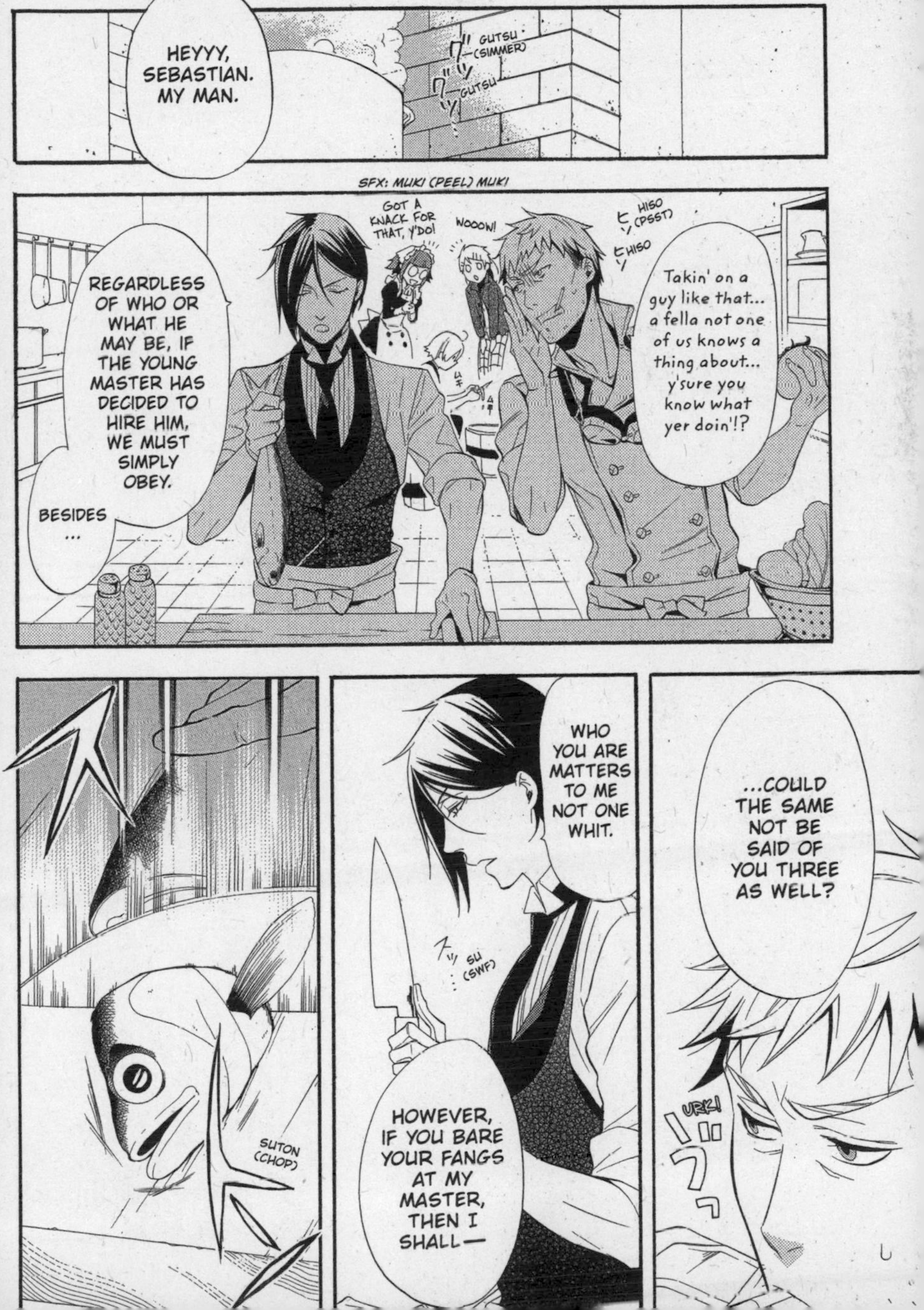
GUTSU (SIMMER)
GUTSU
HEYYY, SEBASTIAN. MY MAN.
SFX: MUKI (PEEL) MUKI
HISO (PSSST)
HISO
Takin' on a guy like that... a fella not one of us knows a thing about... y'sure you know what yer doin'!?
WOOOW!
GOT A KNACK FOR THAT, Y'DO!
REGARDLESS OF WHO OR WHAT HE MAY BE, IF THE YOUNG MASTER HAS DECIDED TO HIRE HIM, WE MUST SIMPLY OBEY.
BESIDES...
...COULD THE SAME NOT BE SAID OF YOU THREE AS WELL?
URK!
WHO YOU ARE MATTERS TO ME NOT ONE WHIT.
SU (SWF)
HOWEVER, IF YOU BARE YOUR FANGS AT MY MASTER, THEN I SHALL—
SUTON (CHOP)

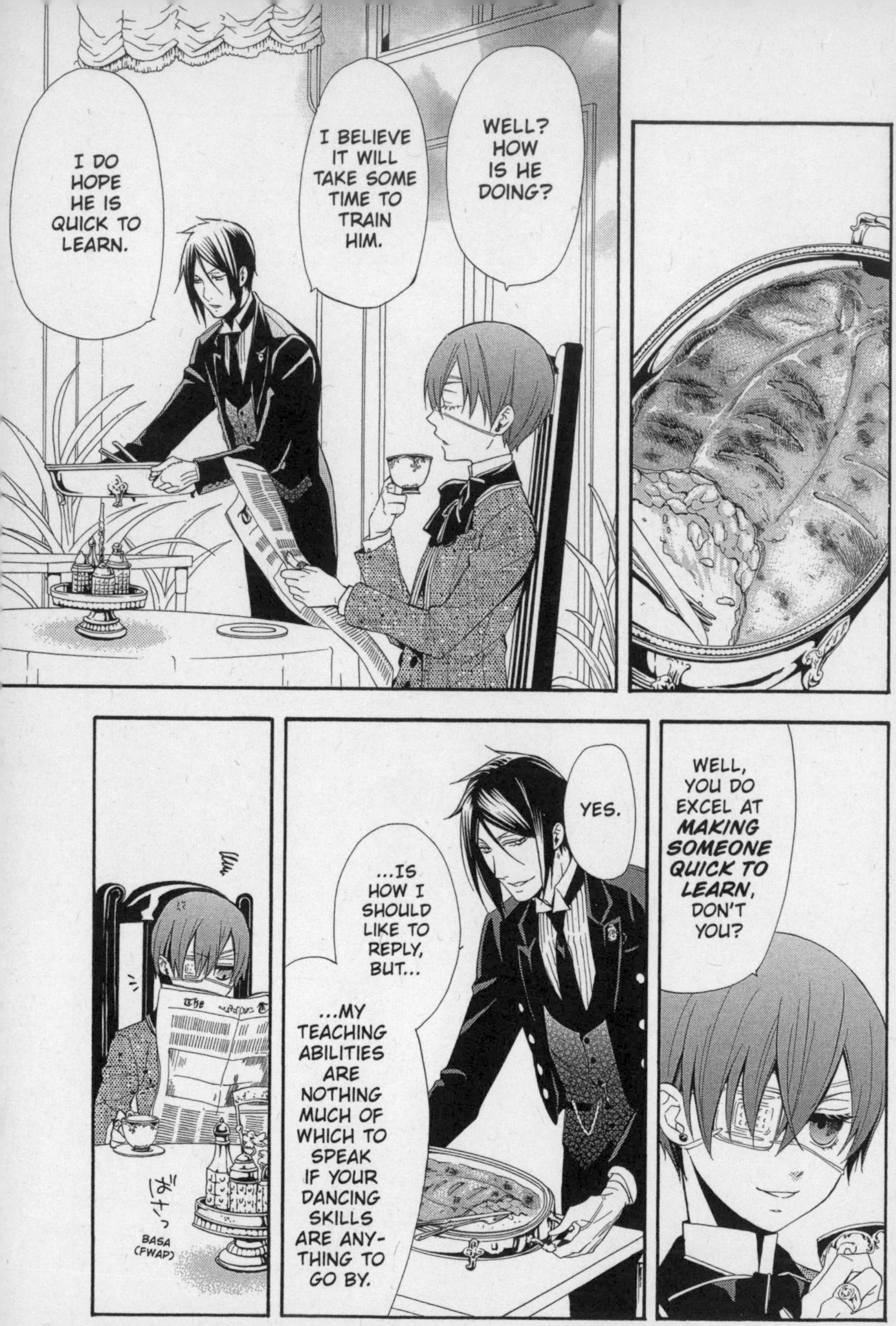
WELL? HOW IS HE DOING?
I BELIEVE IT WILL TAKE SOME TIME TO TRAIN HIM.
I DO HOPE HE IS QUICK TO LEARN.
WELL, YOU DO EXCEL AT *MAKING SOMEONE QUICK TO LEARN*, DON'T YOU?
YES.
...IS HOW I SHOULD LIKE TO REPLY, BUT...
...MY TEACHING ABILITIES ARE NOTHING MUCH OF WHICH TO SPEAK IF YOUR DANCING SKILLS ARE ANY-THING TO GO BY.
BASA (FWAP)

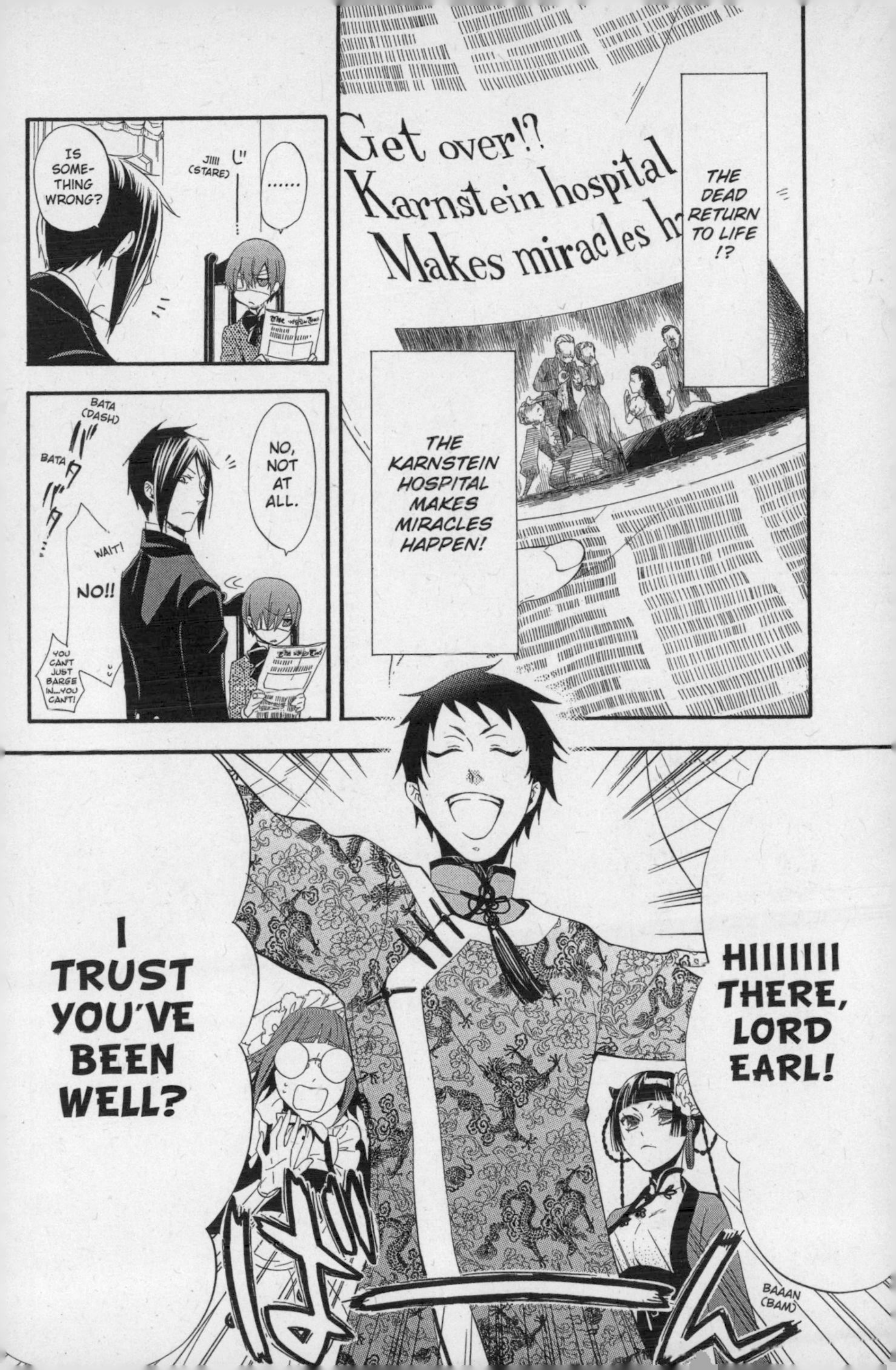
Get over!?
Karnstein hospital
Makes miracles h
THE DEAD RETURN TO LIFE !?
THE KARNSTEIN HOSPITAL MAKES MIRACLES HAPPEN!
......
JIIII (STARE)
IS SOME-THING WRONG?
NO, NOT AT ALL.
BATA (DASH)
BATA
WAIT!
NO!!
YOU CAN'T JUST BARGE IN...YOU CAN'T!
HIIIIIII THERE, LORD EARL!
I TRUST YOU'VE BEEN WELL?
BAAAN (BAM)

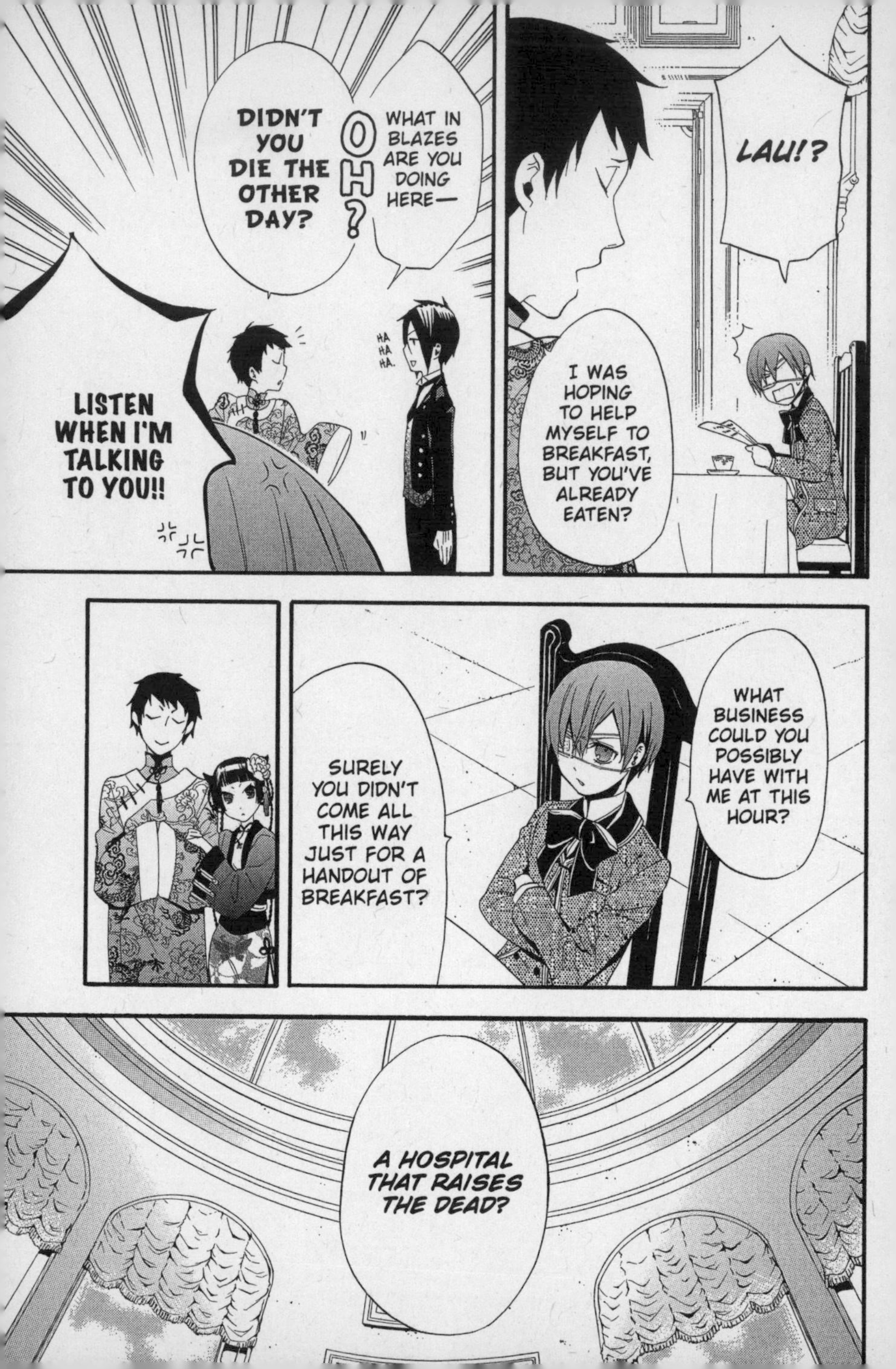
LAU!?
I WAS HOPING TO HELP MYSELF TO BREAKFAST, BUT YOU'VE ALREADY EATEN?
WHAT IN BLAZES ARE YOU DOING HERE—
OH?
DIDN'T YOU DIE THE OTHER DAY?
HA HA HA.
LISTEN WHEN I'M TALKING TO YOU!!
WHAT BUSINESS COULD YOU POSSIBLY HAVE WITH ME AT THIS HOUR?
SURELY YOU DIDN'T COME ALL THIS WAY JUST FOR A HANDOUT OF BREAKFAST?
A HOSPITAL THAT RAISES THE DEAD?

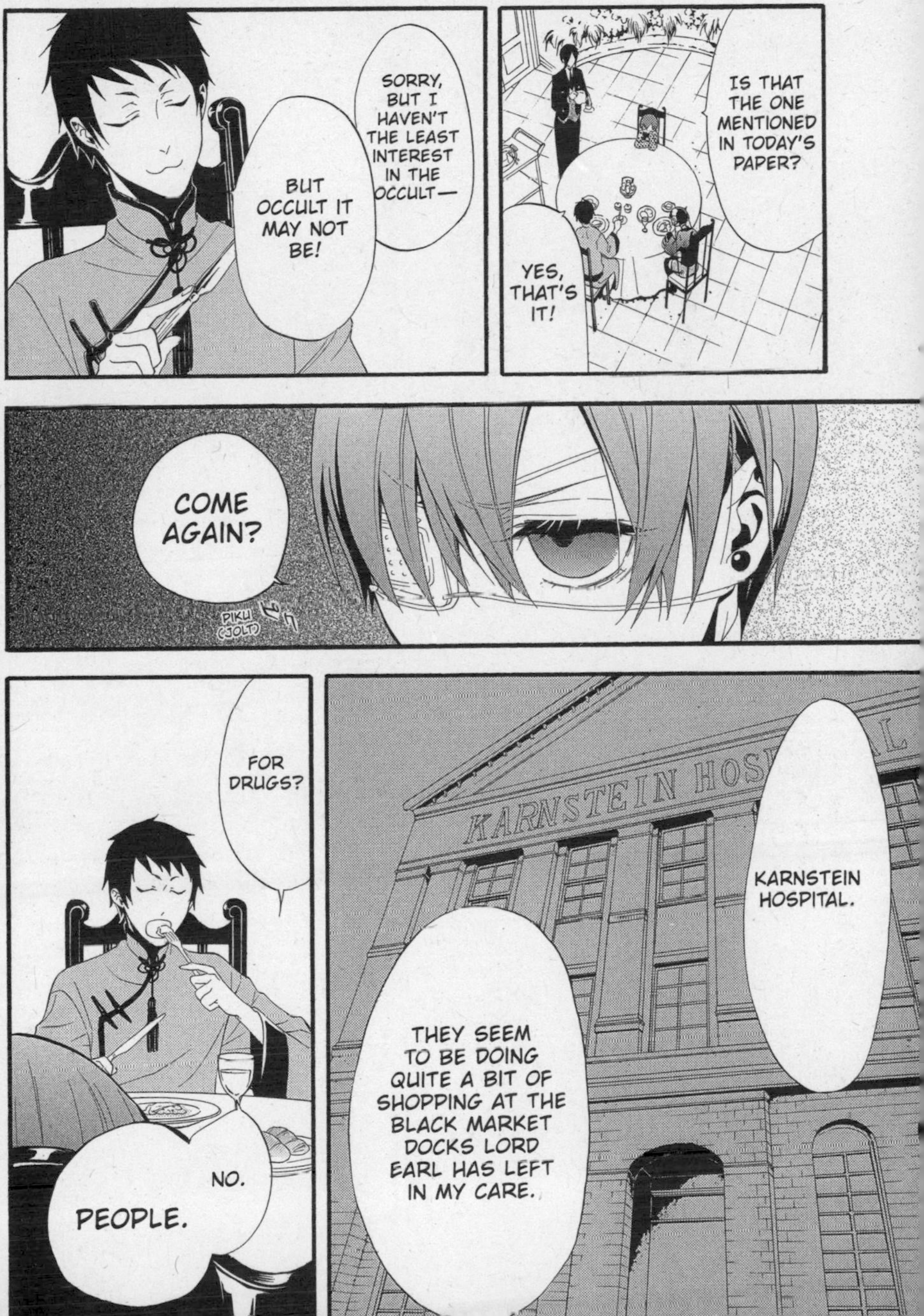
IS THAT THE ONE MENTIONED IN TODAY'S PAPER?
YES, THAT'S IT!
SORRY, BUT I HAVEN'T THE LEAST INTEREST IN THE OCCULT—
BUT OCCULT IT MAY NOT BE!
COME AGAIN?
PIKU (JOLT)
KARNSTEIN HOSPITAL.
THEY SEEM TO BE DOING QUITE A BIT OF SHOPPING AT THE BLACK MARKET DOCKS LORD EARL HAS LEFT IN MY CARE.
FOR DRUGS?
NO.
PEOPLE.

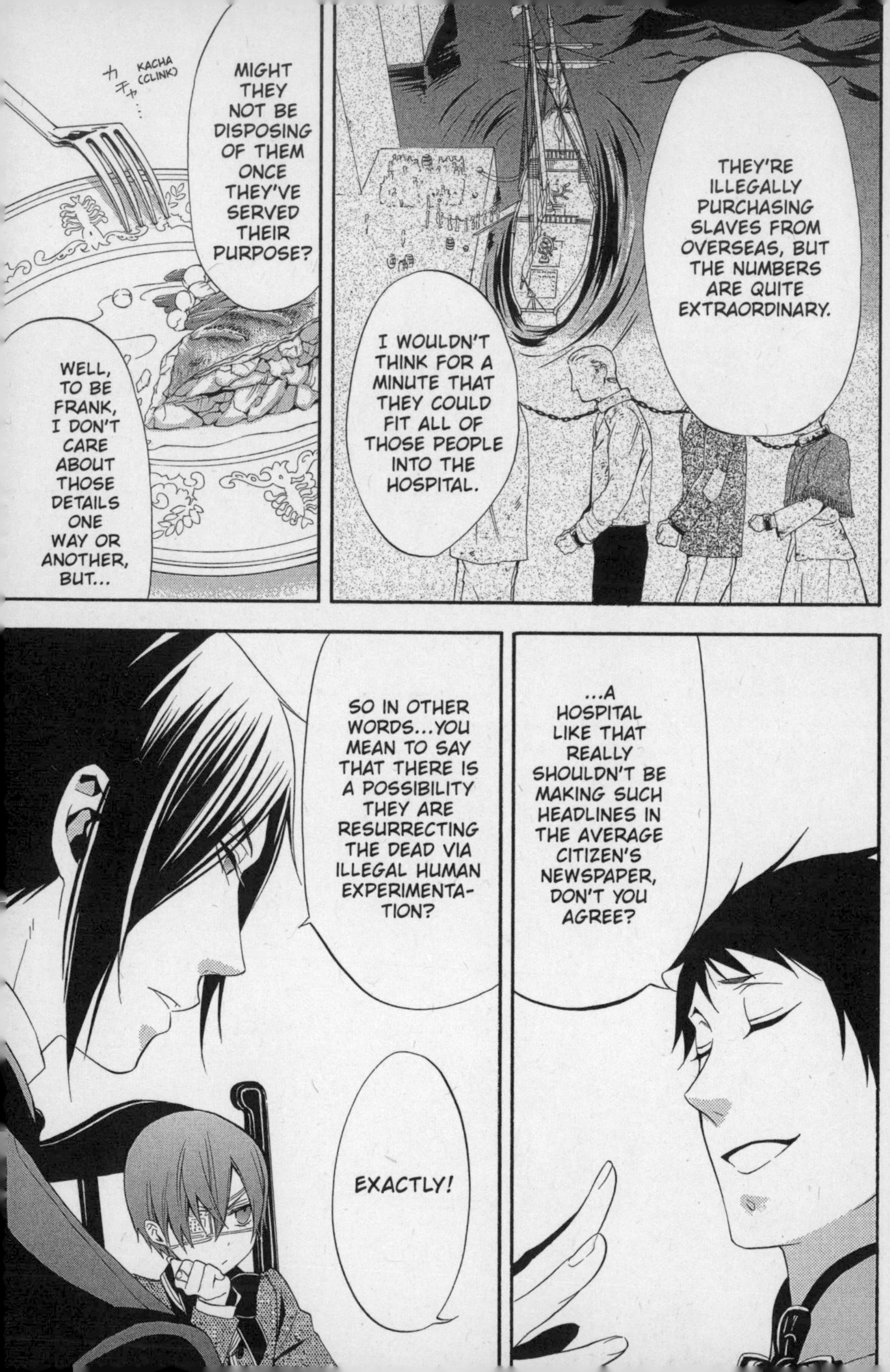
THEY'RE ILLEGALLY PURCHASING SLAVES FROM OVERSEAS, BUT THE NUMBERS ARE QUITE EXTRAORDINARY.
I WOULDN'T THINK FOR A MINUTE THAT THEY COULD FIT ALL OF THOSE PEOPLE INTO THE HOSPITAL.
MIGHT THEY NOT BE DISPOSING OF THEM ONCE THEY'VE SERVED THEIR PURPOSE?
カチャ…
KACHA (CLINK)
WELL, TO BE FRANK, I DON'T CARE ABOUT THOSE DETAILS ONE WAY OR ANOTHER, BUT...
...A HOSPITAL LIKE THAT REALLY SHOULDN'T BE MAKING SUCH HEADLINES IN THE AVERAGE CITIZEN'S NEWSPAPER, DON'T YOU AGREE?
SO IN OTHER WORDS...YOU MEAN TO SAY THAT THERE IS A POSSIBILITY THEY ARE RESURRECTING THE DEAD VIA ILLEGAL HUMAN EXPERIMENTA-TION?
EXACTLY!

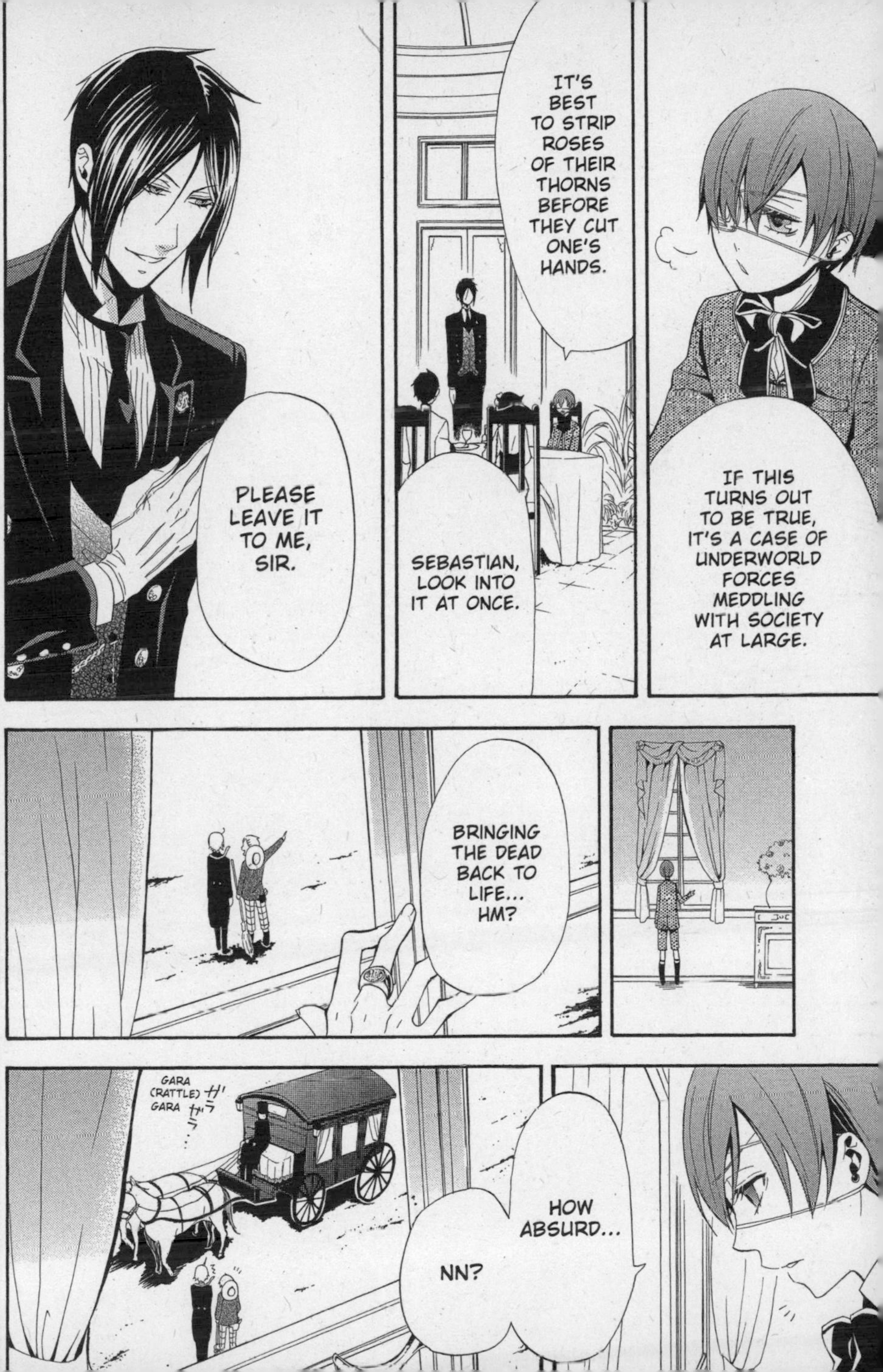
IF THIS TURNS OUT TO BE TRUE, IT'S A CASE OF UNDERWORLD FORCES MEDDLING WITH SOCIETY AT LARGE.
IT'S BEST TO STRIP ROSES OF THEIR THORNS BEFORE THEY CUT ONE'S HANDS.
SEBASTIAN, LOOK INTO IT AT ONCE.
PLEASE LEAVE IT TO ME, SIR.
BRINGING THE DEAD BACK TO LIFE... HM?
HOW ABSURD...
NN?
GARA (RATTLE) GARA
ガラガラ

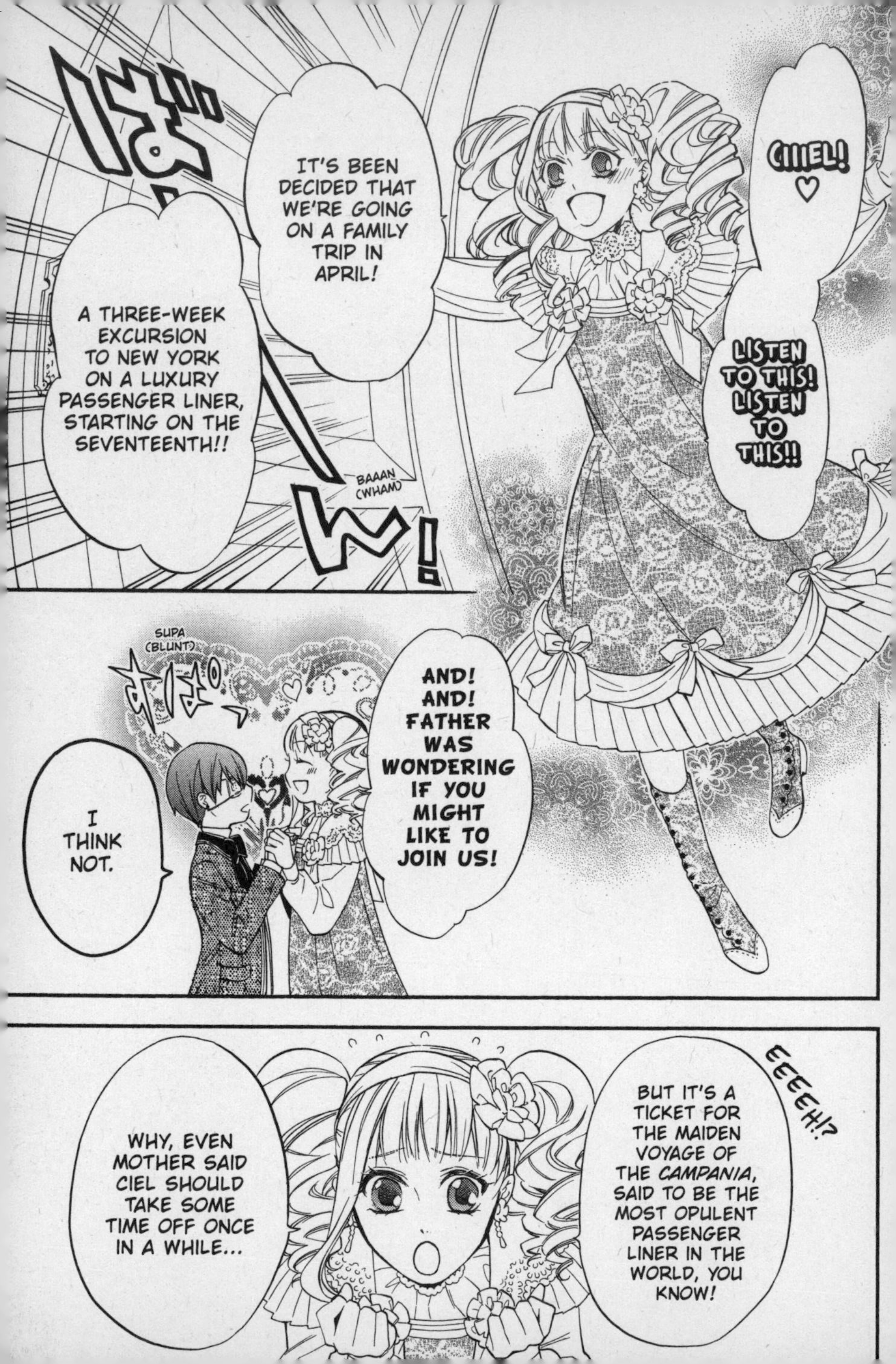
CIIIEL! ♥
LISTEN TO THIS! LISTEN TO THIS!!
IT'S BEEN DECIDED THAT WE'RE GOING ON A FAMILY TRIP IN APRIL!
A THREE-WEEK EXCURSION TO NEW YORK ON A LUXURY PASSENGER LINER, STARTING ON THE SEVENTEENTH!!
BAAAN (WHAM)
AND! AND! FATHER WAS WONDERING IF YOU MIGHT LIKE TO JOIN US!
SUPA (BLUNT)
I THINK NOT.
EEEEH!?
BUT IT'S A TICKET FOR THE MAIDEN VOYAGE OF THE *CAMPANIA*, SAID TO BE THE MOST OPULENT PASSENGER LINER IN THE WORLD, YOU KNOW!
WHY, EVEN MOTHER SAID CIEL SHOULD TAKE SOME TIME OFF ONCE IN A WHILE...

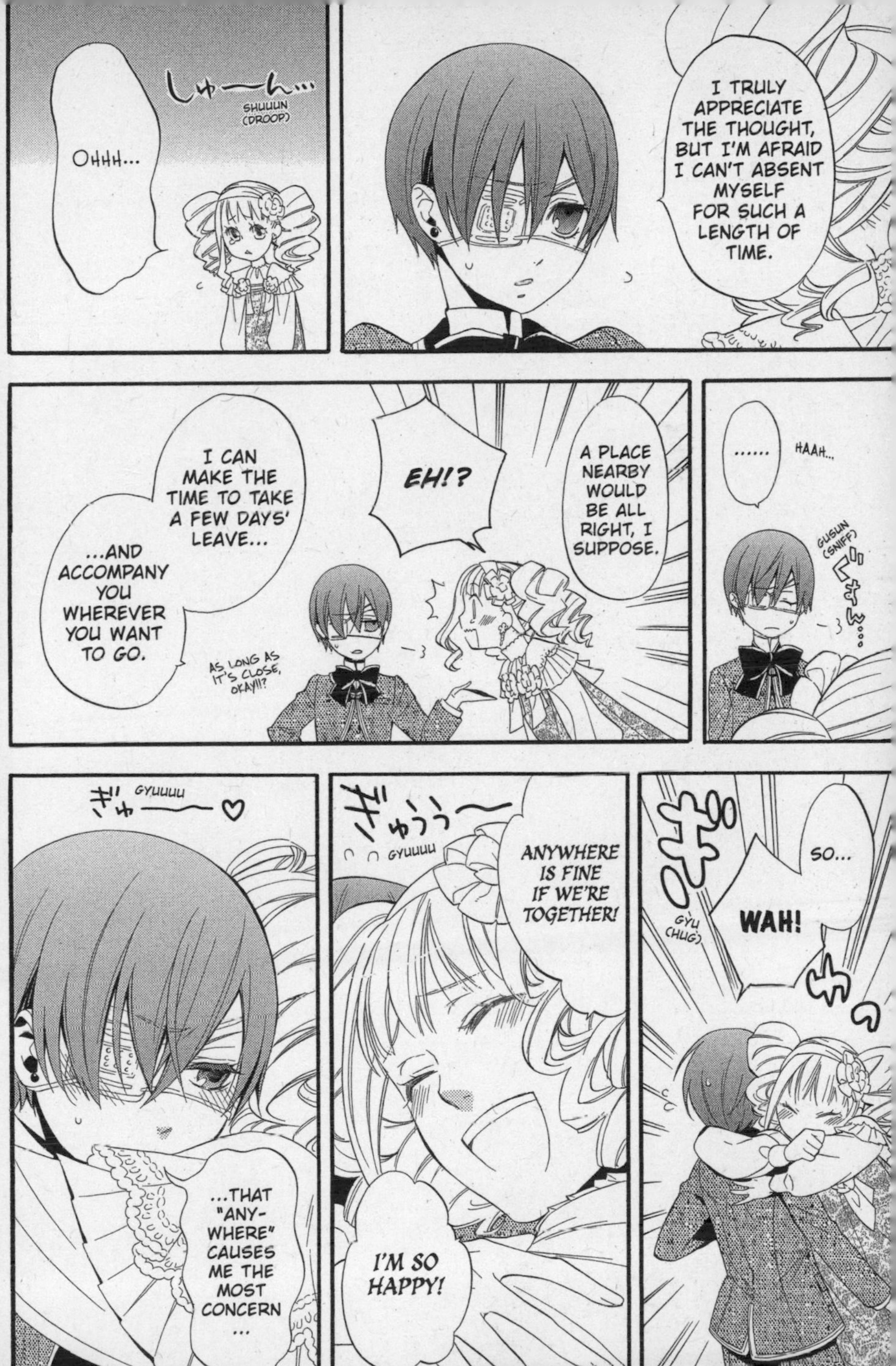
I TRULY APPRECIATE THE THOUGHT, BUT I'M AFRAID I CAN'T ABSENT MYSELF FOR SUCH A LENGTH OF TIME.
しゅーん…
SHUUUN (DROOP)
OHHH...
......
HAAH...
ぐじゅん…
GUSUN (SNIFF)
A PLACE NEARBY WOULD BE ALL RIGHT, I SUPPOSE.
EH!?
AS LONG AS IT'S CLOSE, OKAY!!?
I CAN MAKE THE TIME TO TAKE A FEW DAYS' LEAVE...
...AND ACCOMPANY YOU WHEREVER YOU WANT TO GO.
SO...
ぎゅっ
GYU (HUG)
WAH!
ぎゅううう～
GYUUUU
ANYWHERE IS FINE IF WE'RE TOGETHER!
I'M SO HAPPY!
ぎゅ～～♡
GYUUUU
...THAT "ANYWHERE" CAUSES ME THE MOST CONCERN...

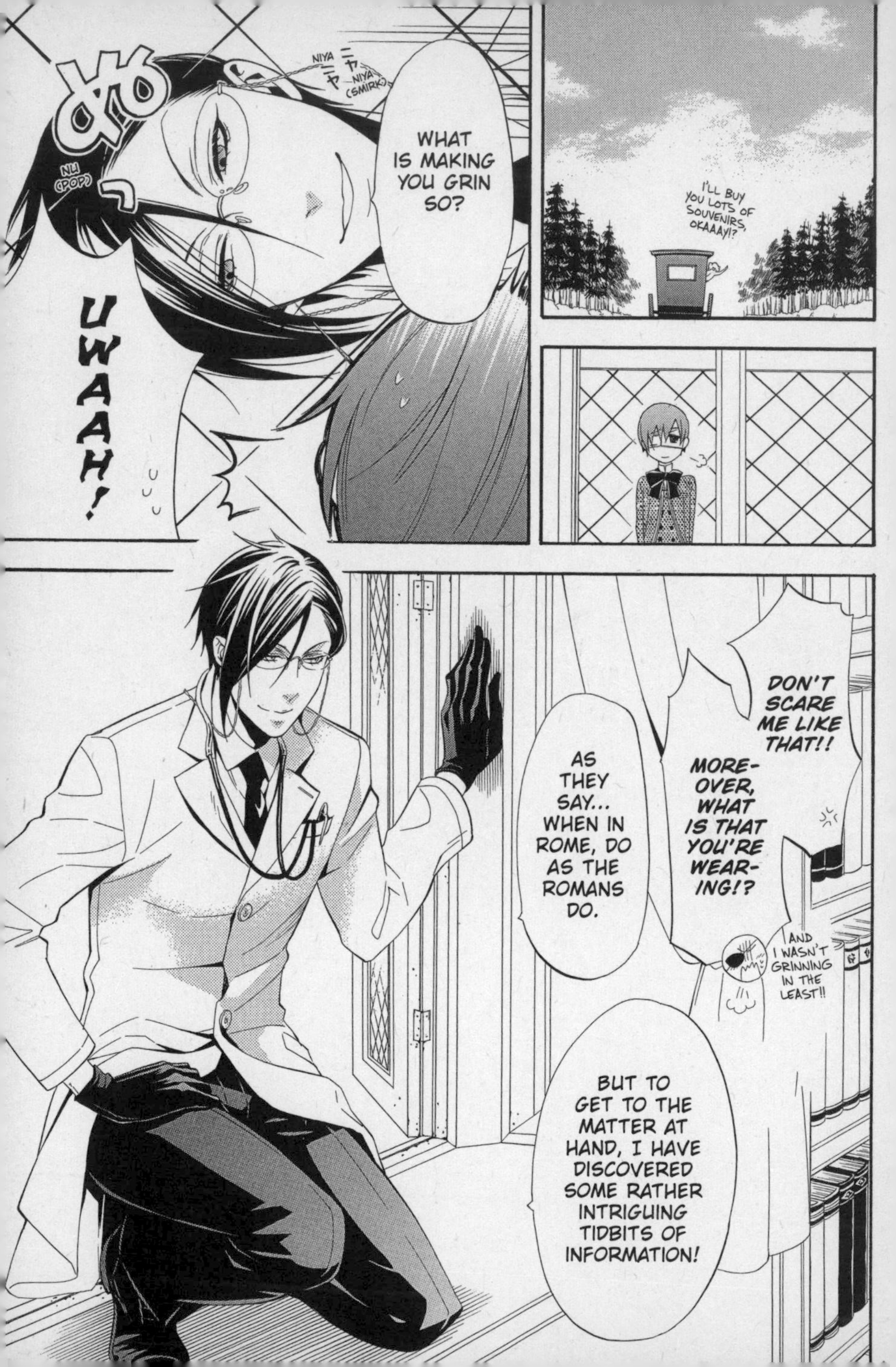
I'LL BUY YOU LOTS OF SOUVENIRS, OKAAAY!?
NIYA NIYA (SMIRK)
WHAT IS MAKING YOU GRIN SO?
NU (POP)
UWAAH!
DON'T SCARE ME LIKE THAT!!
MORE-OVER, WHAT IS THAT YOU'RE WEAR-ING!?
AS THEY SAY... WHEN IN ROME, DO AS THE ROMANS DO.
AND I WASN'T GRINNING IN THE LEAST!!
BUT TO GET TO THE MATTER AT HAND, I HAVE DISCOVERED SOME RATHER INTRIGUING TIDBITS OF INFORMATION!

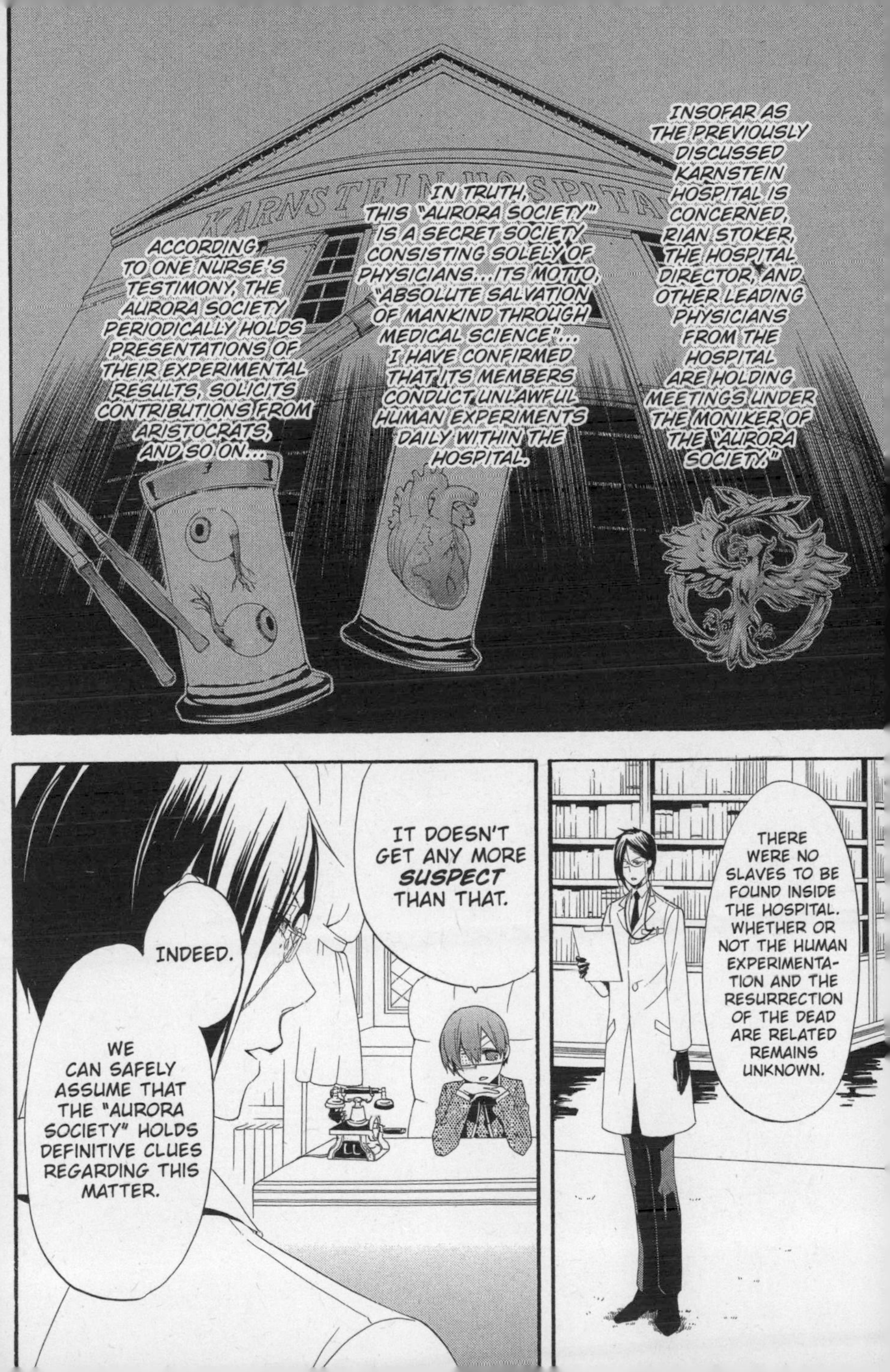
INSOFAR AS THE PREVIOUSLY DISCUSSED KARNSTEIN HOSPITAL IS CONCERNED, RIAN STOKER, THE HOSPITAL DIRECTOR, AND OTHER LEADING PHYSICIANS FROM THE HOSPITAL ARE HOLDING MEETINGS UNDER THE MONIKER OF THE "AURORA SOCIETY."
IN TRUTH, THIS "AURORA SOCIETY" IS A SECRET SOCIETY CONSISTING SOLELY OF PHYSICIANS...ITS MOTTO, "ABSOLUTE SALVATION OF MANKIND THROUGH MEDICAL SCIENCE"... I HAVE CONFIRMED THAT ITS MEMBERS CONDUCT UNLAWFUL HUMAN EXPERIMENTS DAILY WITHIN THE HOSPITAL.
ACCORDING TO ONE NURSE'S TESTIMONY, THE AURORA SOCIETY PERIODICALLY HOLDS PRESENTATIONS OF THEIR EXPERIMENTAL RESULTS, SOLICITS CONTRIBUTIONS FROM ARISTOCRATS, AND SO ON...
THERE WERE NO SLAVES TO BE FOUND INSIDE THE HOSPITAL. WHETHER OR NOT THE HUMAN EXPERIMENTATION AND THE RESURRECTION OF THE DEAD ARE RELATED REMAINS UNKNOWN.
IT DOESN'T GET ANY MORE **SUSPECT** THAN THAT.
INDEED.
WE CAN SAFELY ASSUME THAT THE "AURORA SOCIETY" HOLDS DEFINITIVE CLUES REGARDING THIS MATTER.

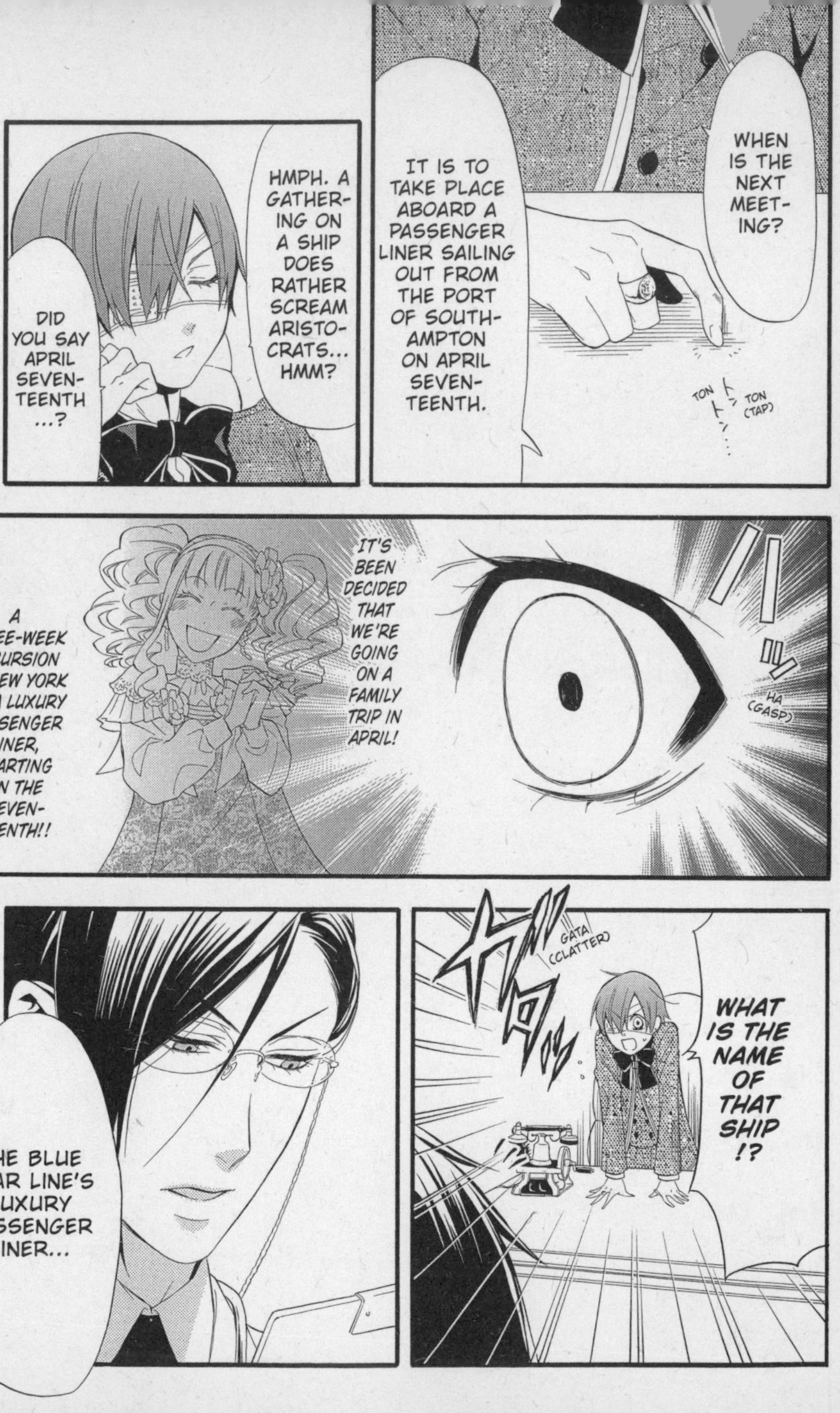
WHEN IS THE NEXT MEETING?
TON TON (TAP)
IT IS TO TAKE PLACE ABOARD A PASSENGER LINER SAILING OUT FROM THE PORT OF SOUTHAMPTON ON APRIL SEVENTEENTH.
HMPH. A GATHERING ON A SHIP DOES RATHER SCREAM ARISTOCRATS... HMM?
DID YOU SAY APRIL SEVENTEENTH...?
HA (GASP)
IT'S BEEN DECIDED THAT WE'RE GOING ON A FAMILY TRIP IN APRIL!
A THREE-WEEK EXCURSION TO NEW YORK ON A LUXURY PASSENGER LINER, STARTING ON THE SEVENTEENTH!!
GATA (CLATTER)
WHAT IS THE NAME OF THAT SHIP!?
THE BLUE STAR LINE'S LUXURY PASSENGER LINER...

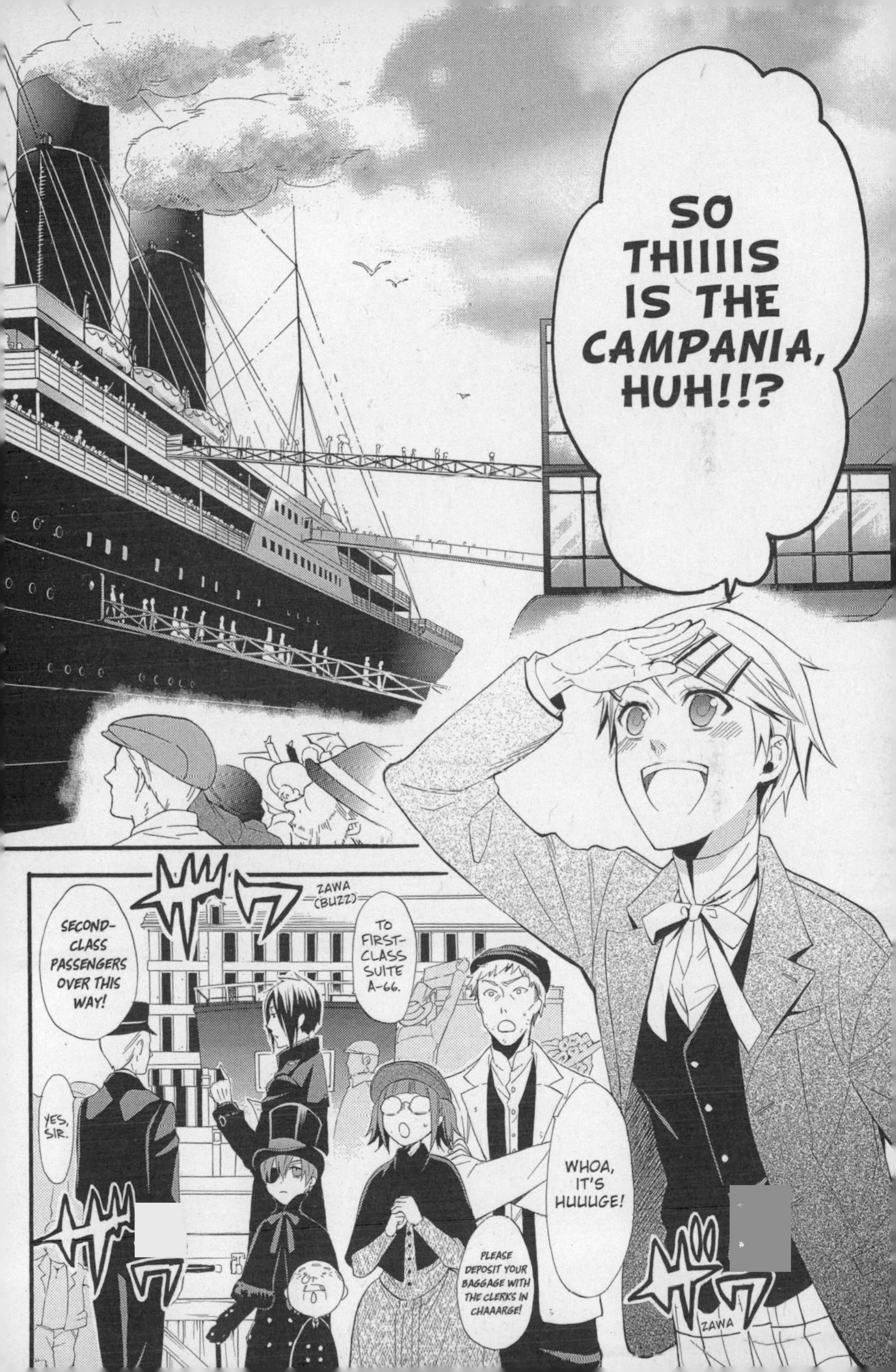
SO THIIIIS IS THE CAMPANIA, HUH!!?
ZAWA (BUZZ)
TO FIRST-CLASS SUITE A-66.
SECOND-CLASS PASSENGERS OVER THIS WAY!
WHOA, IT'S HUUUGE!
PLEASE DEPOSIT YOUR BAGGAGE WITH THE CLERKS IN CHAAARGE!
YES, SIR.
ZAWA

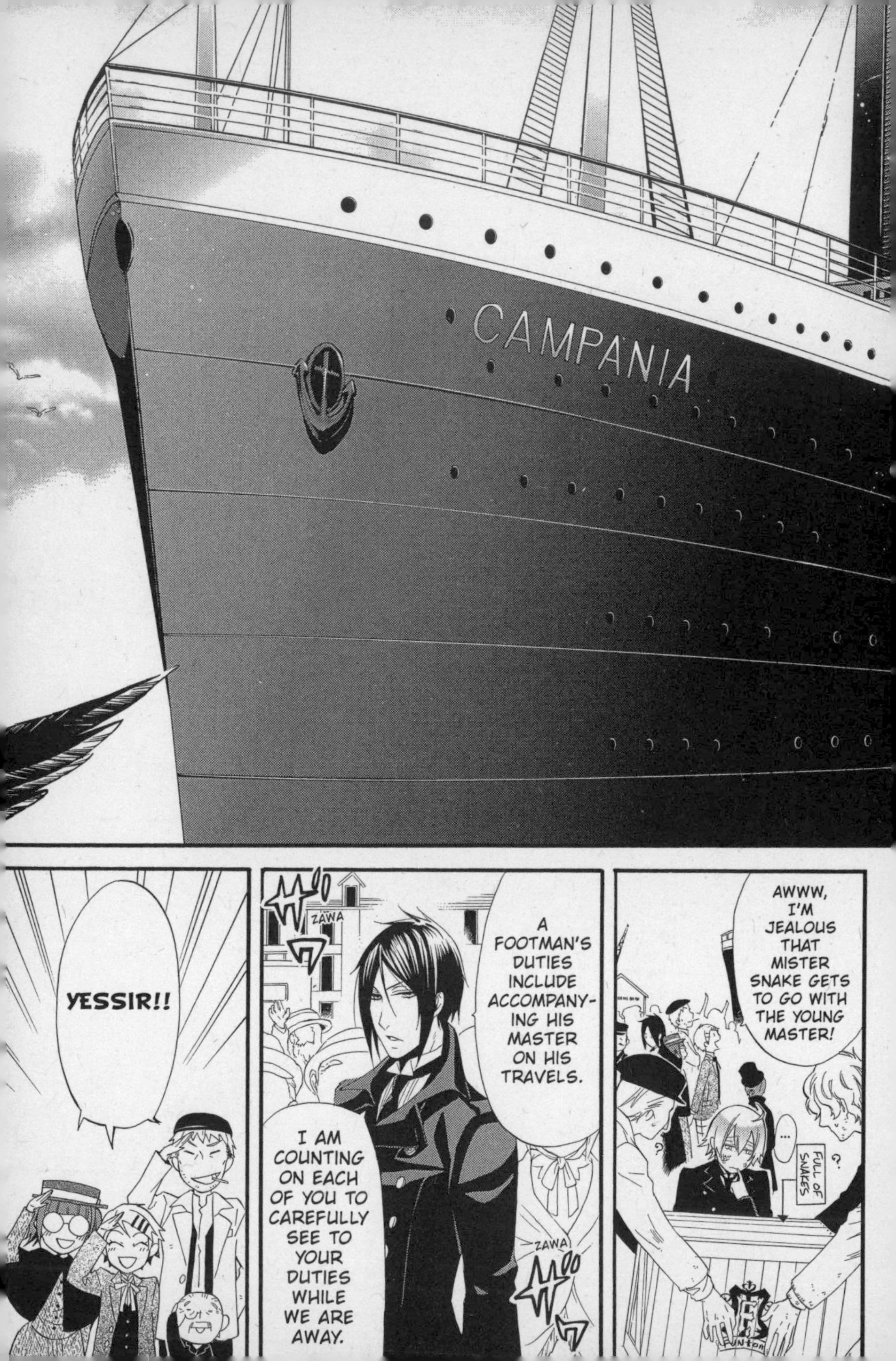
CAMPANIA
AWWW, I'M JEALOUS THAT MISTER SNAKE GETS TO GO WITH THE YOUNG MASTER!
...
FULL OF SNAKES
ZAWA
A FOOTMAN'S DUTIES INCLUDE ACCOMPANYING HIS MASTER ON HIS TRAVELS.
I AM COUNTING ON EACH OF YOU TO CAREFULLY SEE TO YOUR DUTIES WHILE WE ARE AWAY.
ZAWA
YESSIR!!

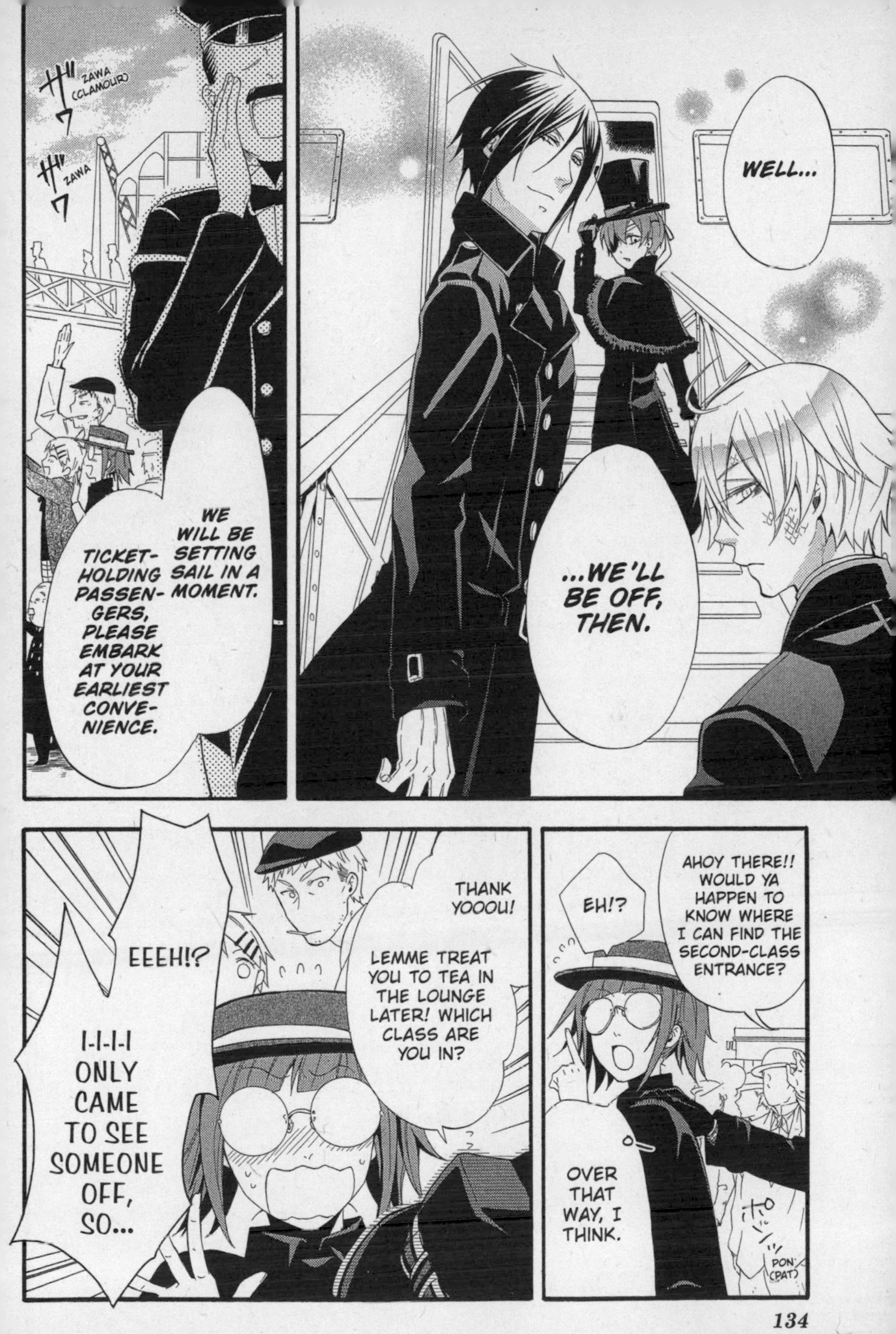
WELL...
...WE'LL BE OFF, THEN.
ZAWA (CLAMOUR)
ZAWA
WE WILL BE SETTING SAIL IN A MOMENT.
TICKET-HOLDING PASSENGERS, PLEASE EMBARK AT YOUR EARLIEST CONVENIENCE.
AHOY THERE!! WOULD YA HAPPEN TO KNOW WHERE I CAN FIND THE SECOND-CLASS ENTRANCE?
EH!?
OVER THAT WAY, I THINK.
PON (PAT)
THANK YOOOU!
LEMME TREAT YOU TO TEA IN THE LOUNGE LATER! WHICH CLASS ARE YOU IN?
EEEH!?
I-I-I-I ONLY CAME TO SEE SOMEONE OFF, SO...

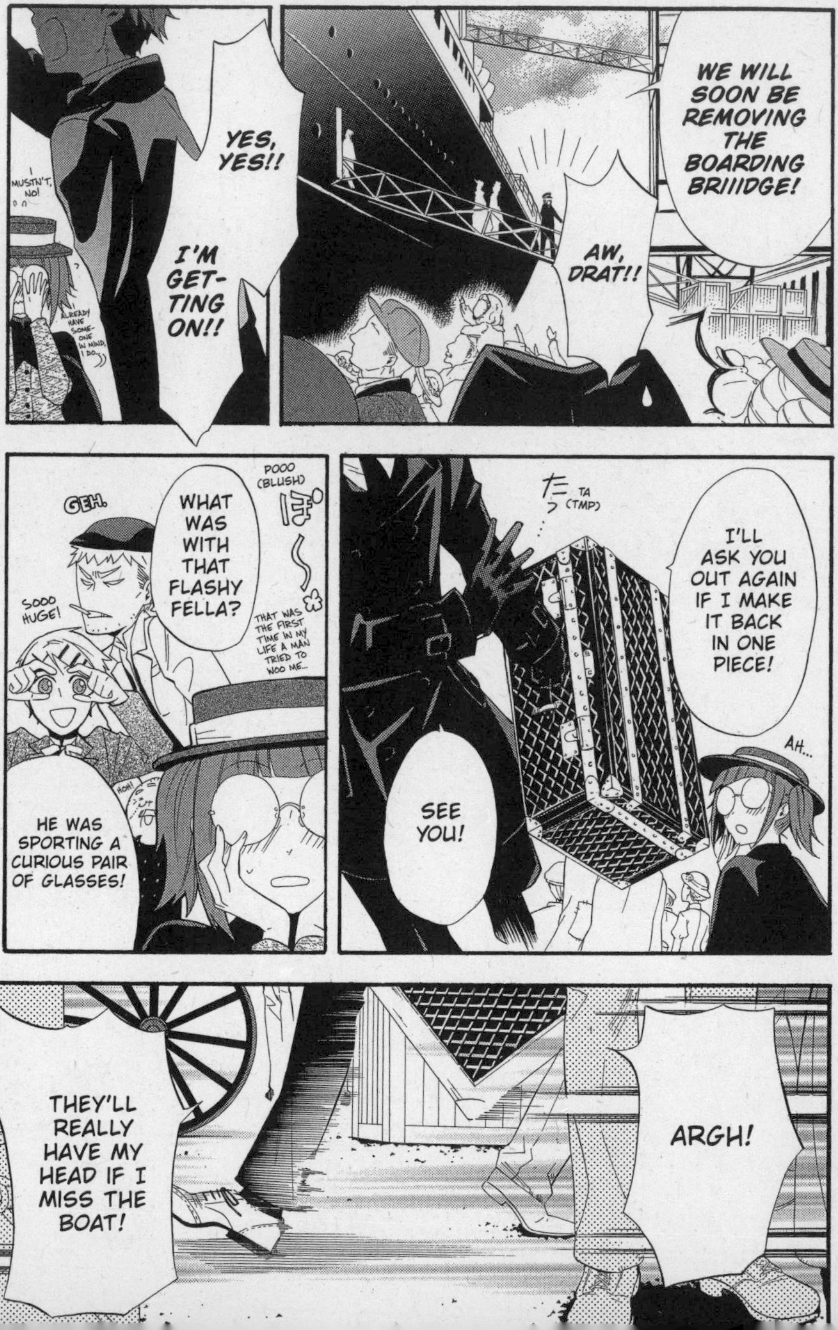
WE WILL SOON BE REMOVING THE BOARDING BRIIIDGE!
AW, DRAT!!
YES, YES!!
I'M GET-TING ON!!
I MUSTN'T, NO!
I ALREADY HAVE SOME-ONE IN MIND, I DO.
たっ TA (TMP)
I'LL ASK YOU OUT AGAIN IF I MAKE IT BACK IN ONE PIECE!
AH...
SEE YOU!
ぽ〜 POOO (BLUSH)
WHAT WAS WITH THAT FLASHY FELLA?
GEH.
SOOO HUGE!
THAT WAS THE FIRST TIME IN MY LIFE A MAN TRIED TO WOO ME...
HOH!
HE WAS SPORTING A CURIOUS PAIR OF GLASSES!
ARGH!
THEY'LL REALLY HAVE MY HEAD IF I MISS THE BOAT!

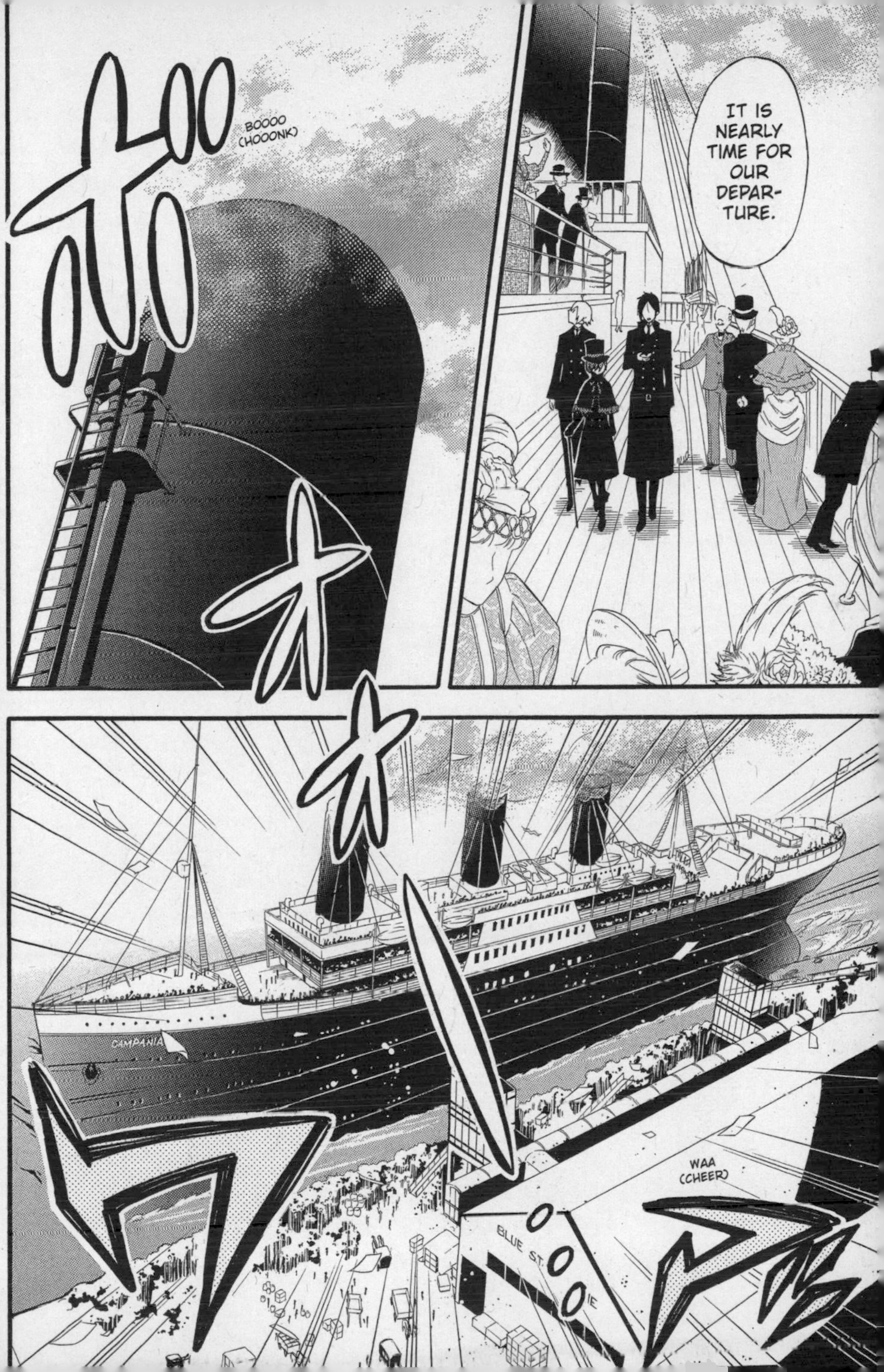
IT IS NEARLY TIME FOR OUR DEPARTURE.
BOOOO (HOOONK)
CAMPANIA
BLUE ST.
WAA (CHEER)

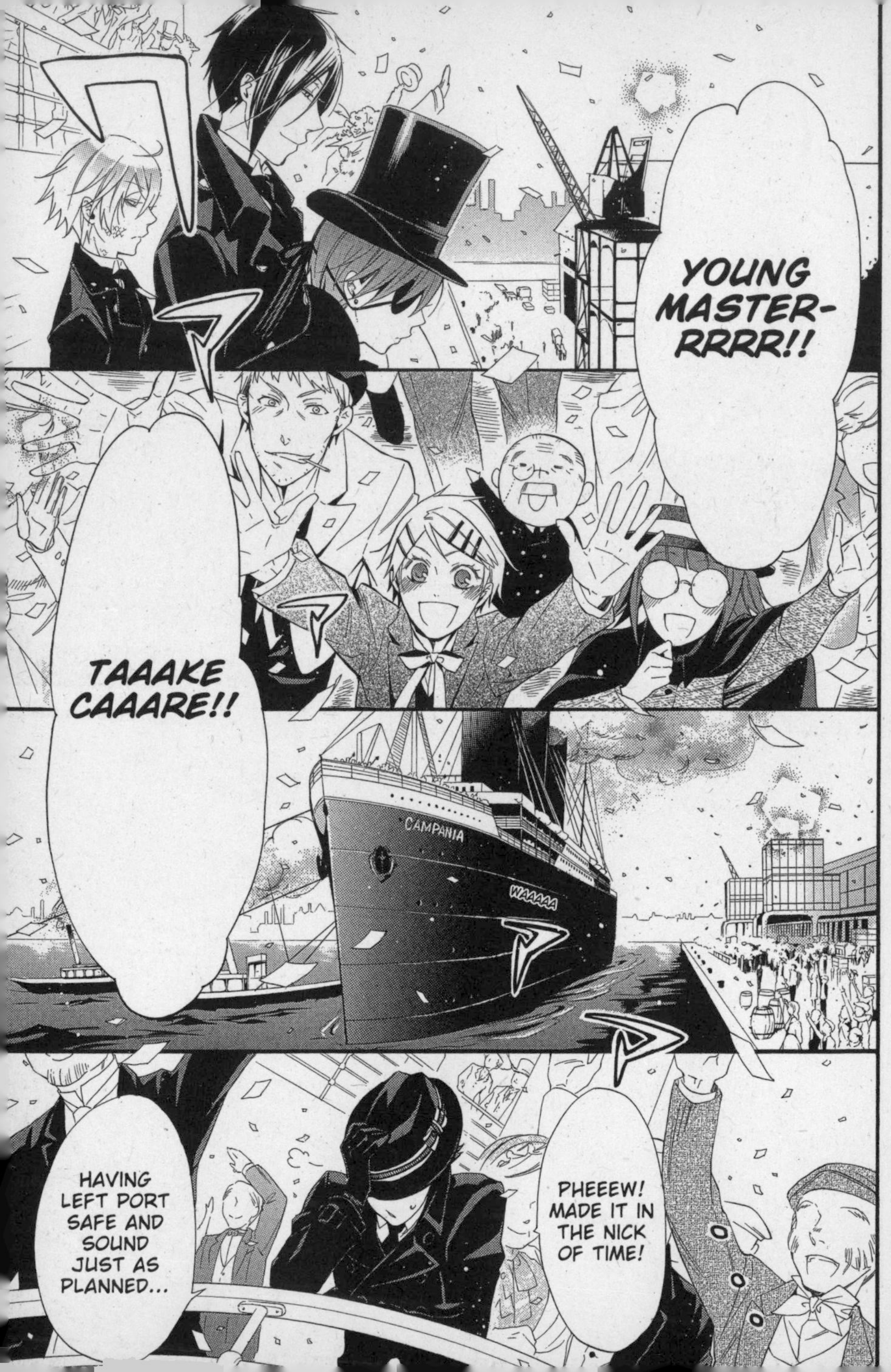
YOUNG MASTER-RRRR!!
TAAAKE CAAARE!!
CAMPANIA
WAAAAA
PHEEEW! MADE IT IN THE NICK OF TIME!
HAVING LEFT PORT SAFE AND SOUND JUST AS PLANNED...

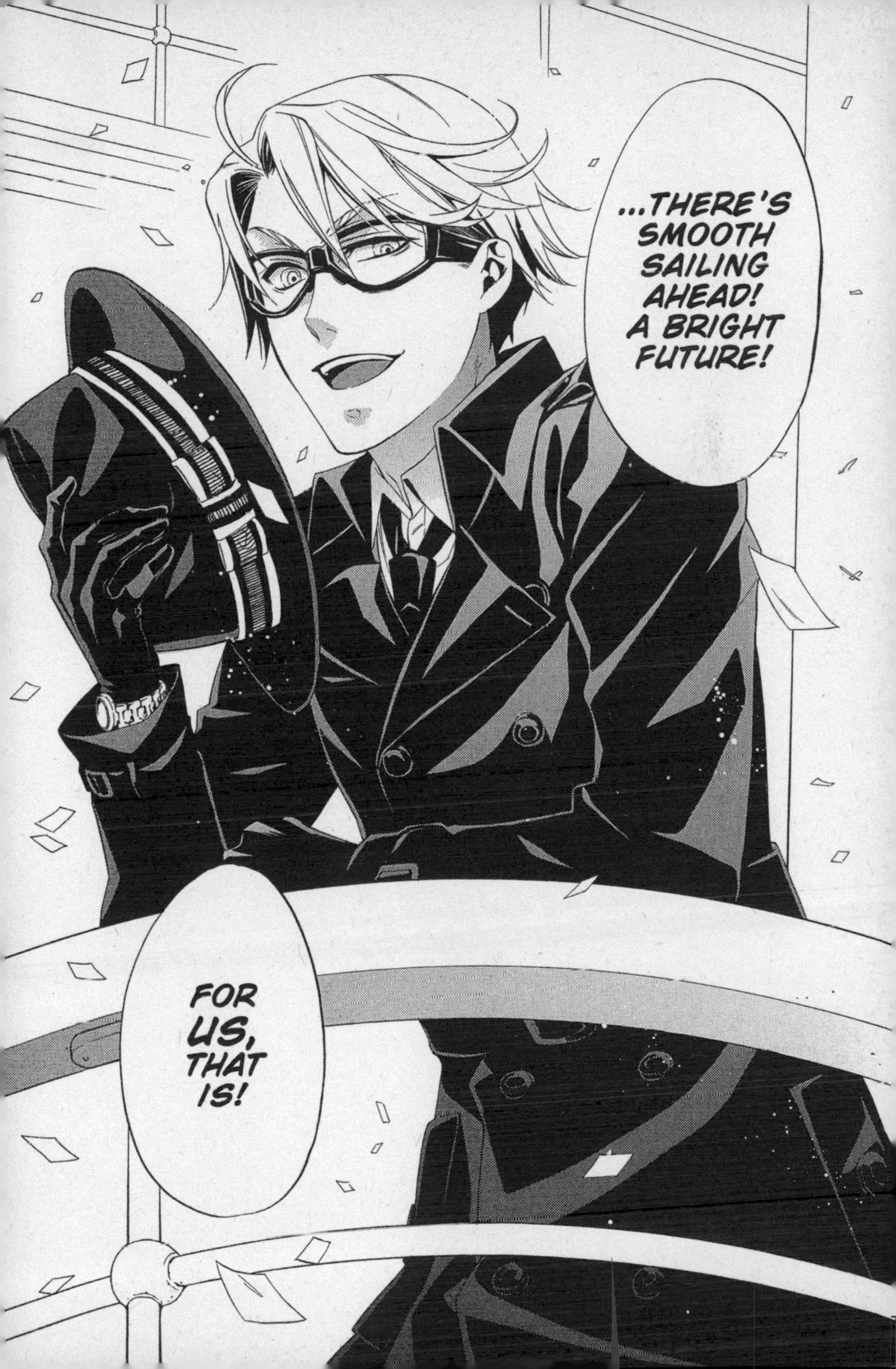
...THERE'S SMOOTH SAILING AHEAD! A BRIGHT FUTURE!
FOR US, THAT IS!

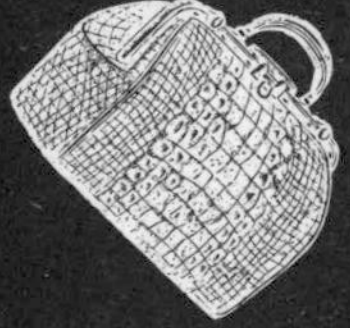

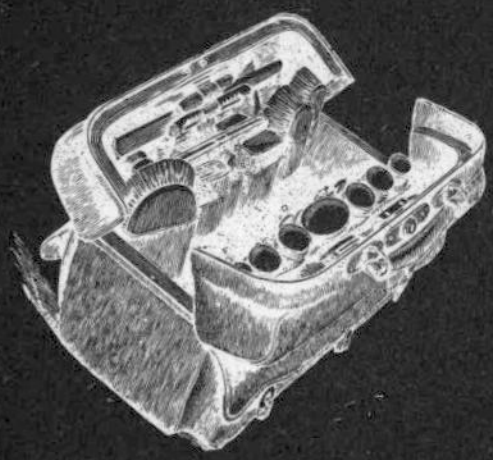

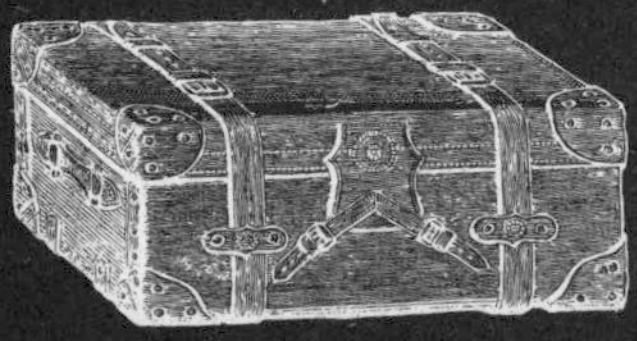

Black Butler

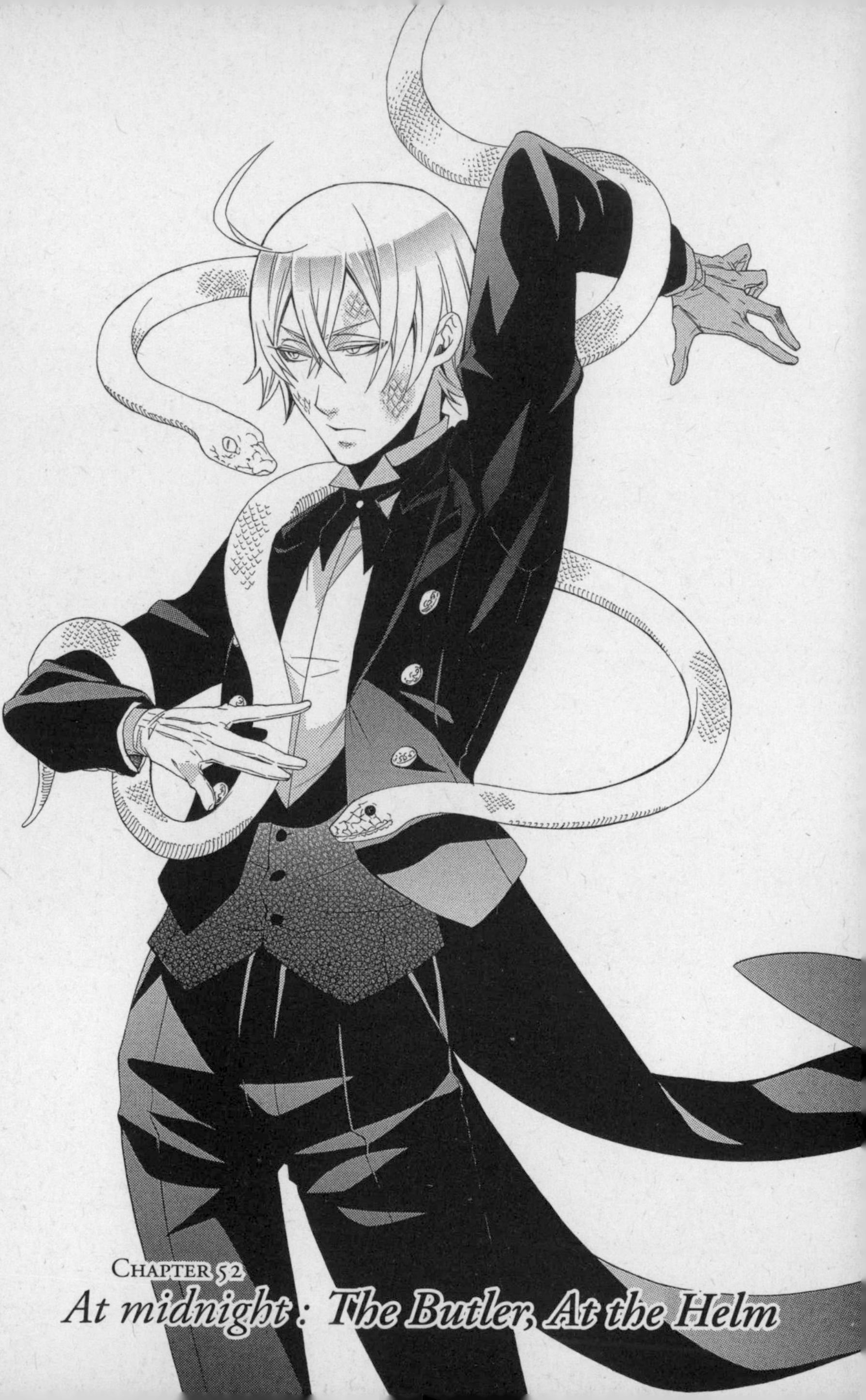

Chapter 52
At midnight : The Butler, At the Helm

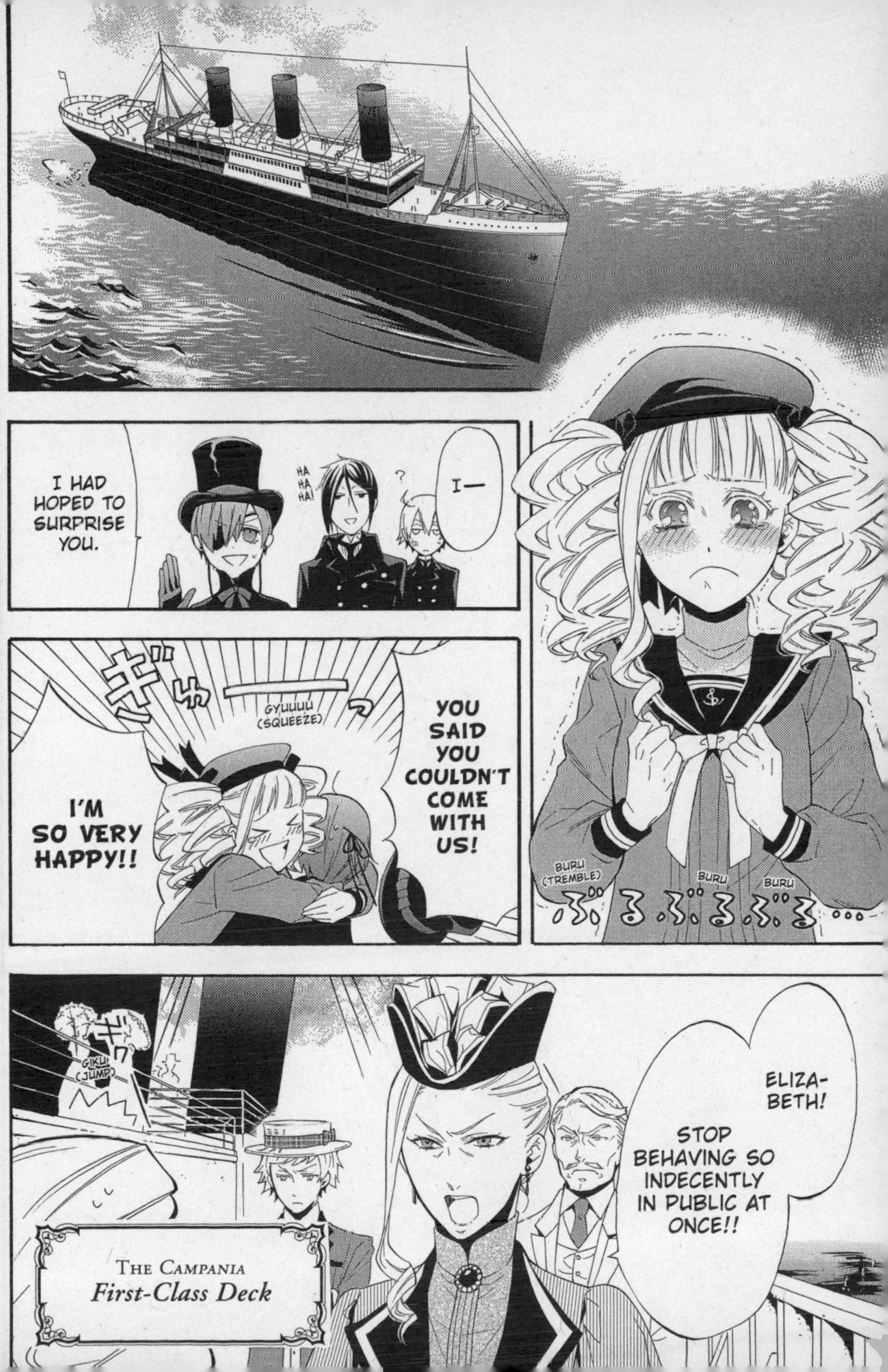
BURU (TREMBLE)
BURU
BURU
I—
?
HA HA HA!
I HAD HOPED TO SURPRISE YOU.
GYUUUU (SQUEEZE)
YOU SAID YOU COULDN'T COME WITH US!
I'M SO VERY HAPPY!!
ELIZA-BETH!
STOP BEHAVING SO INDECENTLY IN PUBLIC AT ONCE!!
GIKU (JUMP)
THE CAMPANIA
First-Class Deck

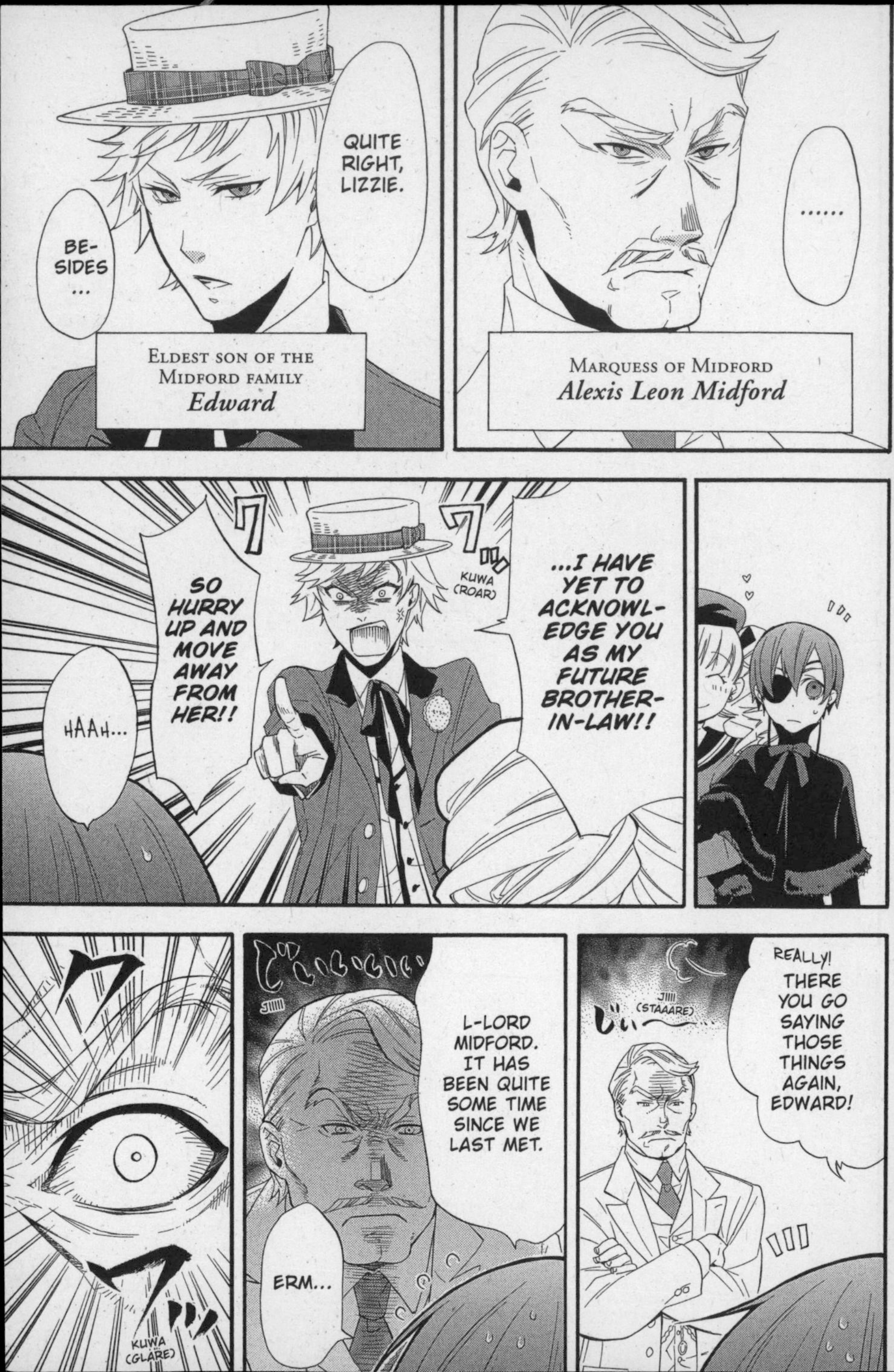
……
Marquess of Midford
Alexis Leon Midford
QUITE RIGHT, LIZZIE.
BE-SIDES ...
Eldest son of the Midford family
Edward
...I HAVE YET TO ACKNOWL-EDGE YOU AS MY FUTURE BROTHER-IN-LAW!!
KUWA (ROAR)
SO HURRY UP AND MOVE AWAY FROM HER!!
HAAH...
REALLY! THERE YOU GO SAYING THOSE THINGS AGAIN, EDWARD!
JIII (STAAARE)
L-LORD MIDFORD. IT HAS BEEN QUITE SOME TIME SINCE WE LAST MET.
ERM...
KUWA (GLARE)

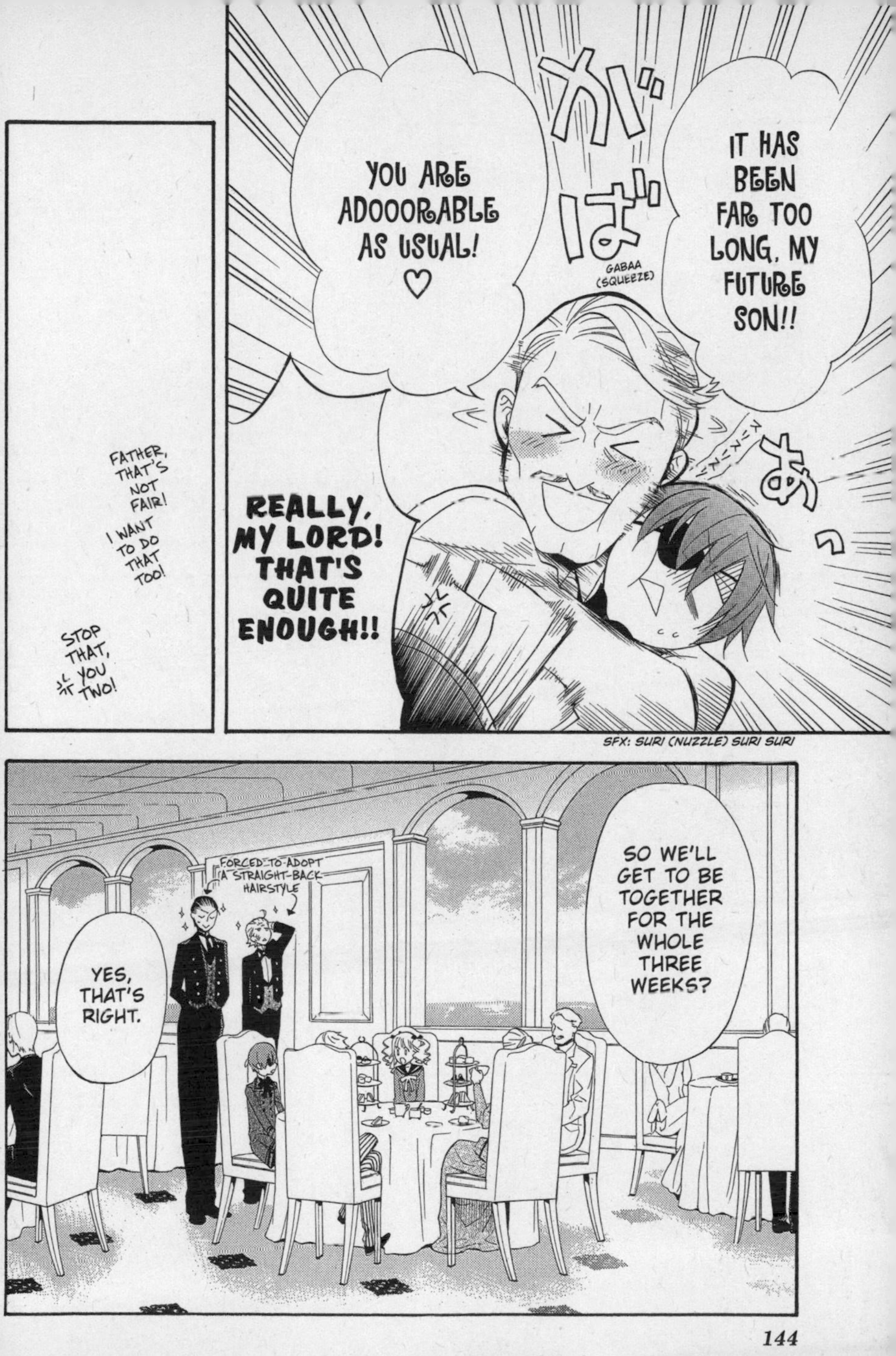

IT HAS BEEN FAR TOO LONG, MY FUTURE SON!!
がば
GABAA (SQUEEZE)
YOU ARE ADOOORABLE AS USUAL! ♡
あっ
REALLY, MY LORD! THAT'S QUITE ENOUGH!!
SFX: SURI (NUZZLE) SURI SURI
FATHER, THAT'S NOT FAIR! I WANT TO DO THAT TOO!
STOP THAT, YOU TWO!
SO WE'LL GET TO BE TOGETHER FOR THE WHOLE THREE WEEKS?
FORCED TO ADOPT A STRAIGHT-BACK HAIRSTYLE
YES, THAT'S RIGHT.

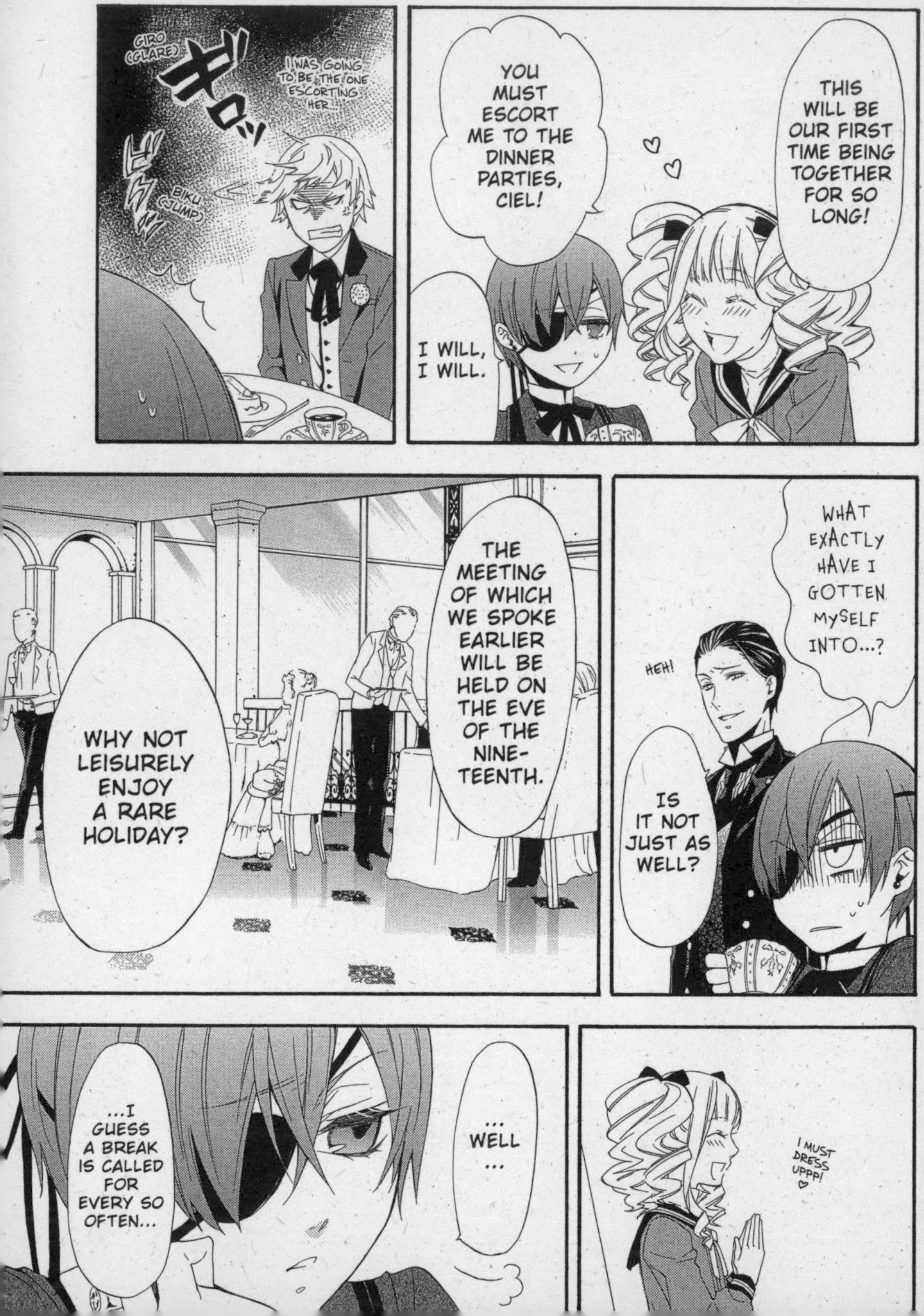
THIS WILL BE OUR FIRST TIME BEING TOGETHER FOR SO LONG!
YOU MUST ESCORT ME TO THE DINNER PARTIES, CIEL!
I WILL, I WILL.
GIRO (GLARE)
ギロッ
I WAS GOING TO BE THE ONE ESCORTING HER...
BIKU (JUMP)
WHAT EXACTLY HAVE I GOTTEN MYSELF INTO...?
HEH!
IS IT NOT JUST AS WELL?
THE MEETING OF WHICH WE SPOKE EARLIER WILL BE HELD ON THE EVE OF THE NINE-TEENTH.
WHY NOT LEISURELY ENJOY A RARE HOLIDAY?
I MUST DRESS UPPP! ♡
... WELL ...
...I GUESS A BREAK IS CALLED FOR EVERY SO OFTEN...

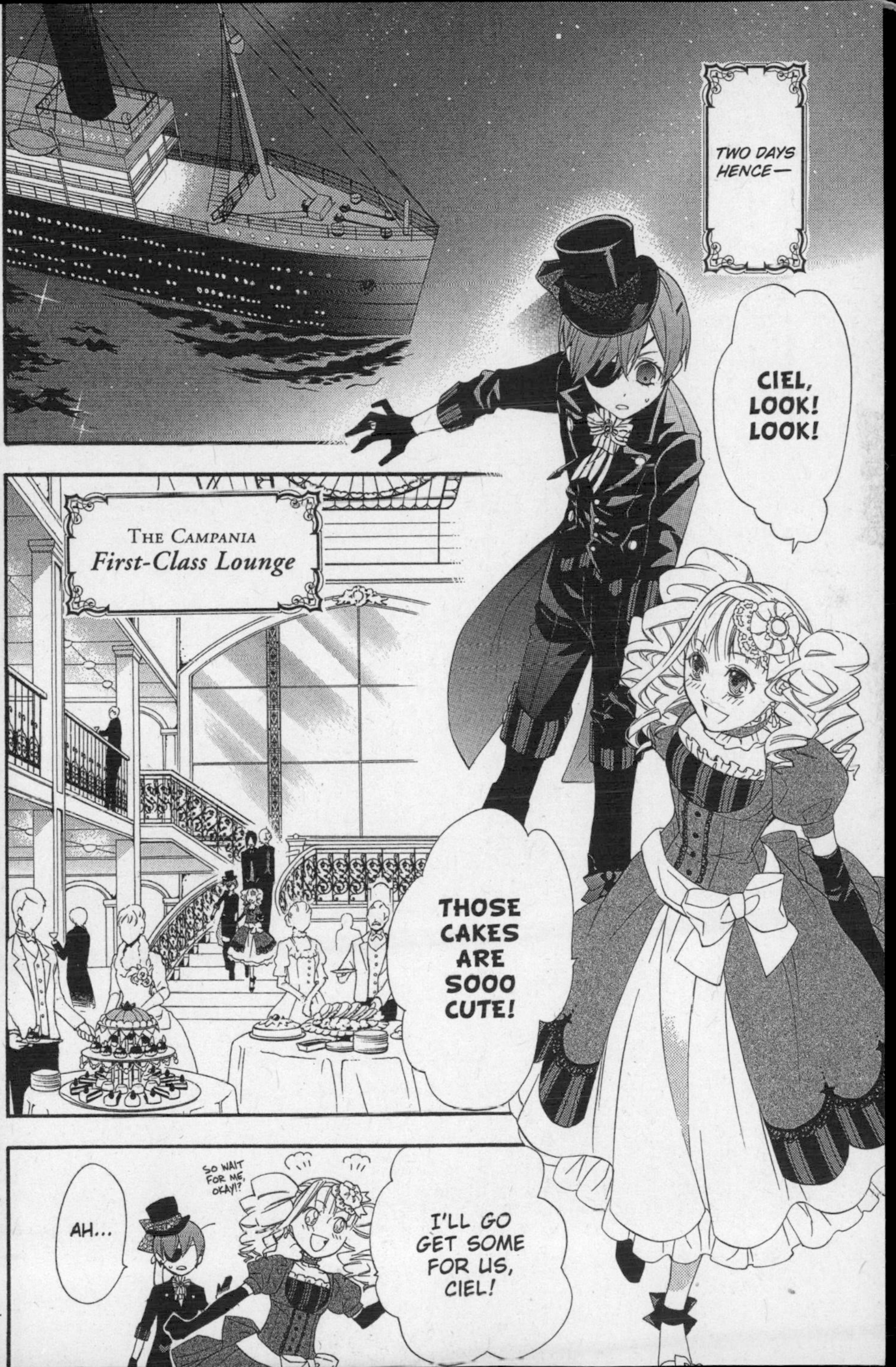
TWO DAYS HENCE—
CIEL, LOOK! LOOK!
THE CAMPANIA
First-Class Lounge
THOSE CAKES ARE SOOO CUTE!
I'LL GO GET SOME FOR US, CIEL!
SO WAIT FOR ME, OKAY!?
AH...

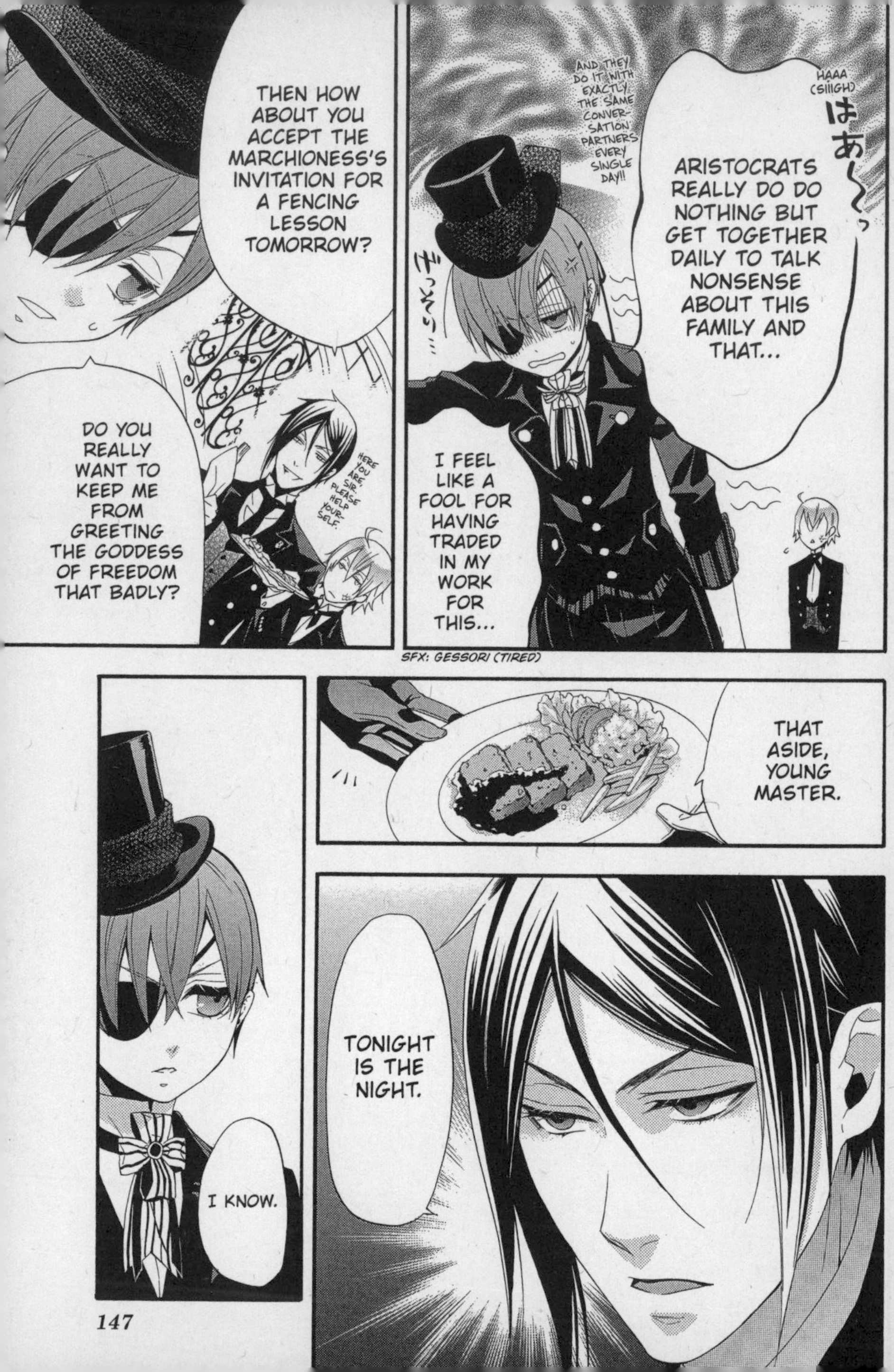
HAAA (SIIIGH)
はあ〜っ
AND THEY DO IT WITH EXACTLY THE SAME CONVERSATION PARTNERS EVERY SINGLE DAY!!
ARISTOCRATS REALLY DO DO NOTHING BUT GET TOGETHER DAILY TO TALK NONSENSE ABOUT THIS FAMILY AND THAT...
げっそり…
I FEEL LIKE A FOOL FOR HAVING TRADED IN MY WORK FOR THIS...
SFX: GESSORI (TIRED)
THEN HOW ABOUT YOU ACCEPT THE MARCHIONESS'S INVITATION FOR A FENCING LESSON TOMORROW?
HERE YOU ARE, SIR, PLEASE HELP YOURSELF.
DO YOU REALLY WANT TO KEEP ME FROM GREETING THE GODDESS OF FREEDOM THAT BADLY?
THAT ASIDE, YOUNG MASTER.
TONIGHT IS THE NIGHT.
I KNOW.

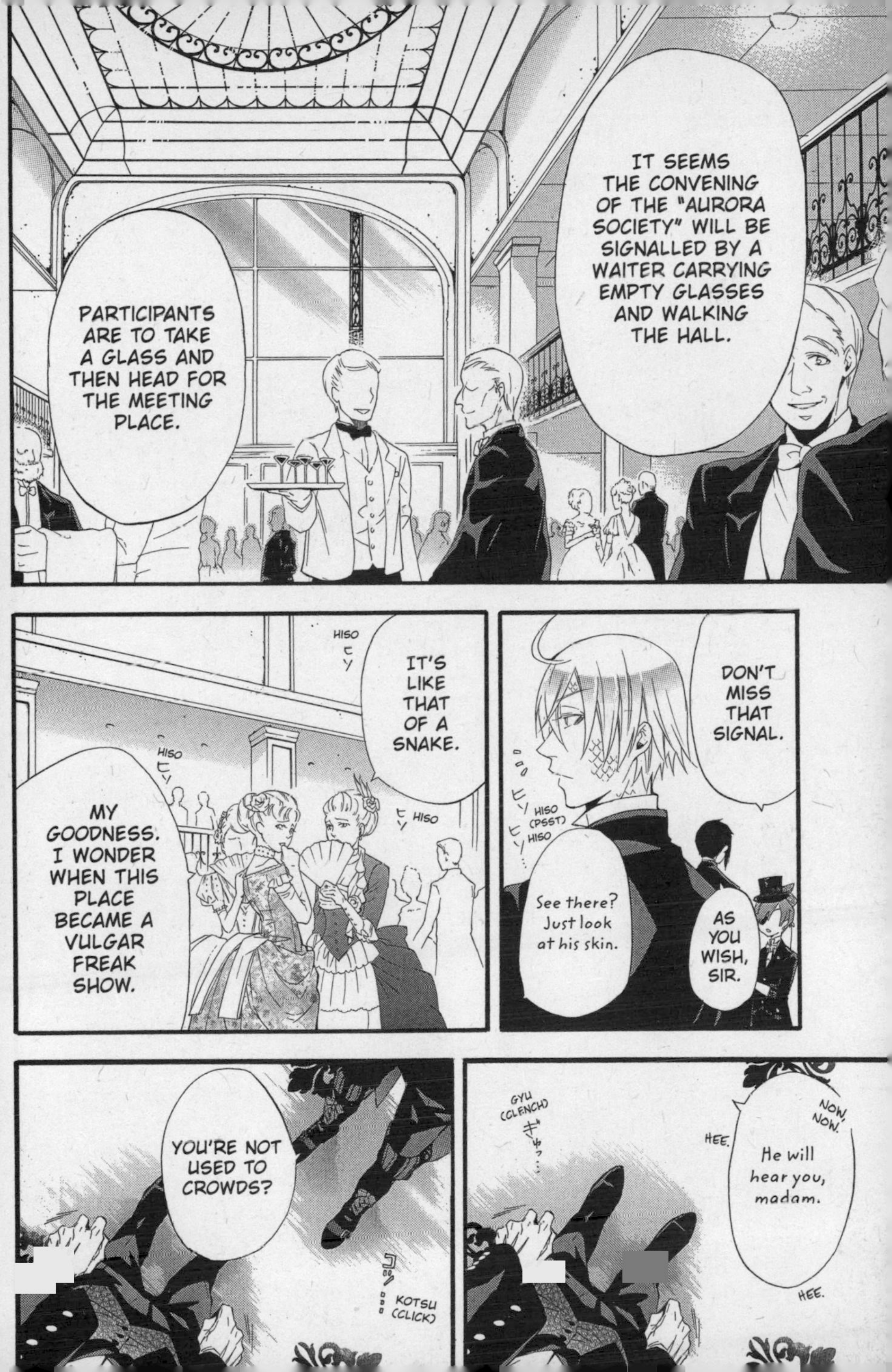
IT SEEMS THE CONVENING OF THE "AURORA SOCIETY" WILL BE SIGNALLED BY A WAITER CARRYING EMPTY GLASSES AND WALKING THE HALL.
PARTICIPANTS ARE TO TAKE A GLASS AND THEN HEAD FOR THE MEETING PLACE.
DON'T MISS THAT SIGNAL.
HISO (PSST) HISO
AS YOU WISH, SIR.
See there? Just look at his skin.
HISO
IT'S LIKE THAT OF A SNAKE.
HISO
HISO
MY GOODNESS. I WONDER WHEN THIS PLACE BECAME A VULGAR FREAK SHOW.
NOW, NOW.
HEE.
He will hear you, madam.
GYU (CLENCH)
HEE.
YOU'RE NOT USED TO CROWDS?
KOTSU (CLICK)

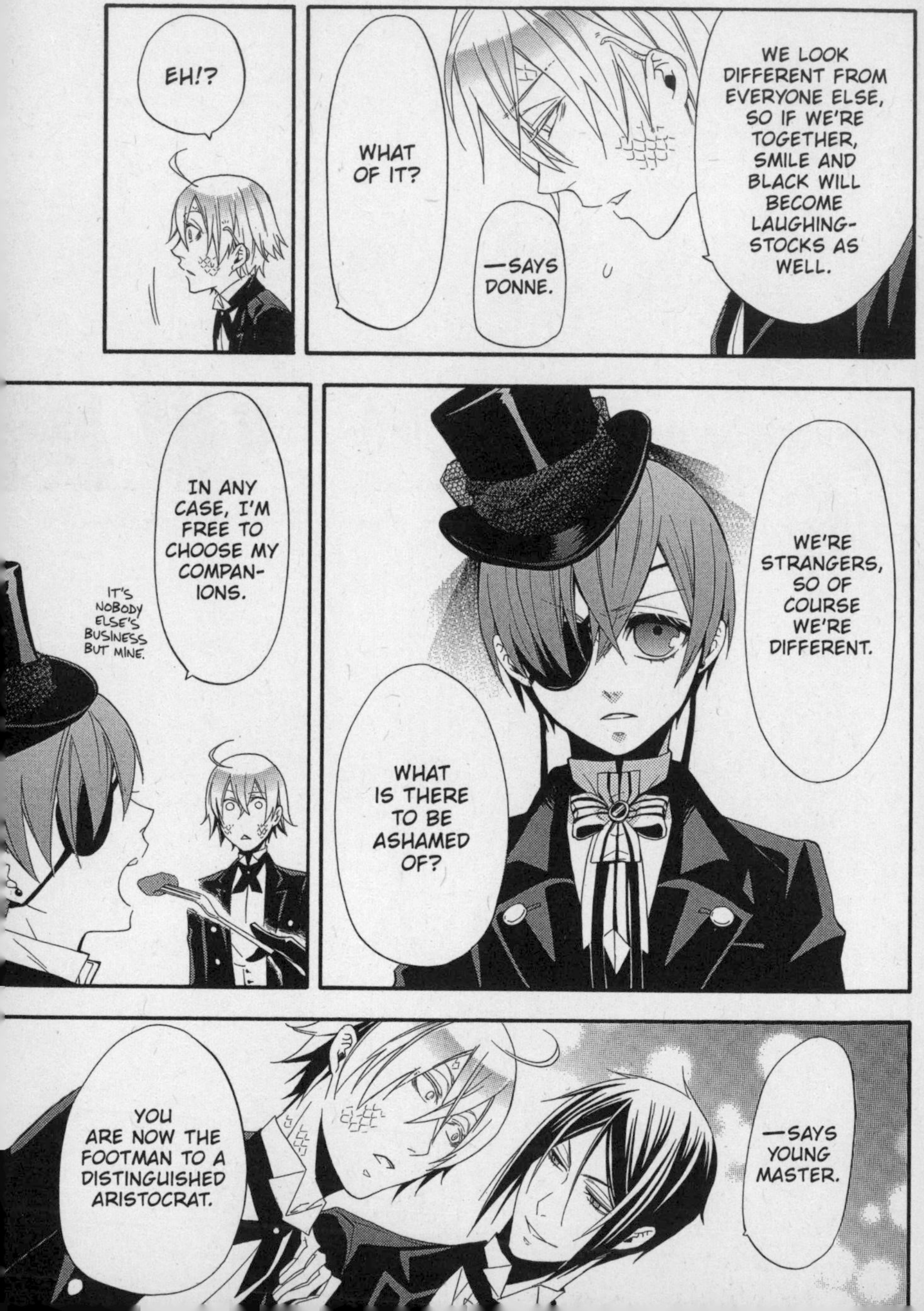
WE LOOK DIFFERENT FROM EVERYONE ELSE, SO IF WE'RE TOGETHER, SMILE AND BLACK WILL BECOME LAUGHING-STOCKS AS WELL.
—SAYS DONNE.
WHAT OF IT?
EH!?
WE'RE STRANGERS, SO OF COURSE WE'RE DIFFERENT.
WHAT IS THERE TO BE ASHAMED OF?
IN ANY CASE, I'M FREE TO CHOOSE MY COMPAN-IONS.
IT'S NOBODY ELSE'S BUSINESS BUT MINE.
—SAYS YOUNG MASTER.
YOU ARE NOW THE FOOTMAN TO A DISTINGUISHED ARISTOCRAT.

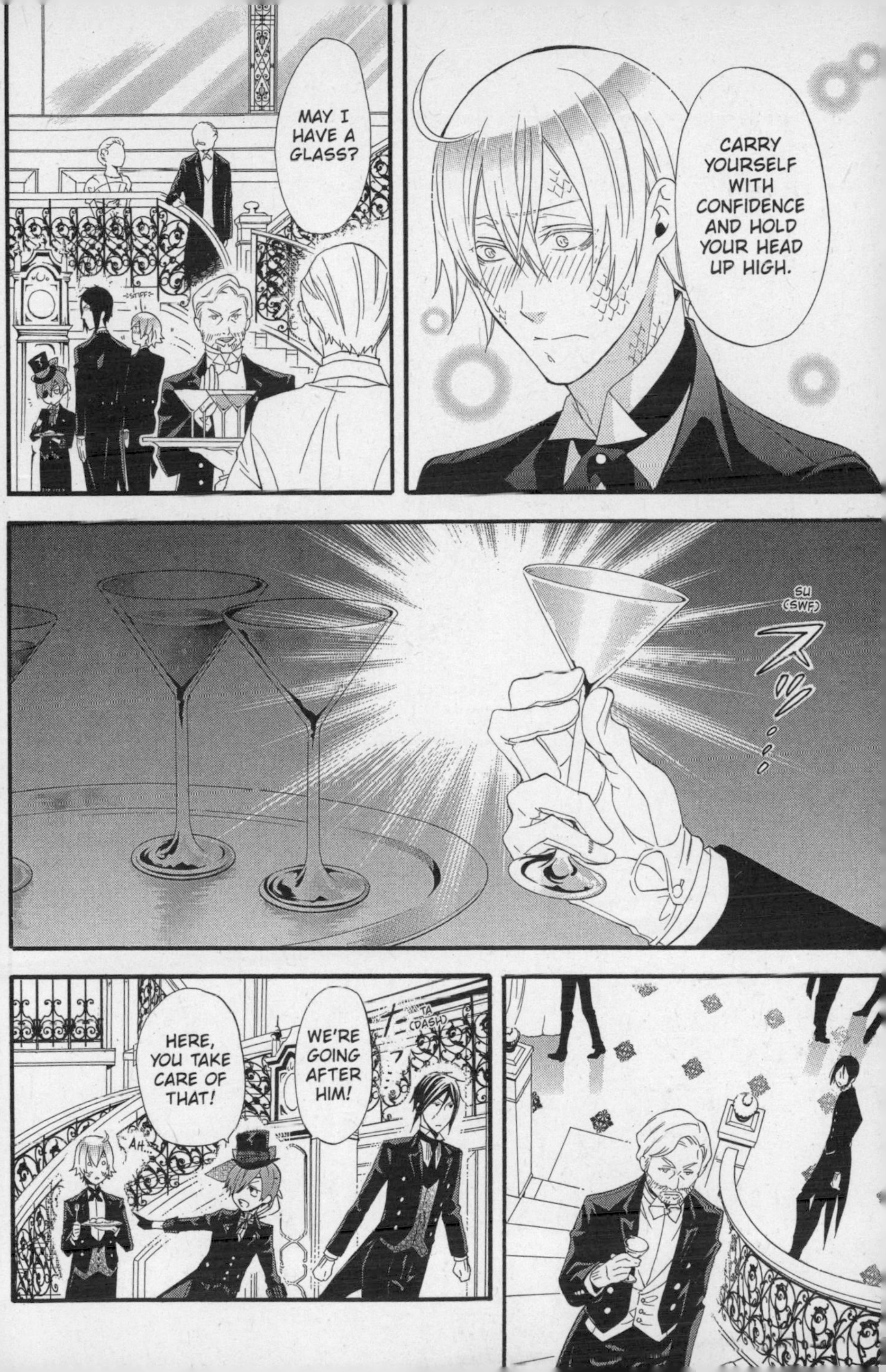
CARRY YOURSELF WITH CONFIDENCE AND HOLD YOUR HEAD UP HIGH.
MAY I HAVE A GLASS?
STIFF
SU (SWF)
TA (DASH)
WE'RE GOING AFTER HIM!
HERE, YOU TAKE CARE OF THAT!
AH...

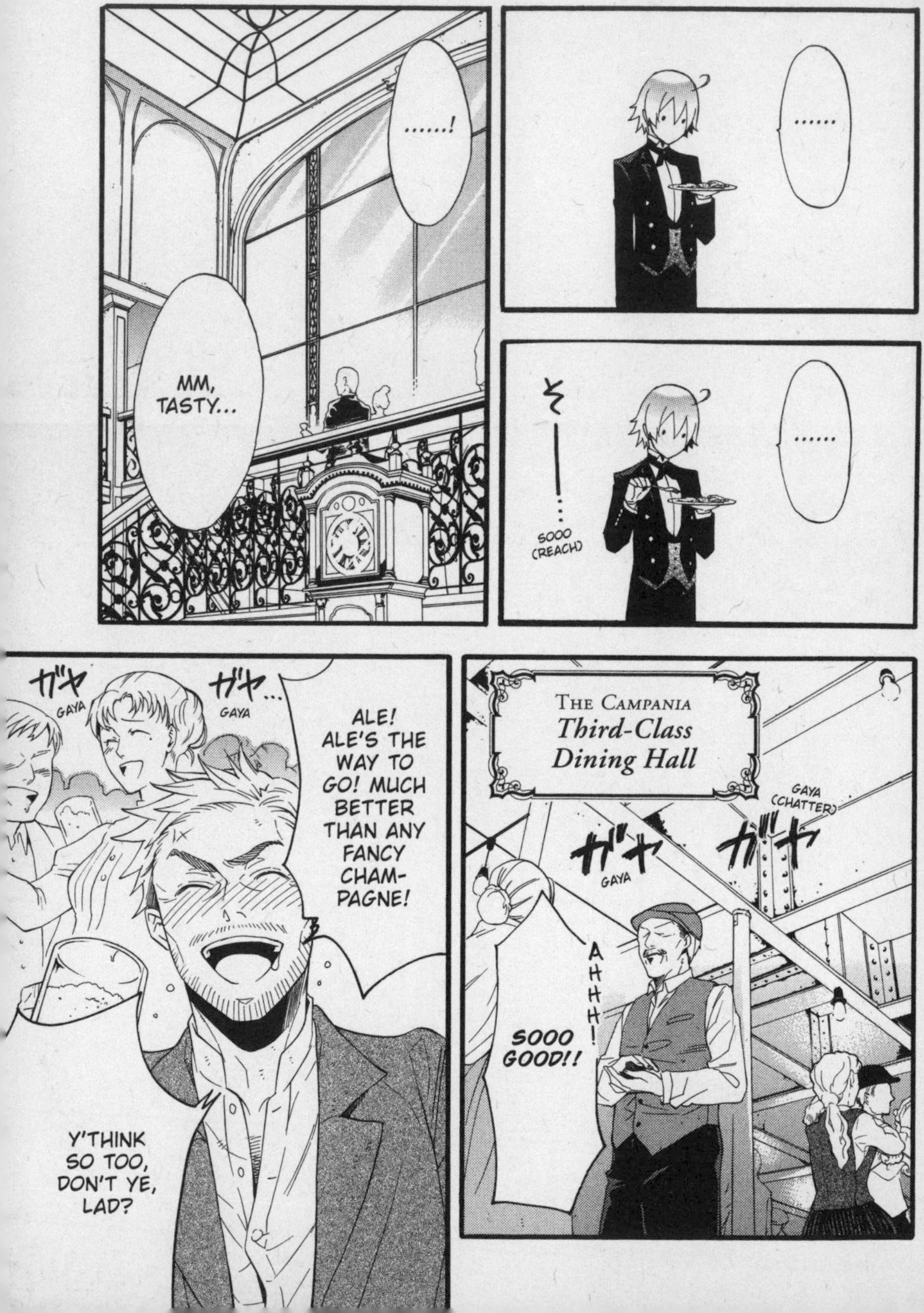

......
そ〜
SOOO (REACH)
......
......!
MM, TASTY...
THE CAMPANIA Third-Class Dining Hall
ガヤ
GAYA (CHATTER)
ガヤ
GAYA
AHHH!
SOOO GOOD!!
ガヤ
GAYA
ガヤ...
GAYA
ALE! ALE'S THE WAY TO GO! MUCH BETTER THAN ANY FANCY CHAM-PAGNE!
Y'THINK SO TOO, DON'T YE, LAD?

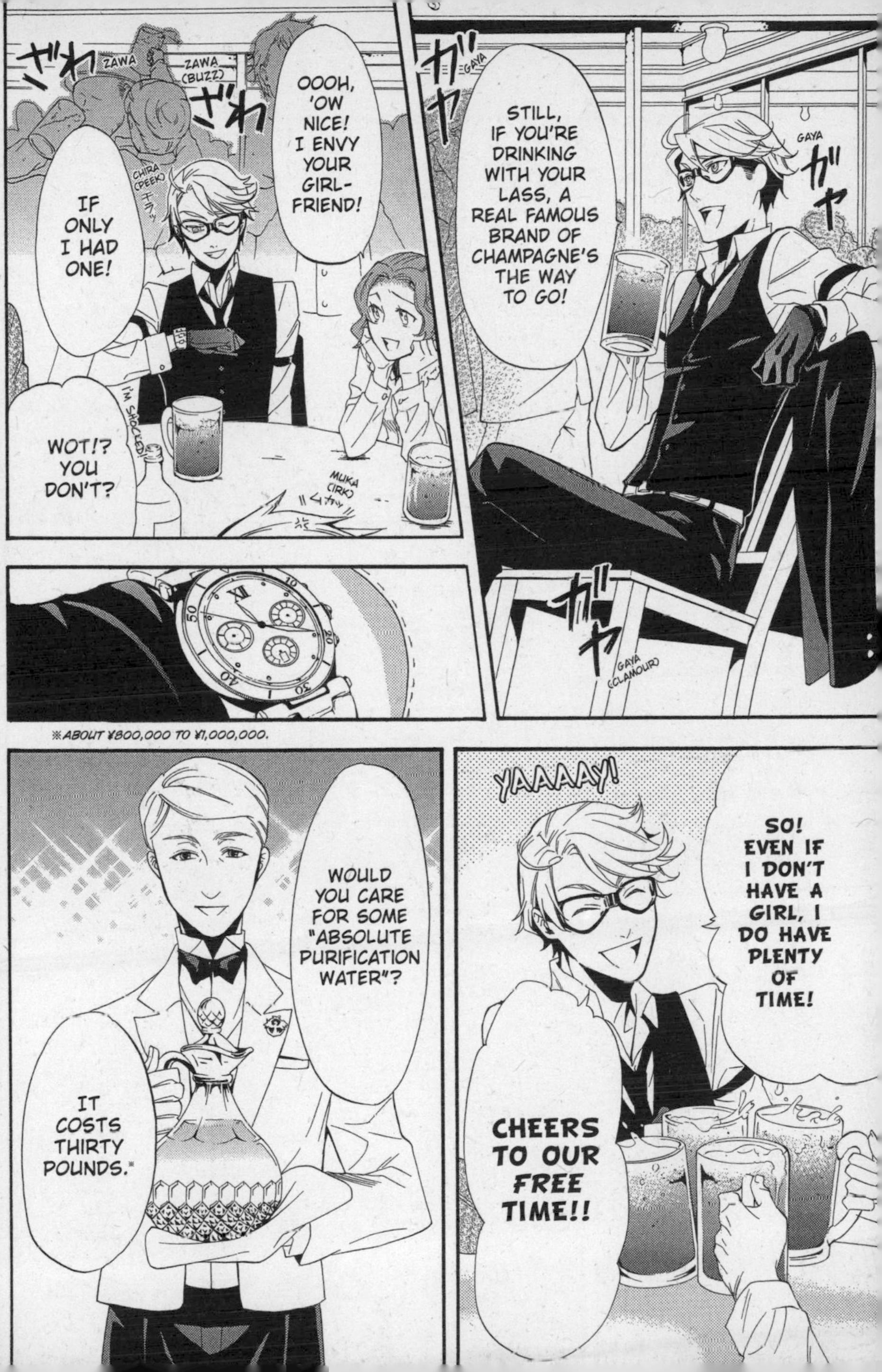
ガヤ GAYA
STILL, IF YOU'RE DRINKING WITH YOUR LASS, A REAL FAMOUS BRAND OF CHAMPAGNE'S THE WAY TO GO!
GAYA ガヤ
ガヤ GAYA (CLAMOUR)
ZAWA (BUZZ) ざわ
OOOH, 'OW NICE! I ENVY YOUR GIRL-FRIEND!
ざわ ZAWA
CHIRA (PEEK) チラッ
IF ONLY I HAD ONE!
MUKA (IRK) ムカッ
I'M SHOCKED
WOT!? YOU DON'T?
YAAAAY!
SO! EVEN IF I DON'T HAVE A GIRL, I DO HAVE PLENTY OF TIME!
CHEERS TO OUR FREE TIME!!
WOULD YOU CARE FOR SOME "ABSOLUTE PURIFICATION WATER"?
IT COSTS THIRTY POUNDS.*

※ABOUT ¥800,000 TO ¥1,000,000.

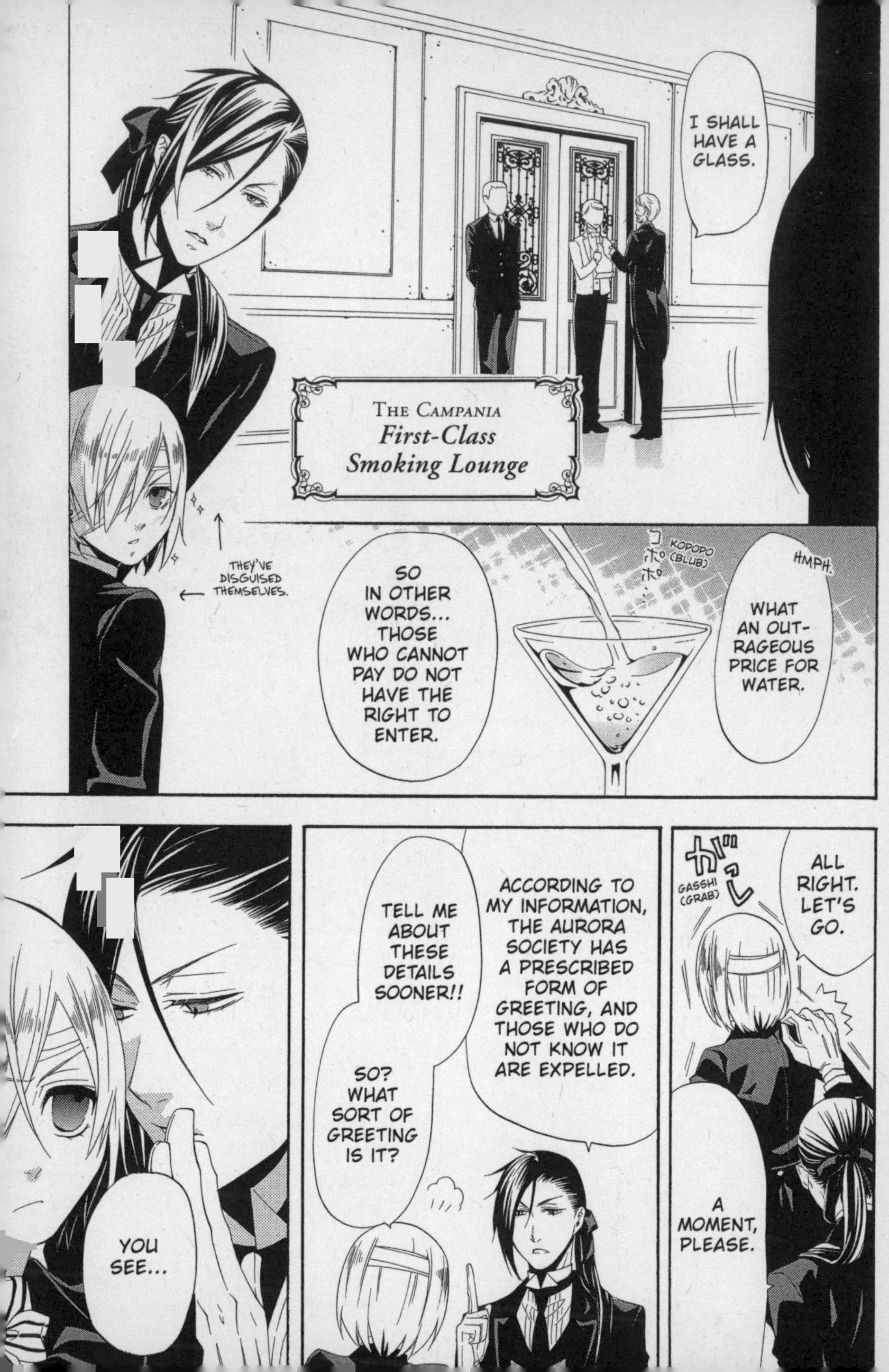
THE CAMPANIA
First-Class Smoking Lounge
I SHALL HAVE A GLASS.
HMPH.
WHAT AN OUT-RAGEOUS PRICE FOR WATER.
コポポ
KOPOPO (BLUB)
SO IN OTHER WORDS... THOSE WHO CANNOT PAY DO NOT HAVE THE RIGHT TO ENTER.
THEY'VE DISGUISED THEMSELVES.
がっし
GASSHI (GRAB)
ALL RIGHT. LET'S GO.
A MOMENT, PLEASE.
ACCORDING TO MY INFORMATION, THE AURORA SOCIETY HAS A PRESCRIBED FORM OF GREETING, AND THOSE WHO DO NOT KNOW IT ARE EXPELLED.
TELL ME ABOUT THESE DETAILS SOONER!!
SO? WHAT SORT OF GREETING IS IT?
YOU SEE...

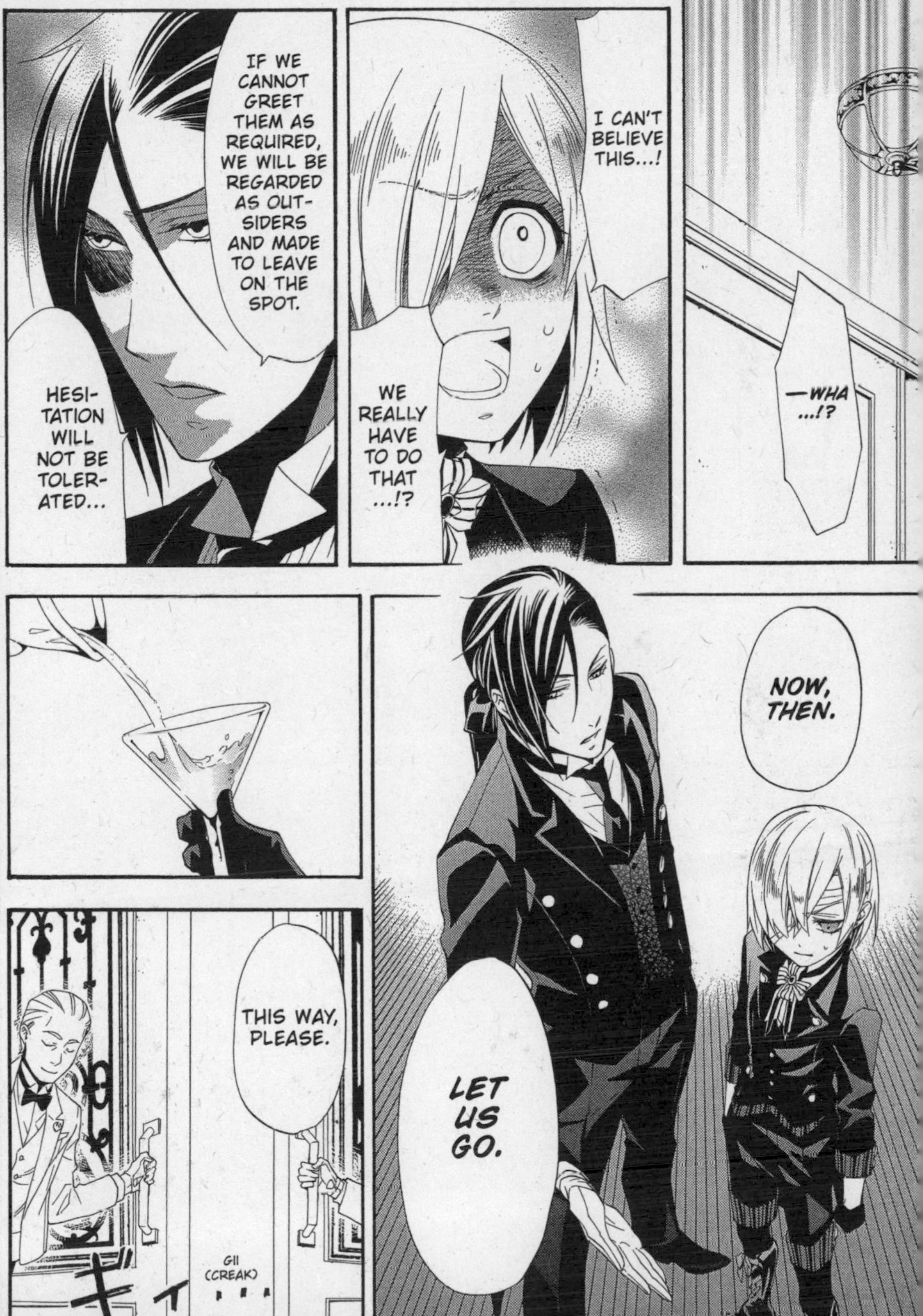
—WHA ...!?
I CAN'T BELIEVE THIS...!
WE REALLY HAVE TO DO THAT ...!?
IF WE CANNOT GREET THEM AS REQUIRED, WE WILL BE REGARDED AS OUTSIDERS AND MADE TO LEAVE ON THE SPOT.
HESITATION WILL NOT BE TOLERATED...
NOW, THEN.
LET US GO.
THIS WAY, PLEASE.
GII (CREAK)

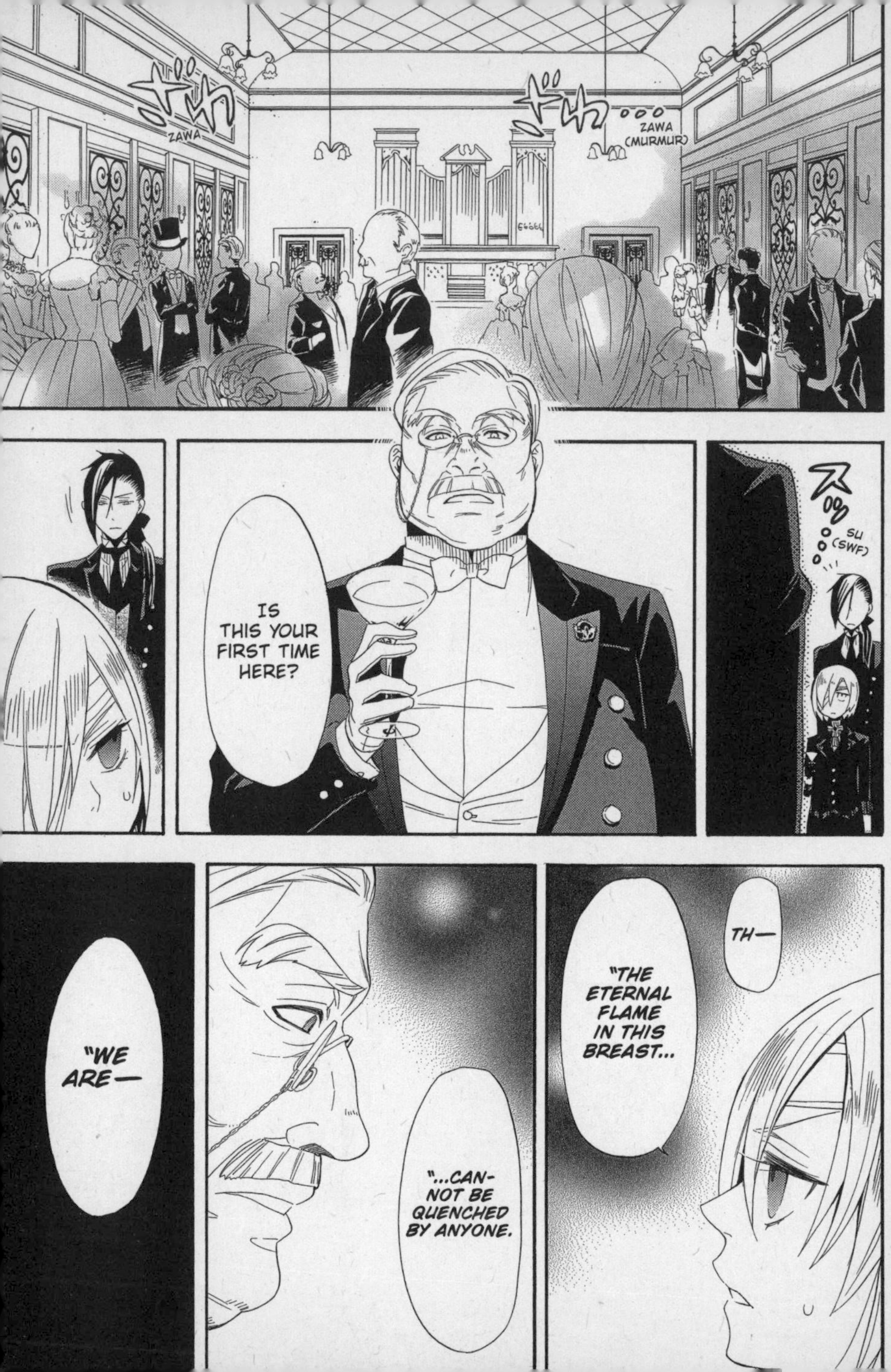
ZAWA (MURMUR)
ZAWA
SU (SWF)
IS THIS YOUR FIRST TIME HERE?
TH—
"THE ETERNAL FLAME IN THIS BREAST...
"...CAN-NOT BE QUENCHED BY ANYONE.
"WE ARE—

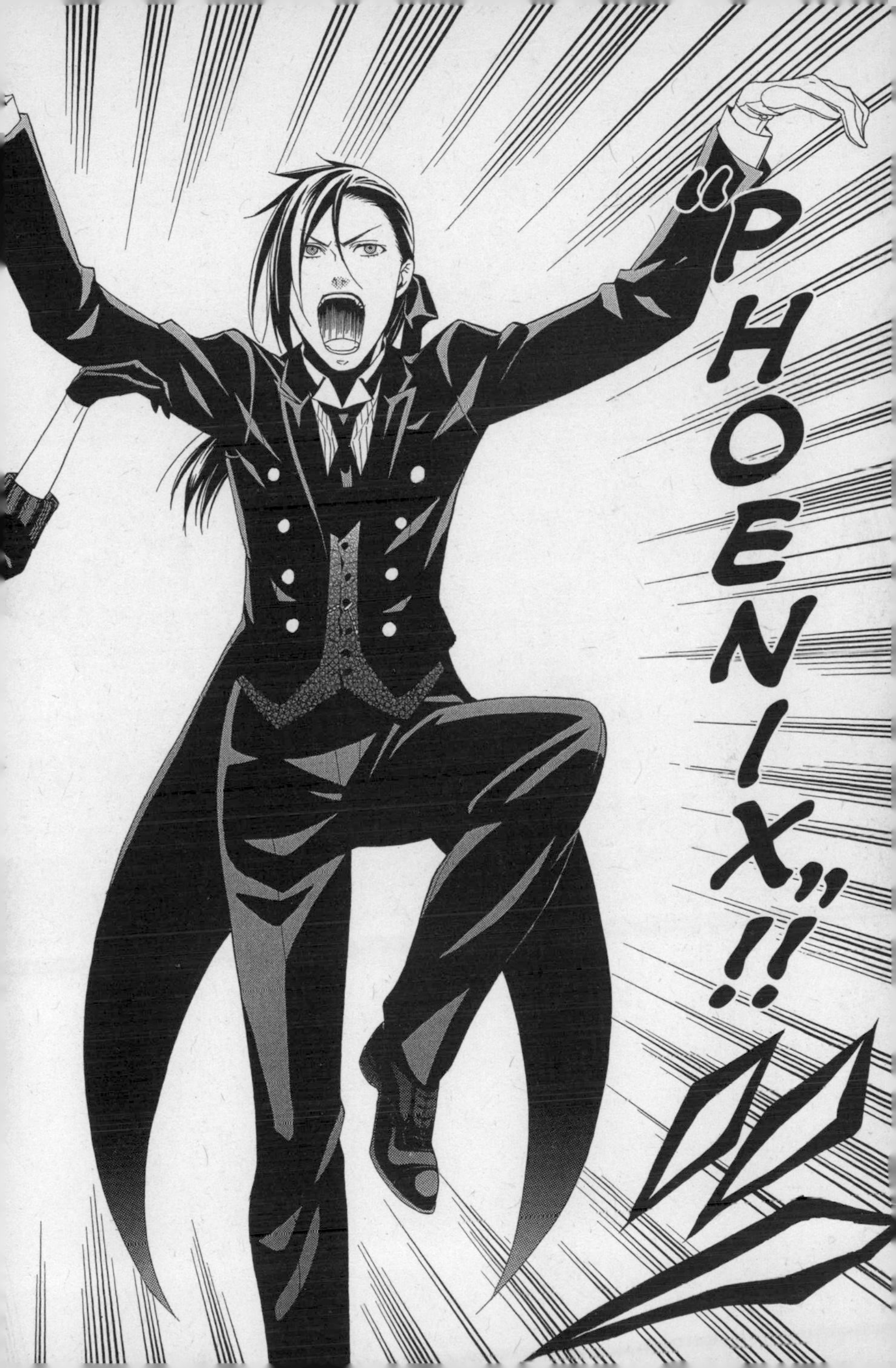
"PHOENIX"!!

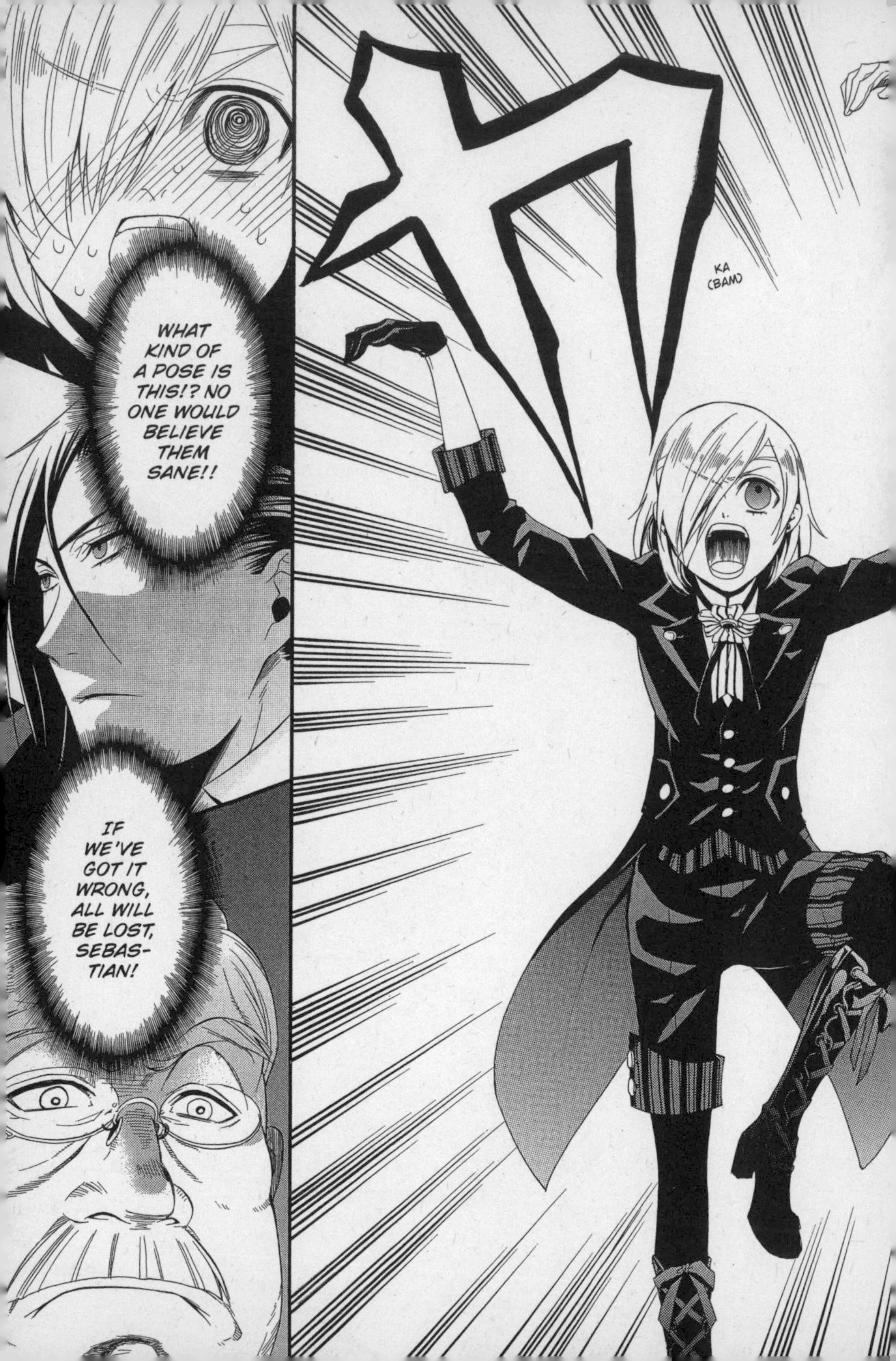
KA
(BAM)
WHAT KIND OF A POSE IS THIS!? NO ONE WOULD BELIEVE THEM SANE!!
IF WE'VE GOT IT WRONG, ALL WILL BE LOST, SEBAS-TIAN!

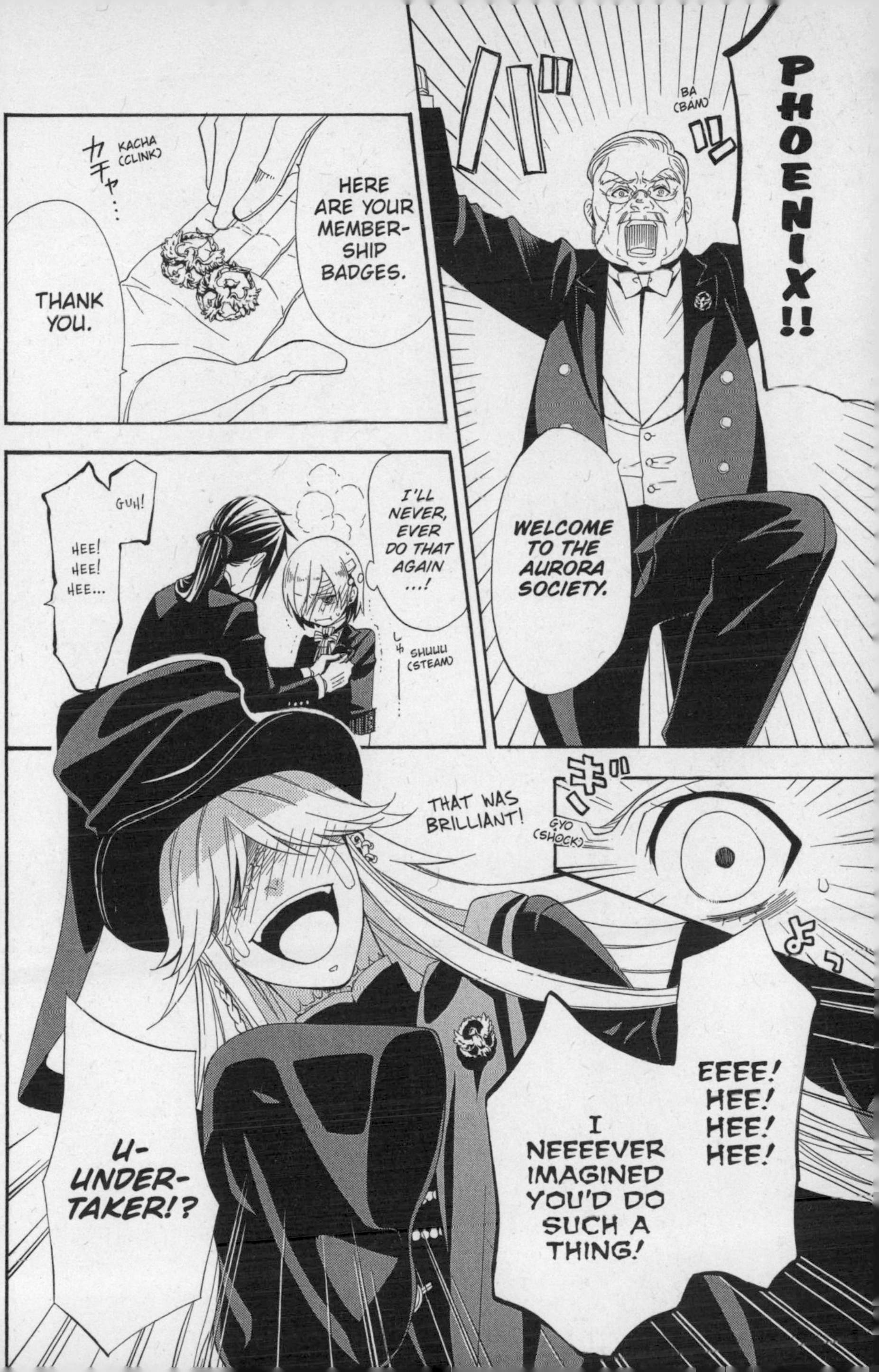
BA (BAM)
PHOENIX!!
WELCOME TO THE AURORA SOCIETY.
カチャ…
KACHA (CLINK)
HERE ARE YOUR MEMBER-SHIP BADGES.
THANK YOU.
I'LL NEVER, EVER DO THAT AGAIN …!
GUH!
HEE! HEE! HEE…
SHUUU (STEAM)
GYO (SHOCK)
THAT WAS BRILLIANT!
EEEE! HEE! HEE! HEE!
I NEEEEVER IMAGINED YOU'D DO SUCH A THING!
U-UNDER-TAKER!?

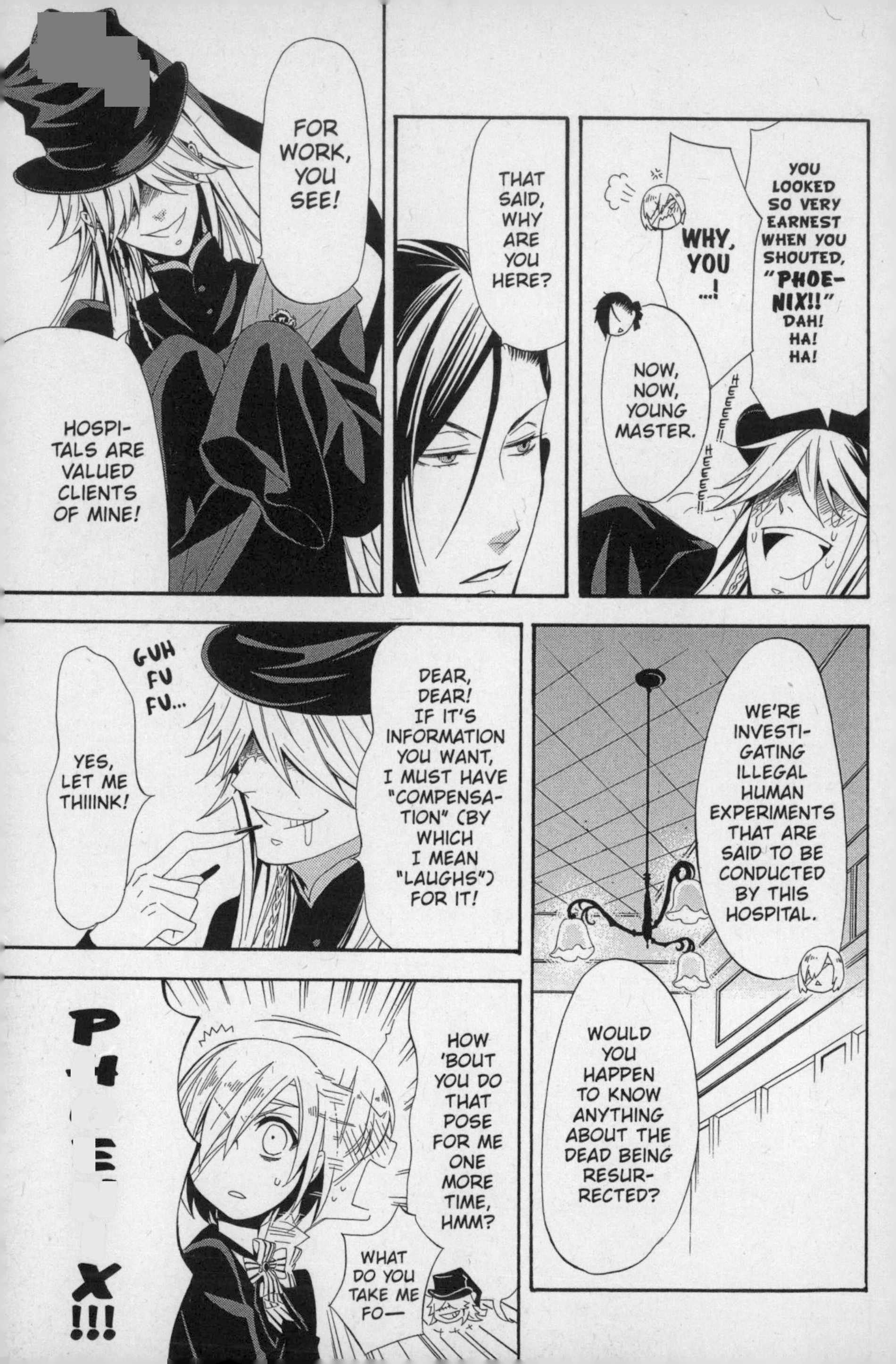

YOU LOOKED SO VERY EARNEST WHEN YOU SHOUTED, "PHOENIX!!" DAH! HA! HA!
WHY, YOU ...!
HEEEE!! HEEEE!!
NOW, NOW, YOUNG MASTER.
THAT SAID, WHY ARE YOU HERE?
FOR WORK, YOU SEE!
HOSPITALS ARE VALUED CLIENTS OF MINE!
WE'RE INVESTIGATING ILLEGAL HUMAN EXPERIMENTS THAT ARE SAID TO BE CONDUCTED BY THIS HOSPITAL.
WOULD YOU HAPPEN TO KNOW ANYTHING ABOUT THE DEAD BEING RESURRECTED?
DEAR, DEAR! IF IT'S INFORMATION YOU WANT, I MUST HAVE "COMPENSATION" (BY WHICH I MEAN "LAUGHS") FOR IT!
GUH FU FU...
YES, LET ME THIIINK!
HOW 'BOUT YOU DO THAT POSE FOR ME ONE MORE TIME, HMM?
WHAT DO YOU TAKE ME FO—
P
X!!!

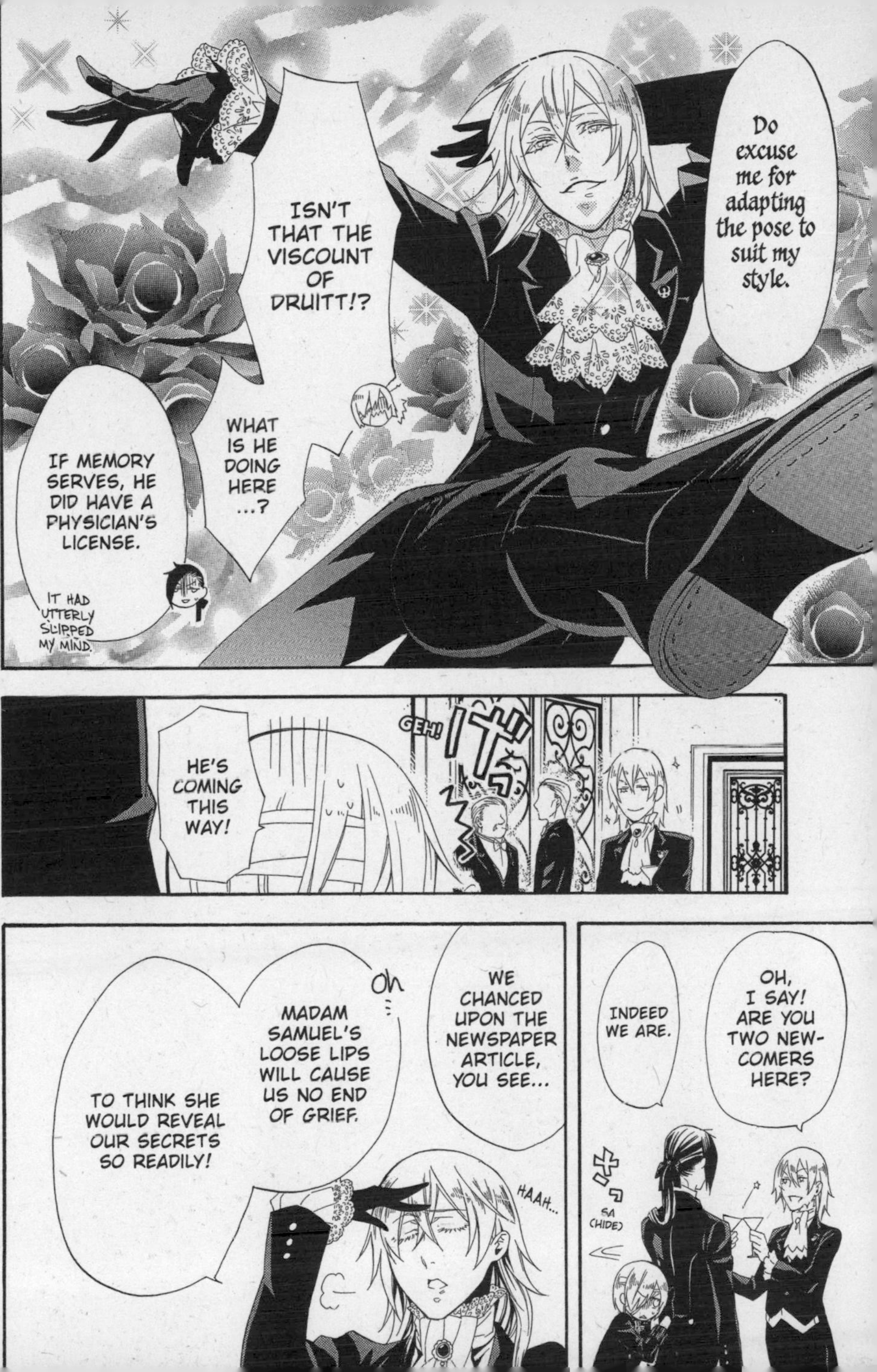
Do excuse me for adapting the pose to suit my style.
ISN'T THAT THE VISCOUNT OF DRUITT!?
WHAT IS HE DOING HERE ...?
IF MEMORY SERVES, HE DID HAVE A PHYSICIAN'S LICENSE.
IT HAD UTTERLY SLIPPED MY MIND.
GEH!
HE'S COMING THIS WAY!
OH, I SAY! ARE YOU TWO NEW-COMERS HERE?
INDEED WE ARE.
SA (HIDE)
WE CHANCED UPON THE NEWSPAPER ARTICLE, YOU SEE...
Oh
MADAM SAMUEL'S LOOSE LIPS WILL CAUSE US NO END OF GRIEF.
HAAH...
TO THINK SHE WOULD REVEAL OUR SECRETS SO READILY!

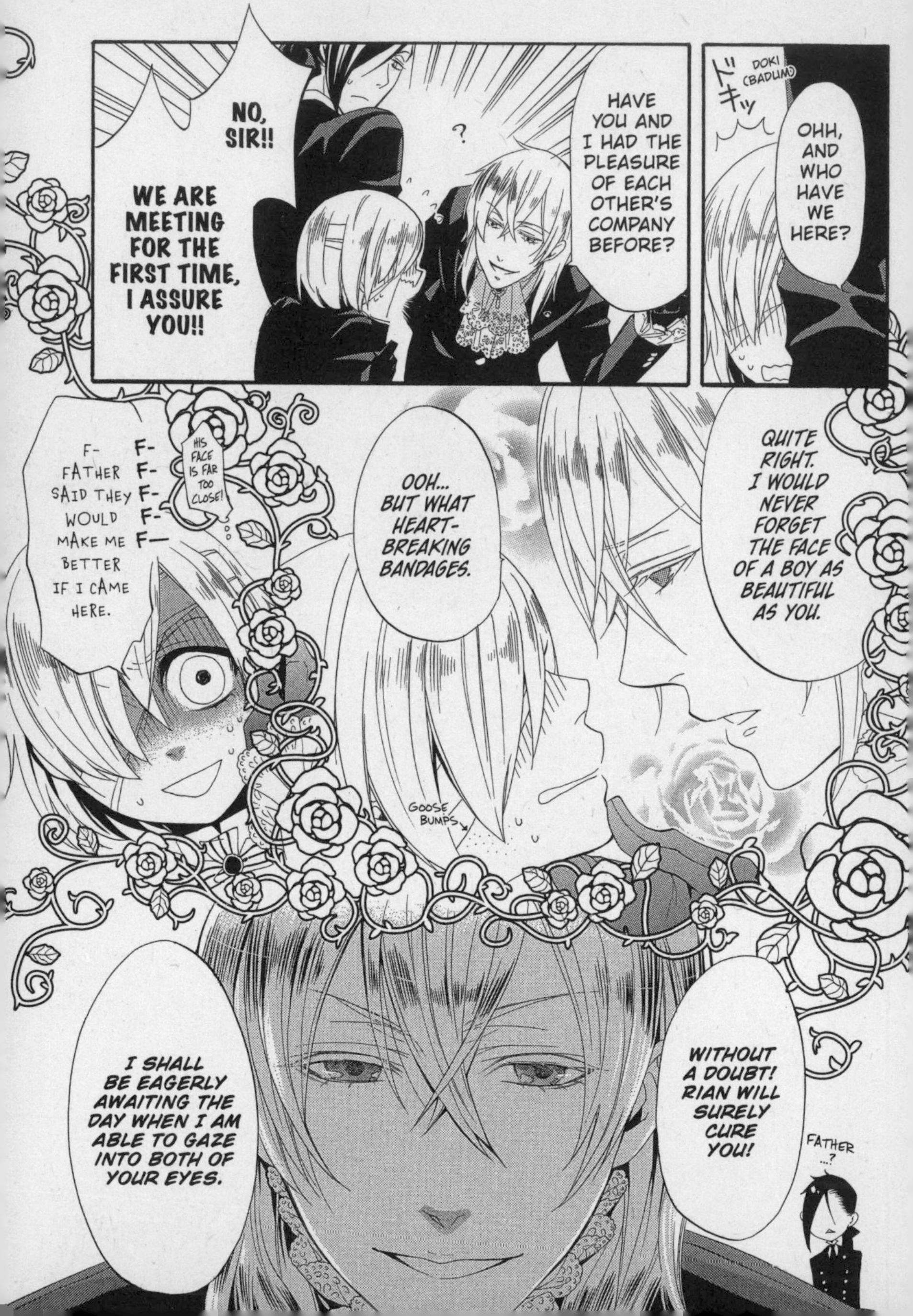
ドキッ
DOKI (BADUM)
OHH, AND WHO HAVE WE HERE?
HAVE YOU AND I HAD THE PLEASURE OF EACH OTHER'S COMPANY BEFORE?
?
NO, SIR!!
WE ARE MEETING FOR THE FIRST TIME, I ASSURE YOU!!
QUITE RIGHT. I WOULD NEVER FORGET THE FACE OF A BOY AS BEAUTIFUL AS YOU.
OOH... BUT WHAT HEART-BREAKING BANDAGES.
GOOSE BUMPS
HIS FACE IS FAR TOO CLOSE!
F- F- F- F- F—
F- FATHER SAID THEY WOULD MAKE ME BETTER IF I CAME HERE.
WITHOUT A DOUBT! RIAN WILL SURELY CURE YOU!
FATHER ...?
I SHALL BE EAGERLY AWAITING THE DAY WHEN I AM ABLE TO GAZE INTO BOTH OF YOUR EYES.

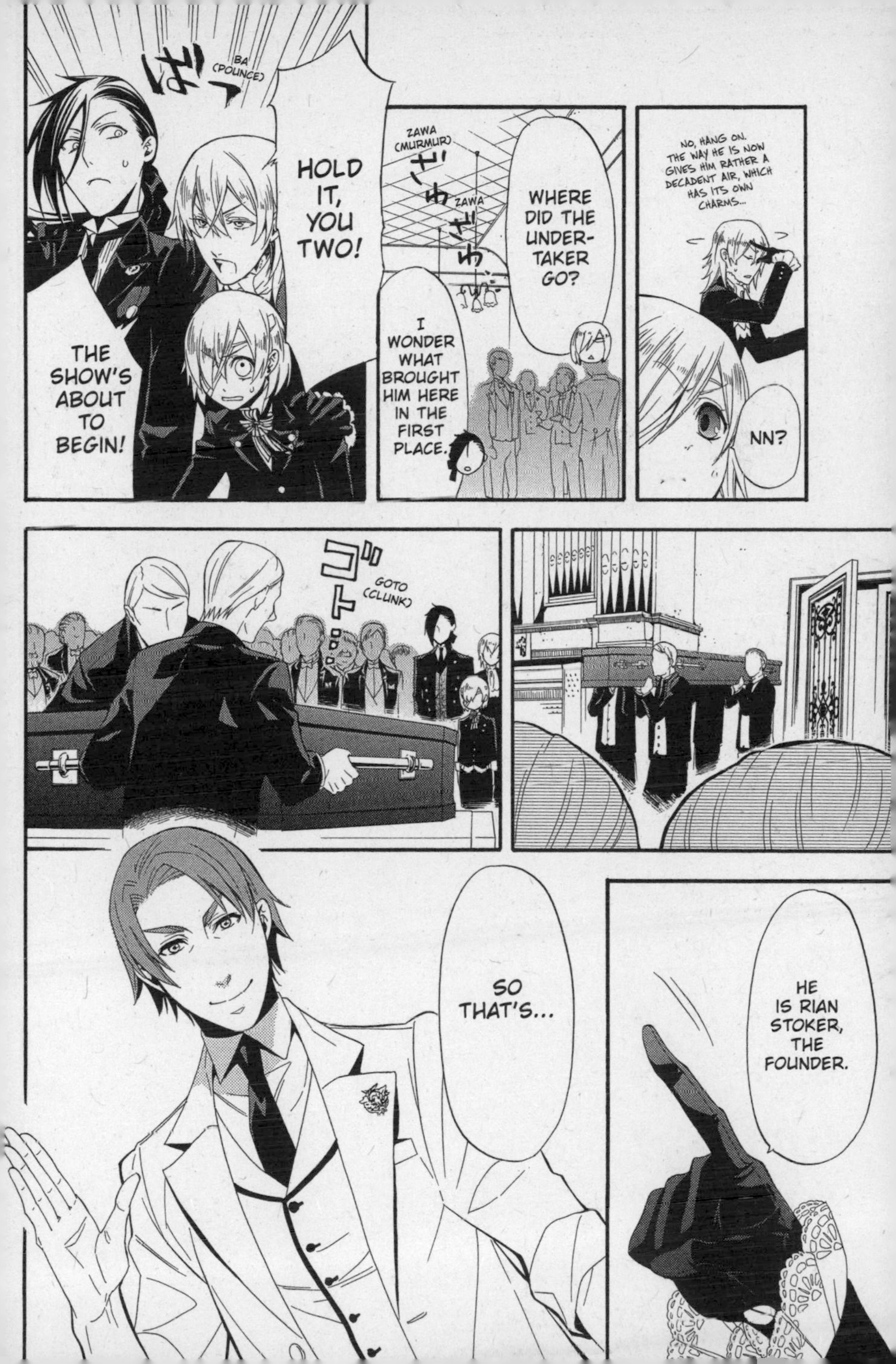

NO, HANG ON. THE WAY HE IS NOW GIVES HIM RATHER A DECADENT AIR, WHICH HAS ITS OWN CHARMS...
NN?
WHERE DID THE UNDER-TAKER GO?
ZAWA (MURMUR)
ZAWA
I WONDER WHAT BROUGHT HIM HERE IN THE FIRST PLACE.
BA (POUNCE)
HOLD IT, YOU TWO!
THE SHOW'S ABOUT TO BEGIN!
GOTO (CLUNK)
HE IS RIAN STOKER, THE FOUNDER.
SO THAT'S...

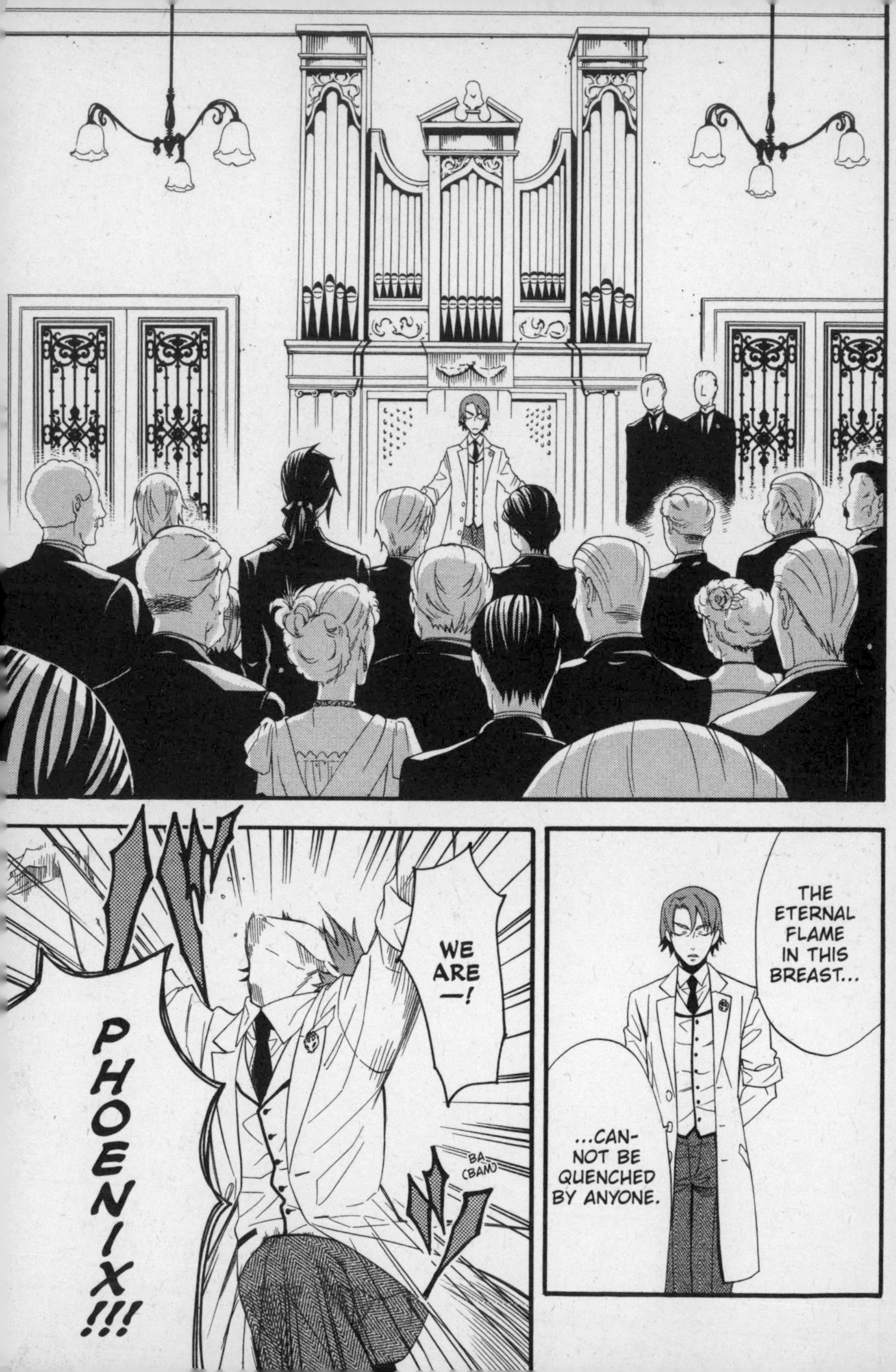
THE ETERNAL FLAME IN THIS BREAST...
...CAN-NOT BE QUENCHED BY ANYONE.
WE ARE—!
BA (BAM)
PHOENIX!!!

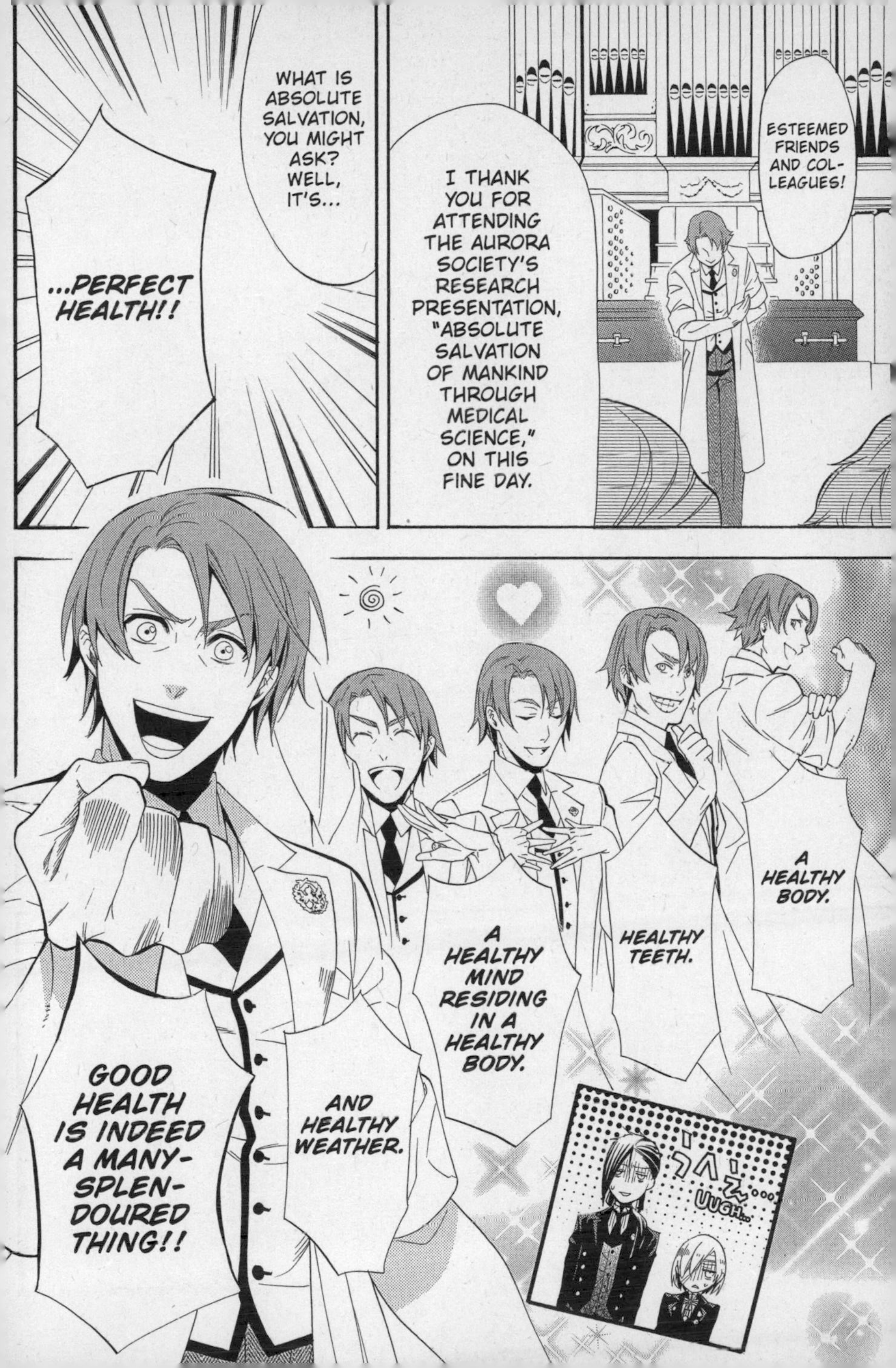
ESTEEMED FRIENDS AND COL-LEAGUES!
I THANK YOU FOR ATTENDING THE AURORA SOCIETY'S RESEARCH PRESENTATION, "ABSOLUTE SALVATION OF MANKIND THROUGH MEDICAL SCIENCE," ON THIS FINE DAY.
WHAT IS ABSOLUTE SALVATION, YOU MIGHT ASK? WELL, IT'S...
...PERFECT HEALTH!!
A HEALTHY BODY.
HEALTHY TEETH.
A HEALTHY MIND RESIDING IN A HEALTHY BODY.
AND HEALTHY WEATHER.
GOOD HEALTH IS INDEED A MANY-SPLEN-DOURED THING!!
UUGH...

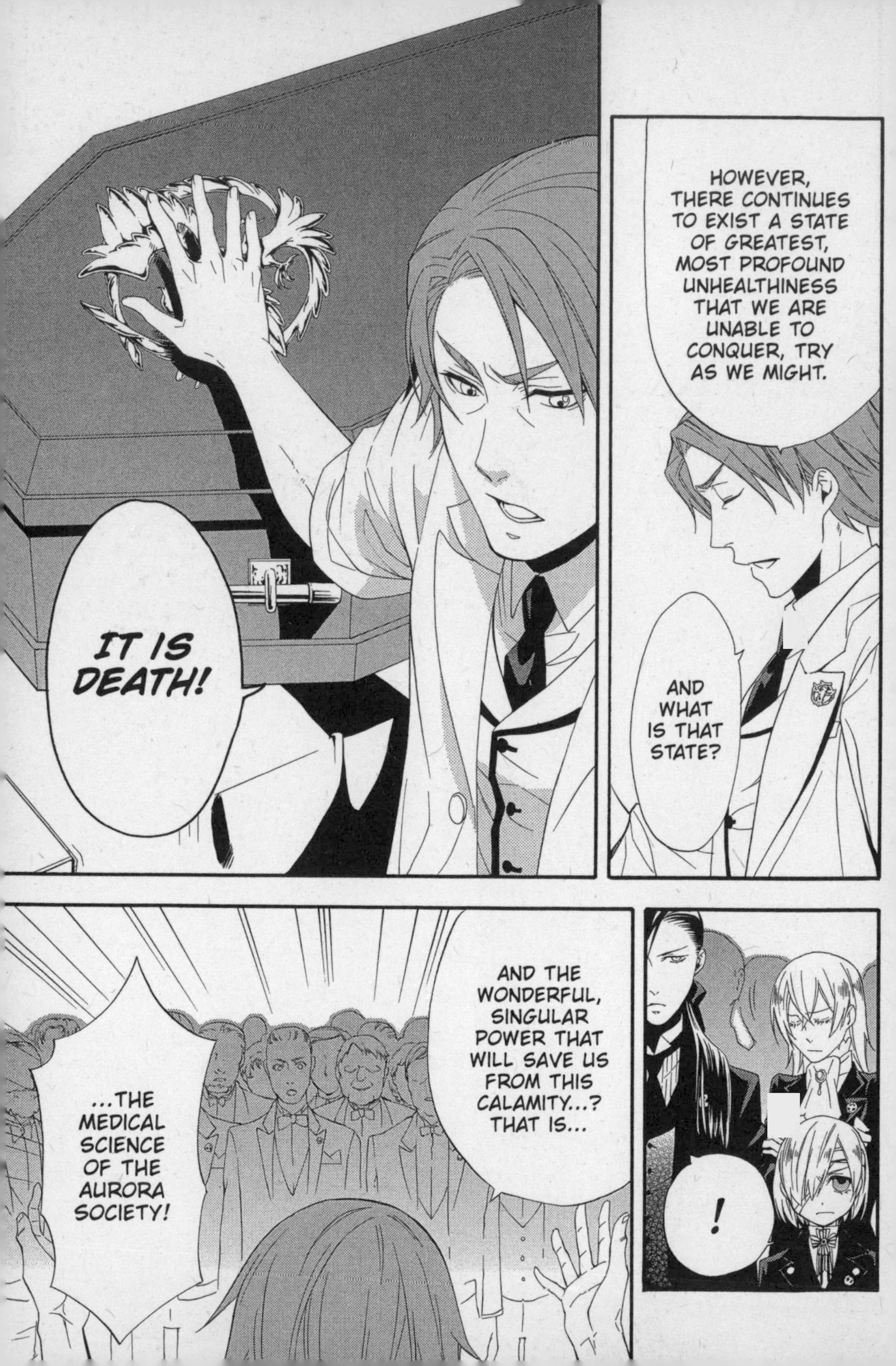
HOWEVER, THERE CONTINUES TO EXIST A STATE OF GREATEST, MOST PROFOUND UNHEALTHINESS THAT WE ARE UNABLE TO CONQUER, TRY AS WE MIGHT.
AND WHAT IS THAT STATE?
IT IS DEATH!
!
AND THE WONDERFUL, SINGULAR POWER THAT WILL SAVE US FROM THIS CALAMITY...? THAT IS...
...THE MEDICAL SCIENCE OF THE AURORA SOCIETY!

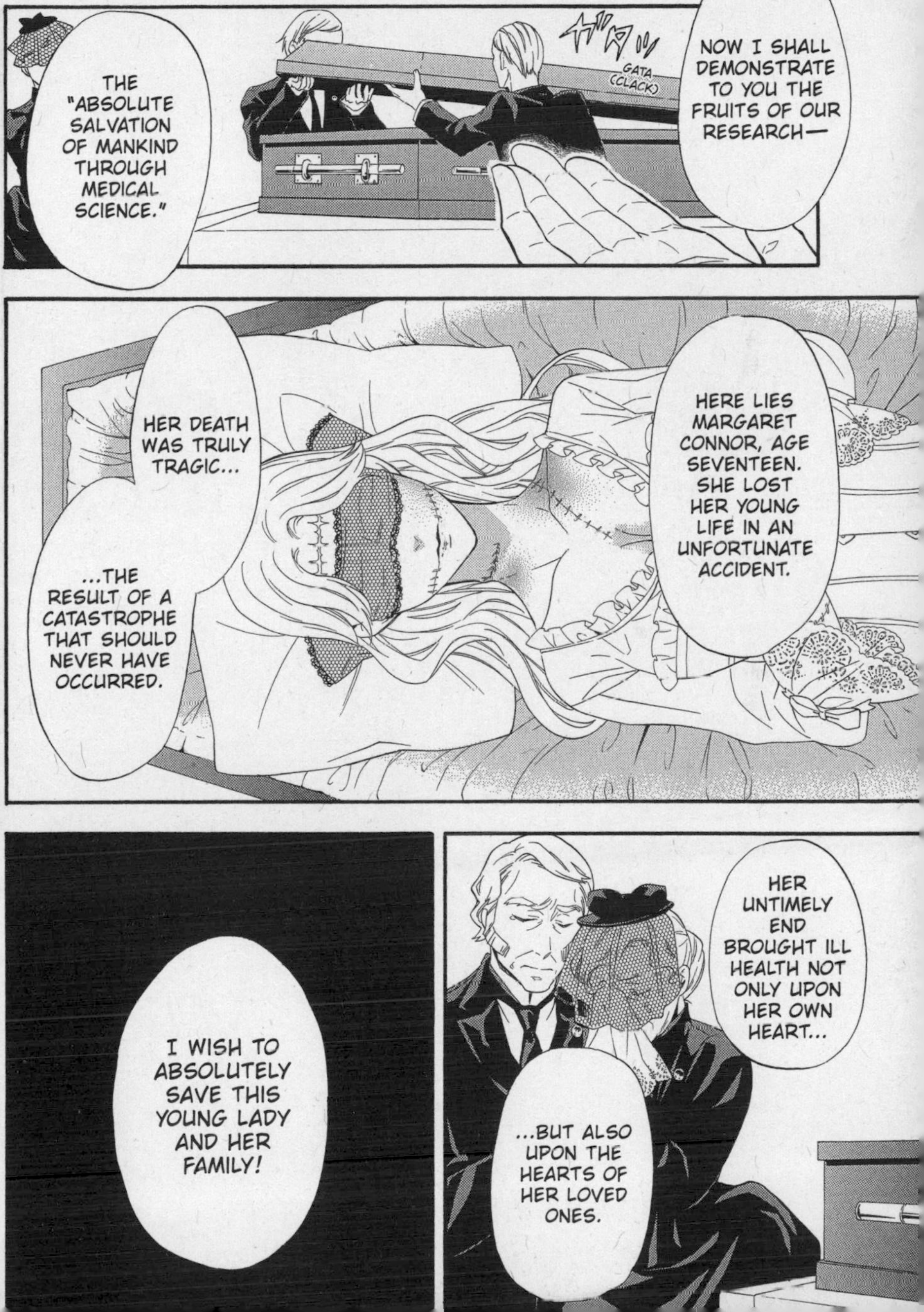
NOW I SHALL DEMONSTRATE TO YOU THE FRUITS OF OUR RESEARCH—
GATA (CLACK)
THE "ABSOLUTE SALVATION OF MANKIND THROUGH MEDICAL SCIENCE."
HERE LIES MARGARET CONNOR, AGE SEVENTEEN. SHE LOST HER YOUNG LIFE IN AN UNFORTUNATE ACCIDENT.
HER DEATH WAS TRULY TRAGIC...
...THE RESULT OF A CATASTROPHE THAT SHOULD NEVER HAVE OCCURRED.
HER UNTIMELY END BROUGHT ILL HEALTH NOT ONLY UPON HER OWN HEART...
...BUT ALSO UPON THE HEARTS OF HER LOVED ONES.
I WISH TO ABSOLUTELY SAVE THIS YOUNG LADY AND HER FAMILY!

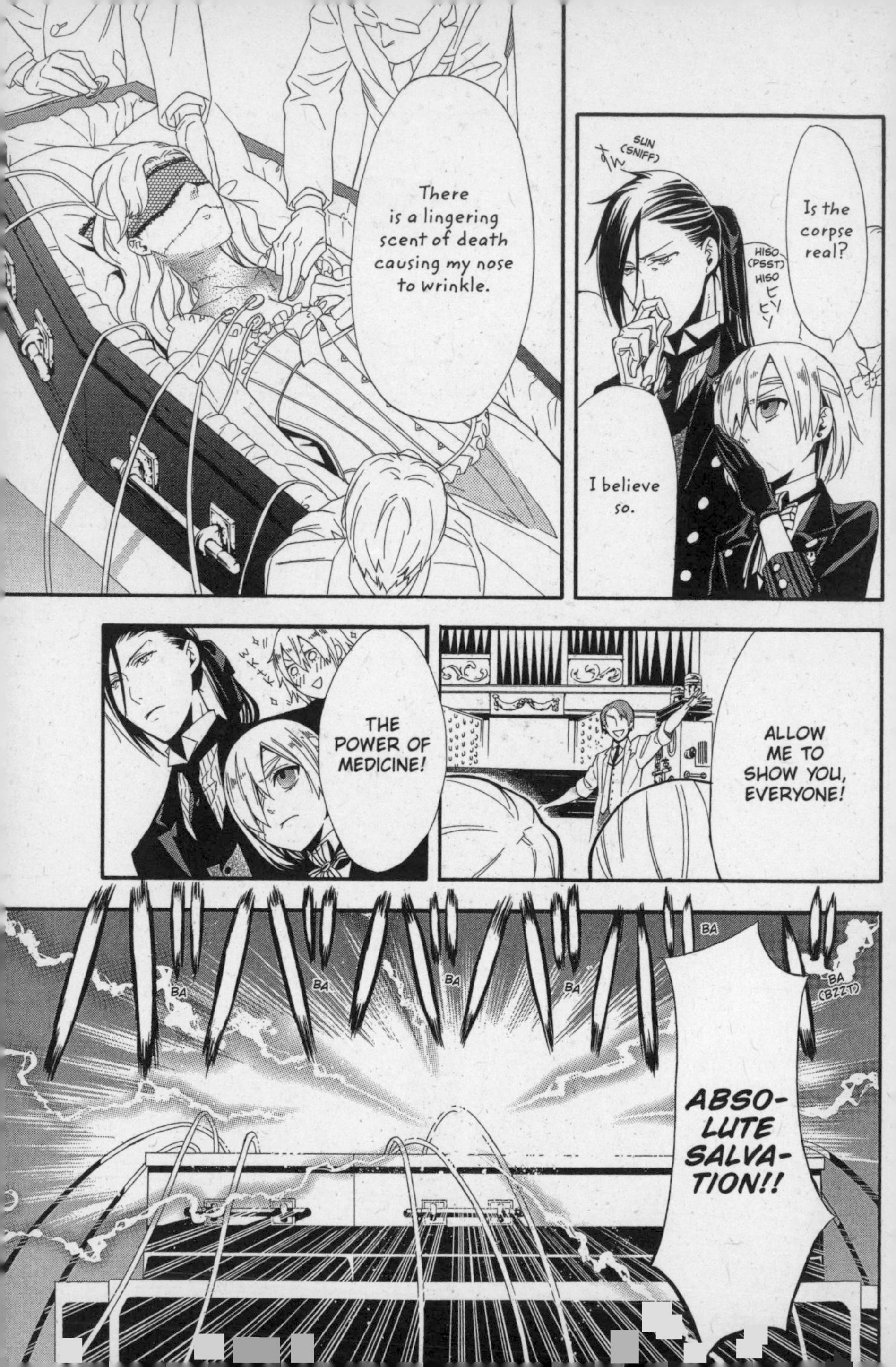
Is the corpse real?
HISO (PSST) HISO
SUN (SNIFF)
I believe so.
There is a lingering scent of death causing my nose to wrinkle.
ALLOW ME TO SHOW YOU, EVERYONE!
THE POWER OF MEDICINE!
BA (BZZT)
BA
ABSOLUTE SALVATION!!
BA
BA
BA
BA

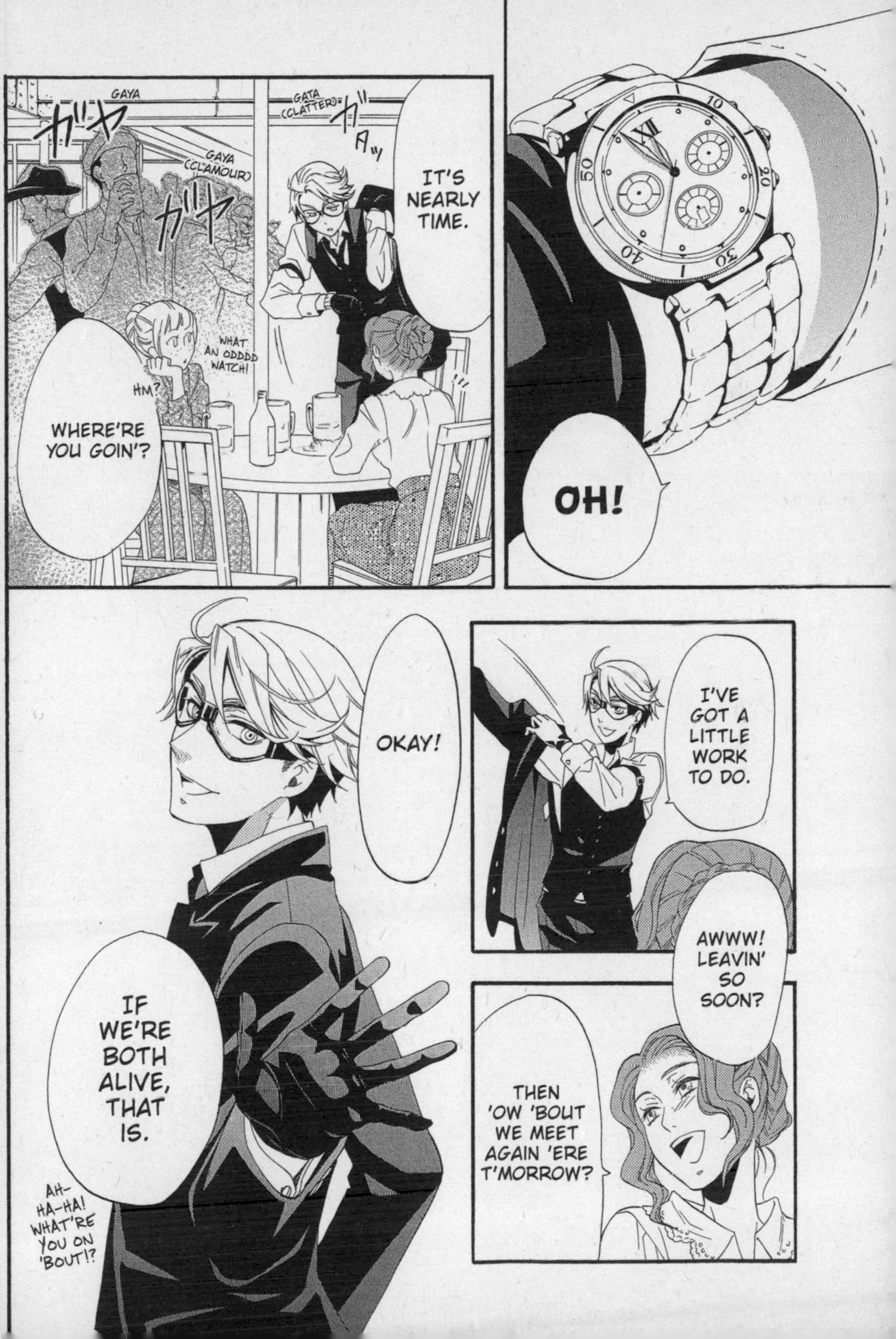
OH!
GATA (CLATTER)
IT'S NEARLY TIME.
GAYA
GAYA (CLAMOUR)
WHAT AN ODDDD WATCH!
HM?
WHERE'RE YOU GOIN'?
I'VE GOT A LITTLE WORK TO DO.
AWWW! LEAVIN' SO SOON?
THEN 'OW 'BOUT WE MEET AGAIN 'ERE T'MORROW?
OKAY!
IF WE'RE BOTH ALIVE, THAT IS.
AH-HA-HA! WHAT'RE YOU ON 'BOUT!?

NOW RISE ANEW FROM THE ASHES, MY DEAR!!

LIKE A PHOENIX!!

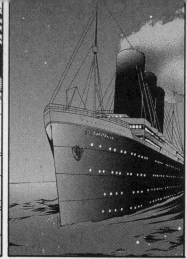

SUU
(RAISE)

PLEASE, TAKE A GOOD LOOK!

OUR MEDICAL SCIENCE CAN OVERCOME EVEN DEATH!!

ZAWA
(MURMUR)

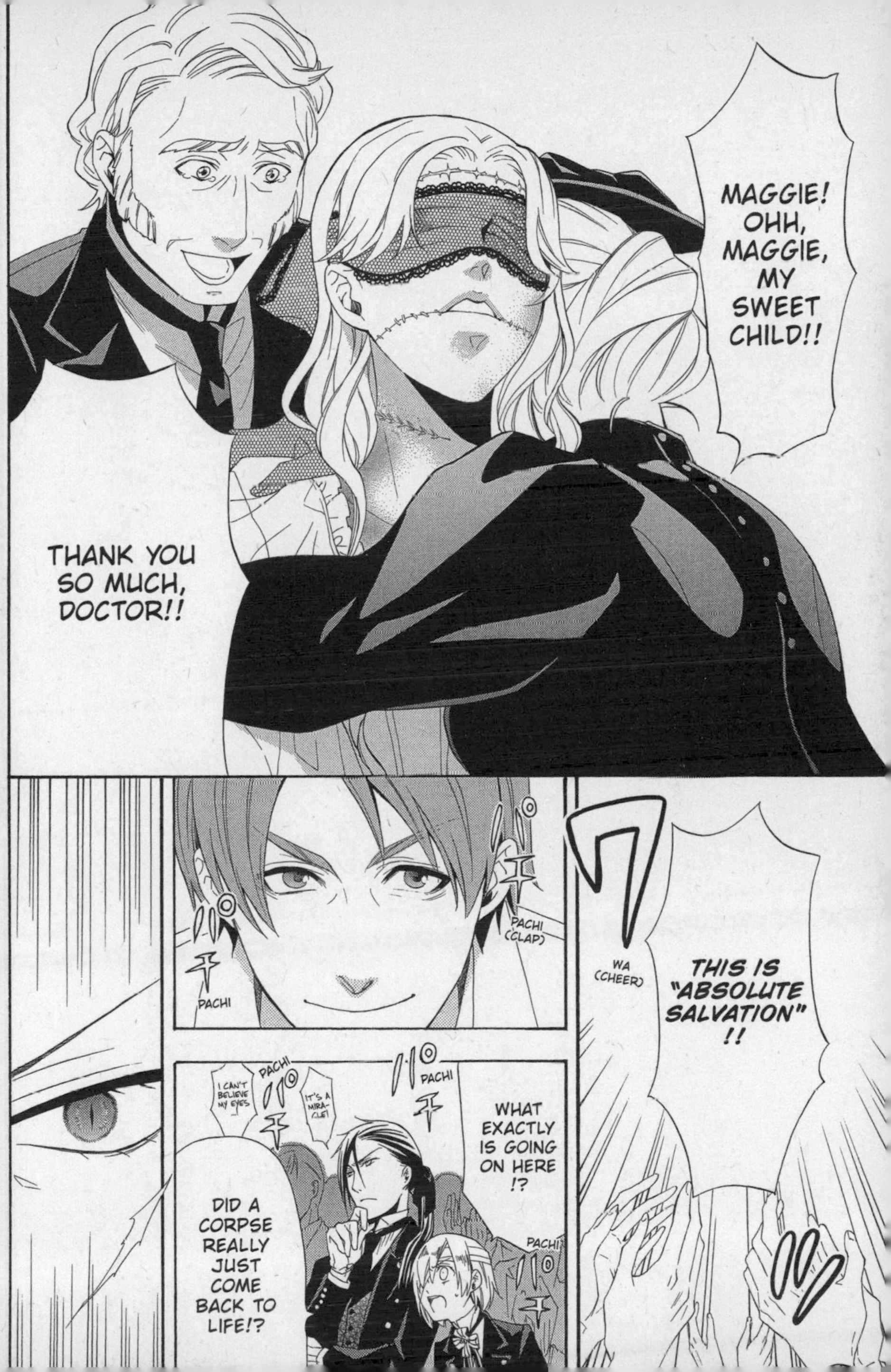
MAGGIE! OHH, MAGGIE, MY SWEET CHILD!!
THANK YOU SO MUCH, DOCTOR!!
WA (CHEER)
THIS IS "ABSOLUTE SALVATION"!!
PACHI (CLAP)
PACHI
WHAT EXACTLY IS GOING ON HERE!?
PACHI
IT'S A MIRACLE!
PACHI
I CAN'T BELIEVE MY EYES...
PACHI
DID A CORPSE REALLY JUST COME BACK TO LIFE!?

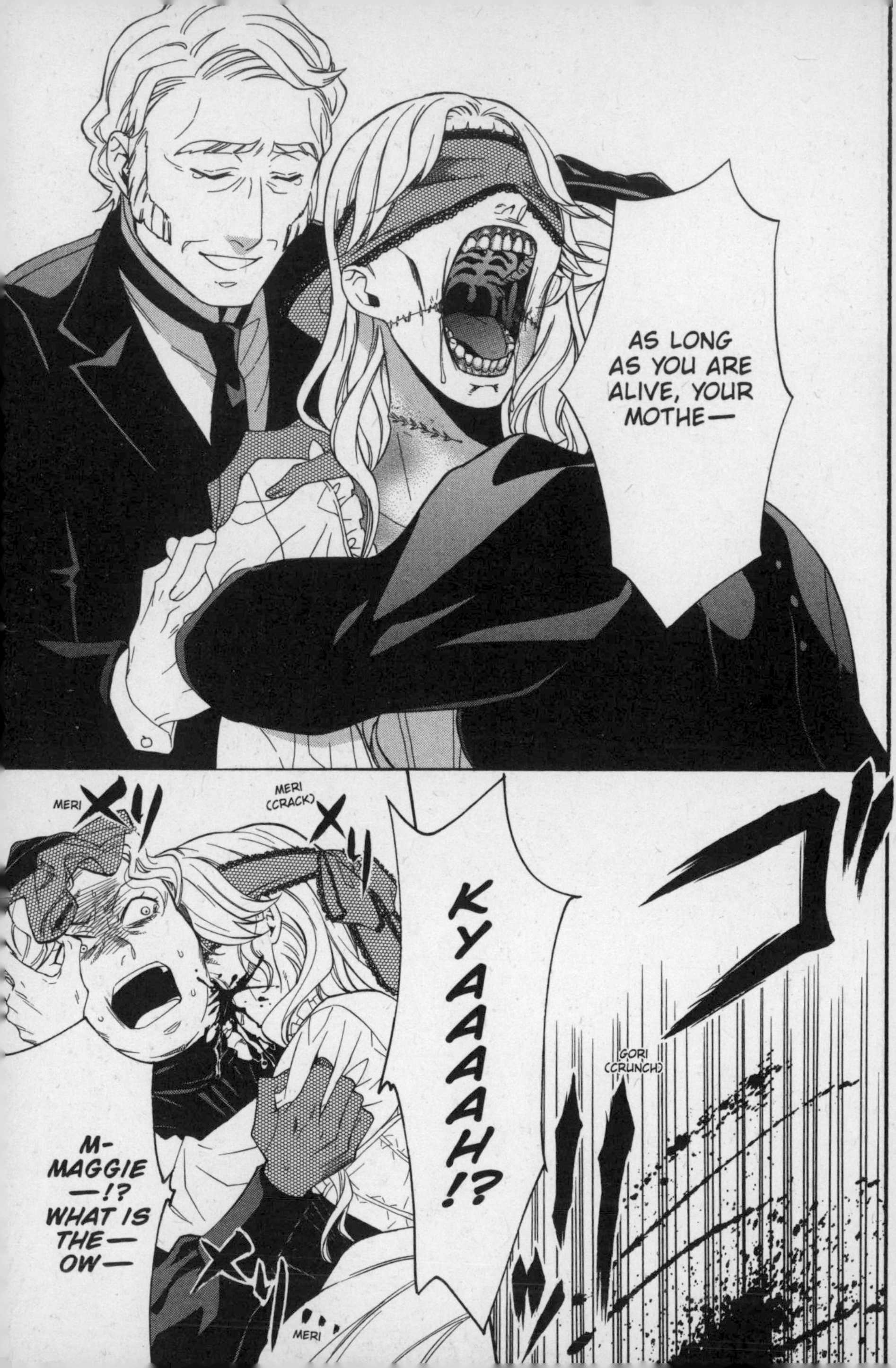
AS LONG AS YOU ARE ALIVE, YOUR MOTHE—
GORI (CRUNCH)
KYAAAAAH!?
MERI (CRACK)
MERI
M-MAGGIE—!? WHAT IS THE—OW—
MERI

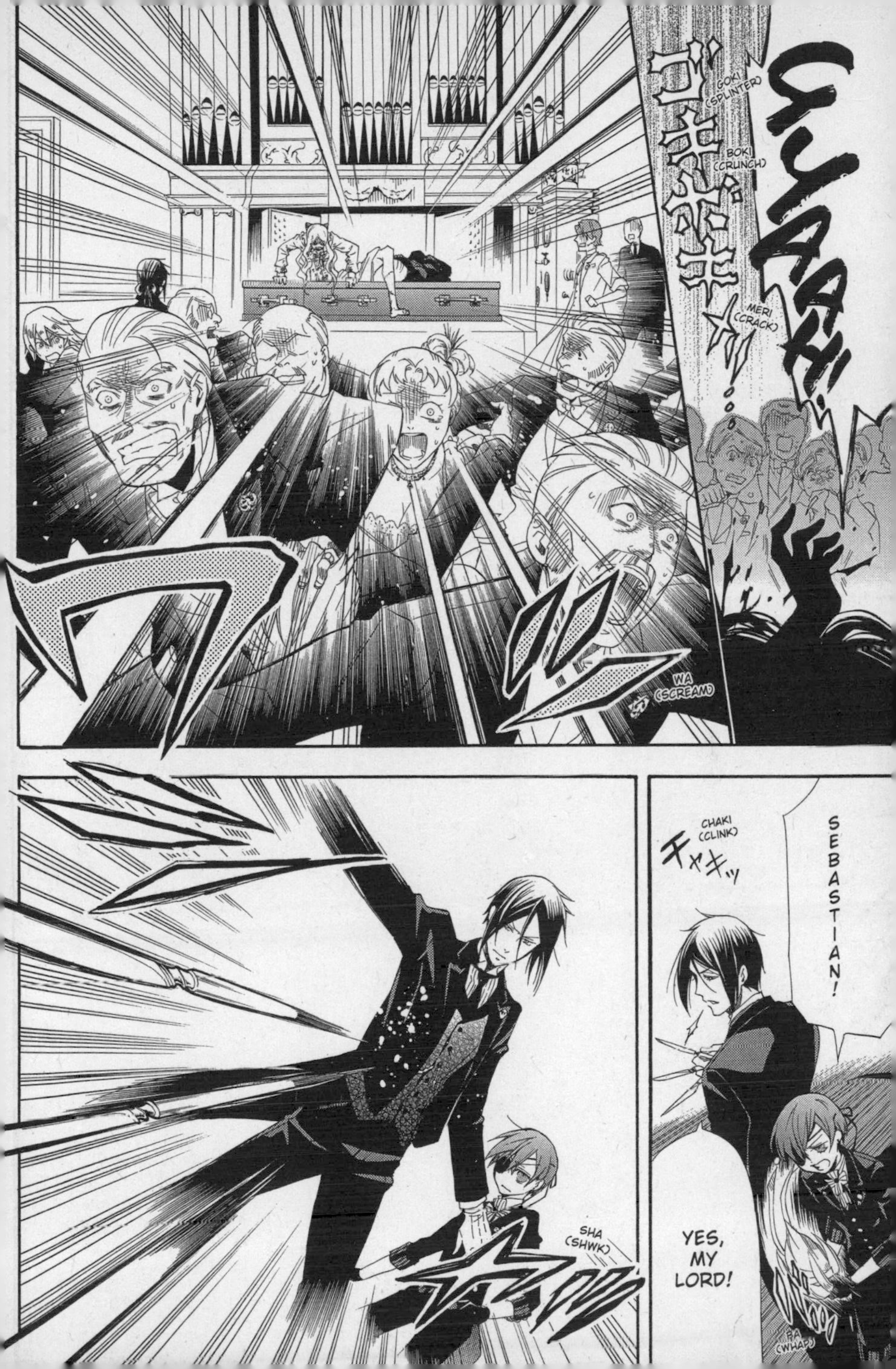
GYAAAH!
GOKI (SPLINTER)
BOKI (CRUNCH)
MERI (CRACK)
WA (SCREAM)
SEBASTIAN!
CHAKI (CLINK)
YES, MY LORD!
PA (WHAP)
SHA (SHWK)

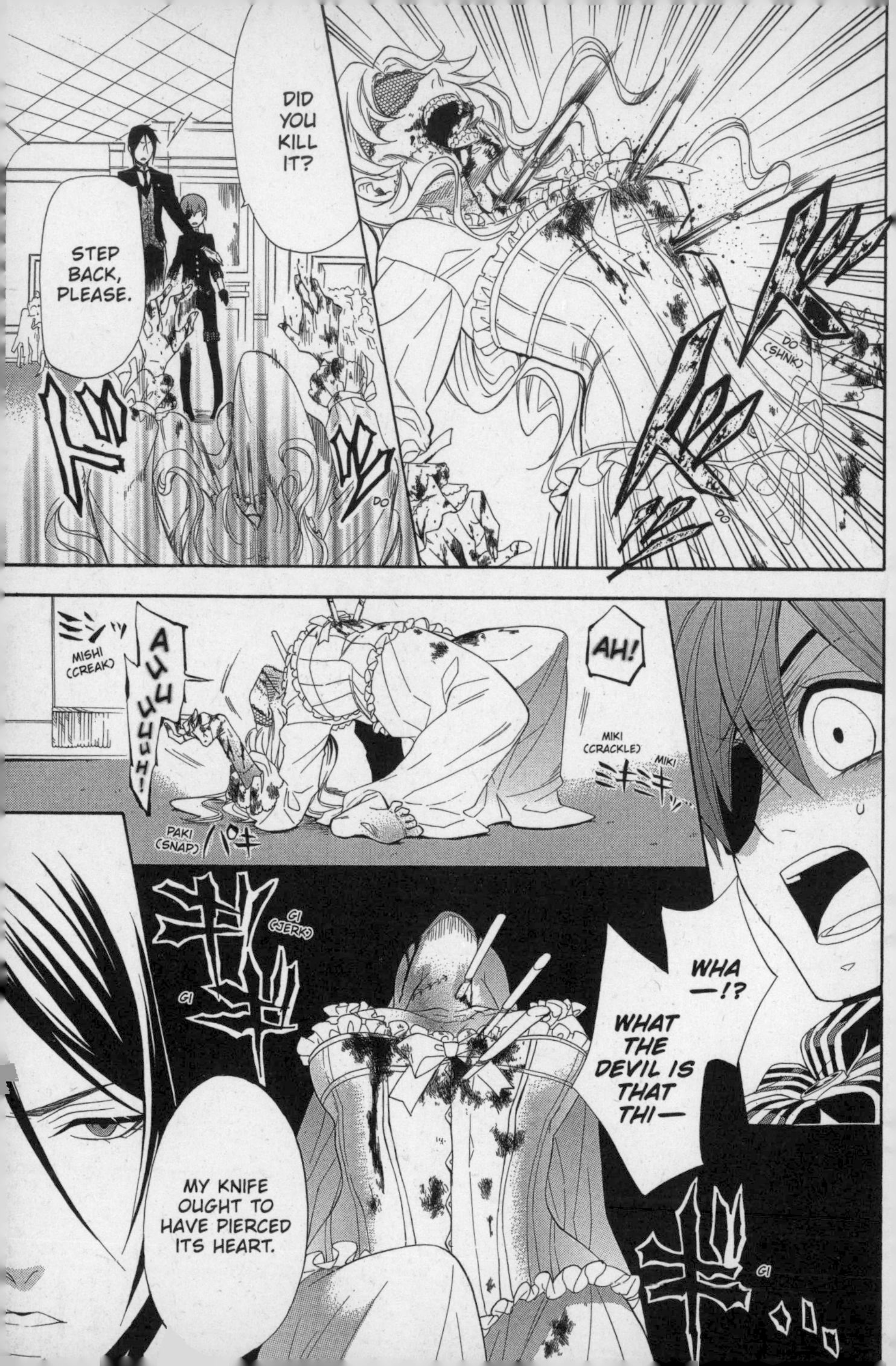

DO (SHNK)
DO
DID YOU KILL IT?
STEP BACK, PLEASE.
DO
AH!
WHA—!?
WHAT THE DEVIL IS THAT THI—
ミシッ
MISHI (CREAK)
AUUUUUH!
MIKI (CRACKLE)
MIKI
PAKI (SNAP)
パキ
GI (JERK)
GI
MY KNIFE OUGHT TO HAVE PIERCED ITS HEART.
GI

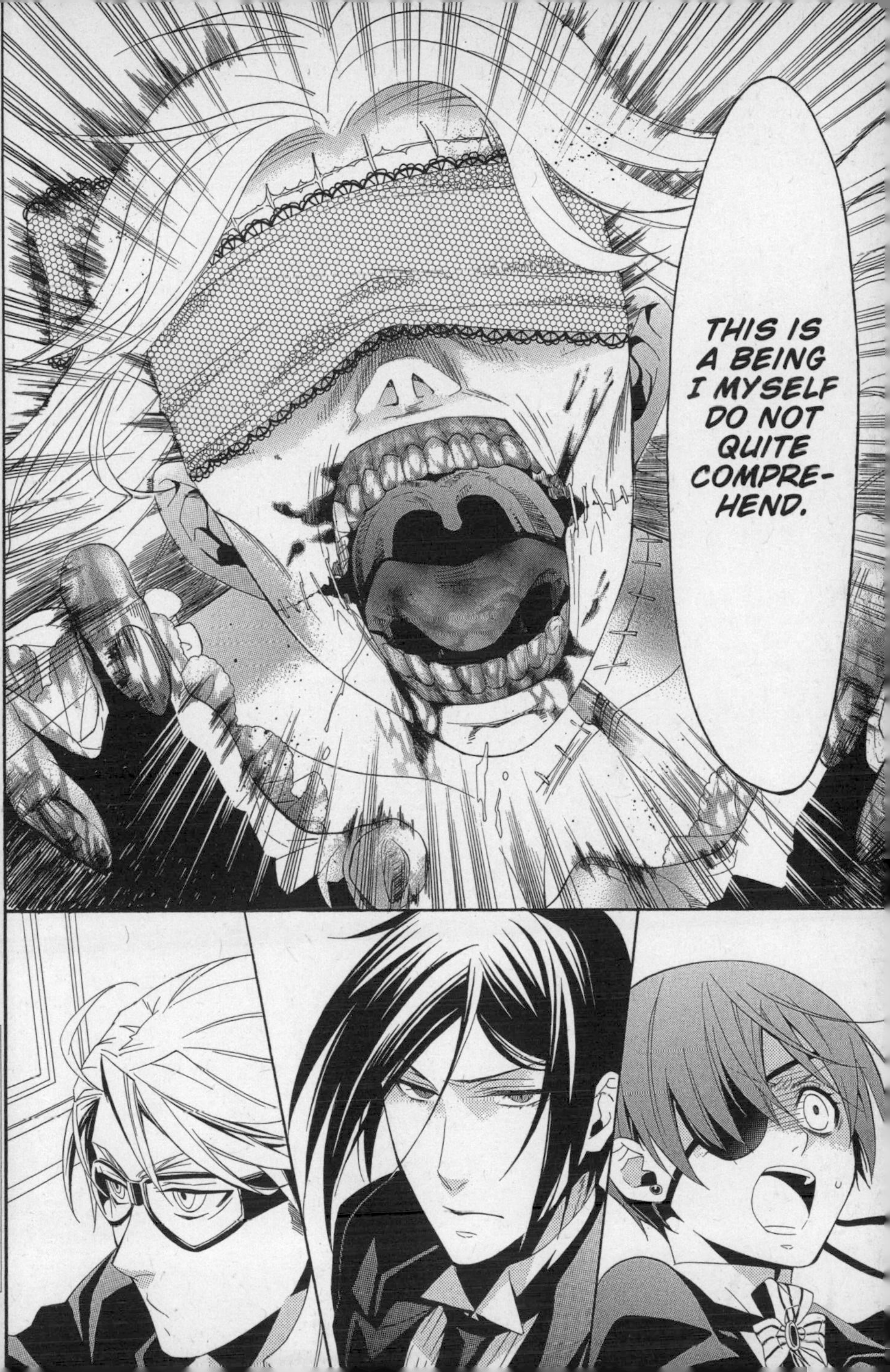
THIS IS A BEING I MYSELF DO NOT QUITE COMPRE-HEND.

⇒ Black Butler ⇐

黒執事

＊

Downstairs

Wakana Haduki

SuKe

7

Saito Torino

＊

Takeshi Kuma

＊

Yana Toboso

❧

SpecialThanks

Yana' s Mother

Sakuya

for You!

Translation Notes

Inside Front and Back Covers
Sukiyabashi Tanaka
A parody of an actual sushi restaurant in Ginza called Sukiyabashi Jiro, which holds three Michelin stars.

Japanese pork dishes
Tonkatsu is pork cutlet that has been breaded and deep-fried. *Shougayaki* is ginger-fried pork. *Tonjiru* is a soup of miso, pork, and vegetables. *Tonshabu* is a kind of hot pot stew with thinly sliced pork among a multitude of other ingredients. *Yakiton* is skewered and grilled pork.

Menu items
Tanmen is ramen with a salty broth topped with stir-fried vegetables and meat. *Chaashuu* sauce flavour is that of braised or barbecued pork. *Chuukadon* is a Chinese-style topping of meat and vegetables over rice. *Oyakodon* is another rice bowl dish made with a topping of both chicken and egg. An *oolong-hai* is an alcoholic cocktail of shochu with oolong tea. The *hai* is short for "highball."

Page 7
Elevenses
A light midmorning snack similar to afternoon tea but for the time at which it is consumed.

Page 9
Fortnum & Mason
A British department store in central London founded in the early eighteenth century, Fortnum's, as it is often called, started out as a grocery and saw rapid growth during the Victorian era. Over the years, it has earned numerous Royal Warrants from the British Crown. An iconic British brand, the store is known for stocking both basic and eclectic, high-quality foodstuffs. It is also home to a renowned tea shop.

Page 9
Second Flush
Tea leaves are harvested throughout their growing season, but teas picked in the first and second flushes, or periods of growth, are often the most prized. A first flush tea has a very delicate flavour while the more robust second flush, which is picked after about roughly a month after the first, is often more popular because it has the same delicacy of flavour but with more body.

Page 36
Hair of the dog
A shortening of "the hair of the dog that bit me," this phrase has been used since the sixteenth century to refer to drinking a small quantity of alcohol to cure a hangover.

Page 64
The Butterfly Effect
The butterfly effect is a tenet of chaos theory, the origins of which began in the late nineteenth century. The example of the ripple effect caused by a butterfly's wings is said to have first been used by the science fiction writer Ray Bradbury who wrote about it in his short story "A Sound of Thunder" in 1952, but the term "butterfly effect" was coined in the 1960s by meteorologist Edward Lorenz.

Page 67
"There is nothing more deceptive than an obvious fact."
This quote appears in Sir Arthur Conan Doyle's "The Boscombe Valley Mystery" featuring his great detective, Sherlock Holmes.

Page 87
Quelmada Island
This small, uninhabited island lies off the coast of Sao Paolo, Brazil, and is home to one of the most venomous species of snake known to man—the golden lancehead pitviper, whose venom is five times more potent than its closest cousin, which itself is the cause of the most deaths by snakebite in South America. It is said that there are anywhere from one to five golden lanceheads per every square meter on the island, which gives the island its nickname: Snake Island.

Page 122
Karnstein Hospital
The true identity of the titular character of Joseph Sheridan Le Fanu's novella *Carmilla* is revealed to be the vampiric Countess Karnstein and much of the action of the story takes place in Karnstein as well.

Page 167
WKTK
An abbreviation of "ワクワクテカテカ" (*waku waku teka teka*), a term to denote anticipation.